THE
SECONDARY
MORTGAGE
MARKET

A Handbook of Strategies

Techniques and Critical

Issues in Contemporary

Mortgage Finance

Edited by
JESS LEDERMAN

PROBUS PUBLISHING COMPANY
Chicago, Illinois

Library of Congress Cataloging in Publication Data

The Secondary mortgage market.

   Includes index.
    1. Secondary mortgage market—United States.
I. Lederman, Jess.
HG2040.25.S43   1987   332.63′244   87-2303
ISBN 0-917253-74-4

Library of Congress Catalog Card No. 87-2303

Printed in the United States of America

1 2 3 4 5 6 7 8 9 0

To My Parents

Preface

The secondary mortgage market is the largest and most rapidly growing segment of the U.S. capital markets. It is also one of the most rapidly changing and least understood sectors of the economy. But perhaps most important of all, from my own personal perspective, the secondary mortgage market is the most exciting—indeed magical—of all markets. Preston Martin, former Vice Chairman of The Federal Reserve, once remarked that the securitization of mortgages is the process of "turning frogs into princes." His fanciful metaphor of transformation captures the drama of this unique market.

Yet, on the surface, what could be more deadly dull than the home mortgage? A series of mind-numbing cash flows, grinding on for 15 or 30 years. Mort-gage, the death payment. But think again: the mortgage cash flow is the life blood of the American dream of home ownership. When we take those cash flows, and use that strange and wonderful alchemy of the secondary market to transform mortgages into a bewildering array of CMOs, REMICs, pass-throughs and pay-throughs, we are not trading pieces of paper—we are trading hopes and dreams.

When Teri Reed, President of The Mortgage Institute, Inc., and I sat down to determine the structure of this book, we agreed not to focus narrowly on any one segment of the market. Rather, we decided to offer a wide-ranging overview of many sectors of the market in an attempt to reveal its breadth and depth and the rich complexities of the world of mortgage finance.

As a result, the book is organized into five sections. Section I features eight chapters that explore the strategies and tactics of secondary marketing—the art of minimizing risk and maximizing profits from the origination and sale of mortgages and mortgage securities. Section II focuses on mortgage backed securities, examining alternative structures and analytical techniques. The final three sections center on three industries that play a pivotal role in mortgage finance. Section III discusses issues in mortgage banking, Section IV explores topics relevant to thrifts and commercial banks, and Section V focuses on the mortgage insurance industry.

Ironically, very little has been written to date on this challenging and complex market. While several excellent monthly magazines are published by the trade organizations, only a small handful of books exist that offer comprehensive discussion and analysis. This book represents a significant addition to this existing body of literature.

Jess Lederman

Foreword

The Secondary Mortgage Market: A Handbook of Strategies, Techniques, and Critical Issues in Contemporary Mortgage Finance covers topics of relevance to individuals and institutions involved in secondary marketing, mortgage-backed securities, mortgage banking, thrift and commercial banking, and mortgage insurance. In order to cover such a broad spectrum of subjects, Jess Lederman and I invited 38 of the most knowledgeable and creative people in the industry to contribute to this book. Many of them have played a formative role in the evolution of the mortgage market.

I wish to express my gratitude to Jess Lederman in his dual role as both editor and author, and to each of the contributing authors. In addition, thanks is owed to Evan Scholl and Tom Gallo of Bear Stearns Mortgage Capital Corporation, for their considerable technical assistance.

Finally, I wish to extend my sincere appreciation to Probus Publishing, for its help and support.

Teri Reed
President
The Mortgage Institute, Inc.

Contributors

Tayna S. Arnold, Vice President, The First Boston Corporation

Harley S. Bassman, Vice President and Senior Trader, Merrill Lynch Mortgage Capital, Inc.

Mary Bruce Batte, Senior Vice President, Barrentine Lott & Associates, Inc.

Roger F. Blood, Senior Consultant, Temple, Barker & Sloan Inc.

Steven J. Carlson, Vice President, Shearson Lehman Brothers

Henry Cassidy, Vice President of Financial Research, Federal Home Loan Mortgage Corporation

Tim Cohane, Senior Vice President, Thomson McKinnon Securities Inc.

Gregory L. Coleman, Executive Vice President and Treasurer, Northeast Savings, F.A.

C. Earl Corkett, Chairman and Chief Executive Officer, The PMI Group of Companies

Diane L. Cortes, Senior Vice President, General Electric Mortgage Insurance Co.

John B. Crosby, Jr., Vice President, Salomon Brothers Inc.

Peter D'Alessandro, Managing Director-Secondary Markets, Howard Taylor & Co.

Richard Ellson, Associate Professor, University of South Carolina

Joseph Garrett, Managing Director, Hamilton Savings Bank

Robert L. Hastings, Chairman, Foremost Guaranty Corporation

Jon G. Holm, Secondary Market Analyst, Mortgage Guaranty Insurance Co.

James A. Hornig, Managing Director, Hunter, Keith, Marshall & Co., Inc.

Joseph Hu, Senior Vice President and Director of Mortgage Research, Shearson Lehman Brothers Inc.

Robert W. Hunter, First Vice President, Northeast Savings, F.A.

Marco Issever, Associate, Prudential Bache Securities

Carol R. Kalin, Associate, Prudential Global Funding

William H. Lacy, President and Chief Executive Officer, Mortgage Guaranty Insurance Co.

Thomas S. LaMalfa, Vice President and Manager, Secondary Market Services, Mortgage Guaranty Insurance Co.

Richard S. Landau, President, Bear Stearns Mortgage Capital Corporation

Jess Lederman, Executive Vice President, Bear Stearns Mortgage Capital Corporation

Norman E. Mains, Ph.D, First Vice President and Director of Research, Drexel Burnham Lambert

Michael F. Molesky, Assistant Vice President, Moody's Investors Service

James F. Montgomery, Chairman and Chief Executive, Great Western Financial Corporation

Kevin J. O'Neil, President, Goldome Realty Credit Corp.

Blaine Roberts, Director of Government Bond Research, Bear Stearns & Co., Inc.

Joel L. Rosenberg, Senior Vice President and Treasurer, ComFed Savings Bank

Peter M. Ross, Senior Vice President, Goldome Realty Credit Corp.

Timothy D. Sears, Shearson Lehman Brothers

Jayne J. Shontell, Vice President, Federal National Mortgage Association

Peter L. Struck, Vice President and Manager of Secondary Marketing, Washington Mutual Savings Bank

Donald B. Susswein, Partner, Thacher Proffit & Wood

Howard Taylor, Chief Executive Officer, Howard Taylor & Company

James Walters, Director of Pricing and Financial Analysis, Bear Stearns Mortgage Capital Corporation

Hunter W. Wolcott, President, Reserve Financial Management Corp.

Contents

SECTION V
THE MORTGAGE INSURANCE INDUSTRY
Introduction 545

Section I:
Secondary Marketing

INTRODUCTION

Section I explores the art and science of secondary marketing from several perspectives.

The first five chapters focus on the more technical, quantitative aspects of the discipline. In each of these chapters the reader will sense the aftershocks of the great interest rate rally of 1985–86: during this period of time market participants became sensitized as never before to the volatility not only of interest rates, but of the mortgage/treasury basis and pipeline fallout ratios as well. Each chapter offers insights into the myriad methods of dealing with these volatilities using futures, exchange-traded and OTC options, and conduit commitments. In Chapter 1, Norman Mains offers an excellent introduction to the dynamics of hedging, analyzing the choices between mandatory and optional hedges, the uses of futures and options, and the issue of basis risk. In Chapter 2, Jess Lederman presents a technique for evaluating alternative hedging using probablistic risk/return analysis. Tanya Arnold makes the argument in Chapter 3 for dynamic versus static hedging, given the uncertainty of mortgage cash flows. Chapter 4, authored by Harley Bassman, focuses on options on mortgage-backed securities, and explores the ways in which they can be customized to meet the specific needs of originators and investors. In Chapter 5, Lederman discusses the many different techniques that originators can use to maximize profits and minimize risk when selling loans to conduits.

The final three chapters of Section I move from the world of high-tech analysis to the artful realm of making deals. Negotiating transactions in the secondary market is more challenging than ever before—the deals are increasingly complex and the participants are more sophisticated. In Chapter 6, Mary Bruce Batte discusses how originators can lay the groundwork for successfully selling loans in the private secondary market. The final two chapters provide a "behind the scenes" look at the way secondary market matchmakers provide liquidity to the market. Howard Taylor and Peter D'Alessandro illustrate the workings of whole loan brokers through several case studies in Chapter 7, while Tom LaMalfa and Jon Holm delineate the role of the mortgage insurers' secondary marketing staffs in Chapter 8.

Chapter 1

NORMAN E. MAINS

Norman E. Mains, Ph.D., is First Vice President and Director of Research for the Institutional Financial Futures division of Drexel Burnham Lambert. Prior to joining Drexel Burnham Lambert, Mr. Mains was a senior economist with the Board of Governors of the Federal Reserve System. He also was an economist with the Investment Company Institute, the national trade association for the mutual fund industry. Mr. Mains received his B.A. and M.A. from the University of Colorado, and was awarded his Ph.D. in economics from the University of Warwick in England.

Hedging Mortgage Loan Originations with Interest Rate Futures and Options: Panacea or Placebo?

NORMAN E. MAINS

INTRODUCTION

Capital market participants are increasingly confronted with a myriad of new instruments and techniques aimed at limiting risk and/or enhancing return. Mortgage market participants, in particular, have been deluged in recent years with increasingly sophisticated analytical approaches designed to transpose the reward/risk profile of mortgage-backed securities in a manner that more closely optimizes the utility preference of a manager or institution. The genesis of much of this transformation was the introduction of interest rate futures in October 1975. The secondary mortgage market underwent a quantum-like change as the introduction of the Chicago Board of Trade's (CBOT) GNMA-CDR interest rate futures contract contributed importantly to a broader and deeper market for the then-nascent GNMA market. Mortgages and mortgage-backed securities were largely viewed in the early 1970s as illiquid instruments, a characteristic that reduced their attractiveness to many capital market participants. The CBOT's GNMA-

CDR contract contributed in this environment to the overall liquidity of the instrument as well as helping to usher in interest rate futures contracts on short- and long-term U.S. Treasury obligations. It is now ironic, to say the least, that the current menu of *actively* traded financial futures contracts lacks a truly viable mortgage-backed security futures contract. Of course, this is in sharp contrast to the continued strong growth in recent years of both financial futures and mortgage-backed securities. Financial futures currently account for approximately two-thirds of all futures trading in the United States. Moreover, Table 1–1 demonstrates that worldwide longer-term interest rate futures contracts had an average daily volume of more than $46 billion in June 1986.

The upper portion of Table 1–1 also shows that the CBOT's two currently active mortgage-backed security futures contracts, the GNMA-CDR and the GNMA-CS (cash settlement), each had an average volume of less than 100 contracts per day in June 1986 versus 213,640 and 22,398 contracts per day, respectively, for the CBOT's Treasury bond and Treasury note futures contracts.* Mortgage market participants seeking to hedge themselves with interest rate futures usually confine their activities to the CBOT's Treasury bond or Treasury note contracts. Such hedgers assume the crosshedge risk associated with a spot (or forward) market position of mortgage-backed securities hedged with a futures market position based on U.S. Treasury obligations, and the potential rewards and risks from such a crosshedge is a principal thesis of this chapter. It begins with an introduction to the dynamics of hedging with either futures or options for mortgage loan originations. Next, it reviews briefly the relative advantages of hedging in various markets. Then the chapter presents a recent example of hedging mortgage loan originations with futures and with options. The chapter concludes with an overview of the merits of the various hedging techniques.

---

*The CBOT has listed four separate GNMA-based futures contracts: The GNMA-CDR (Collateralized Depository Receipt) began trading on October 20, 1975; the GNMA-CD (Certificate Delivery) was launched on September 12, 1978 and is now inactive; the GNMA-II started on March 22, 1984 and is also inactive; and the GNMA-CS (Cash Settlement) contract began trading on May 6, 1986.

Table 1–1
Worldwide Activity in Longer-term Interest Rate Futures Contracts
(June 1986)

Country/ Exchange	Futures Contract	Date Started	Av. Daily Volume[a]	Par Value in US$ (millions)[b]
U.S.-CBOT	Treasury Bonds	2/22/77	213,640	$21,364
	Treasury notes	5/05/82	22,398	2,240
	Municipal bonds	6/11/85	3,506	351
	GNMA-CDR	10/22/75	78	8
	GNMA-CS	5/06/86	67	7
Japan-TSE	Government bonds	10/12/85	34,259	20,453
U.K.-LIFFE	Long gilts	11/18/82	8,228	621
	Short gilts	9/10/85	174	26
	U.S. Treasury bonds	6/21/84	7,006	701
Australia-SFE	Treasury bonds	12/05/84	4,884	336
France-MATIF	Government bonds	2/20/86	4,809	338
Canada-TFE	Government bonds	8/06/85	2	*
Total			229,051	$46,437

a   Number of contracts
b   Non-US$ contracts converted by the monthly average foreign exchange rate
* Less than $500,000

THE DYNAMICS OF HEDGING

The ultimate purpose of a hedge transaction is to reduce the price exposure of a position; such transactions are typically temporary substitutes for the unwinding or offsetting of the original position. For an originator of mortgage loans, the originator is "at risk" to price changes once the mortgage loan commitment has been issued. The originator is obligated to provide a specified amount of funds to a borrower at a given rate of interest. It should be clear to mortgage market participants that the specific nature of the price risk faced by an originator is complex and variable, so it is almost axiomatic to say that a hedging program must be well-planned, clearly defined, and properly executed.

A well-managed hedging program must encompass several basic points to accomplish these goals.

First, the individual or group responsible for the hedging program must carefully *identify* the risk to be hedged. In the case of hedging the price risk of a mortgage loan originator, the individual or group acting as the hedge manager must have as much information as possible with regard to the specific nature of the mortgage commitments in the pipeline.

Second, the hedge manager must *measure* the price risk as accurately as possible, so that the size of the hedge position can be determined with all available information. The measurement of this price risk ultimately will be incorporated into a specific hedge ratio, and the performance efficiency of the hedge will reflect how accurately the hedge ratio was estimated.

Next, the individual or group must make the key *decision* of whether or not to hedge the price risk. Expectations of movements in interest rates over a specified period is an obviously important ingredient in this decision, but the probable response of mortgage loan commitment holders to these changes in interest rates is equally important. It should be recognized also that the hedging decision can entail either all of some portion of the price risk, depending on such factors as the strength of the expectations of interest rate changes, the consequences of adverse price movements, and so on.

Last, if a decision is made to hedge some or all of the pipeline risk, then the hedge manager must select the most appropriate hedge vehicle to transfer the price risk to some other market participant or group of participants.

CHOOSING A HEDGING VEHICLE

The choice of a hedging vehicle for mortgage market participants has become increasingly difficult in recent years. As noted previously, the mortgage-backed security forward market has expanded in recent years at the same time that the mortgage-backed futures market has contracted. And in a closely related development, interest rate option markets—both exchange-traded and over-the-counter markets—have developed rapidly. The individual or group responsible for the hedging process must choose, therefore, among several alternatives based on efficiency, cost, regulatory rules, and other factors. It is very important to recognize that no single solution (such as futures versus options or exchange-traded options versus over-the-counter options) exists that is clearly dominant in all instances for hedging the price risk of mortgage-backed securities. The various hedging methods may improve or deteriorate relative to each other, depending on a variety of factors.

It is easily seen that a mortgage originator faces an asymmetric risk profile once a commitment is issued. The potential borrower has the right, but not the obligation, to "take down" the mortgage loan. If mortgage interest rates decline by a reasonably large amount during the commitment period, then the borrower may elect to recontract the obligation with another lender at a more advantageous rate. If, on the other hand, mortgage intereste rates increase, then the probability rises that the borrower will take down the funds. The lending institution has, for all practical purposes, sold a put option to the borrower with a strike price equal to the commitment rate during the commitment period. Stated somewhat differently, the borrower may put, or sell, the mortgage to the lending institution if the mortgage interest rates remain unchanged or rise, while a decline in such interest rates will mean that the put option is "out-of-the-money" and the borrower may choose not to exercise it during the commitment period.

The mortgage originator is effectively *short* puts on mortgage interest rates, so an obvious hedging solution is to *purchase* puts on mortgage interest rates. Unfortunately, no exchange-traded options on mortgage interest rates currently exist; such option contracts are available only on U.S. Treasury notes and bonds. An alternative hedging strategy is to purchase over-the-counter puts on mortgage interest rates from an institution that offers such instruments to customers. This is certainly the most direct hedging method, although mortgage originators should recognize that the cost of such obligations may be relatively high. The institution selling the obligation to the originator becomes "short" put options in the process, and it is likely that the over-the-counter option dealer will hedge the risk exposure and/or price the option so that it will be profitable unless mortgage interest rates change by an extraordinarily large amount.

ASSESSING CROSSHEDGE RISK

Mortgage originators may want to consider purchasing exchange-traded puts on U.S. Treasury obligations since over-the-counter options are relatively expensive.* If the originator elects to directly hedge the price risk with exchange-traded options, then the hedge manager is assuming the crosshedge risk between U.S. Treasury obligations and mortgage-backed securities. The crosshedge risk can, of course, contribute or detract from the overall hedge results. A narrowing of the yield spread between yields on longer-term U.S. Treasury obligations and mortgage securities will enhance the overall results of the hedge, while a widening of the spread will detract from it. The recent level and variability of the spread can be seen in Figure 1–1. The upper graph presents monthly average yields for GNMA 11s and 10-year U.S. Treasury notes since 1983, while the lower graph shows the spread between them. The top

---

*The largest and most liquid exchange-traded option market is the CBOT's option on Treasury bond futures. The CBOT's options on Treasury note futures contract is also very liquid, in part due to the spreading of both Treasury note futures and options against Treasury bond futures and options.

graph illustrates that GNMA 11s yielded between about 14¼ and 10¾ percent from early 1983 through late 1985, a range of 350 basis points. At the same time, the spread between GNMA 11s and 10-year U.S. Treasury yields ranged between about 65 and 150 basis points, a range of 85 basis points. As noted previously, a narrowing of the yield spread (such as in late 1983 and early 1984) would contribute somewhat positively to the overall hedge results, while a widening of the spread resulted in somewhat less efficient hedge results. It is important to recognize, however, that the month-to-month changes in the levels of the mortgage yields generally were much larger than changes in the spread. Figure 1–1 illustrates also that the change in the spread was much more pronounced in the first half of 1986, as yields on longer-term U.S. Treasuries staged one of the strongest rallies in history. As many mortgage market participants are aware, the rally was much less impressive for mortgage-backed securities and the spreads widened sharply. Against this background, it should be clear that the crosshedge risk may have detracted sizably from overall hedge efficiency in early 1986.

THE LINK BETWEEN SPOT AND FUTURES MARKETS: THE BASIS

A hedger that assumes the risk of a change in the spread between two nonhomogeneous instruments (these differences can be types of instruments, maturities, coupons, and so on) is assuming basis risk. That is, basis risk results when the price risk of a security or position is hedged with a vehicle that has different characteristics. *Basis risk* is a familiar term for futures market participants, since virtually all hedging activity entails using a vehicle that produces a less-than-perfect price change correlation with the underlying position. As noted previously, a goal of a hedger should be to manage the resultant basis risk such that it is considerably smaller than the price risk of the underlying position. Moreover, basis risk need not detract from the efficiency of a hedge. A basis gain can occur, which is, of course, preferable to a basis loss regardless of the magnitude.

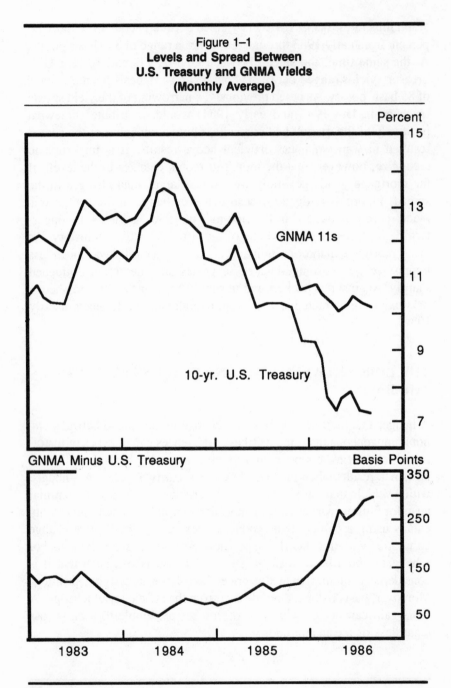

Figure 1–1
**Levels and Spread Between
U.S. Treasury and GNMA Yields
(Monthly Average)**

It should be clear that the basis risk displayed in Figure 1–1 (the yield spread) was not too large throughout most of the 1983–1985 period, so that hedge results were generally acceptable. However, the sharp widening of the spread between U.S. Treasury and GNMA yields in early 1986 may have resulted in relatively poor hedge results. How can hedge managers assuredly assess whether potential basis risk is reasonable? They can't. Hedging is as much of an art as it is a science, and the individual or group responsible for hedging must constantly make judgments about the potential efficiency of a hedge. Managers have certain information and tools at their disposal (such as historical yield relationships, economic forecasts, and econometric models), but the ultimate decision will require managers to make economic judgments based on limited and imperfect knowledge. The principal consolation to this somewhat unsettling statement is that, imperfect as it is, a decision to hedge can be much better in many circumstances than not hedging at all.

FUTURES OR OPTIONS?

It was stated previously that a mortgage originator has effectively written a put option when a mortgage loan commitment is extended to a potential borrower. It was further stated that an obvious hedging strategy for the originator would be to purchase over-the-counter puts on mortgage interest rates, but various factors may make the cost of these options too expensive. Since this is the case, the mortgage originator's hedge manager must assess the potential basis gains or losses from crosshedging mortgage interest rates with longer-term U.S. Treasury yields. If the hedge manger deems the crosshedge (or basis) risk as acceptable, then the manager must choose the amount of the hedge and whether to use futures or options.

The choice between futures or options will depend, once again, on several factors, and neither method of hedging is likely to be dominant in all instances. A major portion, for example, of an option's premium represents time value, so some of the potential expense of hedging with options (both exchange-traded and over-the-counter) will reflect the erosion of this time value with the passage of time. The principal advantage of hedging with options for a mortgage originator is the symmetrical risk profile of commitments: Decreases in mortgage interest rates may result in fewer commitments being exercised. The hedge manager must employ historical data as well as judgment to estimate the interest rate elasticity of the organization's commitments. A relatively high interest rate elasticity suggests a large decline in commitment closings for a given change in interest rates, while a low value suggests much less sensitivity by potential commitment holders. If the latter case appears more appropriate, then the hedge may achieve superior results using futures contracts rather than options. The duration of most mortgage-backed securities are, in addition, closer to the duration of 7- to 10-year U.S. Treasury notes, so the appropriate interest rates futures contract is the CBOT's Treasury note futures rather than its Treasury bond futures contract.

Another use of futures markets would be for option replication. *Option replication* is a technique in which the price characteristics of an option contract are replicated by using option pricing theory and the futures markets. The approach can require frequent rebalancing, so the relatively low transaction costs of financial futures markets are critical. The futures market position is estimated initially based on such factors as strike price and expected volatility; the replicated option position is then rebalanced frequently depending on factors like price movements, changes in volatility, and decay of time value. The overall results should produce a hedging vehicle that is as accurate as an over-the-counter option but at a lower cost to the mortgage originator.

HEDGING A MORTGAGE PIPELINE—AN EXAMPLE

Some of the points emphasized earlier can be demonstrated with a relatively simple example. Suppose that a mortgage banker was committed to make $125 million in mortgages, but the manager was concerned that longer-term interest rates were about to increase. Also assume that the hedge manager reviewed recent commitment behavior and determined that $100 million of the mortgages would close. The mortgage banker intended to sell the mortgages as 9 percent GNMAs. The hedge manager employed recent prepayment data and regressed relative yield changes to determine a hedge ratio of 0.60 Treasury note futures contracts per $100,000 of GNMA 9s. The hedge manager desired to lock in the value of the mortgages on April 16th by hedging the position in the CBOT's Treasury note futures contract. The hedge manager planned to unwind the position in mid-May.

Table 1–2 presents the results of the transaction. The anticipated value of the commitment to make mortgages had a market price of $101^{20}/_{32}$ or $101,625,000 on April 16th. The Treasury note futures were sold at a price of $105^{4}/_{32}$, thereby establishing a hedge position with a value of $63,075,000. The spot minus futures basis was $3^{16}/_{32}$. On May 15th, the $100 million face value of mortgages were taken down although their price declined 4 full points ($4 million) to $97,625,000. At the same time, the short Treasury note futures position declined $5^{29}/_{32}$ to $59,531,320—a gain on the transaction of $3,543,750. The hedge manager's decision to hedge the transaction resulted in the $4 million loss on the spot position being mostly offset by a $3,543,375 gain on the short Treasury note futures position, a net loss of $456,625. The spot/futures basis narrowed from $3^{16}/_{32}$ on April 16th to $1^{19}/_{32}$ on May 15.

Next, suppose that the hedge manager elected to use the CBOT's options on Treasury bond futures contract to hedge the position. The manager determined a hedge ratio 0.40 for 104-strike Treasury bond puts, and these options had a price of $1^{29}/_{64}$ on April 16th, or a value of $581,250. Table 1–3 illustrates that the 104-strike puts rose in price to $8^{12}/_{64}$ on May 15th, so the value of the put position climbed by $6^{47}/_{64}$ to $3,275,000—a gain of $2,693,750. In this instance, the $4 million loss on the spot position was offset by a gain of $2,693,750 on the Treasury bond puts, so that the overall loss was limited to $1,306,250.

A comparison of the results from the two examples demonstrates that the hedge employing futures contracts offset a greater portion of the spot market position loss than the hedge employing options. Suppose, however, that prices of GNMA 9s had increased in value by about 4 points over the period, rather than declined. In this instance, the mortgage originator would have registered a gain of $4,000,000 on the spot

Table 1–2
Hedging a Mortgage Pipeline with Treasury Note Futures

Date	Operation	Quantity	Price	Price Change	Value	Profit/ (Loss)
April 16	Commit to make mortgages	$100,000,000	101–20	—	$101,625,000	—
	Short JUN T-note futures	600	105–04	—	$ 63,075,000	—
May 15	Takedown of mortgages	$100,000,000	97–20	(4–00)	$ 97,625,000	($4,000,000)
	Repurchase JUN T-note futures	600	99–07	(5–29)	$ 59,531,250	$3,543,375

Table 1–3
Hedging a Mortgage Pipeline with Treasury Bond Put Options

Date	Operation	Quantity	Price	Price Change	Value	Profit/(Loss)
April 16	Commit to make mortgages	$100,000,000	101–20	—	$101,625,000	—
	Buy 400 JUN T-bond 104 puts	400	1–29	—	$ 581,250	—
May 15	Takedown of mortgages	$100,000,000	97–20	(4–00)	$ 97,625,000	($4,000,000)
	Sell JUN T-bond 104 puts	400	8–12	(6–47)	$ 3,275,000	$2,693,750

position, *ceteris paribus*, but this would have been offset by approximately a $3,500,000 loss on the short futures position. And, the spot position gain might have been significantly less if a large number of the borrowers chose to recontract their mortgage loans at more advantageous interest rates. The maximum loss on the options hedge would have been limited, on the other hand, to the initial premium outlay ($581,250), so the originator might have enjoyed a major portion of the improvement in interest rates.

CONCLUSION

The relatively simple examples shown in Tables 1–2 and 1–3 demonstrate that hedging mortgage loan commitments can be complex and that no single solution will be superior to others in all instances. Managers faced with the task of hedging the price risk of a mortgage pipeline must weigh a large number of factors against one another to determine which type of instrument will likely result in the highest hedge efficiency. As noted previously, usually changes in mortgage market conditions result in shifts in the appropriate hedging vehicle and technique. Under these conditions, the hedge manager or committee constantly must reassess the goals of the hedging program and make necessary changes when conditions change. This suggests that hedging is unlikely to be either a panacea or a placebo for a mortgage loan originator. The results will be only as good as the efforts devoted to the task.

Chapter 2

JESS LEDERMAN

Jess Lederman is Executive Vice President with Bear Stearns Mortgage Capital Corporation, a wholly-owned subsidiary of Bear Stearns & Co., Inc. Previously he was Vice President of Marketing for Sears Mortgage Securities Corporation. Before joining Sears, Lederman was Director of Pricing and Research for PMI Mortgage Insurance Co.

Bear Stearns Mortgage Capital Corporation is one of the nation's leading private mortgage conduit companies.

Analyzing Alternative Hedging Strategies

JESS LEDERMAN

INTRODUCTION

The contemporary secondary marketing manager has more options than ever before for minimizing risk and maximizing profit opportunities. He or she can choose from an inviting—and often bewildering—array of futures, forwards, puts, calls, mandatories, and standbys. Yet, the fundamental question remains: how should secondary marketing decisions be made? Too often it is easy to fall into one of two traps. Relying on intuition is a common approach. All too often, however, at critical market junctures our instincts can be overwhelmed by those treacherous emotions, fear and greed. And appropriate strategies, oddly enough, can sometimes be counter-intuitive.

An equally dangerous method is one I dub the "black box" approach. Some managers who are fearful of subjective decision making take excessive comfort in the arcane and seemingly infallible computer model. After all, R&D people are constantly inputting data on historical relationships and market volatilities—what's there to worry about? But "go long" can be just as disastrous whether scrawled on a cocktail napkin or neatly typed on a computer printout.

The purpose of this chapter is to discuss a method of analyzing alternative hedging strategies that combines subjective reasoning and quantitative analysis. It is only by balancing these two techniques, by constantly probing, challenging old assumptions, and asking "what if?" that the modern mortgage banker can safely navigate the volatile waters of the contemporary secondary market.

STRATEGIC THINKING

What are the basic risks and returns in secondary marketing?

Let's suppose Acme Mortgage Company typically commits to originate loans with 2.5 points, incurs origination costs of 1 percent, and intends to sell the loans at a price of 99. Acme sees the risks and rewards of the business as follows:

Rewards
- Putting servicing on the books.
- Earning a .5 percent marketing profit if loans are sold at 99.
- Earning a greater marketing profit if loans can be sold at a price of greater than 99.

Risks
- Booking a marketing loss if loans are sold below 98.5.
- Paying substantial pair-off charges (or incurring losses in the futures market) if loans sold on a mandatory basis fail to close.

Table 2–1 associates each of the risks stated above with a specific interest rate scenario and lists the strategies that eliminate the risks and lock in some level of reward. To avoid focusing on too many variables at once, I am ignoring the subjects of basis risk (the risk that the prices of the hedged instrument and the proxy hedge instrument may not move in tandem) and of changes in the value of servicing.

Let's now focus in on three of the simplest approaches—unhedged, 100 percent mandatory (mandatory commitments equal to 100 percent of applications), and 100 percent optional delivery—and see what results they produce over a range of interest rate scenarios.

Table 2–1

Interest Rate Scenario	Risks	Strategies for Eliminating Risk and Capturing Reward
Rates Increase	The value of Acme's mortgage pipeline will fall	Hedge against the possibility of an increase in rates by (a) Committing to sell loans forward on a mandatory basis (either through cash market transactions or in the futures market); and /or (b) Purchasing puts or optional delivery commitments
Rates Decrease	Some or all of the loans in pipeline will not close, resulting in losses on mandatory commitments	Remain unhedged or combine a mandatory position with the purchase of call options

Assumptions

Rate lock given to borrower
at application:

10.75 percent + 2.5 points

Mandatory delivery
commitments:

10.50 percent + 1 point on delivery net to investor (90 percent minimum delivery, 105 percent maximum delivery)

Optional delivery commitments:	11.00 percent + 1/2 percent commitment fee + 1 percent on delivery net to investor
Acme's base servicing fee:	.25 percent
Acme's origination costs:	1.00 percent
Interest rate scenarios:	During any 60 day period rates can increase or decrease by 100 basis points
Loan pricing:	Loans are priced using standard FNMA gold book (12-year average life) assumptions. It is assumed that loans are sold at a premium if rates decline (in reality, Acme is selling the loans at a discount and capitalizing excess servicing, which is assumed to produce the same result as selling the loans at a premium)
Pair-Off Fees:	Pair offs are set equal to the increase in value of a mortgage loan (using loan pricing as described earlier) given the decrease in interest rates between the time of loan commitment and the date of the pair off
Loan Fallout:	Acme's research shows that pipeline fallout (the percentage of applications that fail to close) is directly correlated to changes in interest rates, as follows:

Change In Rates	Fallout Percent
+ 100 bp	2.5
+ 75 bp	5.0
+ 50 bp	10.0
+ 25 bp	15.0
No Change	20.0
− 25 bp	25.0
− 50 bp	35.0
− 75 bp	50.0
− 100 bp	70.0

Using these assumptions, we can now compute the marketing gain or loss that Acme will generate for each combination of hedge strategy and interest rate scenario (Table 2–2).

Table 2–2

	Net Marketing Gain (Loss)		
Change In Yields	Unhedged	100% Mandatory	100% Optional
+ 100bp	(5.548%)	.488%	(3.099%)
+ 75	(3.985)	.475	(3.033)
+ 50	(2.399)	.450	(2.899)
+ 25	(.936)	.425	(1.436)
No Change	.400	.400	(.100)
− 25	1.606	.129	1.106
− 50	2.483	(.505)	1.983
− 75	2.769	(1.765)	2.269
− 100	2.189	(3.929)	1.689

An analysis of Table 2–2 would seem to lead to some fairly obvious conclusions. If Acme expects rates to decrease, it should remain unhedged; conversely, if Acme expects rates to increase, it should rely on mandatory delivery commitments. If rates are expected to stay constant, then Acme is indifferent between an unhedged and mandatory position. Optional delivery commitments do not appear to be optimal under any scenario.

While this analysis seems fairly straightforward, it is obviously naive. For example, if Acme could successfully predict the direction of interest rates 100 percent of the time, its management team would likely be vacationing on the French Riviera instead of staring at their telerate screens, wrestling with hedging decisions. Furthermore, Acme might not have a firm opinion as to whether rates will go up or down, but might simply feel that rates will exhibit a set level of volatility. Will the upside potential of an unhedged position be more than offset by its even greater downside potential? How can this uncertainty be reflected in our analysis?

EXPECTED VALUE

The answer lies in *probabilistic analysis*, through which we will derive the *expected value* of each hedging strategy. Expected value is defined as follows:

$$E = \sum_{s=1}^{9} M_s P_s$$

Where

E = Expected value

s = Interest rate scenarios 1 through 9

M_s = The marketing gain or loss associated with scenarios s

P_s = The probability of scenario s

In other words, the marketing gain or loss associated with a given interest rate scenario is multipled times the probability of that scenario, and the sum of these multiples equals the expected value (E) of the hedging strategy.

In order to carry through this analysis, we must assign probabilities to each interest rate scenario. There is no one right way to do this; techniques vary from inferring the markets' predictions implied by the slope of the yield curve and recent historical volatilities, to econometric analysis, to good old-fashioned guesswork. The important thing is to recognize that, whatever method you employ, you should become involved and establish a comfort level with the probabilities assigned. Every secondary marketing decision either explicitly or implicitly pre-supposes an interest rate forecast. By thinking through the process of assigning probabilities, you will avoid the trap of a) assuming that any given scenario will occur with 100% certainty, or b) blindly accepting "black box"—driven probabilities.

Figures 2–1 through 2–4 are graphic representations of the probabilities assigned to each rate scenario under four different interest rate outlooks. Figure 2–1, which features a neutral outlook with low volatility, presupposes that Acme is neither bullish nor bearish, but shows that rates are likely to fluctuate in a narrow range. Figure 2–2 illustrates a neutral outlook with high volatility and is similarly devoid of a bullish or bearish bias. It assigns considerably higher probabilities to the most extreme rate scenarios. Figure 2–3 presents a bullish outlook, reflecting a 60 percent cumulative probability of rates decreasing versus a 30 percent cumulative probability of rates increasing (rates are twice as likely to fall as to rise). Figure 2–4 gives the bearish outlook, the mirror image of Figure 2–3, with a 60 percent cumulative probability of rates increasing versus a 30 percent cumulative probability of rates decreasing.

Table 2–3 displays the expected value (probability weighted gain or loss) for each hedging strategy under each of the four interest rate outlooks. Several observations can be made from the table:

1. The unhedged strategy produces the highest expected value under every outlook except bearish.

Figure 2–1
Neutral Outlook: Low Volatility

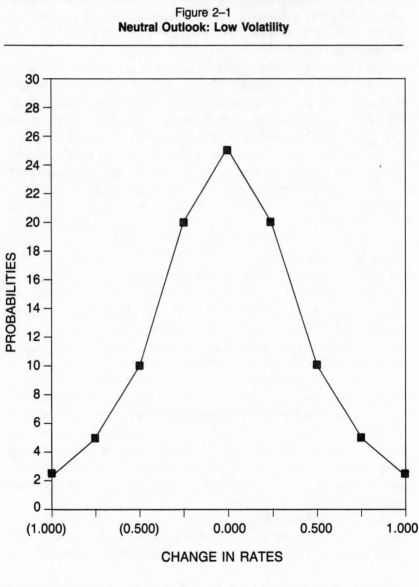

Figure 2–2
Neutral Outlook: High Volatility

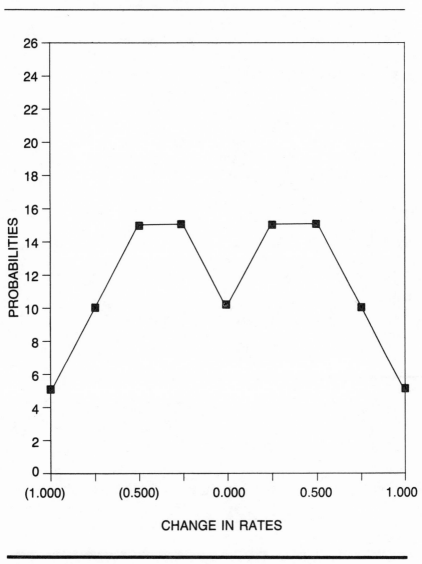

Figure 2–3
Bullish Outlook

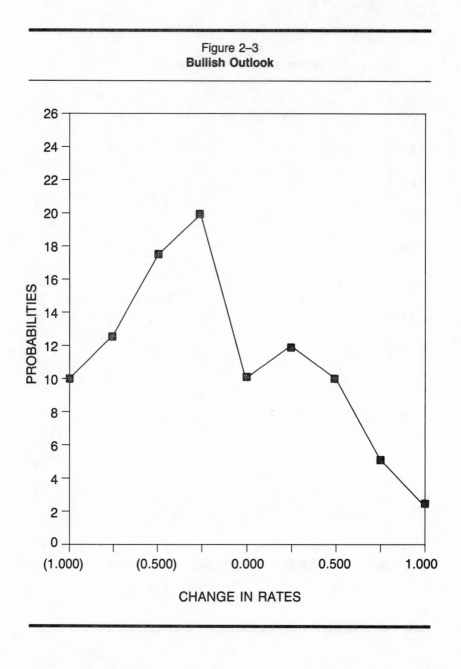

Figure 2–4
Bearish Outlook

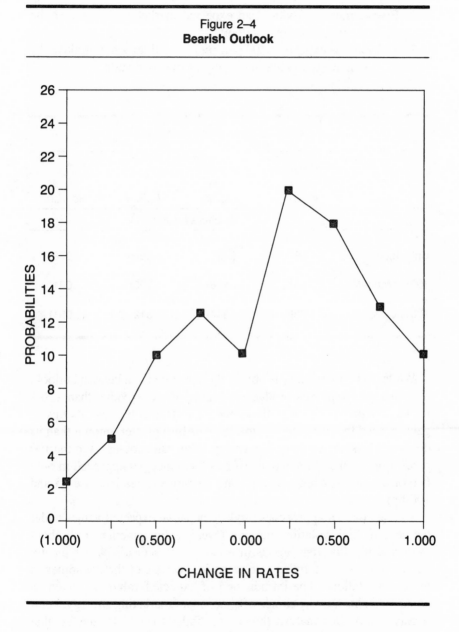

2. Every strategy produces an expected marketing loss under the neutral, high volatility outlook.
3. As might be expected, 100 percent optional does not produce the highest expected value under any of the four outlooks.

	Neutral: Low Volatility	Neutral: High Volatility	Bullish	Bearish
	Expected Value (%)			
Unhedged	.098	(.136)	.666	(.978)
100% Mandatory	.055	(.186)	(.502)	.091
100% Optional	(.256)	(.344)	.312	(1.001)

Table 2–3

While 100% mandatory is obviously best suited to a bearish outlook, the unhedged approach produces a higher expected value than 100% mandatory under the other three outlooks. This is because its upside gains exceed the mandatory's upside gains by a greater amount than its downside losses exceed the mandatory's downside losses. And the 100 percent optional approach outperforms the unhedged approach in only two of the most extreme interest rate scenarios (rates increase 75 and 100 bp).

The fact that all approaches produce negative expected values under the neutral, high volatility outlook reveals a fundamental truth about mortgage pipeline risk: losses in a rising rate scenario will typically exceed gains in a declining rate scenario, because of the phenomenon of pipeline fallout. The introduction of expected value has given us greater insights into the choice of a secondary marketing strategy, but it is only a start. Our analysis thus far has failed to consider the fact that the unhedged approach, while seemingly dominant, has the highest loss potential.

Clearly this downside potential must be taken into account.

THE RISK/RETURN TRADE-OFF

The issue raised above might be restated as follows: How do we assess the trade-off between risk and return? To answer this question it is useful to refer to a classic analytical device used in investment analysis: The risk/return curve.

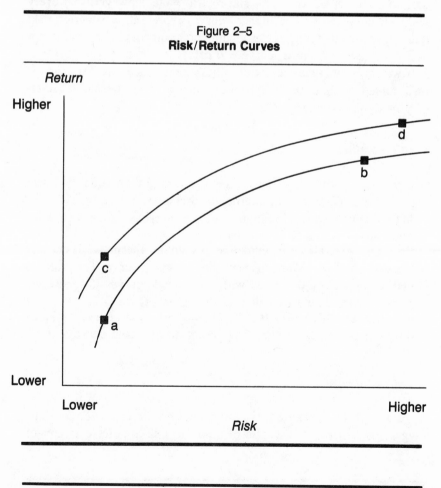

Figure 2–5
Risk/Return Curves

Figure 2–5 displays two typical risk/return curves. As risk increases, so does return; but note that the classic curve is concave to the X-axis, meaning that each increment of risk produces a smaller and smaller increment of return. At the lower left-hand corner of each curve relatively small increases in risk produce significant increases in return; however, as we move to the upper right hand corner, relatively large increases in risk are required to coax additional increments of return. On any given curve one point cannot be said to be "superior" to another.

The choice of any point along a risk/return curve will depend on the desired trade-off between risk and return. Note, however, that every point on curve c–d (the "higher" curve) represents a superior risk/return trade-off than any corresponding point on curve a–b (that is, for any given level of return, curve c–d offers less risk).

If we accept this classic notion of risk/return trade-offs, we can set forth some guidelines that will be useful in analyzing alternative secondary marketing strategies.

First Guidelines

A strategy is optimal if it has a higher return and an equal or lesser degree of risk compared to alternative strategies.

In the example shown in Figure 2–6, alternative B is clearly superior to alternatives A and C.

We might generalize this guideline to state: an alternative is optimal if it lies on a higher risk/return curve than any other curve. The problem is that we are rarely presented with ready-made curves. Suppose we simply are considering two alternatives, as in Figure 2–7.

How can we tell whether B is on a higher risk/return curve (and thus optimal) or is simply an alternative point on the same curve as A?

Second Guideline

If we accept the notion that risk/return curves are concave, then this suggests an answer: If the ratio of return to risk at point B is greater

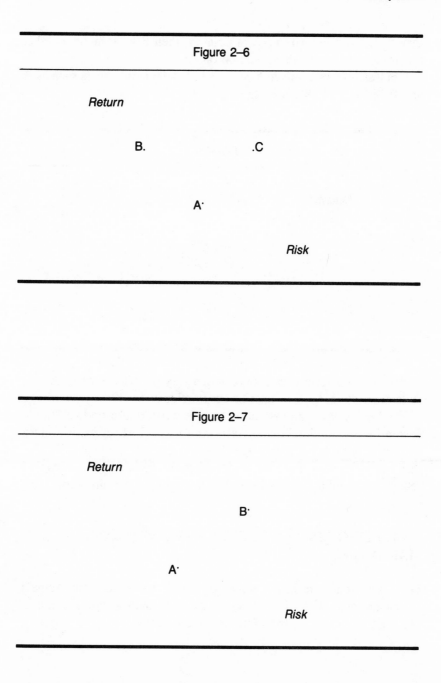

Figure 2–6

Return

B.   .C

A·

Risk

Figure 2–7

Return

B·

A·

Risk

than the ratio of return to risk at point A, then B must be on a higher risk/return curve and thus must be optimal.

It is less obvious, unfortunately, as to whether two points such as A and B in Figure 2–8 are on the same curve:

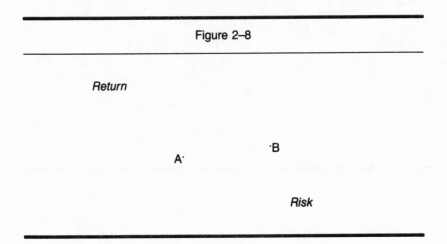

Figure 2–8

Return

A·

·B

Risk

Are we simply viewing a curve with a very flat risk/return trade-off, or is alternative A on a superior curve relative to B?

The best way for an institution to assess risk/return trade-offs is to design its own optimal curve, reflecting its desired set of risk/return trade-offs. That is why the suggestions are labeled "guidelines," rather than rules. For some institutions, for example, there may be no level of return that would justify a level of risk beyond a certain point.

ANALYZING RISK AND RETURN IN SECONDARY MARKETING

Let's now return from the realm of theory and reconsider Acme's secondary marketing alternatives in the light of risk/return analysis. Our first step must be to define risk and return.

Risk

Risk should be a reflection of the potential downside inherent in a given strategy. We shall therefore quantify risk as follows:

$$R = \sum_{s=a}^{j} L_s P_s$$

Where:

R = Risk

s = Interest rate scenarios—a through j, where all such scenarios are associated with a marketing loss

L_s = The marketing loss in scenario s

P_s = The probability of scenario s

Return

Expected Value (E) is a convenient measure of return.

We can now analyze Acme's three alternative strategies in Table 2–4 under each interest rate outlook by applying risk/return analysis.

By looking at Figure 2–9 we can quickly see that the choice between unhedged and 100 percent mandatory depends on Acme's desired risk/return trade-off. The unhedged approach offers a greater return, but also a greater degree of risk. And since the E/R ratio (which measures the slope of the risk/return curve) for unhedged is smaller than for 100 percent mandatory, we have no reason to believe that unhedged lies on a superior risk/return curve. 100 percent optional, of course, lies on a distinctly inferior curve!

Table 2–4

Neutral Outlook: Low Volatility	Risk	Return	E/R
100% Mandatory	.237	.055	.231
Unhedged	.765	.098	.128
100% Optional	.831	(.256)	(.308)
Neutral Outlook: *High Volatility*			
100% Mandatory	.449	(.186)	(.415)
100% Optional	1.119	(.344)	(.307)
Unhedged	1.176	(.136)	(.116)
Bullish			
Unhedged	.695	.666	.988
100% Mandatory	.702	(.502)	(.715)
100% Optional	.709	.312	.441
Bearish			
100% Mandatory	.237	.091	.384
100% Optional	1.494	(1.001)	(.67)
Unhedged	1.66	(.978)	(.589)

Figure 2–9

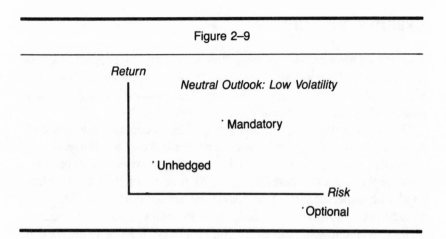

Figure 2–10's representation of the risk/ return characteristics of the three alternatives under the bullish outlook names makes it clear that unhedged is on a superior curve relative to 100 percent optional or mandatory.

Figure 2–10

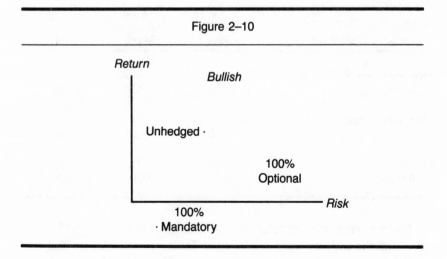

HYBRID STRATEGIES

Thus far we have considered only three very simply secondary marketing strategies. By combining these fundatmental approaches, however, we can create new, hybrid strategies that reduce risk *and* increase return—thus shifting us to a new, superior curve.

Our starting point for this analysis will be to consider the nature of Acme's pipeline risk. Under each scenario there is a relatively high probability that pipeline fallout will average approximately 20 percent. This might suggest, therefore, that 20 percent of Acme's pipeline should be either unhedged or hedged on an optional basis. We have already seen, however, that hedging with optional delivery commitments (given our assumptions for cost) is always inferior to alternative approaches. Armed with this knowledge, we can confidently predict that a strategy of hedging 80 percent of pipeline on a mandatory basis and leaving 20 percent unhedged will produce improved results, as shown in Table 2–5.

Table 2–5

80/20 Mandatory/Unhedged	Risk	Return	E/R
Neutral Outlook: Low Volatility	.121	.181	1.489
Neutral Outlook: High Volatility	.243	(.025)	(.102)
Bullish	.389	(.17)	(.438)
Bearish	.150	.079	.526

By comparing the risk/return characteristics of our new hybrid strategy with the earlier results displayed in Table 2–4, we can see that the 80/20 approach is on a superior curve (lower risk and higher return) under both neutral rate outlooks. And, while it does not help us under a bullish outlook, the 80/20 is a viable alternative (offering less risk in exchange for less return) to 100 percent mandatory under a bearish outlook. In fact, the 80/20 approach offers the lowest level of risk under each of the four rate outlooks.

ACTIVE MANAGEMENT

Thus far the secondry marketing strategies that we have been evaulating have been essentially passive; it is assumed, for example, that an unhedged position remains unhedged no matter what happens to interest rates. I say *essentially* passive, however, because a small degree of hedge management has already entered into our analysis. To illustrate this, consider the 80/20 alternative. Because the investor allows for a 90–150 percent allowable delivery range, Acme can satisfy its mandatory delivery requirement by delivering loans in an amount equal to 72–84 percent of its original pipeline. Obviously, to optimize profits Acme will underdeliver if rates decline and overdeliver if rates rise. In fact, the difference in expected value between optimizing or failing to optimize over or under delivery is over 100 percent under certain interest rate outlooks.

This would seem to suggest that actively managing a hedged position might help set us on a superior risk/return curve. To test this hypothesis, we will analyze each of our four secondary marketing alternatives to see how they perform under active management.

The first step in the analysis is to establish a set of active management guidelines. For example, Acme might establish the following decision rules:

Initial Strategy

Unhedged   If rates increase by 50 basis points, as-
                            sume a 95 percent hedged (mandatory)
                            position. If rates subsequently decline to

	their starting level, pair off mandatory commitments and resume unhedged position.
100 Percent Mandatory	If rates decline by 50 basis points, reduce mandatory coverage to 50 percent of exposure. If rates subsequently increase back to their starting level, resume 100 percent hedged position.
80/20 Mandatory/ Unhedged	If rates increase by 50 basis points, assume a 95 percent hedged position; if rates subsequently decline to their starting level, pair off mandatory coverage in excess of 80 percent. If rates decline by 50 points, reduce mandatory coverage to 50 percent; if rates subsequently increase back to their starting level, resume 80 percent hedged position.

It is important to observe that, given these decision rules, an actively managed position might actually backfire. For example, consider an unhedged position. If rates rise 50 basis points and then subsequently fall, Acme will be faced with a pair-off charge that would have been avoided under a purely passive hedge management program. Clearly, to complete our analysis we will have to quantify the potential for this unfavorable whipsaw phenomenon.

We have already made the assumption that rates will not move more than 100 points in any one direction over a 60-day timeframe. Therefore, if rates increase 50 basis points they cannot fall to a level more than 50 points below their original starting point. Similarly, if rates decrease 50 points they cannot increase to a level more than 50 basis points above their original starting point. Tables 2–6 and 2–7 present a set of probabilities that rates will whipsaw under each interest rate outlook.

Table 2–6
**Probability That Rates Will Reach Final Rate Level
after Increasing 50 Basis Points**

Final Rate Level	Neutral Outlook Low Volatility	Neutral Outlook High Volatility	Bullish	Bearish
+ .25%	.20	.30	.20	.30
No change	.20	.15	.10	.15
− .25%	.05	.10	.05	.10
− .50%	.025	.05	.025	.05

Table 2–7
**Probability That Rates Will Reach Final Rate Level
after Decreasing 50 Basis Points**

Final Rate Level	Neutral Outlook Low Volatility	Neutral Outlook High Volatility	Bullish	Bearish
+ .50%	.025	.05	.05	.025
+ .25%	.05	.10	.10	.05
No change	.10	.15	.15	.1
− .25%	.20	.30	.30	.20

The expected value under the active management alternatives can be calculated by using the following forumla:

$$E_a = \sum_{s=1}^{9} [M_{w,s}\, P_{w,s}) + (M_{n,s}\, (1 - P_{w,s,}))]P_s$$

Where:

E_a = The expected value using active management

s = Interest rate scenarios 1 through 9

$M_{w,s}$ = The marketing gain (loss) experienced, assuming rates whiplash in scenario s

$P_{w,s}$ = The probability that rates will whiplash in scenario s

$M_{n,s}$ = The marketing gain (loss) experienced assuming rates do not whiplash in scenario s

P_s = The probability of scenario s

Table 2-8 displays the return (expected value), risk, and return/risk ratio for the unhedged, 100 percent mandatory, and 80/20 strategies, assuming active management. Figures 2–11 through 2–14 graphically represent comparative risk/return profiles for the three alternative strategies, both with and without active management.

By comparing the results in Table 2–8 with those in Table 2–4, and by analyzing Figures 2–11 through 2–14, we can arrive at conclusions about the effectiveness of the active management strategies under each interest rate outlook.

Neutral Outlook: Low Volitility

Active management of all three alternative strategies leads to a lower level of return under a neutral, low-volatility scenario. This is not surprising; the principal advantage of active management is that it reduces the highest losses that can occur under the more extreme interest rate scenarios. The level of marketing gains generally *declines*, however, for scenarios involving more modest rate fluctuations.

Table 2–8

Netural Outlook: Low Volatility	Risk	Return	Return/Risk
Unhedged	.672	.089	.132
100% Mandatory	.199	.004	.022
80/20	.076	.141	1.858
Neutral Outlook: High Volatility			
Unhedged	.944	(.006)	(.006)
100% Mandatory	.365	(.184)	(.505)
80/20	.152	(.018)	(.12)
Bullish			
Unhedged	.528	.713	1.225
100 Mandatory	.545	(.425)	(.780)
80/20	.258	(.128)	(.497)
Bearish			
Unhedged	1.264	(.67)	(.53)
100% Mandatory	.915	.076	(.39)
80/20	.077	.102	1.321

Figure 2–11
Neutral Outlook
Low Volatility

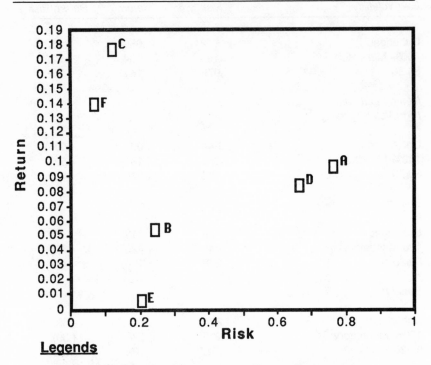

Legends

A: Unhedged (Passive Management Strategy)

B: 100% Mandatory (Passive Management Strategy)

C: 80% Mandatory/20% Unhedged (Passive Management Strategy)

D: Unhedged (Active Management Strategy)

E: 100% Mandatory (Active Management Strategy)

F: 80% Mandatory/20% Unhedged (Active Management Strategy)

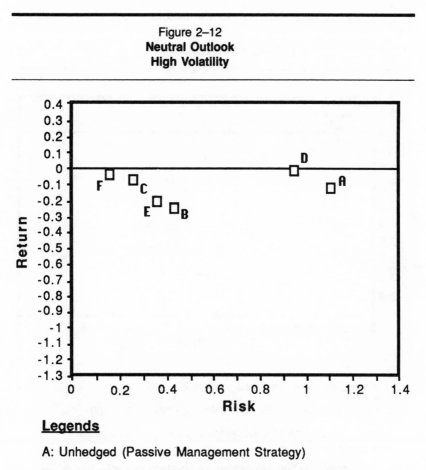

Figure 2–12
Neutral Outlook
High Volatility

Legends

A: Unhedged (Passive Management Strategy)

B: 100% Mandatory (Passive Management Strategy)

C: 80% Mandatory/20% Unhedged (Passive Management Strategy)

D: Unhedged (Active Management Strategy)

E: 100% Mandatory (Active Management Strategy)

F: 80% Mandatory/20% Unhedged (Active Management Strategy)

Figure 2–13
Bearish Outlook

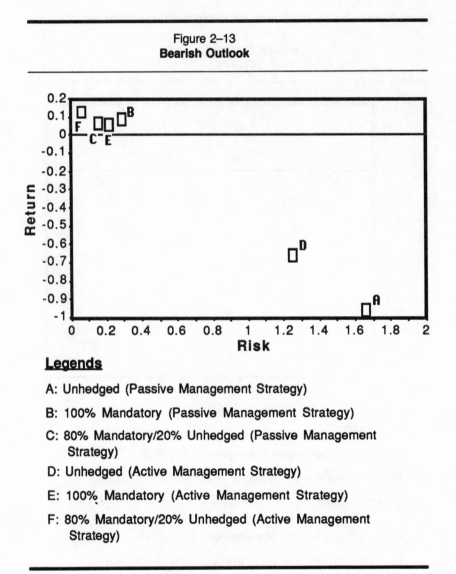

Legends

A: Unhedged (Passive Management Strategy)

B: 100% Mandatory (Passive Management Strategy)

C: 80% Mandatory/20% Unhedged (Passive Management Strategy)

D: Unhedged (Active Management Strategy)

E: 100% Mandatory (Active Management Strategy)

F: 80% Mandatory/20% Unhedged (Active Management Strategy)

Figure 2–14
Bullish Outlook

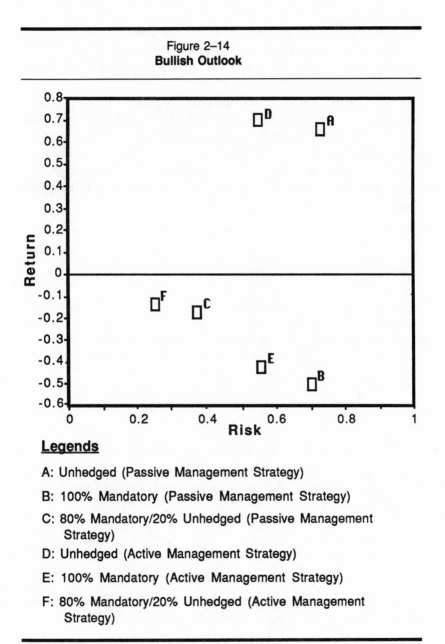

Legends

A: Unhedged (Passive Management Strategy)

B: 100% Mandatory (Passive Management Strategy)

C: 80% Mandatory/20% Unhedged (Passive Management Strategy)

D: Unhedged (Active Management Strategy)

E: 100% Mandatory (Active Management Strategy)

F: 80% Mandatory/20% Unhedged (Active Management Strategy)

Although active management decreases the level of return, it also decreases the level of risk. In fact, as we shall see, active management leads to a lower level of risk under every strategic alternative and under all four rate outlooks.

The next step is to analyze our new position on the risk/return curve. The 80/20 mandatory/unhedged approach clearly lies on the optimal curve. The 80/20 actively managed version can be viewed as an acceptable alternative for Acme if it prefers a lower risk profile. It is interesting to note that the actively managed 100 percent mandatory approach would appear to lie on a curve that is *inferior* relative to the 100 percent mandatory nonactively managed approach.

Neutral Outlook: High Volatility

Not surprisingly, under the neutral high-volatility outlook active management leads to increased return *and* decreased risk under all strategies. Unhedged and 80/20 mandatory unhedged can be viewed as risk/return alternaives, with 100 percent mandatory falling on an inferior curve.

Bullish

Return increases and risk decreases for all four alternative strategies under a bullish outlook. The actively managed unhedged approach is clearly superior.

Bearish

The actively managed 80/20 mandatory unhedged strategy emerges as the optimal approach under the bearish interest rate outlook.

CONCLUSION

Probabilistic analysis, expected value, and risk/return analysis are important tools for institutions involved in the secondary market. Hedging mortgage pipeline risk requires a disciplined blend of subjective reasoning and rigorous quantitative analysis. It is only by carefully considering the implications of each alternative hedging strategy that secondary marketing managers will successfully minimize risk and maximize profits.

Chapter 3

TANYA S. ARNOLD

Tanya Arnold is a Vice President with The First Boston Corporation in New York. She is a member of the Fixed Income Research Dept., responsible for synthetic products. Previously Ms. Arnold was involved in the development of the interest rate swap market, and was a member of First Boston's corporate finance and mergers and acquisitions departments. She holds a degree in mathematics from Yale University and an M.B.A. from Harvard.

The Current Status of Hedging Tools for Mortgage-Backed Securities

TANYA S. ARNOLD

Hedging mortgage backed securities (MBS) is a tricky business. The 1985–1986 rally caused an unprecedented number of failed hedges, as the percentage of MBS securities at a premium increased from 5 percent to over 75 percent. Many investors who thought they were hedged discovered they were not. But the dramatic rally was not the culprit—it only made certain types of hedges fail more quickly. The culprit in failed hedges was typically a static hedging technique.

MBSs by their very nature are dynamic; that is, their cash flows are uncertain. Existing hedging tools cannot remove this uncertainty. Static hedges can be designed only against *expected* cash flows for MBS. If actual cash flows vary from expected cash flows (as they did in the rally) a hedge will likely require modification. This is the definition of a *dynamic hedge*. Dynamic hedges have outperformed static hedges for discount as well as premium MBS.

Figure 3–1 shows the result for both a static and a dynamic hedge of GNMA 8s (a discount security) using Treasury note futures. GNMA 8s had a price of 96 in March 1986 and ranged in value from 89 to 97 through September. The static and dynamic hedges structured in March consisted of the sale of $700,000 September 1986 Treasury note futures per $1 million GNMA 8s. In the static hedge, this futures position was held constant. In the dynamic hedge, the futures position was altered as the market changed. Specifically, as the GNMA 8s rose in value, T-note futures were sold. As the GNMA 8s fell in value, T-note futures were purchased. The benefit of dynamic hedging is clear; the dynamically hedged value of the GNMA 8s ranged from 93 to 96, versus 91 to 96 in the static case—a reduction in residual (or unhedged) risk of 25 percent.

Figure 3–1
Dynamic Hedge Analysis
GNMA 8 Vs. T-Note Futures September 86

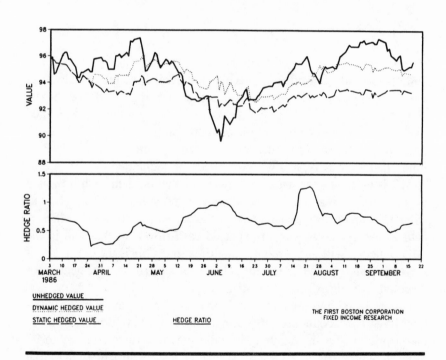

UNHEDGED VALUE
DYNAMIC HEDGED VALUE
STATIC HEDGED VALUE   HEDGE RATIO

THE FIRST BOSTON CORPORATION
FIXED INCOME RESEARCH

Hedges for MBSs may be one-way or two-way. A one-way hedge offsets the change in the value of an asset in one direction only; for example, it may limit the downside of the asset value. A two-way hedge moves in both directions, with a change opposite in value to that of the asset. Examples of one-way and two-way hedges for fixed rate MBS include:

One-Way Hedges

- Purchase puts
- Purchase calls and short futures
- Purchase calls and short cash
- Purchase interest rate caps or interest rate floors

Two-Way Hedges

- Short futures, forwards, or cash
- Pay fixed/receive floating interest rate swaps

Figure 3–2 illustrates the price/yield relationship for MBS. As interest rates rise, the price of the MBS declines much like that of an ordinary bond. If rates fall, however, escalating prepayments cause the price to rise less rapidly, and eventually to flatten out. This price/yield behavior is termed *negative convexity*. It is an important consideration in structuring MBS hedges.

To see why it is important, consider a static two-way hedge. Such a hedge position is risky because premium MBSs may prepay at par when the hedge is at a loss. Consider an investor who purchases an MBS at 100 and enters a static two-way hedge. If the MBS trades to a premium—for example 107—the hedge should have a loss of 7, since it is designed to move opposite in value to that of the asset. Without prepayments, the value of the MBS plus hedge is 100 (107 less a loss of 7 on the hedge). If the security were to prepay in full, however, the investor would receive only 100 from the MBS rather than the 107

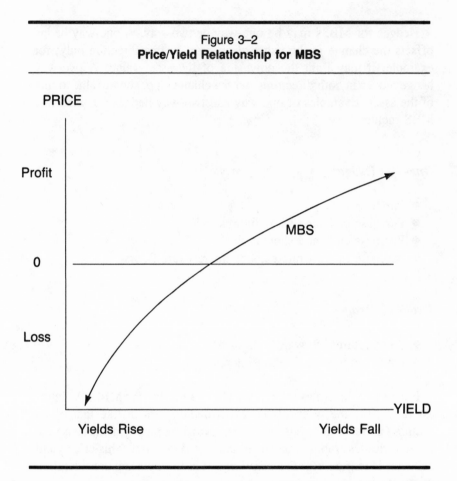

Figure 3–2
Price/Yield Relationship for MBS

market value. The value of the MBS plus hedge in this case is 93 (100 minus the loss of 7 on the hedge) rather than the desired 100. It is easy to see that as long as there are any prepayments, this static hedge will produce some amount of net loss. This further illustrates the need to manage MBS hedges dynamically.

Figure 3–3 illustrates the result of the most common one-way hedge for MBS—the purchase of a put option. By comparing the graphs in Figures 3–2 and 3–3, it is clear that the long put position protects the

Figure 3–3
**Price/Yield Relationship
Long MBS, Put**

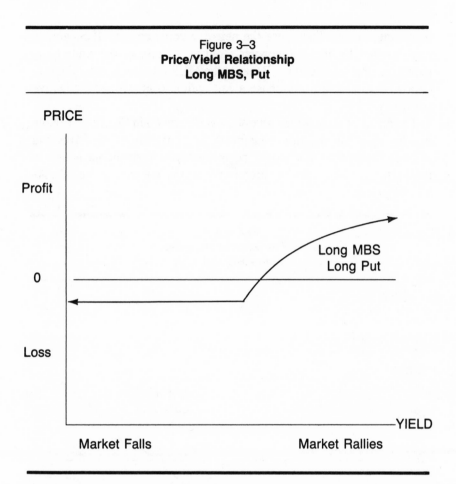

downside value of the asset when the market falls. It must be noted, though, that for falling markets the hedge produces a slight loss. This is due to the premium that must be paid to purchase the put. Many hedgers employ this put strategy with the philosophy that the put can be purchased with some of the high yield from the MBS. In fact, it is common to see the put premium expressed in basis points.

With the put strategy, the investor's upside is retained. However, it remains limited by the negative convexity of the MBS. The rising prepayment levels that cause the negative convexity of MBSs are, in turn, caused by the homeowner's option to prepay the underlying mortgage (that is, to call it). Because the MBS investor is short this call option, it is natural to purchase a call option to improve the negative convexity.

The result of adding the call option is illustrated in Figure 3–4. Note that the long call position transforms the convexity of the MBS and restores the upside that would be present in a noncallable bond. In return, the investor must pay premiums for both the put and the call. As

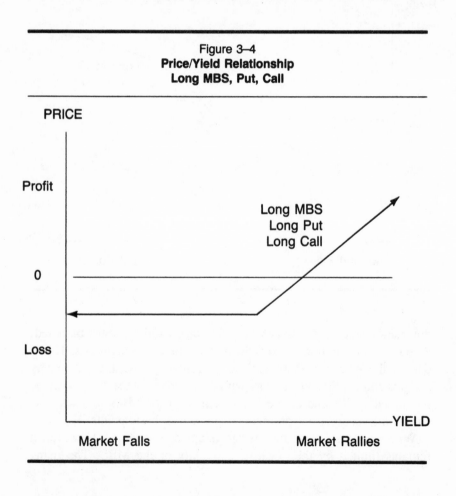

Figure 3–4
Price/Yield Relationship
Long MBS, Put, Call

PRICE

Profit

Long MBS
Long Put
Long Call

0

Loss

YIELD

Market Falls   Market Rallies

before, these premiums may be stated as a reduction in the MBS yield.

Although a long call position is not normally taken against a long position in fixed-rate assets, it is clearly a solution to the negative convexity of MBS. A long call position may be used in both one-way and two-way hedges, but its use is limited by the available term of options contracts. Although exchange-traded and over-the-counter call options are available on instruments with maturities ranging from 3 months to 30 years, the term of option contracts typically does not exceed 1 year. Therefore, options must be rolled over for hedges that exceed 1 year or proxies for longer-term options must be used. Proxies for long-term call options are interest rate floors, corporate bond warrants, and long zeros.

A popular technique used by financial institutions to hedge incremental MBSs is risk-controlled arbitrage. Typically, fixed-rate MBSs are purchased and then funded in the repo market. To remove the interest rate exposure between the fixed-rate asset and the floating-rate liability (rollovers in the repo market) a hedge is structured that may include interest rate swaps, interest rate caps, futures and/or options (see Table 3–1 for a numerical example). The hedge is designed against the expected cash flows of the MBS and should be adjusted (made dynamic) if actual cash flows vary from expected cash flows. Steps in the process are:

1. Purchase $700 MM GMNA 9 percent at 96–08/32.
2. Place the securities on three-month reverse-repo.
3. Use the interest rate swaps shown in Table 3–1, paying fixed-rate and receiving three-month LIBOR.

There is little doubt that dynamic management improves the performance of hedges, given the uncertainty of MBS cash flows. Dynamic management, however, may require frequent hedge adjustments, making the bid-ask spread of the hedging tool a key consideration. In addition to the cost factor, several other factors merit study. Round lots, available contract maturities, the term of the contract, potential risks created by spread shifts between the MBS and the hedging tool markets, and changing yield curve shape risk are the other key factors.

Table 3–1
Risk Controlled Arbitrage for GMNA 9s*

Maturity	Amount ($MM)	Rate
1	15	7.510
2	30	7.960
3	30	8.413
4	30	8.664
5	550	8.795

* The HTG corporate bond equivalent yield of the GNMA 9s is 9.71% and the all in cost of the interest rate swaps is 8.75%. Therefore, the spread between the GNMA 9s and the swaps is 96 basis points.

Assumptions:

1. GNMA 9.00% prepay at 0.35% SMM.
2. Residual gaps are borrowed or invested at the term liability curve.
3. LIBOR offsets the cost of reserve-repo.
4. Five-year analysis

Table 3–2 summarizes these factors for the various hedging tools. Unfortunately, no hedging tool is perfect. Trade-offs exist; for example, in return for the high liquidity and small lot size of financial futures, hedgers must accept intermarket spread risk and a maximum term of one year.

It is important to understand what the available MBS hedging tools can and cannot do. None of the hedging tools can transform the uncertainty of the MBS cash flow, its final maturity, or its credit risk. The properties that can be transformed for MBS are described in Table 3–3. A pattern is worth noting:

- Futures, forwards, and interest rate swaps all transform the same properties of MBS.
- Options, interest rate caps, and interest rate floors all transform the same properties of MBS.

The effectiveness of a hedge may be judged from the percentage of total interest rate risk removed. Its complement is the residual, or basis

Table 3–2
Key Aspects of Hedging Tools for MBS

Risk Management Tool	Available Contract Maturities	Longest Term	Round Lot	Bid-Ask Spread (in basis points)	Yield Curve Shape Risk	Intermarket Spread Risk
Exchange traded futures	3 Mo., 10 Yr., 30 Yr.	1 yr.	$100K	up to 2	Yes	Yes
Forwards	3 Mo.–30 Yr.	12 mos.	$ 10 MM	up to 25	No	No
Exchange traded options	3 Mo., 10 Yr., 30 Yr.	9 mos.	$100K	up to 4	Yes	Yes
Over-the-counter options	3 Mo.–30 Yr.	1 yr.	$ 1 MM	up to 4	No	No
Interest rate swaps	1–10 Yrs.	10 yrs.	$ 5 MM	up to 10	No	Yes
Interest rate caps/floors	1–12 Yrs.	12 yrs.	$ 10 MM	15	Yes	Yes

Table 3-3
Hedging Tools for MBS

Property	Futures	Forwards	Options	Interest Rate Swaps	Rate Caps/ Floors
Coupon/Rate of Interest:					
Transform from fixed to floating (or vice versa)	X	X		X	
Set/remove minimum or maximum rate			X		X
Payment of coupon:					
Transform to more frequent or less frequent payments	X	X		X	
Principal:					
Set/remove option characteristic			X		X

risk, of the hedge. For MBS hedges, effectiveness is unquestionably limited by the factors described in Table 3–3 as well as by the very nature of the MBS. It is worth noting that basis risk on hedges against all securities has increased in the past two years and not only against MBS.

Table 3–4
The Effectiveness of Hedging

Market Segment	Typical Effectiveness Two Years Ago	Typical Effectiveness Today
Long Treasury Bond	98%	90%
Long Corporates		
High Quality	90%	80%
Lower Quality	70%	60%
GNMAs	75%	65%

Given the difficulty of hedging MBS, investors may prefer to cope by locking in a minimum reinvestment rate for future prepayments. To do this, investors in fixed-rate MBS would both purchase floating-rate notes, floating rate certificates of deposit, and/or adjustable rate mortgages as future prepayments occur and execute one of two transactions:

- Purchase an interest rate floor on the index of the floating rate securities to be purchased when prepayments occur or
- Enter into an interest rate swap in which a fixed rate is received and a floating rate based on the index of the floating rate securities is paid, and purchase an interest rate cap on the floating index.

Either transaction creates a minimum rate at which future prepayments may be reinvested. Similar to a long call position, this strategy provides insurance for the consequences of rising prepayment levels during a market rally. As with a risk controlled arbitrage, this hedge requires that the prepayment schedule, or at least the average life, of the associated MBS be estimated in advance.

The available hedging tools are not able to remove all of the interest rate risk in MBS. But the basis risk that remains is caused only partially by the hedging tools; the balance is due to the uncertainty of the MBS cash flows. One thing is certain, however: dynamic hedging helps.

Chapter 4

HARLEY S. BASSMAN

Harley S. Bassman is currently Vice President and Senior Trader of over-the-counter mortgage-backed security options for Merrill Lynch. He created the OPOSSMS™ (Options to Purchase or Sell Specified Mortgage-backed Securities) product shortly after joining the firm in 1985. He was previously a trader involved in equity futures/options arbitrage and over-the-counter treasury options. He received his MBA in finance and marketing from the University of Chicago in 1983.

Hedging with Options on Mortgage-backed Securities

HARLEY S. BASSMAN

In what seems like the distant past (but was only a little over a decade ago), a regulated financial community intermediated short-term funds into long-term mortgage money for the home-buying public. Interest rates were relatively stable, accompanied by a positive sloping yield curve. But as inflation increased and the pace of deregulation accelerated, bond price volatility injected risk into the mortgage finance market. Mortgage originators, skilled at evaluating potential loan commitments, no longer desired to absorb the price risk during the commitment window. They needed a way to hedge without giving up the spread they were working for. The investment banking community, constantly looking for new opportunities, quickly developed a vehicle to respond to this need. For a fee, they would stand by the mortgage originator to accept his or her loans at a fixed price if interest rates were to rise during the term of the commitment. The banker's promise to stand by the originator guaranteed a price floor for the loan product, effectively locking in a profit and removing price risk.

This was the birth of the "stand by market" that subsequently flourished in the late seventies. A secondary market was created to broker risk among those institutions whose loan production was in disequilibrium with their desire to take securities into their portfolios. Mortgage bankers, for example, who had no desire to hold loans would effectively be paired with large thrifts whose deposit inflows were greater than loan production. Unfortunately, as contingent claims analysis was still in its infancy and forward pricing was not yet efficient, the curve inversion of 1981 that nearly destroyed the thrift industry sent the stand-by market reeling.

With the heightened need for price volatility protection, a new breed of "techno-trader" emerged. Consequently, options on mortgage-backed securities appeared as a new derivative evolving from the standy-by market concept. As a standy-by is nothing more than a put, advanced option theory has laid the groundwork for today's liquid and efficient MBS options market. Via a network of financial dealers, you can now buy or sell puts and calls on almost all mortgage-backed securities.

The real virtues of options can quickly be discerned by reviewing the basic option fundamentals. A *call* is the right—not the obligation—to purchase a given security at a fixed price over a certain time. In the same vein, a *put option* is the right to sell a given security at a fixed price over a certain time. Compare this with the other types of securities with which you are more familiar. The three most common trading instruments are cash securities, which settle immediately, and futures and forwards, which specify a transaction that settles at a later date. All three of these securities—cash, futures, and forwards—have one thing in common: they all have one-for-one risk/return profiles. That is, if the security you own rises one point in price, you will make one point. Similarly, if its price falls a point, you will lose the same. Therefore, when involved with these securities, you are limited to being long, short, or flat. Your risk/return curve is described by a 45-degree line. Unfortunately, not everyone has investment needs or market outlooks that are so black and white. Most of us rest in between the shades of gray. This is where options fit in. Using options, you can add a new dimension to your investment arsenal. With options you can buy and sell pieces of the risk/return curve. Call buyers, for instance, purchase only the upside move on a security for a small fee. Call sellers are willing to give up this portion of the curve in exchange for a more immediate increase in short-term return. Some people believe the market will rise three points from its present level and stop. To satiate these investors, it is possible to purchase exactly this three-point range for a small fee. Others may believe the market will rise over the next two to three months and then fall after that. This market viewpoint can also be translated into profits via options.

These examples illustrate how options can be applied to today's complicated money management, but more specifically, why should you use over-the-counter mortgage-backed securities (MBS) options? After all, you can't find them on Quotron, and they don't appear in the paper. Why can't you use the futures options on the CBT?

One of the primary uses of the options is hedging. *Hedging* is the decrease or removal of risk. When one uses Treasury futures to hedge mortgages, one may actually be *increasing* risk. Suddenly, you have introduced three new sets of variables into the equation. First of all, you will incur *basis risk*, that is, the price spread between the futures contract and the 30-year Treasury. A second type is *curve risk*, which is the yield spread between the 10-year and 30-year Treasuries. Finally, you have to contend with the *intermarket spread*, the yield spread of mortgages to the 10-year Treasury from which we price our product. These relationships are all volatile, any of which can move as much as one point in a day. This type of hedging is more effective in Las Vegas. As long as you are not hedging an 8 percent 15-year Treasury (the specification for the CBT contrac), you are exposed to this risk.

The best reason to be involved in the OTC options market is that it offers a pure, customized product. Unlike futures options, with fixed strikes and only four expirations a year, you can specify the security type, coupon, strike, and time horizon. This complete flexibility means that investors can match their financial needs more accurately.

Investors, traders, mortgage bankers, and other participants in the mortgage finance community ultimately derive their worth from how effectively they can manage risk. As the preceding discussion demonstrated, options—especially OTC MBS options—are a vital necessity to anyone involved in the mortgage market. Options are the best way to maximize profit while being an effective risk manager.

Mortgage bankers require options to hedge potential price risk. Managers of these operations must determine how much of their profits depend upon the stability of the market. They must decide how much added income can be derived by not hedging a portion of their production and how big a bet they are placing on the direction of interest rates. A risk manager in this type of operation needs a concise business plan to deal with the exogenous risks of a volatile market. You must ask directly how important interest rate movement is to profitability. Once this is determined, options can then place the firm at its desired risk level.

Investors in mortgage-backed securities have different needs. How important is current income relative to capital gains? What portion of the yield curve do you favor? For money managers, what is the underlying goal of the investor? As portfolio managers are invariably net long, options are the vehicle of choice to fine tune the position without churning the account. Risk managers of money invested in mortgages need to set their goals and compare these to their market opinion. Once these goals are set, options can be used to help execute. For example, option strategies can be employed to maintain the desired duration of your portfolio in the face of volatile prepayments and yield curve movements.

Active traders of mortgage securities also require options. A prudent trader should know the profit and loss potential of his or her position over a range of yield levels. Ideally, the potential profit and loss should be analyyzed to the point that the trader can graph the risk/return profile of the position. Options can then be added to modify this curve to reflect the trader's market opinion and risk level.

This ability to fine tune risk is one of the most important attributes of options. With options you can reduce exposure without having to realize a loss. It enables you to lock in a profit without giving up additional upside. You can also use options to manage unwanted risks while maximizing profits from your established business plan.

With the realization that MBS options are a smart trader's tool in today's financial environment, you are ready to create some option strategies. At first, only four option positions are apparent: long or short puts and calls. But this is only true for the uninitiated. From these positions come a plethora of option combinations that can mold any position to match your market opinion or risk requirements. These possibilities notwithstanding, there is a basic flow to the MBS options market that encompasses 70 percent–80 percent of all trading. The first of the two most common uses of options is the purchase of puts by mortgage bankers, builders, and other creators of mortgage products who are at risk if interest rates rise. Typically, mortgage bankers give loan commitments to home buyers, guaranteeing them an interest rate over a certain period of time. The purchase of a put is a perfect hedge that removes price risk and locks in a profitable spread to the banker. In its simplest form, one can view this business as a basic retail operation in which MBS option dealers sell puts wholesale to mortgage bankers who then retail them to home buyers. Admittedly, mortgage banking operations are more compex, but we can see how using options has negated most of the potential price risk and left the banker with more time to exercise expertise in making loan commitments.

The other most common use of options involves the selling of calls by savings and loans, thrifts, pension and mutual funds, and other holders of mortgage-backed securities. This fee-generating trade is executed to increase short-term yield. Astute and timely call selling programs can add 300–500 annualized basis points to one's return, while more systematic call-writing programs can add 100–150 basis points with significantly lower exercise risk.

Even though these two trades account for most of the volume, there are many more option uses available.

Investors who have cash available currently, or who foresee the inflow of funds at a future date and would not mind owning securities at current yield levels, *often sell puts*. Because of the structure of forward pricing, the put seller is placed in the position of either keeping the fee unencumbered if rates fall or owning securities 40–50 basis points cheap to the current market if rates rise. Although not for everyone, this trade is quite popular with large institutions that want to acquire assets at attractive yields.

Mortgage bankers who have underestimated the fallout characteristics of their pipelines often buy calls to cover the forward sale of mandatory commitments. This is known as a *synthetic put* and is often used to cap potential losses when pipeline fallout is excessive yet allows for the possibility of profit if rates rise.

Mortgage funds that own a large amount of premium securities often buy calls on discounts to hedge prepayment risk. If rates fall and prepayments rise, the profits on the discount calls will negate these losses. If rates rise, premiums will do better and all that will be lost is the call fee. This is called a *prepayment hedge*.

More complex strategies include the purchase of a put and the sale of a call at different strikes on the same security. This position limits capital loss or appreciation over the time horizon while current income is derived from the security. This is known as a collar agreement.

This chapter was intended to demonstrate the broad potential for option usage. Remember, it was not so long ago that this same type of primer was written for financial futures. At the time people were skeptical, education was required, and investment charters had to be rewritten to allow for their use. Now, the bond contract is the most liquid and actively financial traded instrument in the world. Over the next decade, options no doubt will follow the same pattern. With their superior risk/return characteristics, option volume will overtake that of futures. If the last 10 years has been the decade of futures, the next decade will be that of the option.

Chapter 5

JESS LEDERMAN

Jess Lederman is Executive Vice President with Bear Stearns Mortgage Capital Corporation, a wholly-owned subsidiary of Bear Stearns & Co., Inc. Previously he was Vice President of Marketing for Sears Mortgage Securities Corporation. Before joining Sears, Lederman was Director of Pricing and Research for PMI Mortgage Insurance Co.

Bear Stearns Mortgage Capital Corporation is one of the nation's leading private mortgage conduit companies.

Techniques for Selling Loans to Conduits

JESS LEDERMAN

INTRODUCTION

The heightened interest rate volatility and proliferation of mortgage products since 1979 has challenged the skills of most secondary marketing managers. Over the past few years, the most successful mortgage bankers have developed sophisticated marketing strategies using forwards, Fannie Mae, and Freddie Mac commitments and futures and options to minimize risks and maximize profits. These instruments, however, have been useful primarily in hedging government and conforming production. Until the mid 1980s the secondary market for nonconforming products was undependable, and under such conditions it was difficult to develop a flexible marketing strategy.

The development of private conduits in the mid-1980s, however, has provided a consistent source of funds for a diverse menu of mortgage products featuring nonconforming loan limits. These conduits offer mortgage lenders an array of marketing strategies that complement the choices available for government and conforming loans.

A secondary marketing manager once remarked that "The key to any successful marketing strategy is having as many options as possible for a block of loans." Conduits have helped to maximize their clients' profit opportunities by providing a comprehensive selection of commitment options, and lenders have evolved many different strategies using those options. This chapter describes some of the most important strategies and analyzes how they differ according to lender size, loan type, market conditions, and attitude toward risk.

SINGLE LOAN VERSUS BULK COMMITMENTS

Because conduit minimum commitment requirements are typically as low as $30,000, lenders can purchase small commitments to cover individual loans or higher-volume commitments to cover blocks of their pipeline or anticipated future production. Lenders who exclusively use *single loan commitments* (SLCs) for a particular product tend to have one or more of the following characteristics:

- A preference to precisely match commitment terms and dollar amount to loan amount and anticipated term to closing
- A reluctance to pay commitment fees
- Relatively low and/or unpredictable origination volumes
- Decentralized marketing (branch offices call in commitments)
- A low priority for the development of a marketing strategy that incorporates bulk commitments

Single loan commitment strategies are often logical outgrowths of the first three characteristics. The fourth characteristic is an operational tactic employed by lenders who use an SLC strategy. Such lenders must be careful; unless firm controls and organizational discipline are in place, the potential for expensive mistakes is high.

I encourage lenders who identify with the fifth characteristic to evaluate their secondary marketing strategies and make sure that important opportunities are not being missed. While SLC strategies are well-suited to many lenders, the bulk commitment approach sometimes offers greater flexibility, is applicable to a wide variety of situations, and is not necessarily dependent on high origination volume.

Lenders who frequently use the bulk commitment approach tend to have one or more of the following characteristics:

- A portfolio approach to managing pipeline risk, looking at probable dollar exposure by product over a multimonth time horizon
- Substantial builder business
- Relatively high and/or predictable origination volume

SINGLE LOAN COMMITMENT STRATEGIES

Short-Term Mandatories

One group of lenders primarily makes use of short-term (30- and 60-day) mandatories. Some originate uncovered loans, taking down mandatories as loans close. If rates are set prior to closing, this is a high-risk approach that is best suited to improving markets. Others initially hedge their rate exposure by going short in the futures market or buying puts in the options market. Shorting futures in an improving market can lead to a net loss if loans fail to close. The cost of buying puts should be carefully compared to the cost of purchasing a short-term optional delivery commitment.

Lenders who purchase mandatory delivery commitments for unclosed loans often have a preference for avoiding the commitment fees associated with optional delivery commitments. This has an implicit cost, however, that lenders sometimes overlook. If a lender has adopted an SLC strategy because production volume is spotty, there is a high probability that loan fallout will result in nondelivery, because no substitute loan will be available. A pair off with the conduit will result, with the lender paying the conduit's hedging loss, if any. Because the probability of loan fallout is greatest in an improving market, and the conduit's hedge will lose money when rates decline, the pair off can be costly.

The implicit cost of this mandatory delivery approach is calculated as follows:

$$C = P \times H$$

Where

C = implicit long-run cost of mandatories on unclosed loans

P = probability of loan fallout

H = expected average hedging loss

For example, if fallout probability is 20 percent and the expected average hedging loss is 2 percent, the implicit cost over time will average .4 percent.

Some lenders hedge against fallout on mandatories by buying call options, because the gain on the option should approximately offset the loss on the conduit's hedge in a declining rate environment. Both the implicit cost (C) and the cost of call options should be compared to the cost of a short-term, optional delivery commitment.

Short-Term Optionals

Recouping Commitment Fees. A number of lenders take down 60- or 90-day optionals to hedge a rate-lock given to the borrower at application. Because delivery is not mandatory, loan fallout is not a problem. Commitment fees paid to the conduit, however, must be recouped over time. Two ways to do this are:

1. Charge the borrower an application fee equal to the commitment fee.
2. Increase points collected at closing after factoring in a fallout percentage.

While approach 1 is self-explanatory, approach 2 is slightly more complicated and is illustrated in Table 5–1.

In this example, the lender must collect an extra .5 percent (above and beyond points collected to cover delivery fees and origination expenses) at closing to cover a .375 percent commitment fee if loan fallout averages 25 percent. Obviously, this approach warrants a conservative estimate of fallout probability.

Table 5–1

Variable	Description	Hypothetical Valve
C	Commitment fee	.375%
P	Probability of loan fallout	25%
D	Delivery fees and origination expenses	2%
X	Additional points collected at closing to cover commitment fees	$C/(1-P) = .5\%$
T	Total points collected	$D+X = 2.5\%$

Maximizing Profits. Some lenders who use an SLC approach with 60- and 90-day optionals will always deliver against their optional delivery commitment if loans close, regardless of whether rates have subsequently declined. Significant profit opportunities will almost certainly be missed by following this tactic. The net result of delivering closed loans into a new mandatory should always be compared to delivery into the original optional. Even if rates have not declined, mandatories often feature higher delivery prices than optionals. Lenders who allow branches to call in commitments must pay particular attention to assure that delivery is made into the most profitable commitment option.

BULK COMMITMENT STRATEGIES

Long-Term Standbys

Many mortgage bankers have at some point negotiated a long-term (90 days or more) standby in the private secondary market to cover nonconforming production. Both the availability and the terms of private market standbys have historically been hard to predict. Most conduits continuously offer standardized long-term standby delivery commitments, which make planning a consistent secondary marketing strategy considerably easier. There are several reasons why lenders take down bulk long-term standbys:

- To cover builder commitments
- To minimize interest rate risk on blocks of loans in pipeline
- To lock in rates at cyclical lows, thus maximizing profit potential on future production
- To help manage the introduction of new products

Leveraging Long-Term Optionals

Longer-term optionals are typically not inexpensive; for example, up-front fees for six-month optional delivery commitments are often 1 to 2 percent. If 100 percent of production were hedged with optionals, the entire commitment fee would have to be recovered on every loan, presumably through points collected on the back end or through excess servicing revenues. However, most mortgage bankers attempt to reduce their effective commitment fees on a per-loan basis by leveraging long-term optionals. The basic concept is to use a given dollar commitment to hedge a greater volume of actual production.

For example, Optimum Mortgage Banking Corp. anticipates one-year ARM origination volume to average $2 million per month. Optimum is concerned that rates might rise in coming months, although they are not sure whether the rate increase will occur immediately or further out in the future. Because their top priority is coverage for loans currently in pipeline, they purchase a six-month standby for $4 million (sufficient to cover two months' origination volume) for a 1 percent fee, or $40,000. If rates remain stable or decline, Optimum will take down new mandatories over the ensuing six months and will ultimately have hedged $12 million of production with a $4 million standby. On a per-loan basis, the effective commitment fee has been reduced to .333 percent:

$$1\% \times 4/12 = .333\%$$

If rates increase sharply at the beginning of the commitment term, Optimum will deliver the first two months' production into the standby and then purchase new coverage.

The following formula can be used to compute the expected effective fee:

$$S = (P \times F) + ((1 - P) \times F \times (VS/V))$$

Where

S = expected effective commitment fee

P = probability that rates will increase, thus warranting delivery into standby

F = commitment fee

VS = dollar volume of standby

V = anticipated origination volume over term of standby

New Program Introduction

It is often useful to secure a long-term optional to cover production at the introduciton of a new program. This accomplishes the following:

- Guarantees availability of funds for products for which the market is otherwise not liquid
- Provides rate stability: given the proliferation of products that most lending officers are expected to sell, consistency in pricing can help win acceptance in the field
- Allows for more effective coverage than mandatories, because the behavior of new product pipeline is often difficult to predict

BULK MANDATORIES

With a regularly rolling pipeline, mortgage bankers can use mandatories to hedge their positions. This is important, because mandatory commitments are more cost-effective than optionals.

Sophisticated lenders with consistent volume in a given product line will closely track the progress of loans from application through closing and will develop a sense (some intuitively, some statistically) for the relationship between the probability that loans will close and the age of loans in pipeline. As the age in pipeline increases, lenders will roll loans out of their current coverage—whether unhedged (no coverage), or a short position in futures or puts—and into mandatories. Lenders will minimize the risk of loan fallout and subsequent nondelivery by either:

- Buying mandatories only for core loans with the highest probability of closing and using optionals to cover the remainder of the pipeline
- Buying call options to hedge against the possibility of loan fallout in an improving market

INDEXED RATE STANDBYS

The last strategy involves the use of a standby commitment structure that is frequently called an *indexed rate standby*. This standby structure is an extremely useful supplement to other long-term optional delivery commitments. Under an indexed rate standby, lenders lock in a spread and delivery price for a given product. A *spread* is the difference between an index value and the net rate required by the conduit. For fixed-rate loans, the index values are typically based on Fannie Mae or Freddie Mac net yields. For ARMs, the Treasury indexes are used. The standby is typically convertible at any point during the commitment term to a short term mandatory delivery commitment. The lender locks in a net rate equal to the current index value plus the established spread when the standby is converted to mandatory.

There are numerous advantages to the indexed rate standby:

- It can be designed to cover multiple products under one commitment.
- It offers greater predictability and reduced volatility of rate changes. While conduits normally reprice daily, under an indexed rate standby prices are typically fixed for a week. This offers both administrative and potential arbitrage advantages. For example, if rates were to rise sharply in midweek, delivery into an indexed rate standby can be more profitable than delivery into other short-term commitments. Because an indexed rate standby can cover multiple products, the potential for such arbitrage profits is increased.
- While lenders typically think of standbys as a hedge against an increase in rates, the indexed rate standby can be used to maximize the benefits of a *decline* in rates for adjustable-rate mortgage (ARM) products. Historically, rates in the spot market for ARMs have tended to move more sluggishly than the Treasury indexes. This means that investors' required spreads relative to the index widen in an improving market and tighten in a declining market. Because the indexed rate standby locks in a fixed spread over the Treasury index, it can produce substantial profit opportunities in a declining rate environment.

CASE STUDIES

Case Study 1: Single Loan Mandatory Delivery Commitments: Using Pair Offs to Manage the Risk of Loan Fallout

ABC Mortgage Banking Corp. originates $50 million of fixed-rate loans a year, but only a small portion of total production is nonconforming. Because nonconforming production is spotty, ABC prefers to take down commitments on a loan-by-loan basis. It prefers to avoid paying up-front commitment fees, and looks for the commitment option that offers the lowest yield while still allowing sufficient time to close loans. For these reasons, ABC typically takes down 60-day mandatory delivery commitments to cover individual loans in pipeline. If for any reason loans do not close and no substitute loans are available to fill the commitment, it notifies the conduit and a pair off results, with ABC paying the conduit's hedging loss, if there is any. Table 5–2 illustrates ABC's experience over a one-year time period.

Analysis. In the first quarter, the conduit allows a 90-105 percent delivery range on mandatory commitments. Because ABC delivered more than 90 percent of the commitment amount, no pair off was necessary.

During the second quarter, mortgage rates declined and ABC experienced substantial fallout. Because a conduit's hedge will lose money when rates drop and because actual deliveries fell short of the minimum required by $600,000, a pair off was necessary. The conduit lost 2 percent on its hedge and therefore charged a pair-off fee equal to 2 percent of $600,000, or $12,000.

Although ABC's actual third-quarter deliveries were less than the minimum required, rates increased and the conduit did not experience a loss on its hedge. Therefore, no pair-off fee was charged.

During the fourth-quarter, deliveries fell short of the required minimum, and a slight drop in rates led to a small pair-off fee.

Results. Following are the results of using pair offs:

Total Applications/Mandatory Commitment Volume:	$4,800,000
Total loans closed:	$3,300,000
Fallout percentage:	31 percent
Pair-off fees:	$13,575
Pair-Off Fees as a Percentage of:	
Commitment volume:	.28 percent
Loans closed:	.41 percent

Because ABC calculates that fallout percentages and pair-off fees are relatively predictable over the long run, it feels that this mode of operation has the advantages of an optional delivery commitment while ABC pays the equivalent of a relatively low commitment fee on the back end rather than up front.

Case Study 2: Single Loan Optional Delivery Commitments; Recouping Commitment Fees

XYZ Mortgage Banking Corp. originates adjustable rate mortgages. It gives borrowers a rate lock at application and then takes down 60-day optional delivery commitments on a loan-by-loan basis. Because delivery is not mandatory, loan fallout is not a problem, and unlike ABC Corp., XYZ knows up front the exact cost of obtaining coverage. Unlike ABC, however, XYZ must pay an up-front commitment fee (.375 percent), because it is using optional rather than mandatory delivery commitments.

While some of XYZ's competitors charge the borrower an application fee equal to the cost of the commitment, XYZ prefers to avoid charging application fees. Instead, it backloads the commitment fee by increasing points collected at closing, after adjusting for estimated fallout. Because the commitment fee is .375 percent and XYZ believes that fallout will average 25 percent, total points collected are increased by .50 percent. This calculation is made by dividing .375 percent by a decimal equal to 1.00 less the estimated fallout percentage (.375/

Table 5–2

	(a) Mandatory Commitments (Equal to Application Volume) ($000)	(b) Minimum Required Delivery (90% of Commitment) ($000)	(c) Mortgage Rate (%)	(d) Loans Closed and Delivered ($000)	(e) Delivery Shortfall ($000)	(f) Conduit's Hedging Loss (%)	(g) Pair-offs Fee ($)
IQ	400	360	13.500	375	0	0.00	0
IIQ	1,500	1,350	13.125	750	600	2.00	12,000
IIIQ	650	585	13.250	385	200	0.00	0
IVQ	2,250	2,000	13.125	1,790	210	.75	1,575

Table 5–3

	(a) Optional Commitments (Equal to Application Volume) ($000)	(b) Loans Closed and Delivered ($000)	(c) Fallout Percentage (%)	(d) Commitment Fees Paid (.375 × a) ($)	(e) Excess Points Collected (.5% × b) ($)	(f) Net Gain (Loss) (e − d) ($)
IQ	2,000	1,500	25%	$ 7,500	7,500	—
IIQ	1,500	1,400	7%	5,625	7,000	1,375
IIIQ	2,500	2,100	16%	9,375	10,500	1,125
IVQ	4,000	2,000	50%	15,000	10,000	(5,000)
Total	10,000	7,000	30%	37,500	35,000	(2,500)

$(1.00 - .25) = .50)$. XYZ prices to sell at a 1.5 percent discount to the conduit and needs to retain 1 percent to cover costs, so total points charged equal 3 percent. Table 5–3 shows XYZ's experience over a one-year time period.

Analysis. Over the course of the year, fallout averaged 30 percent, which was higher than XYZ's estimate. The result was an unanticipated loss of $2,500. In effect XYZ ended up paying .025 percent more for the $10 million of commitments taken down throughout the year.

Case Study 3: Combining Bulk Mandatory and Optional Commitments

Acme Mortgage Banking Corp. recently decided to begin using a conduit for nonconforming fixed-rate product. With $5 million in pipeline and new production averaging $1–$2 million per month, it has opted to use bulk commitments rather than the loan-by-loan approach favored by the ABC and XYZ companies. After analyzing the status of loans in pipeline, Acme's secondary market manager prepares the report contained in Table 5–4.

The secondary market manager is concerned that rates may be highly volatile over the next few months and is anxious to secure the right type and amount of coverage.

Analysis. After checking conduit rates and prices, the manager prepares the analysis in Table 5–5.

Acme's options.
- Remain uncovered: This is too risky. For every .25 percent increase in required yield in the secondary market, Acme would lose 1.5 points. On the other hand, Acme could take down some kind of coverage for the $4.1 million of probable exposure and remain uncovered on the $900,000 of projected fallout.

Table 5–4

Loans Closing Within	Exposure with 0% Fallout ($000s)	Probable Exposure After Projected Fallout ($000s)
30 days	1,000	1,000
60 days	3,000	2,400
90 days	1,000	700
Total	5,000	4,100

Table 5–5

	Required Yield	Fee
Mandatory		
30 days	13.200	—
60 days	13.250	—
90 days	13.30	—
Optional		
60 days	13.250	.500
90 days	13.450	.750

- Use mandatory commitments exclusively: Generally, Acme tries to avoid paying fees and attempts to obtain the lowest possible yield. About 80 percent of the loans in pipeline will close, so most of Acme's exposure can be hedged with mandatories. But what about the $900,000 of potential fallout? Acme could go mandatory on the whole $5 million and simply pay pair-off fees if fallout results in nondelivery.
- Combine mandatory and optional commitments: Finally, mandatory commitments for the loans with the highest probability of closing could be used. Then, optional delivery commitments could be used for all or a portion of the $900,000 that is less certain. Sixty-day optionals increase total costs by .500 percent, and 90-day optionals increase total cost by 1.63 percent (factoring in the higher required yield plus the commitment fee, all expressed in price.) But at least Acme's costs would be known up front, and it would not face the uncertainties of the other options.

Conclusion. If Acme could be sure rates were heading up, covering the whole $5 million with mandatories exclusively would make sense because the probability of incurring pair-off fees would be remote: the conduit's hedge will rarely lose money in a declining market, and a higher percentage of loans will tend to close. But this is a volatile market, and a drop in rates of .375 percent, for example, would result in a pair-off fee of almost 2.25 percent—more than the cost of either optional commitment. And the same reasoning could be applied to covering only $4.1 million with mandatories and going uncovered on the remaining $900,000. This would make sense in an improving market. But if rates increase, and fallout is not as heavy as anticiapted, Acme could easily lose more than the cost of the optional delivery commitment fees. Therefore, it is recommended that Acme take down the coverage shown in Table 5–6.

The probability of large unanticipated marketing losses or pair-off fees is thus minimized, with up-front commitment fees reduced on a per-loan basis to fewer than 10 basis points.

Table 5–6

Commitment Term	Mandatory ($000s)	Optional ($000)	Total ($000s)
30 days	1,000	—	1,000
60 days	2,400	500	2,900
90 days	700	250	950
Total	4,100	750	4,850

Percentage of Total Exposure Hedged with Commitments: 97 percent.
Total Commitment Fees Paid: $4,375.
Commitment Fees as a Percentage of Total Exposure: .09 Percent.

Case Study 4: Using Bulk Long-Term Optional Delivery Commitments

Optimum Mortgage Banking Corp. uses the conduit to cover one-year ARM production. In early July, its secondary marketing manager became extremely concerned that recent tightening by the Federal Reserve might lead to sharply higher rates in the months ahead. He therefore decided to take down long-term optional delivery commitments to protect both loans in pipeline and future production through the end of the year.

One-year ARM production has been averaging $3 million per month, so Optimum's secondary marketing manager needs to cover $18 million of loans over the next six months. The highest priority, however, is $5 million of loans in pipeline. The strategy will be to take down only slightly more than $6 million of standby coverage. If rates move sharply higher in the next 60 days, Optimum can deliver the $6 million into the standbys and take down new coverage. If rates stay stable or decline, Optimum can deliver loans into the conduit's 30-day mandatory delivery commitment option. Thus, Optimum will have the potential to "leverage" its standbys, that is, use a given dollar amount of standbys to cover a greater volume of actual production. The manager is interested in the program arrayed in Table 5–7.

Table 5-7

Program Type	Base Initial Net Rate	Base Price	Commitment Fee
30-Day Mandatory	10.375	98.50	—
90-Day Mandatory	10.500	98.00	.75
180-Day Optional	10.500	97.50	1.00
180-Day Indexed Rate Standby	Index + .75	98.50	1.00

The following price adjustments apply. If loans are delivered with initial net rates above the base initial net rate, increase the base price by .125 percent for every .125 percent above the base initial net rate. If loans are delivered with initial net rates below the base initial net rate, reduce the base price by .250 percent for every .125 percent shortfall in initial net rate.

Optimum's secondary market manager decides to take down $3 million of the 90-day optional, $3 million of the 180-day optional, and

$2 million of the 180-day indexed rate standbys. At the start of the commitment period, the manager is basing his pricing on the conduit's 30-day mandatory delivery commitment, offering a street rate of 10.50 percent, plus 3 points. Optimum services for .25 percent and would thus deliver at 10.25 percent, or .125 percent below the posted net rate of 10.375 percent. This means that Optimum would deliver at a price of 98.25 percent. The manger estimates that orgination costs are 1 percent; therefore, origination costs plus discount to the conduit total 2.75 percent, leaving a .25 percent marketing profit. If Optimum can leverage the standby, this .25 percent will cover most, if not all, of the commitment fees.

Analysis. Table 5–8 shows what actually happened over the next six months.

Results. The following results were achieved using bulk long-term optional delivery commitments:

A.	Total loans closed:	$16,700,000
B.	Total commitment fees paid:	72,500
C.	Marketing gain (loss):	9,950
D.	Net Gain (Loss) (C – B)	(62,550)
E.	Net Loss as a Percentage of Loans Closed	(.375 percent)

By delivering into the 90- and 180-day optionals, Optimum was able to minimize marketing losses in September and October. The indexed rate standby proved particularly useful in December, when the one-year index dropped more sharply than the conduit's 30-day mandatory rate. While lower-than-anticipated volume and extremely volatile rates prevented Optimum from fully recouping commitment fees, it emerged safely from difficult market conditions with a net marketing loss of only .375 percent.

Table 5–8

	July	August	September	October	November	December
Loans Closed ($000)	3,200	2,300	3,000	2,500	3,700	2,000
Gross Rate + Points (%)	10.5+3	10.5+3	10.5+3	11+3	10.875+3	10.625+3
Conduit 30-Day Mandatory:						
Base Initial Net Rate (%)	10.375	10.375	10.875	11.500	10.875	10.500
Base Price (%)	98.5	98.5	98.5	98.5	98.5	98.5
One-Year Index (%)	9.75	9.875	10.250	10.875	10.25	9.25
Commitment Option Chosen	30-Day Mandatory	30-Day Mandatory	90-Day Optional	180-Day Optional	30-Day Mandatory	180-Day Indexed Rate Standby
Net Rate Delivered to Conduit	10.25	10.25	10.25	10.75	10.625	10.375
Price Paid to Acme	98.25	98.25	97.50	97.75	98.00	98.875
Calculation of Marketing Gain or Loss						
Points Collected (%)	3.00	3.00	3.00	3.00	3.00	3.00
Less Origination Cost (%)	1.00	1.00	1.00	1.00	1.00	1.00
Less Discount on Sale (%)	1.75	1.75	2.50	2.25	2.00	1.125
Net Gain (Loss) (%)	.25	.25	(.50)	(.25)	—	.875
Marketing Gain (Loss) ($)	8,000	5,750	(15,000)	(6,300)	—	17,500

Chapter 6

MARY BRUCE BATTE

Mary Bruce Batte is Senior Vice President of Barrentine Lott & Associates, Inc., Vienna, Virginia, a mortgage finance consulting and eduction services company. She advises clients on secondary market sales, purchases, strategies and techniques.

Increasing Your Access to the Private Secondary Market

MARY BRUCE BATTE

The period 1982–1986 has seen tremendous growth in secondary market trades with investors other than the quasigovernmental secondary market corporations. While there are many benefits to private market transactions, seasoned players in this sector are raising their standards and seem determined to concentrate on quality organizations and products. Mortgage sellers who cannot adequately demonstrate track records of sound capitalization, experience, adequate quality control, and superb servicing will find it increasingly difficult to deal in the private market. The best private market investors are looking for a higher standard of professionalism among the sellers they deal with. The ability to expedite the deal is critical. Lengthy, drawn-out negotiations with sellers who must be educated to the market and who aren't sure what they want are unlikely to result in sales.

Tapping the private market for dollars involves more effort and attention to detail because of the need to negotiate and craft the transaction without the benefit of the agencies' structured programs. Often, the buyer plans to resell the loans being purchased, causing sellers to satisfy not only the buyer's needs, but also those of the ultimate investor. From the buyer's point of view, failure of the seller to deliver loans that meet the specifications of the contract and/or adhere to the agreed-upon schedule can mean losses. The need to reject loans and send others back for further information or correction increases the cost of execution for both parties and makes future transactions less likely.

Investors who are always in the market want to develop strong, ongoing relationships with quality sellers that they can rely upon for good execution. They also want to see sufficient financial strength to handle repurchases that might be specified in their sales agreements. The ability to service loans for investors according to schedule and to submit the servicing reports required in the desired format is a prerequisite to establishing a relationship.

Sellers view execution the same way. Poor execution can reduce the profitability of a transaction while the parties argue over original loan terms and contest their underwriting. Even more serious is the failure of the investor to fund at all. Some investors may fail to fund due to inadequate financial capability, while others may be interested in booking fees, but less interested in buying loans when interest rates increase.

Some sellers have soured on the private market because of repeated poor execution, investors' whims, inconsistent underwriting policies, and funding problems.

There are a number of steps that you as a seller can take to increase your access to private market investors, improve your marketing to this sector, and protect yourself against hazards.

DEFINING INVESTOR CRITERIA

The first action is to define criteria for selecting investors. Some sellers believe that every investor's money is the same color and that examining the investor's financial strength pursuant to an immediate transaction is unnecessary. While it is true that financial strength becomes more and more important the further forward the trade is set, sellers can be burned on immediate transactions with weak or unethical buyers. The market can move quite a distance in the 30 or 60 days it might take for delivery and review or post-funding loan audits.

As a matter of policy, you should request and review current financials, the most recent audited financials, and at least three quarters of quarterly reports to regulators if the investor is a regulated financial institution. Analysis of financials, however, is only half the equation. Ask the investor about its outstanding volume of commitments and how it expects to fund those commitments. Weigh the investor's ability to shoulder the market risk involved in forward transactions, especially those for fixed-rate, long-term products. Is the investor taking a risk it can afford, or is it speculating and placing the seller's shop in a risky position?

Once financial standards for investors have been determined, establish a policy of checking the potential buyer's reputations. If the investor is dishonest, unreasonable, or unknowledgeable, a favorable ongoing relationship probably cannot be established. As a matter of policy, ask investors to provide references and check them. Then you should snoop a bit by consulting others in the market who are familiar with the investor. Mortgage insurance companies, investment banking firms, and active sellers can be useful here.

If you are transacting only on a serving-related basis, checking the buyer's servicing record can be critical to protecting your relationships with customers.

Another purpose of asking for references is to find out if the buyer's underwriting policies are reasonable and are applied consistently. The most valuable reference on this issue is another seller active in the same market, because an investor may be experienced in underwriting loans from one part of the country and oblivious to factors that are unique to your market.

Beyond checking references, establish a policy of visiting potential investors in advance of paying for coverage. The secondary marketing trader should take along the firm's top underwriter, shipper, and perhaps the head of loan production if a new or complicated product is being considered. Some sample files that require judgment calls in underwriting can be helpful, as well.

An important criterion for selecting investors is the prospect for repeat business. One-time transactions are rarely beneficial from a total cost prospective unless the price is considerably better than you could receive from a repeat investor. There is a considerable cost of time and money to negotiate the deal and review the agreement. The first deal with an investor will usually entail a more thorough review of the loans and perhaps a prior approval process.

Another consideration is restricting activity to only those investors whose underwriting, documentation, and packaging requirements match yours. If your requirements are those generally expected in the secondary market, and an investor is insisting on a requirement that is extraordinary, making such a change in your system can reduce its efficiency. A further concern would be whether the requirement might render the loans unacceptable to a larger portion of the secondary market.

SELLING YOUR COMPANY

Developing general marketing materials for your company, a formal standard loan package offering format, sample files for each product, and a preferred sales and servicing agreement can save you time, put your company in a better position to negotiate, and increase your firm's professional image.

The marketing package should be designed to tell your company's story in terms of your markets, products, resources, and track record. It should include financial information on your company, background information on the top managers, a brief description of when the company was started, how it has grown, and its expected current year and future volume. Describe its orientation; operations (wholesale or retail); the number of branch offices; the manner in which processing is handled; and, most importantly, underwriting and quality control.

Next, describe its servicing volume and whether it currently services loans for other investors. The package also should include information on the markets your company is active in and pertinent information on industry, employment, and economic trends that will affect the values of your properties and the performance of your loans. Information on your company's products—whether they are standard or feature numerous "bells and whistles"—is critical as well.

Loan quality is a critical concern to investors. Not only should marketing materials address the issue of your company's underwriting guidelines (for example, whether they are FNMA or FHLMC), but also its quality control program. Your company's performance in terms of delinquency and foreclosure statistics on a product-by-product basis is also important information that should be included.

Your company's sales points can be packaged in a brochure or a company folder with individual pieces that are updated as needed. If this information is put together in a concise, attractive manner and is readily available to potential investors, the company can streamline its initial contact and increase the probability of making a good first impression.

Being able to develop professional-looking, quality loan offerings depends on the firm's ability to capture accurate and complete information about the loans moving through its pipeline and in warehouse. Handwritten lists or delays for computerized lists immediately put sellers at a disadvantage when selling loans that have closed. Sellers should be in a position to send listings to investors immediately after an investor has expressed an interest. It is critical that the seller have the capability to also provide information summarizing the key features of the offering, including: average original principal balance, range of principal balances, number and amount of any jumbos included in a largely conforming package, range and distribution of rates, dollar amount and percentages of the package comprising each loan to value category, maximum principal balance per LTV category, mixture of property types by total dollar amount, locations of the properties by city and state, seasoning of loans in the package, range of underwriting ratios, and mortgage insurance coverage. In the case of adjustable-rate loans, the seller also needs the capability to provide all information pertaining to periodic adjustment or payment caps, adjustment dates, distribution and range of gross margins, and the maximum note rate that can be charged per loan.

Having access to information in the pipeline can help secondary market traders project the parameters of loan packages that they are likely to deliver in the future and therefore the parameters of the commitments that they are trying to develop with investors.

Sample files for each product can be useful in approaching potential investors. Special company folder jackets, summary sheets, and clearly

Xeroxed documents are a must. The purpose of the sample files is to demonstrate the quality of your company's loans and the documentation it uses. Be sure to clarify whether the sample files you are sending to an investor are actual files available for sale or are representative samples typical of your production.

SALES AND SERVICING AGREEMENTS

The next critical step is to develop your firm's own sales and servicing agreements. While many investors have their own agreements and will not consider using those of the seller, they are often willing to modify them. The exercise suggested here can expedite the agreement amendment process. On the other hand, many investors simply use standard agreements of the U.S. League of Savings Institutions and will consider using the seller's agreements as a starting point for negotiations.

Too often, sellers are concentrating on the price and key elements of the transaction they are negotiating and don't adequately review the sales and servicing agreements. Most standard agreements, in their effort to be neutral to seller and servicer, fail to address details that can have a considerable impact on the real value of the transaction being negotiated. The sales and servicing agreement should address all details that are relevant to the transaction, including characteristics of the loans.

Language such as "FNMA/FHLMC underwriting will apply," is an open invitation to disagreements, because the agencies no longer have the same guidelines. Then, too, language such as "FHLMC guidelines will apply," is frequently adopted, while both parties have different interpretations of what FHLMC underwriting entails. The investor, for example, may not be willing to accept *every* aspect of FHLMC underwriting in the refinance loan area and may insist on a minimum amount of property ownership for cash out loans. If this difference is not uncovered until the closed loans are delivered, one party is going to be hurt.

In addition, if jumbo loans are contemplated, very detailed underwriting guidelines need to be spelled out, because the agency guidelines may not be adequate for either the investor or the seller.

Another area often neglected is that of buyback or substitution rights. Time, prices, and expiration of the rights must be spelled out clearly. It is important to clarify the buyback/substitution process and to determine whether prior approval will be required and the amount of review the time the investor may take. Conditions under which an investor can reject a loan that has been cleared through the prior approval process should be detailed.

Delivery dates and the length of time after expiration of the commitment that can be allowed for submission of final documentation must be addressed, as well as funding—not only when, but in what form.

The manner in which disputes over underwriting will be handled is another critical area. Some sellers now insist that if more than 25 percent of loans are rejected, a third party will underwrite the loans, or a proportional part of the upfront fees will be returned.

In the servicing area, the standard agreements—if they are to be the starting points—should be carefully examined to see that all issues of importance are addressed, including whether there will be subservicer rights, whether servicing can be pulled without cause, the compensation to the servicer if servicing is pulled without cause, what constitutes cause and whether there is any redress, how various collected fees will be shared, such as late fees, assumption fees, conversion of ARM to fixed-rate mortgage fees, and so on. The agreements should spell out not only remittance and reporting dates, but also the exact formats to be used and the penalties, if any, for failure to comply.

As sellers go through the process of developing a sales and servicing agreement that will form the basis of all future transactions, they should think about elements that can be added to strengthen the appeal for the buyer without undue risk or cost to the seller.

As important as determing what the seller wants in an agreement is identifying those investor-driven provisions that the seller simply can't live with. Issues such as whether the seller is willing to provide modified MBS-style servicing (where principal and interest are advanced to the investor, whether collected or not, for a period of time) should be evaluated because of its increasing popularity. Whether loans can be sold with recourse, or in the form of participations with subordinate interests, should be discussed with management to determine the circumstances under which these approaches might be considered.

For sellers who are active in trading whole loans with investment banking firms that buy as principal, review of the basic Thacher Proffit and Wood agreement is an important part of this exercise. The agreements are lengthy and vary somewhat from house to house. If the seller already is familiar with the basic agreement and has considered its impact on the company, negotiations with investment banking firms can be expedited.

Of course it would be naive to believe that there will be more than a few deals along the way where the investor agrees to the seller's agreements without changes. So it is important, as a matter of groundwork, to establish a streamlined decision-making process for considering exceptions to the basic agreements. The process obviously should involve all key managers affected by the proposed changes, including servicing, origination, and accounting. If everyone understands the process in advance, negotiations with investors can proceed in an orderly, expedited fashion and the review process shouldn't bog down.

Two other actions are critical to improving sellers' access, as well as their negotiating skills. Secondary marketing professionals have little patience for sellers who have little or uncertain authority and have no feel for how their product really stacks up against the national market.

Secondary marketing representatives—whether a senior vice president or trader—must have a clear understanding of their negotiating parameters before approaching investors. It is generally ineffective for management to specify narrow requirements that constitute a wish list rather than what is realistic in the market. The process of determining parameters for a particular series of calls to investors has to start with secondary marketing giving a clear reading of the primary and secondary market conditions that will form the basis of negotiating parameters. Prioritizing the seller's needs can lead to more effective negotiating. Traders need to understand what is impossible from the company's perspective and what might be acceptable—and under what conditions. It is impossible to effectively negotiate when every aspect of the deal must be taken back to higher management.

It is the kiss of death to a secondary marketing representative to assure an investor that one set of factors will be acceptable for a deal and then have upper management disavow it. If the company's policy is that all deals must be confirmed by one or more officers of the company, the marketing representative must take special care to communicate this to the investor.

While calling and negotiating with investors provides the excitement of secondary marketing, laying a solid basis for the transaction at hand and building ongoing relationships can ultimately bring mortgage sellers more valuable commitments and access to a broader segment of the market.

Chapter 7

HOWARD TAYLOR
AND
PETER D'ALESSANDRO

Howard Taylor is founder and Chief Executive Officer of Howard Taylor & Company. Peter D'Alessandro is Managing Director–Secondary Markets. Founded in 1979, the Rochester, New York based firm has gained national prominence in the whole-loan sector of the Secondary Mortgate Market. The company's commercial division is very active in commercial originations nationwide, and maintains offices in Albany, New York and Boca Raton, Florida.

Creativity in Negotiated Transactions: Working with Whole Loan Brokers

HOWARD TAYLOR AND PETER D'ALESSANDRO

Since the founding of Howard Taylor & Company, our corporate aim has been to put buyers and sellers together in deals that make good economic sense for all parties concerned. Our strength has been in tailoring transactions to meet the specific needs of both buyer and seller. While at times this task is difficult, as each entity must act and negotiate in a manner that maximizes their own profit, it is through the ability to bring such transactions to fruition that whole loan brokers must earn their reputation. Brokers can't just let deals happen, they must make them happen. Our entire staff of secondary market account executives strives daily to fulfill this objective, as does the managing director and chief executive officer of the firm.

We start by listening. We listen to what our client wants to accomplish conceptually. We also want to understand our client's motives. Is there a better way to accomplish the same desired result? Having grasped the basic 'why's and 'wherefores,' we now move to the mechanics of the transaction, the details. Our industry demands accuracy. There is no room for assumptions or shooting from the hip. Individuals and institutions that subscribe to this mode of operation eventually fall victim to the process of natural selection. Whole loan brokers must be acutely aware of the importance of accuracy and detail in every secondary market transaction, be it a small package of adjustable rate second mortgages or a $50,000,000 package of fixed rate mortgages being brought to market on a competitive bid basis. The volume is not crucial, the accuracy is!

As an intermediary in a transaction, a broker must be able to objectively view both sides of the transaction, while at the same time negotiate with buyer and seller toward a common ground. The broker must also act as a catalyst in bringing a transaction to fruition and provide the creativity necessary to revive a deal when it is all but dead.

An actual transaction will help illustrate these points. Our client in this transaction was a large, northeast life insurance company with virtually no experience in the residential secondary mortgage market. Since we do not want to reveal the life company's true identity, let's call it the "Good Life Insurance Company." Our account executive had been discussing the possible sale of this package for several weeks and had given the seller a list of the parameters necessary in order to obtain an optimal price.

Having done all the necessary number crunching, the package was brought to market in the early part of June, with a bid date set for mid-June. Even within the realm of non-conforming, this package was rather unique. It was composed of FHA, VA, and Conventional loans aggregating to ± $15,000,000. The loans had been originated and were currently being serviced by at least thirty different correspondents. The package was scattered nationwide and carried an overall WAM of approximately 48 months. Given the seasoning of the package, it was no surprise that the average loan size barely exceeded $4,000, a servicer's nightmare! Our seller had a very strong preference for a servicing released transaction (in this instance, servicing can actually take on a negative value).

Given the unique composition of this package, many investors who had initially expressed a strong interest became less and less reachable as bid day approached.

On the bid day, the competition quickly narrowed down to two possible winners, both of whom were brought in through Howard Taylor & Company. All others had non-competitive bids or had dropped out of the bidding entirely. As we discussed our two bids with Good Life, it appeared that, even though we had the best bids, neither would be suitable. Bid A was very strong, but required the seller to retain servicing; Bid B was a servicing-released bid (which was the seller's preferred sale method), but the bid was a bit light on price. Things seemed bleak at this point, but we were committed to make this deal work; there had to be a way. We had all worked too hard to merely accept failure and walk away.

Our account executives went back to the drawing board, reviewed all of the data, reworked the numbers, and reviewed the motives and objectives of each player. In further discussion with Investor A, we found that the reason its pricing was so aggressive was because it had a dire need for short WAM paper. On the other hand, because Investor A's servicing operation was small scale and regionalized, nationwide servicing would have been prohibitively expensive, resulting in a "servicing-released" bid.

In further discussion with Investor B, we found that its servicing capability was far more advanced than that of Investor A. Due to Investor B's high servicing volume and a nationwide network of offices, it enjoyed economies of scale that are not available to a small servicing operation. Consequently, Investor B was more willing to undertake servicing (at a price, of course) than was its competitor.

After studying all the parameters of the situation, a possible solution emerged. In looking at the spread between our two bids, it became evident that a deal could be consummated, but would necessitate a tri-party transaction. Our negotiations shifted from a "buyer-seller" format to a "buyer-seller-servicer" format. After several days of negotiation and discussion, we were able to hammer out a viable solution that left everyone a winner.

We structured the deal so that Good Life would sell the entire package to Investor A on a servicing released basis. Investor A simultaneously executed an agreement with Investor B in which B agreed to service the package for a "healthy" servicing spread plus a one-time fee of 1.70 points. The final result was a deal that worked well for all.

In another recent transaction we were confronted with a situation that called for both persistence and extended negotiations. The seller was a small midwest savings & loan with good intentions, but limited secondary market experience and no sense of urgency. In order to appreciate the persistence and perseverance necessary to bring this deal to fruition, we must start at the very beginning. This transaction began in mid-July when our client, during a routine call from his Howard Taylor & Company account executive, expressed a possible interest in selling a small portfolio of "below water" residential mortgages in order to take advantage of the institution's current tax situation. Given their tax status they were able to take a $200,000 to $300,000 "hit" on the transaction. Though by no means a large transaction, it was certainly feasible, so we asked the seller to send us a computer breakdown of the portfolio and recent financials for review.

The portfolio totalled approximately $4,000,000, comprised of various coupon levels. The account executive worked the numbers and came up with a coupon mix that would maximize the amount of product sold, given the "maximum loss" constraint. The seller took this information to its August board meeting and was granted approval to proceed with this sale. Once notified, we began to preliminarily market the package to our investors who we thought might have an interest in a smaller transaction. To those that expressed an interest in persuing the package, we sent computer printouts, sample loan files, etc. We also made sure they understood that this transaction would probably not move along with the same expediency as most secondary market transactions. Though we had no way of knowing at the time, this would be a major understatement.

The seller requested preliminary bids to take into its September board meeting to get a rough indication of pricing levels, a request which we accommodated. The board reacted favorably to the preliminary pricing and wanted firm bids for the October board meeting. By the time the October board meeting rolled around, Howard Taylor & Company had secured an investor with an aggressive bid ready to purchase the package.

Upon adjournment of the October board meeting the seller calmly notified us that his board had decided not to sell, not due to price, but rather due to lack of reinvestment ideas! Needless to say, our investor was more than a little unhappy with this surprise ending. We immediately had a heart-to-heart conversation with our seller, explaining to him that it is "not customary" in secondary marketing to bring a transaction this far and then "pull" the package, especially for a reason other than price.

Although the seller could certainly understand our reasoning and thought it made perfect sense, our contact (who was a vice president) said there was nothing he could do; the matter was out of his hands, and the only person who would have even a remote chance of reversing the board's decision was the bank president. Naturally we wanted to speak directly with the president, but first we had some in-depth discussion with our investor and came up with several reinvestment scenarios for the seller. In addition, our investor liked the package enough to increase its bid slightly. Armed with our reinvestment scenarios and improved bid, we proceeded to call the president of the savings & loan. After a lengthy discussion, the president finally agreed that the deal made sense and that he would contact the board members individually by phone and try to get a reversal of the original decision. As it turned out, our persistence and patience paid off; we were able to close the deal!

Needless to say, our investor was also pleased with the outcome. This was a situation that could have left the buyer, seller, and the broker very unhappy. Instead, due to some tactful intervention and 'T.L.C.,' we were able to close the deal, and more importantly, establish a good working relationship between the buyer and seller.

The foregoing cases are just two of many in which we as brokers were instrumental in making the deal happen. The secondary market broker is a vital element in the negotiation process for many reasons. He or she must prescreen buyers and sellers before initiating a transaction or making an introduction. Given the importance of first impressions, it becomes most vital that things get off on the right foot. This is where we must do our homework to be sure that the needs and objectives of all the players in a potential transaction are reasonable and compatible. Once the deal is in motion, we stay on top of it to make sure things move along as they should. This includes the exchanging of financials between buyer and seller, providing the buyer with sample loan files that are a fair representation of the overall portfolio, the formulation and negotiation of the commitment letter, and ultimately, a timely funding.

Naturally, we consider the commitment letter to be a critical point in the deal-making process and, therefore, always request that a copy be sent to our office. We immediately review the letter for accuracy and to spot areas that may require further negotiation or clarification. Experience has shown us that many times buyers or sellers will be more willing to express their true thoughts on a particular matter to the broker than to the other principal in the transaction. Therefore, by having an intermediary in the transaction, useful information that may have otherwise been repressed can now be interjected either directly or indirectly to enhance the negotiation process.

A fully executed commitment letter is the successful culmination of the negotiation process and certainly represents an accomplishment in and of itself. At Howard Taylor & Company, however, we don't stop there. We stay in the deal right through funding. We're not happy until the buyer and seller are happy. Our objective is not to merely close deals, although we certainly do our share. Our objective is to build relationships—relationships that work and relationships that last!

Chapter 8

THOMAS S. LA MALFA
AND
JON G. HOLM

Tom LaMalfa has worked as an analyst in the mortgage markets since joining MGIC in 1976. As Vice President-Manager, Secondary Market Services, he is responsible for coordinating economic, regulatory and legislative research for MGIC's capital markets operation. Tom has written numerous articles for various mortgage and industry-related publications and co-authored a book entitled A Guide to Secondary Marketing. *He recently served as an author and contributing editor to* The Handbook of Mortgage Banking.

Tom holds a Bachelor's degree in political science and economics and a Master's degree in housing economics from the University of Wisconsin. Prior to joining MGIC, he worked as a housing analyst for the Milwaukee County Board, a municipal analyst for a consulting firm, and served as an Alderman.

Jon Holm has co-authored the MGIC Secondary Market Newsletter with Tom LaMalfa since 1979. Mr. Holm spent 4 years in MGIC's real estate accounting department and previously worked in bank examining and manufacturing and savings and loan accounting. He holds a B.B.A. in finance.

The Role of Mortgage Insurance Companies in the Secondary Market

THOMAS S. LaMALFA AND JON G. HOLM

The involvement of mortgage insurance companies (MICs) in the secondary mortgage markets dates back to the 1960s, prior to the founding of Ginnie Mae or Freddie Mac and before Fannie Mae operated outside of the government loan market. It began as a service to mortgage companies that needed help selling their loans, at a time when the word *market* in the phrase secondary mortgage markets was still written in a singular case. In the almost two decades since then, MICs have sold tens of thousands of whole-loan packages, the market's traditional sales vehicle, totalling tens of billions of dollars for their insurance customers. In the process, MICs have helped hundred of buyers and sellers form long-lasting relationships with one another. Many of these relationships have existed for ten or more years. MICs were pioneers in the development of the private-placement aftermarket for conventional loans, and, in a similar fashion a decade later, were pioneers in the development of conventional mortgage-backed securities.

This chapter has several objectives: first, to tell the story of the still-evolving role of the MICs in the secondary mortgage markets; second, to describe the functions of the MIC trader so that new and experienced users of these services can extract the most mileage from them; and third, to review some of the reasons why mortgage lenders use the MIC networks. To eliminate comparative necessities, focus will be on the role of the secondary market group at MGIC. However, it should be noted that MGIC is not alone in the secondary market services it provides its customers. Indeed, most of the major MICs have similar operations that provide comparable services. For this reason readers can conclude that the similarities between MIC secondary market operations are greater than their differences.

The focal point of the MGIC operation is its trading network. MGIC's nationwide network consists of 9 regional offices staffed by 15 traders. In addition, it includes a small management/support staff in its home office. The regional offices are linked electronically among themselves, as well as with the home office. The latter sets policy; directs, coordinates and monitors its regional activities; and provides research and other support services for both its traders and customers.

Staff consists of trading personnel and nontrading support staff. "Traders," or secondary market account executives as they are formally called, have strong academic backgrounds in finance complemented by many years of mortgage lending and sales experience. They are well-paid professionals who understand mortgage banking, local and national mortgage and housing market conditions, and mortgage finance. In addition, all are licensed securities brokers who can speak knowledgeably about a diverse range of topics, from state laws affecting mortgage transactions to cash flow analysis, and from pricing to packaging.

The trader's primary function is to assist his or her company's customers to fulfill their secondary market objectives. Although these objectives may vary substantially from one customer to another, generally the most basic need is to find an investor outlet for a seller or a quality investment for a buyer. Using the resources of the network, the trader can work with either party to satisfy the investment or disposition need. Thrifts form the bulk of MGIC's investor base, but continued efforts are being made to attract funds from nontraditional mortgage buyers such as life insurance companies and pension funds. Periodically during the 1980s, MICs have worked or attempted to work with Freddie Mac and Fannie Mae on master commitments under which the MICs would market purchase commitment programs. Few attempts have rendered much in the way of success, however.

In order to find investors willing to buy a seller's production or to provide it with the forward or standby coverage necessary for the mortgages it hopes to produce, the trader must find financial institutions who have excess funds to invest in mortgage loans. Traders do this by knowing both the supply/demand characteristics of the markets they cover and the individual customer accounts within their territories. (A *territory* may consist of an area as small as a metropolis or as large as three or four states, depending largely on the level of mortgage activity.) More often than not, investors with excess funds are found in mature markets with light primary market demand and slow economic growth.

Once identified, traders must strive to develop a good working relationship with one or more of an institution's investment decision makers. In addition, they must get to know: the types of product the investor purchases; the profile of preferred sellers; which institutions are currently servicing loans for the investor; whether loans are purchased servicing released and/or servicing retained; what investment markets the investor likes or dislikes; what its yield and fee requirements consist of, and so forth. Knowing this, traders can discreetly assist the investor in meeting its investment objectives.

Traders must also obtain an in-depth understanding of their clients that are selling loans. Sell-side concerns different from those noted on the buy side. For instance, traders must know the type of loans the seller originates, the strengths and weaknesses of the markets in which it originates, the quality of the mortgages it produces, its servicing capabilities, reputation, and a wide range of details about its financial strength. Knowledge about the seller's lending, underwriting, and quality control practices are also useful, because they often shed light on its delinquency and foreclosure experience. MGIC, like other MICs, will not assist sellers with poor track records in lending or with blemished secondary market records.

Since the whole loan market is large, fragmented, and essentialy unregulated, traders must be careful to resolve any misunderstandings that could later end up as problems. Indeed, knowledge of the customers on both sides of a transaction is of paramount importance and puts

traders in a position from which they can operate effectively and efficiently. As matchmakers, the last thing traders want is to unnecessarily
alienate the seller or jeopardize a relationship with the investor.

The telephone is the trader's chief tool. With it and a list of account
names and numbers, the trader can prospect to find one or both sides of
a transaction. Depending on the customer's level of market involvement, traders may contact an assigned account monthly, weekly, or
even more frequently. Since there are many tens of other fee brokers
scouring the marketplace, traders must earn a reputation as secondary
marketing professionals with something special to offer. Doing deals
alone may not be enough for many customers. Sometimes deal making
is simply the culmination of a wider array of services that traders must
provide. To be successful, they must understand local markets and the
entire national mortgage market. Among other things this would include: required yield on different types of mortgage products; the types
of coverage available at various prices; and continuously updated pricing offered by profile of the products and mortgage originators. Additionally, they must be able to: (1) integrate the impact of economic
factors on production levels; (2) assist both buyers and sellers in developing marketing strategies; and, (3) proficiently communicate information on market conditions, activity levels, and developing trends.

The secondary marketing network is critical in supporting the trader
in these areas because it provides and constantly updates the information the trader needs to put participants together in a trade. For example, assume there is a shortage of floating-rate forward coverage, but
strong demand for it. Recognizing this, the trader can alert investors to
the situation while devising a plan through which they can best take
advantage of the imbalance.

To provide an example of how this all works, let's dissect a sale.
Let's start from the point at which a seller calls a trader to indicate that
a package of whole loans is available for immediate delivery. Upon
receipt of the sell offer, the trader fills out a form (Figure 8–1) that
outlines the pertinent data about the loans and the seller: the type of
loans available; their location; the composition of the package by dollar
amount and loan-to-value ratio; yield and fee data; the seller's track

record; the number and dollar amount of loans the seller is servicing; the principal and back-up contact persons, and so on. If the offering came from a reliable seller to whom the trader has sold loans before, the trader relays the information to the other regions. Simultaneously, the trader enters it into the computer as an "offer." This log-in process serves as a backup should one or more of the traders not hear the initial communication of the offering.

After the offer is "looped," the trader highlights the strengths and weaknesses of the offering and addresses any specific questions gener-

Figure 8–1

Offer   MGIC

☐Fee   ☐Priority

S/M AE:	Division	Date

Seller	Location
Contact Person	Telephone No ( )

Product Type:
☐Fixed Rate
☐ARM (_____ Yrs./Index _____ /Margin _____ /Caps _____)
☐Other _____ Property Location _____

YLD	PTS	DEL	AMT	LTV		P/W	Properties		
		IMMED		80's	to $	INS	SFD	☐00 ☐2nd ☐INV	
		FWD							
		STBY		90's	to $	INS	TWN	☐00 ☐2nd ☐INV	
		FLOW		95's	to $	INS	Condo	☐00 ☐2nd ☐INV	

Comments: _____ Investors Contacted: _____

Form #71-1437 (9/85)   (Use reverse side if needed)

ated by other traders about the offering or the seller. Many inquiries request data such as: (1) the range of note rates included in the package; (2) the margins, caps, and indexes on ARM offerings; (3) the geographic concentration of the package; (4) seasoning; and (5) the seller's net worth, delinquency and servicing record. When all queries are addressed, traders begin contacting potential investors who they think may be looking for similar loans. At the point at which an investor is located, a trader representing the investor contacts the trader representing the seller to indicate that a possible sale is in the works. Any additional questions are resolved and the name and phone number of the investor is given to the sell-side trader (or vice versa, depending upon the agreement between the investor and the trader). Details on the investor are provided to the seller, which is instructed to contact the investor within a short time frame. This assumes both parties are experienced, frequent secondary market participants. Should this not be the case, the trader may set up a four-way conference call to introduce the parties, resolve any questions, and talk through the follow-up responsibilities.

The next step involves follow-through with the buyer and seller by the respective traders. The trader on the sell side checks to see that contact was made and to determine what action was agreed upon by each party. The buy-side trader checks to determine if the specifics of the offering were identical to those initially received by the trader representing the seller. If there are no significant discrepancies, the trader establishes a mutually agreeable timetable and delineates the specific responsibilities of each party.

This might include the exchange of an offering letter, physical delivery of documents, an exchange of the servicing agreement, and so forth.

From then on, traders exercise a monitoring role. They check on the agreed-upon execution of the commitment, the property inspection, the underwriting review, and finally the actual funding of the transaction. After the deal is completed, traders submit a transaction report to be verified by home office personnel. Once a sale is confirmed as bona fide by the parties involved, traders are compensated.

Even though completed sales are the principal measure of a trader's job performance, their responsibilities extend considerably further. They are also responsible for helping their customers stay abreast of local and national mortgage market developments, market conditions, new products, marketing strategies, investment and/or sales opportunities, agency developments, and more. Through such services the MIC also may be able to earn new insurance.

The home office support staff exists to provide the nontrading services that traders are expected to provide to their customers. Through traders, lenders can request historical data, access research on a wide array of mortgage-related subjects, or simply talk with someone who is knowledgeable about a problem or concern. In addition, the support staff is the link between the trader and the customers for all of the other services offered by the MIC. At MGIC this would include: project services, optimal delivery analysis, servicing evaluation, portfolio analysis, conduit participation, and mortgage securities services. Although a discussion of each of these services is beyond the scope of this chapter, a brief explanation of mortgage securities services seems in order, because many of the MICs provide similar assistance.

In general, mortgage securities services offer customers a complete line of investment services from a single source. They include: (1) aggregator services, (2) designated underwriting, (3) funding agent services, and (4) master servicing. As an aggregator, the MIC will help investors design a commitment to accommodate their cash flow, yield, and safety requirements. This allows the investor to tap new markets and new originators without the expense of adding people, offices, or systems. Designated underwriting services put the onus of loan evaluation on the MIC. Loans can be evaluated on the basis of Fannie Mae/ Freddie Mac standards or using the investor's criteria. The investor simply spells out guidelines and all loans are underwritten to those specifications. As a funding agent, the MIC collects and remits the investor's delivery fees. Master servicing assures the investor that the performance of individual subservicers is being monitored and that payments from the subservicers are remitted in a regular, timely fashion. Mortgage securities services can be contracted for individually or as a package.

The information network is further enhanced by using computers.

Besides listing loan package bids and offers, software accesses money and capital market data, news reports, posted yield/price requirements for the agencies and conduits, and customer profiles and histories. This database, in conjunction with a free-flow of anecdotal information, reports, and statistical data, keeps the trader close to the market's pulse.

While the number of markets and market participants in the conventional secondary market is constantly expanding, the MICs' niche has been in the traditional private-placement, whole-loan sector of the market. The advent of new players; the devleopment of a plethora of private conduit operations; changes in the economic, financial, and regulatory environment; and the introduction of new trading vehicles and products is gradually changing the MICs' secondary market operations and promises to alter them even more in the years to come. Conduit sponsorship, the trading of conventional pass-through securities, and accessing trading desks are among the ideas currently being pursued.

One of the more significant policy changes to descend in the mid-1980s was the move to collect fees in lieu of mortgage insurance payback (the traditional vehicle) for secondary market trading services. Many major MICs have gone to the imposition of direct hard-dollar fees to cover expenses. This partially reflects the market's heightened demand for placement assistance, but also indicates the broader array of products—construction loans, commercial and multifamily loans, sales of servicing, and soon—that the trader is now being asked to market. Since insurance payback is difficult to earn on these products, fees have been collected as compensation for trading assistance.

Despite the entrance of new players and new markets, the importance and size of the whole-loan market remains substantial. HUD statistics indicate, possibly contrary to the beliefs of many, that whole-loan activity remains considerable. Whole-loan sales in 1985 totalled $81.9 billion, compared to $57.6 billion two years earlier. With aggregate conventional mortgage sales totalling $145 billion in 1985 and $96 billion in 1983, it is quite apparent that the private-placement, whole-loan market remains a significant sector within the secondary market.

Investors access the MIC trading networks to obtain: (1) investment-grade mortgage products, (2) yield, (3) income, and (4) portfolio balance. Contrary to common rumors, quality, investment, grade, whole-loan packages of $500,000 to $20 million are almost always available or readily found. Quality is ensured because investors can underwrite loans to their standards. Moreover, if they are MIC-insured loans, they undergo three evaluations—from the originator, the investor, and the MIC. If proper due diligence is important to the investor, whole loans are the ideal. Unlike pass throughs, the documents and the properties can be viewed, touched, inspected, examined, and reviewed for a determination of quality. Furthermore, products that may not be available locally—ARMS for instance—can usually be found, either for immediate or deferred delivery.

Yield is the second reason investors use the MIC networks. Whole loans, as of mid-1986, yield approximately 100 basis points more than pass throughs and 200 basis points more than treasuries with comparable maturities. For example, as of September, 1986, whole loans with 15-year maturities were priced to yield 9.625 percent–9.75 percent net, compaed to current-coupon, 15-year pass-through securities, which yield 8.55 percent–8.90 percent. Figures 6–2 and 6–3 compare yields on 30-year fixed-rate mortgages (FRMs) to 10-year treasuries and 15-year FRMs to 7-year treasuries. Yield pickups off of treasuries on whole loans are depicted for the period from January through mid-April, 1986.

Another reason why investors use the MIC's secondary market networks is fee income. Unlike alternate investments, whole loans provide commitment and/or delivery fees. Fees of .5 percent to 2 percent of the outstanding principal balance are common, depending on the product, yield, and type of commitment. Many investors book the fees as income in the period received.

Geographic and product risk dispersion (of the mortgage portfolio) is a fourth reason why investors use the MIC trading operations. Investment managers can geographically balance their portfolios in order to mitigate losses should their local economy slump. With the wide and rapid fluctuations seen in local markets in recent years, this factor deserves greater attention. Texas-based investors, for example, who used the secondary markets as a portfolio management tool, are less

Figure 8–2
**Yields on 30-Yr. Private Sector Whole Loans vs.
10-Yr. Treasury Yields
Jan. 1, 1986 - August 15, 1986**

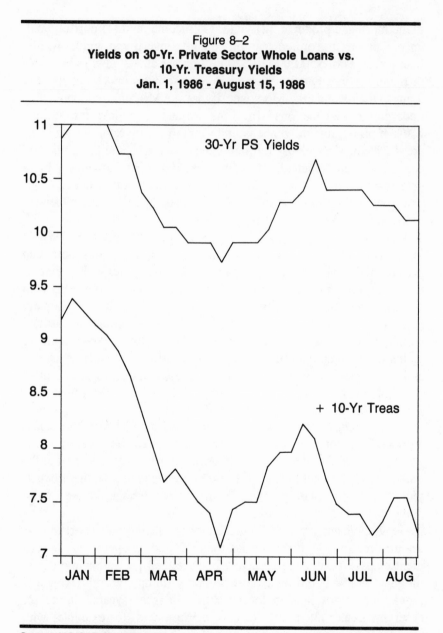

Source: MGIC, Federal Reserve.

Figure 8–3
Yields on 15-Yr. Private Sector Loans vs.
7-Yr. Treasury Yields
Jan 1, 1986 - Aug 15, 1986

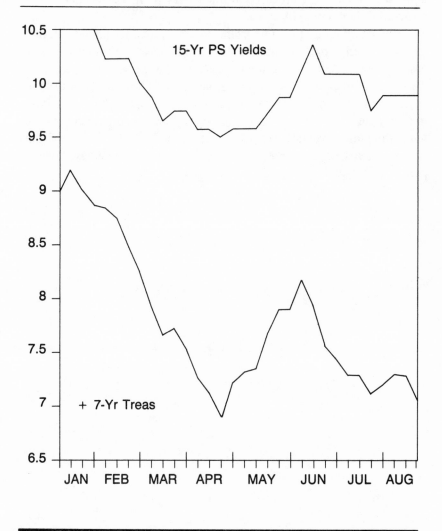

Source: MGIC, Federal Reserve.

likely to be as adversely affected by the high foreclosure rates and property value depreciation resulting from the recent drop in oil prices than those who rarely, if ever, invested in loans outside of the state. In the same fashion, products that may be desired but that are not available locally can be purchased from sellers in markets where their origination is commonplace.

Early recognition of the importance of a vibrant aftermarket in mortgages for market participants and the nation as a whole led the MICs to assume a pioneering role in the development of the secondary market. This commitment has grown over time. It has allowed MICs to help augment the flow of capital to meet the nation's goal of "a decent home in a suitable environment" for countless millions of American families while helping to satisfy suppliers' and users' needs in one of the nation's largest credit markets. Each MIC and every trader has played a part in this evolving saga.

Section II:
Mortgage-Backed
Securities

INTRODUCTION

The diversity and complexity of the mortgage-backed securities (MBS) market offer substantial opportunities for the experienced—and treacherous pitfalls for newcomers. Simply keeping up with the ever-expanding menu of exotic MBS instruments can be a daunting prospect, but failure to keep abreast of this dynamic market can mean forfeiting profit potential and risking painful losses.

The 11 chapters in Section II offer insights into many different facets of the MBS market. In Chapter 9, Richard Landau explains the evolution of mortgage-backed securities from the early 1970s to the mid-1980s. The next two chapters reflect some of the same aftershocks of the rally of 1985–86 that were encountered in Section I. Chapter 10, authored by Joseph Hu, discusses the relative value of MBS in the aftermath of the rally. In Chapter 11 Steve Carlson and Timothy Sears offer a new approach to determining the duration of MBS that is appropriate to an environment characterized by rapidly changing rates. While Chapters 10 and 11 focus on prepayments primarily as a function of relative interest rates, Chapter 12, authored by Blaine Roberts and Richard Ellson, examines how the analysis of regional economic data can lead to a better understanding of prepayment probabilities.

Section II: Mortgage-Backed Securities

While the Government National Mortgage Association (GNMA) enjoys a virtual monopoly over the securitized market for government product, more vigorous competition exists in the conventional sector. Among the greatest rivalries of all time, one might include, along with Mohammed Ali and Joe Frazier and the New York Yankees and the Boston Red Sox, Fannie Mae and Freddie Mac. These two quasi-federal agencies dominate the market for conventional MBS. In Chapter 13, Henry Cassidy and Patricia Dodson demonstrate how Freddi Mac PCs can be used in a variety of financing strategies, while in Chapter 14 Jayne Shontell delineates the advantages of the Fannie Mae MBS.

During the 1980s, the pace of change in the MBS market greatly accelerated. The last five chapters of Section II focus on some of the most significant developments of this decade. One of the most important trends is undoubtedly the securitization of assets other than single-family residential mortgages, and John Crosby traces the evolution of securities backed by commercial mortgages in Chapter 15. The collateralized mortgage obligation (CMO), a dramatic breakthrough in MBS design, is the subject of the next two chapters. James Hornig examines the pros and cons of public versus private placements of CMOs in Chapter 16. In Chapter 17, Marko Issever and Carol R. Kalin discuss the creation of synthetic CMOs through the use of interest rate swaps.

While the first non-agency MBS was issued during the 1970s, it was not until the mid-1980s that the private sector MBS began to come into its own. The development of standards that allowed privately issued MBS to be rated was critical to the development of this market. In Chapter 18, Michael Molesky presents an overview of how rating agencies view mortgage credit risk.

The landmark Tax Reform Act of 1986 opened up many new opportunities for MBS participants by authorizing Real Estate Mortgage Investment Conduits (REMIC). The implications and uses of REMIC are the subject of Chapter 19, authored by Donald Susswein.

Chapter 9

RICHARD S. LANDAU

Richard Landau is President of Bear Stearns Mortgage Capital Corporation. Previously, he was Executive Vice President and Director with Dean Witter Reynolds, Inc. responsible for all mortgage trading, research, finance, as well as Sears Mortgage Securities Corporation. Mr. Landau has been involved with mortgage securities with several Wall Street firms over the past 14 years. He received his B.A. from Brown University in mathematical economics and his M.B.A. from New York University.

The Evolution of Mortgage-backed Securities

RICHARD S. LANDAU

In the early 1970s, mortgage-backed securities (MBSs) were synonomous with GNMAs. Mortgage bankers would aggregate $1 million of FHA/VA 30-year fully amortizing, single-family residential mortgage loans, place the loans with a custodian, obtain a GNMA guaranty, and then sell the resultant GNMA pass-through security either directly to a thrift institution or to one of a handful of Wall Street dealers. Total volume of GNMA issuance for the years 1970–1975 inclusive was approximately $21 billion.

In the mid-1970s, the Federal Home Loan Mortgage Corporation (FHLMC) became an active participant in the mortgage-backed securities marketplace. Fully amortizing, single-family residential conventional loans were brought by Freddie Mac and subsequently re-issued with a government agency backing as FHLMC Participation Certificates (PCs). There were perhaps a dozen FHLMC dealers who initially participated in the FHLMC auctions.

During the same time period, the Federal National Mortgage Association (FNMA) was a dominant portfolio investor in conventional mortgage loans through its auctions of optional commitments. Mortgage originators purchased stand-by commitments from FNMA to hedge their conventional mortgage loan pipelines. In periods of rising interest rates, FNMA purchased a tremendous percentage of newly originated mortgage loans through the exercise of these optional commitments. At that time, thrift institutions were the only other major source of mortgage funds.

In September 1975, the Chicago Board of Trade initiated its first financial futures contract, the GNMA CDR. Despite the CDR's eventual demise, it spurred the development of Treasury bond, bill, and note futures contracts, as well as other financial futures contracts traded today.

Thus, by the mid-1970s, mortgage-backed securities were for the most part GNMAs, FHLMC PCs, and a small volume of assorted mortgage-backed bonds and mortgage pay-through bonds. The latter two mortgage security structures were the initial inventions of the nascent mortgage finance industry, which was searching for an efficient method to liquify existing mortgage portfolios.

Any chronology of the evolution of mortgage-backed securities that omits the Bank of America's effort in 1977 to standardize a conventional pass-through security would be unfair. Though a viable secondary market for the Bank of America pass through never developed, the concept of nongovernmental participants creating their own mortgage-backed securities was the forerunner of today's private conduits.

In the late 1970s Wall Street firms made a major commitment to their then fledging mortgage-backed securities departments. Larger distribution networks created additional demand for mortgage-backed securities from institutional investors other than thrift institutions. Insurance companies, pension funds, and money managers all became aware of this new segment of the fixed-income market by the late 1970s and had begun to allocate a portion of their investment portfolios to mortgage-backed securities, mostly GNMAs and some FHLMC PCs.

Without doubt, the single largest contribution to the maturity and depth of the emerging mortgage-backed securities business occurred in 1981, when both Freddie Mac and Fannie Mae began their swap programs. The ability of portfolio lenders to swap seasoned whole-loan mortgage inventory into newly issued FHLMC PCs and FNMA MBSs enabled the swapping institutions to create more standardized—and thus more liquid—collateral.

The adverse interest rate environment of the early 1980s created such financial pressures within the thrift industry that new accounting practices were promulgated. Regulatory (RAP) accounting treatment accelerated swapping entire thrift portfolios of discount whole loans for FHLMC PC's or FNMA MBS's.

The combination of the GNMA, FHLMC, and FNMA mortgage-backed securities programs during 1981–1983 created new issue volumes of approximately $19 billion, $54 billion, and $83 billion in those three years respectively.

It was during this same period that Wall Street began to seriously dissect the actual cash flow characteristics of a mortgage loan. Yields were no longer based on the standard 12-year prepay assumption, and mortgage research became a necessity in order to profitably trade mortgage securities.

This mortgage quantification surge created the "speed game," whereby mortgages are classified by their potential future prepayment speeds. Age, location, initial coupon rate, present interest rate environment, and the shape of the yield curve all potentially influence future prepayment rates.

Additional financial pressures on the thrift industry to match the duration of assets and liabilities fostered the popularity of the adjustable-rate mortgage (ARM). The combination of the huge volume of ARMs being originated and the emergence of private conduits such as RFC (Residential Funding Corporation) and Sears Mortgage Securities as daily participants in the mortgage marketplace set the stage for the first ARM security in 1984. Subsequently, GNMA, FHLMC, and FNMA also created their own versions of ARM securities.

In 1984, new mortgage originations included 1-year ARMs (of all sizes and shapes); 3-year and 5-year ARMs; and fixed-rate, 15-year and 30-year maturity mortgage loans with varying payment amortizations, in addition to the level payment self-amortizing loan. Negative amortization in 1-year ARMs as well as 30-year, graduated-payment mortgages seized a certain percentage of new originations, and these mortgages were used as collateral for new mortgage-backed securities. As interest rates began to decline in mid-1984, and then continued their dramatic descent throughout 1985, the 15-year mortgage became more popular with borrowers who wanted to reduce their total interest costs and rapidly build home equity.

The mortgage-backed securities market has experienced more rapid change in the short time between 1984 and 1986 than it did during the whole period from 1970 to 1983. The emphasis on mortgage investment for the rapidly expanding mortgage-backed securities investor base led to the creation of the collateralized mortgage obligation (CMO). The multiclass pass-through attempt by Dean Witter/Sears Mortgage Securities in 1984 was the forerunner to the 1986 Real Estate Mortgage Investment Conduit (REMIC) legislation, which could conceivably create more mortgage-backed securities issuance and secondary volume than its parent, the CMO.

The dramatic decline in interest rates in late 1984 through 1986 created an acute awareness of the concept (much talked about but not totally understood) of negative convexity of mortgage-backed securities. Options-type pricing for mortgage securities became necessary to properly evaluate the risk inherent in the call option feature of the underlying mortgage. This attention to convexity led to an increase in the use of mortgage-backed options and treasury note and bond options to hedge mortgage-backed securities position.

In 1986, excess servicing became a major issue as mortgage servicers and financial auditors realized that past capitalized gains of excess servicing have disappeared with prepayment acceleration. Securities evidencing an ownership in a strip of excess servicing have been created, as well as stripped coupons in which different classes of investors receive differing pro rata shares of the underlying interest and principal of specific mortgage pools.

The ability to strip cash flows from a diversified portfolio of mortgage loans and treat the resultant mortgage-backed securities as qualifying real estate assets under REMIC should better define investment strategies for each type of mortgage-backed security investor.

As if all the actual mortgage-backed securities that have evolved are not enough, the PhDs of mortgage research have created market in synthetic securities using mortgage-backed securities to provide investors higher returns relative to a given amount of interest rate risk or the same return with reduced interest rate risk.

Whatever happened to plain old GNMA mortgage-backed securities? In reality, more than twice the amount of GNMA mortgage-backed securities were issued in the first nine months of 1986 (over $62 billion) than in any single year except for 1983.

The volume of overall mortgage-backed securities issued in the first nine months of 1986 (approximately $200 billion) was almost 60 percent of the total issued from 1970 through 1985 (approximately $335 billion). In essence, the varied world of mortgage-backed securities has expanded beyond anyone's wildest imagination.

One underlying theme pervades this entire 16-year period, and it remains as true today as in the past—*the mortgage-backed securities industry is still in its infancy*. We can all look forward to even faster growth in the future.

Chapter 10

JOSEPH HU

Joseph Hu is Senior Vice President and Director of Mortgage Research for Shearson Lehman Brothers Inc.

The author wishes to acknowledge the assistance of his colleagues, Jerry M. Dell'Isola, Suzanne P. Franks, Jane Isaacson, and Timothy D. Sears in the prepartion of this report.

Evaluating Mortgage Pass-Through Securities

JOSEPH HU

OVERVIEW

The dramatic decline in interest rates during 1986 boosted housing activity but wreaked havoc in the mortgage securities market. Declining interest rates stimulated sales of existing homes, which in turn raised prepayments on mortgage pass throughs backed by mostly seasoned mortgages. Interest rates on these mortgages ranged from substantially above to below the current market rate. More importantly, as interest rates declined, homeowners refinanced their higher-rate mortgages, causing prepayments for premium-coupon pass throughs to rise. Since all mortgages are prepaid at par, rising prepayments hindered the performance of premium coupons whereas they enhanced the return on discount coupons.

As of September 1986, more than 50 percent of all outstanding mortgage securities traded four to five points over par, tripling the level of only a year before. These premium-coupon securities became increasingly unattractive to investors because of their sharply rising prepayment rates. Particularly, investors' concern of persistently high prepayments restricted the price appreciation of higher-coupon pass throughs. In fact, during 1986, whenever the market rally gathered further momentum, high premiums—particularly those with coupon rates of 12 percent and above—not only ceased to appreciate, but began to sustain price losses. Consequently, mortgage pass throughs turned in a dismal performance during one of the most powerful bond market rallies in history.

Premium coupons are not the only coupons that have difficulty following the trail of the bull market. Robust housing activity during the mid-1980s has generated a huge volume of mortgage originations, leading to a gigantic supply of newly issued mortgage pass throughs. This new issuance exerted substantial downward pressure on the price of mortgage securities and raised mortgage yields. The combined effect of high mortgage prepayments and a huge supply of originations dramatically cheapened the relative value of mortgage pass throughs for virtually all coupons. During 1986, mortgage-to-Treasury yield spreads widened to historically high levels. (See Appendix, The Spectacular Widening of Mortgage-to-Treasury Yield Spreads.)

Are mortgage securities necessarily cheap because of these wide spreads? Will these spreads remain wide? Only time can provide the answers to these questions. There are, however, various analytical tools that, if used properly, can shed light on the relative value of mortgage pass throughs. Nevertheless, the proper use of these tools requires the awareness of the following critical issues: (1) the computation and interpretation of the yield on mortgage pass throughs, (2) the limitation of using historical mortgage-to-Treasury yield spreads and total returns to analyze the relative value of mortgage pass throughs, (3) the use of horizon analysis as a necessary step in evaluating mortgage pass throughs, (4) the analysis of break even prepayment rates as a means to determine the intra-market relative value of mortgage pass-throughs, and (5) the importance of incorporating prospective views on housing and mortgage finance to project the long-term value of mortgage pass throughs.

MARKET FINDINGS

This chapter addresses these issues and presents the relative value of mortgage pass throughs by coupon sector. Market information, as of

August 29, 1986, for Government National Mortgage Association guaranteed mortgage pass throughs (GNMAs) is used as a point of illustration, although the discussion is also entirely applicable to pass throughs guaranteed by the Federal National Mortgage Association (FNMA) and the Federal Home Loan Mortgage Corporation (FHLMC).

The major conclusions of this chapter follow.

• The yield of a mortgage pass through is computed under a specific prepayment assumption that remains constant for the entire term of the security. Over the past few years, the computation has evolved from a simplistic 12-year prepaid-life to a more sophisticated constant prepayment rate (CPR) assumption. However, the CPR assumption varies among users, and a slight variation in the CPR substantially changes the yield of a pass through, particularly when its price is significantly above or below par (see Tables 10–1 and 10–2).

• Mortgage-to-Treasury yield spreads, computed on the basis of historical CPRs, had served well as past indictors of the relative value of mortgage securities. A mortgage security has value if its current yield spread over a comparable Treasury is considered wide by historical standards (see Table 10–3). During 1986, however, the sharp drop in interest rates and the near-record strength of housing activity reduced the reliability of this measure. Investors attempting to determine relative value for mortgage pass throughs should supplement the study of yield spreads with an analysis of total returns for a given holding period (see Tables 10–4a and 10–4b). Mortgage securities may be viewed as cheap only when they match the returns of comparable Treasuries and still exhibit historically wide yield spreads. Nevertheless, the combined analyses of yield spreads and total returns tells only half of the story because it is, after all, confined to a historical context. To complete the story, relative value analysis has to incorporate projected future returns on mortgage pass throughs. Mortgage securities will only have true value when they have the potential to outperform comparable Treasuries under various projected interest rate scenarios.

• A horizon analysis enables investors to project future returns on mortgage pass throughs and Treasuries. The analysis requires assumptions about what will happen to the slope and level of the Treasury and

Table 10–1
Mortgage Yields of Selected Coupons Computed under Various Assumptions

Price	GNMA 8%				GNMA 9%				GNMA 12%			
	30/12*	FHA†	12-Mo.‡	1-Mo.	30/12*	FHA†	12-Mo.‡	1-Mo.	30/12*	FHA†	12-Mo.‡	1-Mo.
90	9.41%	9.87%	8.52%	10.21%	10.47%	10.78%	10.73%	10.79%	13.65%	13.99%	15.37%	18.53%
95	8.66	8.86	8.86	9.02	9.68	9.82	9.79	9.82	12.75	12.89	13.52	14.94
100	7.96	7.95	7.95	7.94	8.95	8.94	8.94	8.94	11.92	11.91	11.85	11.71
105	7.30	7.10	7.11	6.94	8.27	8.14	8.17	8.14	11.15	11.01	10.34	8.78
110	6.68	6.33	6.34	6.03	7.62	7.41	7.45	7.40	10.43	10.19	8.96	6.11

* Assumes a 30-year maturity with a 12-year prepaid life.
† Assumes a 100% FHA experience.
‡ Assumes a constant prepayment rate (CPR) of the previous 12 months (July 1985–July 1986); 1-Mo. assumes a CPR of the previous month (July 1986).

Table 10–2
**Add-on Factors in Basis Points for
Various Mortgage Yields**

Mortgage Yield		Add-on	Mortgage Yield		Add-on
6.73% –	7.06%	10bps	9.63%–	9.86%	20 bps
7.07 –	7.39	11	9.87 –	10.13	21
7.40 –	7.70	12	10.14 –	10.33	22
7.71 –	8.01	13	10.34 –	10.55	23
8.02 –	8.30	14	10.56 –	10.77	24
8.31 –	8.58	15	10.78 –	10.99	25
8.59 –	8.85	16	11.00 –	11.20	26
8.86 –	9.12	17	11.21 –	11.41	27
9.13 –	9.37	18	11.42 –	11.62	28
9.38 –	9.62	19	11.63 –	11.82	29
			11.83 –	12.01	30

mortgage yield curves, morgage prepayment rates, and the reinvestment rate over a horizon period. The horizon analysis presented in this chapter suggests that, if interest rates either remained unchanged or rose by 100 basis points from their levels as of September 1986, the 11.5 percent–13.5 percent GNMAs would far outperform lower coupon GNMAs and all Treasuries. If interest rates declined 100 basis points, however, these coupons would significantly underperform their lower coupon counterparts as well as intermediate and long-term Treasuries; however, they would still exceed the returns of short-term Treasuries (see Table 10–5).

• As an alternative to valuing mortgage securities versus Treasuries, a break-even analysis offers an assessment of value for various coupons relative to the benchmark coupon. The benchmark is defined as the coupon whose price is closest to par. Traditional break-even analysis computes the prepayment rate for each coupon so that it will have the same cash flow yield as that of the benchmark coupon. This traditional analysis, however, fails to recognize the term structure of interest rates.

Table 10–3
Bond Equivalent Cash Flow Yields and Yield Spreads Over
Comparable-Duration Treasuries for Selected GNMAs, August 29, 1986

Coupon	Price 8/29 (32nds)	3 Mo CPR (%)	Bd Eq Yield (%)	Mod Dur (yr)	Comp Treas Mat (yr)	Comp Treas Dur (yr)	Comp Treas Yield (yr)	Comp Dur Treas 8/29	12. Mo. Yld Sprd to Comp Dur Treas (Basis Points) High	Low	Avg
8.0%	97–09	7.8	8.64	5.0	7	5.3	6.72	191	207	112	72
8.5	98–11	8.0	8.92	5.1	7	5.3	6.72	220	241	117	91
9.0	100–12	7.3	9.03	5.5	7	5.3	6.72	231	238	115	75
9.5	102–23	7.1	9.10	5.5	7	5.3	6.72	238	246	118	84
10.0	104–30	3.1	9.43	7.1	10	6.8	6.93	249	250	120	90
10.5	106–28	3.7	9.67	6.8	10	6.8	6.93	269	269	126	101
11.0	106–27	11.7	9.54	4.4	5	4.3	6.42	312	312	201	118
11.5	106–28	30.9	8.83	2.2	3	2.7	6.12	225	324	204	129
12.0	107–12	36.8	8.02	1.9	2	1.8	5.92	210	352	207	135
12.5	107–16	43.8	7.60	1.6	2	1.8	5.92	167	364	206	125
13.0	107–22	49.3	7.23	1.4	2	1.8	5.92	130	372	201	81
13.5	108–17	49.4	7.09	1.4	2	1.8	5.92	116	367	128	70

Source: Shearson Lehman Mortgage Securities.

Table 10–4a
Total Holding Period Returns for Selected GNMAs
August 30, 1985–August 29, 1986

Coupon	Purchase Price (32nds)	Selling Price (32nds)	Price Change (%)	Principal Paydown (%)	Coupon Return (%)	Reinvest (%)	Total Returns (%)
8.00%	83–06	97–09	16.94	0.19	9.37	0.44	26.95
8.50	85–26	98–11	14.60	0.12	9.64	0.45	24.81
9.00	87–26	100–12	14.31	−0.02	10.03	0.42	24.74
9.50	90–14	102–24	13.61	−0.14	10.30	0.41	24.18
10.00	93–00	104–30	12.84	−0.24	10.55	0.41	23.55
10.50	95–06	106–28	12.28	−0.29	10.85	0.40	23.24
11.00	98–00	106–27	9.02	−0.45	10.95	0.45	19.98
11.50	100–08	106–28	6.61	−0.59	11.14	0.48	17.63
12.00	102–18	107–12	4.69	−0.69	11.35	0.48	15.84
12.50	104–22	107–16	2.69	−1.00	11.41	0.57	13.66
13.00	106–22	107–22	0.94	−1.35	11.42	0.66	11.67
13.50	108–08	108–18	0.29	−1.88	11.40	0.79	10.60
Treas. 2 yr	100–14	102–17	2.08	NA	9.09	0.30	11.47
3 yr	100–14	106–11	5.88	NA	9.46	0.18	15.52
5 yr	99–10	110–29	11.67	NA	9.69	0.34	21.71
7 yr	101–02	116–19	15.37	NA	10.27	0.25	25.88
10 yr	101–11	122–11	20.72	NA	10.36	0.20	31.28
30 yr	101–11	134–22	32.90	NA	10.48	0.20	43.58

Table 10–4b
Total Holding Period Returns for Selected GNMAs
March 31, 1986–May 30, 1986

Coupon	Purchase Price (32nds)	Selling Price (32nds)	Price Change (%)	Principal Paydown (%)	Coupon Return (%)	Reinvest (%)	Total Returns (%)
8.00%	95–24	91–12	−4.57	0.10	1.37	.00	−3.09
8.50	97–25	93–15	−4.41	0.08	1.42	.00	−2.90
9.00	100–06	95–20	−4.55	0.05	1.47	.00	−3.03
9.50	102–02	98–14	−3.55	0.02	1.52	.00	−2.01
10.00	104–14	101–22	−2.63	−0.02	1.56	.00	−1.09
10.50	106–06	104–16	−1.59	−0.06	1.62	.00	−0.03
11.00	106–25	104–30	−1.73	−0.11	1.68	0.01	−0.15
11.50	107–00	104–30	−1.93	−0.22	1.75	0.01	−0.39
12.00	107–27	105–20	−2.06	−0.34	1.80	0.01	−0.58
12.50	108–00	105–27	−2.00	−0.47	1.86	0.01	−0.59
13.00	108–06	106–15	−1.62	−0.60	1.92	0.02	−0.28
13.50	108–12	106–24	−1.50	−0.65	1.99	0.02	−0.14
Treas. 2 yr	100–12	99–18	−0.81	NA	1.22	0.00	1.16
3 yr	102–15	100–27	−1.59	NA	1.32	0.00	−0.26
5 yr	107–07	104–03	−2.91	NA	1.44	0.00	−0.94
7 yr	97–15	93–30	−3.62	NA	1.17	0.00	−1.65
10 yr	110–10	104–28	−4.93	NA	1.36	0.00	−2.96
30 yr	127–08	115–16	−9.23	NA	1.23	0.00	−7.26

Source: Shearson Lehman Mortgage Securities

Table 10–5
**A One-Year Horizon Analysis for Selected GNMAs and Treasuries,
as of August 29, 1986**

Total Returns (%) Assuming Treasury Yields

Coupon	Assumed CPR (%)	Rise 100 Basis Points				Remain Unchanged					Fall 100 Basis Points				
		Flat	Para	Steep	Comp Treas (Yr.)	Assumed CPR (%)	Flat	Para	Steep	Comp Treas (Yr.)	Assumed CPR (%)	Flat	Para	Steep	Comp Treas (Yr.)
8.00%	6	3.0	3.9	2.6	2.3 (7)	7	7.6	8.5	7.1	6.9 (7)	10	13.6	12.7	14.0	6.7 (5)
8.50	6	3.2	4.1	2.8	2.3 (7)	7	7.9	8.9	7.4	6.9 (7)	10	13.9	13.1	14.4	6.7 (5)
9.00	3	3.3	3.3	0.5	0.9 (10)	4	8.1	9.2	7.5	6.9 (7)	8	14.8	13.8	15.3	6.7 (5)
9.50	3	4.1	4.1	1.3	0.9 (10)	4	8.6	9.8	8.1	6.9 (7)	9	14.1	13.2	14.6	6.7 (5)
10.00	1	3.2	3.2	0.0	0.9 (10)	5	8.8	8.8	6.1	7.0 (10)	10	12.6	11.7	13.1	6.7 (5)
10.50	1	4.0	4.0	0.8	0.9 (10)	5	9.1	9.1	6.3	7.0 (10)	20	7.9	7.6	8.6	6.2 (3)
11.00	5	6.2	7.2	5.7	2.3 (7)	10	8.8	10.1	9.3	6.7 (5)	35	6.1	6.0	6.5	6.2 (3)
11.50	10	12.0	13.2	12.4	3.1 (5)	25	8.9	9.7	9.5	6.2 (3)	40	7.2	7.2	7.7	6.0 (2)
12.00	20	10.2	11.2	10.9	4.5 (3)	30	8.8	9.6	9.6	6.0 (2)	45	6.8	6.8	7.2	6.0 (2)
12.50	25	10.7	11.5	11.3	4.5 (3)	35	8.9	9.6	9.6	6.0 (2)	45	7.8	7.8	8.2	6.0 (2)
13.00	25	12.6	13.4	13.2	4.5 (3)	35	10.2	10.9	10.9	6.0 (2)	45	8.7	8.7	9.1	6.0 (2)
13.50	25	13.3	14.1	13.9	4.5 (3)	35	10.5	11.2	11.2	6.0 (2)	45	8.7	8.7	9.1	6.0 (2)

Interest rate sub-scenarios:

Flat (rise, unchanged): Mortgage yield curve flattens—yields for various coupons rise another 50, 40, 30, 20 and 0 basis points over the comparable 2-, 3-, 5-, 7-, and 10-year Treasuries.

Steep (rise, unchanged): Mortgage yield curve steepens—yields for various coupons rise 0, 10, 20, 30 and 50 basis points over the comparable Treasuries.

Flat (decline): Mortgage yield curve flattens—yeidls for various coupons decline another 0, 10, 20, 30 and 50 basis points over the comparable Treasuries.

Steep (decline): Mortgage yield curve steepens—yield for various coupons decline another 50, 40, 30, 20 and 10 basis points over the comparable Treasuries.

Para (rise, decline, unchanged): Mortgage yield curve undergoes a parallel shift to the Treasury yield curve.

Source: Shearson Lehman Mortgage Securities

In an environment characterized by a positively sloped yield curve, premium coupons need not yield the same as the benchmark coupon in order to be equally attractive. By incorporating the slope of the yield curve, the "revised" break-even analysis generates prepayment rates for premium coupons such that their yield spreads to comparable-duration Treasuries equal that of the benchmark to the 7- or 10-year Treasury. The revised break-even prepayment analysis indicates that prepayment rates for 10 percent–11 percent coupons could still increase significantly from their mid-1986 levels and remain as attractive as the benchmark coupon. This large cushion indicates value for these securities. The revised break-even prepayment rates for all other premiums, however, were lower than their mid-1986 levels, indicating that they were rich to the benchmark. The analysis also suggests that discount coupons were rich to the benchmark (see Table 10–6).

● The prepayment experience of 13 percent–15 percent GNMAs between 1983 and 1986 indicates the likely prepayment pattern for lower coupons (11 percent–12.5 percent) in a falling interest rate environment. The experience shows that the CPR for a premium coupon rarely stayed at an annualized rate of 45 percent for a long period of time when its underlying mortgage rate was 400 basis points above the market rate. The prepayment rate generally stayed below 30 percent when the spread was below 300 basis points, and 20 percent when the spread was less than 200 basis points (see Figures 10–1 and 10–2, pages 166–67.)

● The sharp drop in mortgage rates during the early part of 1986 created a tremendous opportunity for many homeowners to refinance. As a result, in mid-1986 prepayment rates for premium coupons surged to record-high levels. Over the long run, however, several social, economic, and institutional factors will prevent them from remaining at these levels. These are: the high cost of refinancing; the long period of residence after refinancing necessary to recoup up-front costs; limited appreciation in housing prices in certain regions over the past few years due to plummeting oil and farm prices; the tightening of mortgage underwriting criteria, and the potential cutback in mortgage insurance activity from government agencies.

● The unprecedented prepayment uncertainty compounded with the

Table 10–6

Break-Even Prepayment Rate Analysis for Selected GNMAs
August 29, 1986

Coupon	Price (32nds)	3 Mo. CPR (%)	BEPR (%)	RBEPR (%)	RBEPR 3 Mo. CPR	BECFY on RBEPR (%)	Yield Value (bps) 1% CPR	Yield Value (bps) 4/32nds
8.0%	97–09	7.8	22.3	22.3	14.5	9.03	2	3
8.5	98–10	8.0	15.7	15.7	7.6	9.03	1	3
9.0	100–12	7.2	NA	NA	—	9.03	1	2
9.5	102–23	7.1	9.3	9.3	2.2	9.03	3	2
10.0	104–30	3.1	10.7	6.8	3.7	9.24	5	2
10.5	106–28	3.7	12.0	9.1	5.4	9.24	6	2
11.0	106–26	11.7	18.2	21.7	10.1	8.73	7	3
11.5	106–28	30.9	23.6	30.3	−0.6	8.43	9	5
12.0	107–12	36.7	26.9	34.8	−2.0	8.24	11	6
12.5	107–16	43.8	31.1	38.4	−5.4	8.24	12	7
13.0	107–21	49.3	34.7	41.5	−7.8	8.24	13	8
13.5	108–17	49.3	35.2	41.3	−8.0	8.24	15	8

BECFY: Bond equivalent cash flow yield
BEPR: Break-even prepayment rate
RBEPR: Revised break-even prepayment rate

Source: Shearson Lehman Mortgage Securities.

flood of new issuance severely depressed the price of mortgage pass throughs. The valuation process described in this chapter suggests benchmark GNMAs were cheap in mid-1986. While both discount and high-premium coupons were relatively rich to the benchmark, they were cheap to their comparable Treasuries. Therefore, mortgage pass throughs offered a variety of investment opportunities. As of mid-1986, high premiums with coupon rates of 11.5 percent or above were well suited for investors with an investment horizon of two to three years. Low-premium coupons (9.5 percent–11 percent) should have been particularly attractive to intermediate or long-term yield-oriented investors, such as portfolio and mutual fund managers. Investors should have also considered a weighted mix of premium and discount coupons to suit their maturity preference and achieve desired yields.

COMPUTING AND INTERPRETING MORTGAGE PASS-THROUGH YIELDS

The yield of a mortgage pass-through security is the discount rate (that is, its internal rate of return) that equates the present value of its future cash flow to its price. It is a measure of yield to maturity. However, since the prepayment behavior of the mortgages backing the pass through oscillates with changing social, economic, and demographic conditions, the security has an uneven cash flow and an uncertain maturity. (The maturity is measured both in terms of weighted average life and duration). The yield computation of a pass-through security, therefore, requires certain prepayment assumptions to specify the pattern of its future cash flow. As the prepayment assumptions change, the yield can change substantially.

During the 17-year existence of mortgage pass throughs, investors have implemented various prepayment assumptions to compute yield. These assumptions have changed through time as market participants improved their understanding of the intrinsic characteristics of mortgage pass throughs. Initially they computed yield on a "quoted" basis. Quoted yield assumed that all mortgage securities, regardless of age, had a 30-year remaining maturity. It also assumed that mortgages would experience only amortized repayment of principal, without receiving any unscheduled prepayments before the end of the first 12 years. At the completion of the 12th year, however, all of the remaining balance was prepaid at once. While this "30/12" assumption now seems unrealistic, at the time when mortgage securities were first developed it was a simple and straightforward technique. Table 10–1 shows quoted yields of selected GNMA coupons, along with other yields computed using later-developed assumption methods.

Another early, although slightly sophisticated, method of calculating mortgage yields assumed that underlying mortgages replicate the prepayment experience of FHA-insured mortgages. A specific pool of mortgages was assumed to prepay at a multiple or a fraction of FHA experience, depending on the expectation of their future prepayments. For example, the prepayment rate for a mortgage pool may be assumed to be 150 percent or 75 percent of the "FHA experience." While this method took variations of annual prepayments into consideration, most mortgages, conventional mortgages in particular, rarely duplicate the FHA experience on a year-to-year basis. (Again, yields computed on a 100 percent FHA experience for selected GNMAs are shown in Table 10–1.)

Recently, investors have devised a more advanced way of calculating mortgage yield, known as "cash flow yield." This yield assumes that the future cash flow of a mortgage security conforms to the average CPR of its recent past and applies this average to its remaining term. Naturally, this yield varies with the period over which the average CPR is computed. Conservative investors would use the average CPR of the past 12 months to encompass a complete seasonal cycle of housing activity; others would be a six-, three-, or even one-month CPR to project the future cash flow yield (see Table 10–1).

Cash flow yield is a more realistic measurement of mortgage yield than any of its forerunners, particularly when housing activity and interest rates are relatively stable. Since discount coupons prepay mostly as a result of housing transactions, a stable housing market produces steady prepayment rates on a seasonally adjusted basis. Premium coupon prepayment rates, however, are basically the result of mortgage refinancings, which rarely occur without sharp declines in interest rates. For this reason, the cash flow yield gained wide acceptance prior to 1985. Throughout that period, interest rates fluctuated between 12–14 percent. Prepayment rates surged only for those securities with a coupon rate of 14 percent or higher because the drop in interest rates was never sharp enough to justify refinancing of lower coupons; by the same token, the decline in mortgage rates was never significantly enough to trigger a record high in housing activity.

The powerful bond market rally of 1986, however, created considerable confusion in the computation and the interpretation of cash flow yield. The dramatic decline in interest rates led investors to expect a sharp rise in prepayment rates both as a result of the brisk housing market and the strong incentive for refinancing. Past prepayment rates—even those of the previous month—were considered too low for the projection of future cash flow. Thus, market participants began to compute cash flow yields based on their own *expected* prepayment rates. Inevitably, these expectations vary from one participant to another and many are substantially higher than past experience might indicate. However, the resulting yields implicitly assume that the expected prepayment rate will persist throughout the remaining life of the underlying mortgages. This assumption stands on shaky ground. Any pricing of premium coupons based on unsustainably high prepayment assumptions will depress the value of these securities.

EXAMINING MORTGAGE-TO-TREASURY YIELD SPREADS

The traditional way of evaluating the relative value of a mortgage pass through compared its quoted yield, regardless of coupon, to that of the risk-free yield on the constant maturity, 10-year Treasury. A mortgage security was considered cheap if its current spread over the 10-year Treasury was wider than its average over a given period, say the past 12 months. Conversely, a lower-than-average spread meant that the security was relatively rich.

This technique is still valid, although the cash flow yield ha replaced the quoted yield. Also, not all coupons are compared to the 10-year Treasury; the benchmark and discount coupons are compared to either the 7- or 10-year Treasury. Premium coupons, because of their shorter duration, are compared to the 2-, 3- and 5-year Treasuries depending on their specific prepayment assumption. This new method of evaluating mortgage securities with respect to various sectors of the Treasury curve assumes that comparable duration securities have roughly the same price volatility, although not necessarily similar convexity.

Furthermore, since mortgage securities are instruments that pay monthly, their yields are computed on a monthly compounding basis. In order to make a mortgage yield directly comparable to a Treasury yield (semiannual compounding), the cash flow yield must be expressed in a slightly higher "bond-equivalent" yield. Table 10–2 presents the add-on factor used when mortgage yields are converted to bond-equivalent yields., Table 10–3 provides bond-equivalent cash flow yields based on past three-month prepayment rates and yield spreads to comparable-duration Treasuries for selected GNMA coupons.

Mortgage-to-Treasury yield spreads should be examined in a stable interest rate environment to analyze the relative value of mortgage securities. The sharp decline in interest rates during 1986, however, rendered this approach inaccurate, particularly for premium coupons. Using unusually high prepayment rates to project cash flows created confusion through a wide range of projected yield spreads for premium coupons over comparable-duration Treasuries. These spreads suggested that most premium coupons could be rich if prepayment rates continued to soar, but they also could be exceedingly cheap if prepayment rates leveled off. How should investors deal with the uncertainty of premium coupons? The answer lies in the investment objectives and the length of holding period of these securities. That is, yield spread analysis can be meaningful only when it is supplemented with a total return analysis over a given horizon period.

MEASURING TOTAL RETURNS OVER HORIZON PERIOD

The total return of nonmortgage, fixed-income securities over a given holding period consists of three components: price appreciation (or depreciation), coupon return, and reinvestment of the coupon prepayment during the holding period. Mortgage securities have an additionally important component—paydown of principal, both amortized repayment and prepayment. Thus, for mortgage securities, reinvestment return includes interest earned on both the coupon and the principal. More importantly, because mortgages are always prepaid at par, the paydown of principal enhances the return on discount coupons but retards the performance of premium coupons.

During 1985–1986, as interest rates plummeted, prepayment rates for discount coupons rose significantly, although not as much as did premium coupons. As shown in Table 10–4a, during this period discounts far outperformed premiums (despite the fact that premiums have higher coupon returns) for basically two reasons: price appreciation and principal return. In fact, these two factors reinforce each other. Falling interest rates raise the price of discounts; in the meantime, they also raise prepayments, which further enhances their total returns. In contrast, declining interest rates impair the performance of premium coupons by accelerating principal paydown, which in turn limits price appreciation. This limitation is generally referred to as "price compression" of premium coupons.

Table 10–4a shows that during 1985–1986 GNMA 8s returned a stunning 27 percent, dwarfing the 10.6 percent return produced by GNMA 13.5s. While the market appreciation of GNMA 8s was the decisive factor for their superior returns, the 1.9 percent negative return due to principal paydown was also a detrimental factor undermining the GNMA 13.5s' performance. During late-April and mid-May of 1986, however, as interest rates ascended moderately, GNMA 13.5s outperformed GNMA 8s (see Table 10–4b). The marginal price decline of GNMA 13.5s resulting from "price decompression" enabled them to maintain their posture in the market retreat. In relation to the magnitude of the price change and the coupon return, the principal paydown was not as important a factor for both coupons because of their short holding period.

The experience of 1985–1986 has shown that in a declining interest rate environment mortgage securities with a longer duration (discount and benchmark coupons) generally outperform those with a shorter duration (premium coupons). The difference is primarily due to the expectation of rising prepayment rates. This situation, of course, reverses itself when interest rates rise.

The total return analysis described above evaluates mortgage securiites more completely than yield spreads because it takes into consideration the price change, the principal paydown, and the reinvestment of cash flow generated during the holding period. However, it still tells only half of the story becaue it evaluates mortgage securities in a historical context. To complete the story, the total return concept should become a horizon analysis, which would assess the prospective performance of mortgage securities under various interest rate scenarios over a predetermined horizon; for example, premiums deemed cheap because of their exceedingly poor performance and wide spreads to comparable-duration Treasuries may remain cheap if they continue to underperform Treasuries under various interest rate scenarios. On the other hand, discounts that are currently rich because of their outstanding returns and narrow yield spreads may remain rich if they are expected to continue outperforming Treasuries under reasonable sets of interest rates and prepayment assumptions.

CONDUCTING A HORIZON ANALYSIS

A horizon analysis assesses the prospective performance of a mortgage security over a predetermined holding period under four basic assumptions:

1. The slope and the level of the Treasury yield curve at the end of the horizon period
2. The prepayment rate during the horizon period
3. The yield spread between mortgage securities and comparable duration Treasuries, (along with projected prepayment rates this assumption provides the selling prices of mortgage securities)
4. The reinvestment rate during the holding period for the principal paydown and coupon payment

The numerical example provided in Table 10–5 demonstrates the potential performance of selected GNMAs over a one-year period. During this period, the Treasury yield curve either remains unchanged, or rises/declines 100 basis points, respectively. Within each scenario, mortgage yields are assumed to move either parallel or further from the Treasury yield curve, resulting in a flattened or steepened curve. An annualized constant prepayment rate that is consistent with the interest rate assumption is projected for each GNMA coupon. The analysis further assumes a 6 percent initial reinvestment rate for the principal paydown and the coupon return. Depending on the interest rate scenario, the reinvestment rate will either rise or decline 100 basis points during the horizon period.

As shown in Table 10–5, if both the Treasury and mortgage yield curves remain unchanged between September 1986 and September 1987, all GNMAs would outperform their respective comparable-duration Treasuries. The winning factors favoring mortgage securities are the large yield advantages for discount and benchmark coupons and the assumed slowdown in prepayments for premium coupons. All GNMAs would maintain their lead against comparable Treasuries if the mortgage curve were to flatten, with yields on the shorter-duration coupons rising up to 50 basis points, and Treasury yields were to remain unchanged. If, however, mortgage yields rose up to 50 basis points on longer-duration coupons, then only GNMA 10s and 10.5s would be slightly outdistanced by the 10-year Treasury.

If interest rates rise 100 basis points, high-premium coupons (11.5% and up) would be by far the best performers, outshining all Treasuries and all other mortgage securities. Their performance would be equally stunning regardless of whether mortgage yields rise further on the short- or long-duration coupons. As interest rates rise, prepayments for premium coupons decline, which in turn substantially boosts their cash flow yields, making them attractive to investors. Thus, in a market retreat, while all other securities suffer price losses, premium coupons experience price increases. This "price decompression" contrasts with their behavior during the market rally of 1985–1986. During that period, price appreciation of premium coupons was often severely restricted because of the expected surge in their prepayments, whereas other securities experienced tremendous price gains.

In a rising interest rate scenario, GNMA 11s and below would also outstrip their comparable 7- or 10-year Treasuries. While these mortgage securities would suffer significant price losses, their large coupon returns would enable them to outrun Treasuries. However, GNMA 10s and 10.5s would fall behind the 10-year Treasury in exceptional cases where the mortgage curve steepens, and yields on long-duration coupons rise further above the Treasury curve.

If, on the other hand, interest rates decline another 100 basis points, the benchmark and discount coupons would become the stellar performers due to their substantial price appreciation. GNMA 9.5s and 10s would also produce sizable returns because ther slight premium would still provide room for further appreciation. More significantly, all high premiums would also trounce the 2-year Treasury. These bearish coupons perform so impressively in a bullish scenario primarily because their prepayment rates are not expected to respond significantly to further interest rate declines. (This expectation is elaborated on in the later discussion on the prospective view of prepayment rates.) These coupons experienced record high prepayments in 1986, and interest rates on their underlying mortgages were already far above prevailing market rates. Any further decline in rates, therefore, would only contribute a small degree of additional prepayment risk. Consequently, given more or less the same prepayment rates but declining mortgage yields, high premiums would also experience some price increases.

It appears, based on the horizon analysis, that as of mid-1986 mortgage securities were potentially better performers in relation to Treasuries and thus had increased value. In particular, those with 11.5 percent and higher coupons almost always outperform two- and three-year Treasuries in the three interest rate scenarios. In most cases, they also outstrip the five-year Treasury; discounts also have the potential to provide greater returns than the 7- and 10-year Treasuries in most scenarios. Benchmark and low premium coupons are clearly better performers in a steady or falling interest rate environment.

ANALYZING BREAK-EVEN PREPAYMENT RATES

The break-even prepayment rate is the rate at which a mortgage security provides the identical cash flow yield to that of the benchmark security. The benchmark security is defined as the GNMA coupon that is priced closest to par. On August 29, 1986, for example, the benchmark GNMA had a coupon rate of 9 percent that was priced at 100–12 to provide a bond equivalent cash flow yield of 9.03 percent.

Investors may assess the potential value of a security by comparing its break-even prepayment rate to the actual prepayment rate. Since mortgages prepay at par, an increase in prepayments would raise the yield for discount coupons but lower the yield for premium coupons. If the break-even rate for a discount coupon should far exceed the most recent prepayment rate, the security may be considered rich to the benchmark because its prepayment rate has to increase substantially in order to raise the yield to the same level as that of the benchmark coupon. On August 29, 1986, for example, GNMA 8s were priced at 97–09 and yielded 8.64 percent (see Table 10–3). This was considered rich because its prepayment rate would have to increase substantially to 22.3 percent in order to bring its yield up to 9.03 percent. This rate is nearly three times above the three-month prepayment rate of 7.8 percent (see Table 10–3). Historically, prepayment rates for discount GNMAs have rarely exceeded 6 percent, even at the peak of housing cycles.

Conversely, a premium coupon is considered cheap to the benchmark if its most recent prepayment rate lies far below, and seems unlikely to approach, the break-even rate. If the premium coupon is yielding far above the benchmark, its prepayment rate would have to be raised to equate its yield with that of the benchmark. To illustrate this point, Table 10–3 shows that GNMA 11s, at a price of 106–27, were yielding 9.54 percent based on a three-month prepayment rate of 11.7 percent. The 11 percent coupon appeared cheap as compared to GNMA 9s because its prepayment rate could jump substantially to 18.2 percent and still be equally attractive to the benchmark coupon, providing a 9.03 percent yield.

This traditional break-even analysis, however, suffers a serious shortcoming when it is applied to premium coupons because it does not recognize that rising prepayment rates shorten the duration of premium coupons. Since shorter-duration securities provide lower yields than longer-duration securities, in a positively sloped yield curve environment, premium coupons need not yield the same as the benchmark. A more realistic break-even analysis, therefore, would incorporate the term structure of interest rates and compare mortgage securities to their respective comparable-duration Treasuries.

The revised break-even prepayment rate (RBEPR) does exactly that. It produces a cash flow yield for a specific mortgage security whose spread to the comparable-duration Treasury is the same as that of the benchmark GNMA to the 7- or 10-year Treasury. Both the traditional and revised approaches use the same security as the benchmark coupon. On August 29, 1986, the benchmark GNMA 9s yielded 231 basis points over the 7-year Treasury (See Table 10–3).

The numerical differences between the traditional and revised approaches for selected GNMAs are shown in Table 10–6. For example, in order for GNMA 11s to yield the same as the benchmark GNMA 9s, the traditional break-even prepayment rate would have to be 18.2 percent. At that prepayment rate, however, GNMA 11s would have a much shorter duration than the benchmark coupon. Incorporating the slope of the Treasury yield curve, the RBEPR approach finds the prepayment rate such that GNMA 11s' yield spread to the comparable-duration Treasury is the same as that of the benchmark over the 7-year Treasury. For GNMA 11s, the RBEPR turns out to be significantly higher, 21.7 percent, with a much lower cash flow yield of 8.73 percent. This yield, however, is also 231 basis points over the 3-year Treasury.

It should be noted that, in the example just given, the revised break-even approach implicitly assumes that a yield spread of 231 basis points is adequate for the compensation of prepayment risk in all coupons. This assumption seems reasonable for discount coupons. However, one can invariably argue that, regardless of the shorter duration, to compensate for the inherent risk of fast prepayments premium coupons should provide greater yield spreads to comparable Treasuries than do discount and benchmark coupons. While this argument has intuitive appeal, it is difficult to determine the appropriate spreads. The yields for premium coupons that are selected by the RBEPR approach can thus be viewed as minimum yields. The derived prepayment rates can therefore be viewed as the upper limits for premium coupons to break even with the benchmark coupon.

Within the context, the RBEPR approach is particularly useful in analyzing the relative value of premium coupons. The difference between the RBEPR and the actual rate may be viewed as a prepayment cushion. If the RBEPR for a premium coupon is significantly higher than the past three-month prepayment rate, then the premium coupon can sustain further increases in prepayment and still provide a yield that is competitive with the benchmark. Consequently, the premium coupon may be viewed as relatively cheap and therefore an attractive investment. Based on this concept, as of mid-1986 the GNMA 10 percent–11 percent coupons were cheap, but 11.5 percent and higher coupons were rich to the benchmark GNMA 9s. In terms of discount coupons, their relatively higher RBEPRs also suggest that GNMA 8s and 8.5s were rich to the benchmark.

FUTURE PREPAYMENT RATES: A PROSPECTIVE ASSESSMENT

The most important aspect in the evaluation of mortgage securities boils down to one central point—determining future prepayment rates for the underlying mortgages. Mortgages prepay because of two basic factors: home sales and refinancing. In general, home sales account for the bulk of prepayments for discount coupons, whereas refinancing dominates prepayments for premium coupons. Both factors depend on the level and the movement of market interest rates as well as other social, economic, and demographic factors. The past experience of high coupon prepayment rates, along with some fundamental considerations, is presented in the following discussion.

Historical Prepayment Levels

By studying mortgage securities' past prepayment experience, one can infer the potential future prepayment behavior under certain interest rate assumptions. For example, prepayment rates for high-premium coupons depend primarily on the difference between the interest rate on the underlying mortgage and the current mortgage rate. Therefore, as shown in Figure 10–1, the future prepayment rate of GNMA 12s (which as of August 29, 1986, was 300 basis points above the benchmark rate of 9 percent) should correspond to the prepayment behavior of GNMA 15s in an environment where the benchmark GNMA was 12 percent. Alternatively, the potential prepayment speed of GNMA 12s should approximate the prepayment rate of GNMA 14s when the benchmark rate was 11 percent, as shown in Figure 10–2. In fact, the prepayment rate of any premium coupon is relevant as long as the differential between its coupon rate and the benchmark rate was 300 basis points at the time.

One potential shortcoming of this approach, of course, is that interest rates over the past three years did not decline as dramatically—and remain as low—as they have in the past year. Prepayments usually lag the decline in interest rates, and, if interest rates drop only briefly, the corresponding rise in prepayments may not fully reflect the potential impact of a prolonged market rally on prepayments. One should realize the shortcoming of this approach, and compensate for it by simultaneously analyzing the prepayments of several coupons, as described earlier, in different interest rate environments.

Fundamental Constraints on Prepayment Rates

Between late 1985 and early 1986 mortgage rates fell more than 200 basis points, creating a great opportunity for refinancing. Never before had refinancing become as worthwhile for so many people in such a short time. As a result, prepayment rates for premium coupons soared to levels of 50 percent–60 percent. The sharp decline in mortgage rates

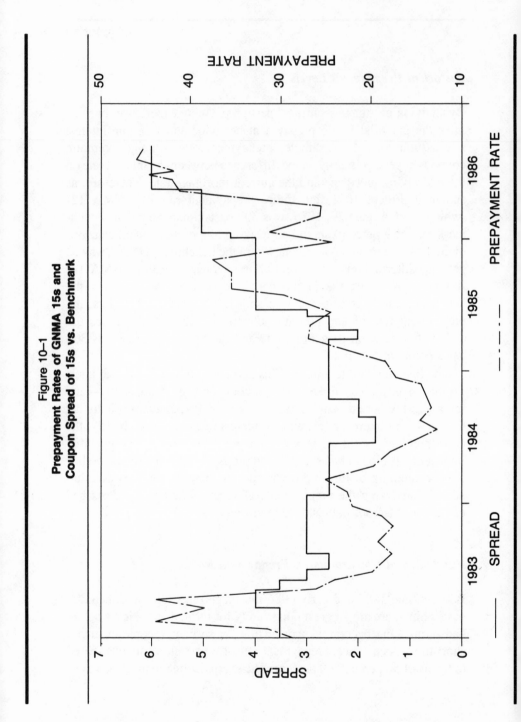

Figure 10–1
Prepayment Rates of GNMA 15s and
Coupon Spread of 15s vs. Benchmark

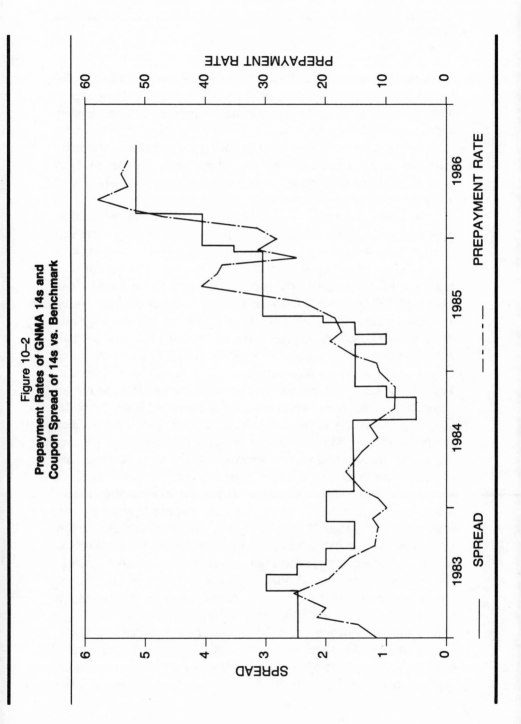

Figure 10–2
Prepayment Rates of GNMA 14s and
Coupon Spread of 14s vs. Benchmark

also raised housing affordability to record levels and sparked an explosion of housing activity. The combined demand for mortgage credit, both for refinancing and home purchases, buried mortgage lenders under a blizzard of paperwork. The resulting bottlenecks delayed the mortgage origination process and sustained prepayment rates at historically high levels. Eventually, however, prepayment rates are likely to taper off as steady refinancings reduce existing mortgagors to a core of less interest-sensitive borrowers.

Even though these borrowers appear likely to refinance on the basis of mortgage rate differentials, several other socioeconomic factors will prevent them from doing so. First, many borrowers are reluctant to absorb the necessary up-front costs of refinancing. The cost of refinancing a FHA mortgage averaged about $3,400 for an average loan amount of $57,000. Aside from the monetary cost, borrowers seeking to refinance must also spend time shopping for the best mortgage rate and obtaining necessary documentation for the new mortgage. Second, other borrowers do not plan to remain in their present homes long enough to allow the interest savings to offset the cost of refinancing. Typically, it takes two and one-half to three years in order to recoup refinancing costs. Homeowners have beome increasingly more mobile, however, and now evaluate refinancing opportunities over a much shorter timeframe. These borrowers would not benefit from refinancing, despite the short-term interest savings. Third, some borrowers are either unaware of existing refinancing opportunities or unwilling to act accordingly. Some borrowers may even lack the sophistication to recognize these opportunities, while others are resigned to making every single payment on their 30-year mortgages. As a result, falling interest rates are unlikely to induce this core of interest-insensitive borrowers to refinance. Consequently, many high coupon pools remain outstanding. For example, more than $2 billion of the $7.6 billion of GNMA 15s (originated entirely in the 1981–1982 period) remained outstanding as of mid-1986, despite a 600 basis point drop in mortgage rates.

In addition, borrowers also face a major institutional constraint. Recent underwriting standards for conventional loans have been tightened markedly. Lenders have become less willing to originate mortgages with loan-to-value (LTV) ratios greater than 80 percent. The tightened standards, therefore, would prevent highly leveraged home-owners, who have not accumulated sufficient equity in their homes, from refinancing conventional mortgages. Consequently, refinancing decisions also depend on house price appreciation. If the value of the home did not increase, or even fell since it was purchased, as happened in oil patch and farming states, the homeowner may not have sufficient cash to refinance at the same or lower LTV ratio.

Over the long term, additional instituional constraints may increase the core of interest-insensitive borrowers. As of September 1986, the Department of Housing and Urban Development is drafting regulations that will exclude closing costs from the single-family loan amount that the FHA will insure. Consequently FHA borrowers will no longer be able to amortize their closing costs, and higher up-front costs will deter many low-income borrowers from refinancing. During 1985–1986, borrowers who could not meet the higher up-front costs associated with conventional mortgages turned to the FHA program. The Reagan administration's efforts to reduce the role of government in the housing and mortgage finance industry may lead to further restrictions in the FHA program. For example, its fiscal 1987 budget proposal included an increase in the mortgage insurance premium from 3.8 percent to 5 percent and included a requirement that it be paid in cash. Although these changes required congressional approval and were later withdrawn, they may resurface in the future.

INVESTMENT IMPLICATIONS

Mortgage pass throughs are high-yielding, high-quality investments with an outstanding balance exceeding $400 billion. Their wide range of coupons appeal to a variety of investors with different maturity preferences and interest rate outlooks.

Based on the various evaluation tools presented in this chapter, benchmark GNMAs were extremely cheap to the 7-year Treasury in mid-1986. Although the benchmark GNMA matched the comparable Treasury in total return during 1985–1986, they still showed a substantial yield spread over Treasuries. Moreover, their future returns were likely to exceed comparable Treasuries under almost all interest rate scenarios. Furthermore, as housing activity moves into low gear and the demand for mortgage credit peaks out, the benchmark's historically wide spread will begin to tighten. This expected tightening in spreads suggests that the benchmark coupon had value. Of course, on the other hand, a slowdown in housing activity will subtract value from the discount coupons. While most premium coupons were modestly rich to the benchmark according to break-even analysis, a prospective long-term decline in prepayments still indicates value for these securities.

High-premium coupons (11.5 percent and above) with historically high prepayments can be viewed as short-term investments suited for a two- to three-year investment horizon. These high premiums are particularly attractive for bearish investors. Rising interest rates will sharply slow prepayments and substantially raise their cash flow yields. Further, in a market retreat, the price decompression will enable high premiums to outperform both lower coupon securities and Treasuries. Of course, if interest rates continue to rise over an extended period, high-premium coupons will no longer be short-term instruments.

Without taking a stand on future interest rates, low-premium coupons (9.5 percent–11 percent as of mid-1986) should be most desirable for yield-oriented investors such as mutual or trust fund managers. These securities are subject to significantly lower prepayment risk and yet are the highest yielding coupons among all pass throughs. Furthermore, if interest rates were to rise significantly, coupons in the range of 9.5 percent–11 percent would most likely become the new benchmark. Newly issued securities will therefore carry these coupon rates, thus enlarging the reservoir of supply that is important for fund managers.

Discount coupons, on the other hand, are ideal investments in a bullish interest rate environment. Their long maturity and excellent potential for price appreciation make them well suited for strictly performance-oriented investors. Moreover, with their relatively long-term and steady cash flows, discounts also fit the investment needs of portfolio managers.

Mortgage pass throughs have also been purchased by trade-oriented investors. The market perceptions of future interest rates and prepayments coupled with specific supply and demand factors often create wide swings in the price spread among various types and coupons of mortgage securities. These fluctuating price spreads have created arbitrage opportunities for these investors.

APPENDIX: THE SPECTACULAR WIDENING OF MORTGAGE-TO-TREASURY YIELD SPREADS

During the first half of 1986, yield spreads between mortgages and Treasuries widened dramatically to historical highs. As shown in Figure A–1, the differential between primary market mortgage rates and the 30-year Treasury widened to 350 basis points—twice as high as the average of the past 2 years. Similarly, in the secondary market, the bond equivalent cash flow yield spread of benchmark GNMA 9s versus the 10-year Treasury topped 240 basis points, matching the historically wide spread reached when the benchmark coupon was 15 percent, (Figure A–2).

This dramatic widening of yield spreads constrasts sharply to the pattern that existed between 1982 and mid-1984, when spreads tightened substantially. Both periods, however, witnessed significant declines in interest rates. During the 1982–1984 period, primary market mortgage rates versus the 30-year Treasury narrowed from over 400 basis points to below 80 basis points. At the same time, yield spreads between benchmark GNMAs and the 10-year Treasury tumbled from 240 to 70 basis points. Why didn't the mortgage market follow the Treasury market during the 1986 rally? The main answer probably lies in the absolute level of interest rates. While long-term Treasuries ralied 400 basis points during 1982, they did not fall below 10 percent by mid-1984 before rising back to almost the prerally level. Similarly, during this period, mortgage interest rates never dropped below 12.5 percent.

In the 1986 rally, however, long Treasuries were below 10 percent to begin with and by mid-April they had nearly touched 7 percent, while mortgage rates fell to an eight-year low of 9.8 percent. Since mortgages prepay at par, mortgage-backed securities appreciate less than Treasuries in a rallying market. Thus, as interest rates continued to

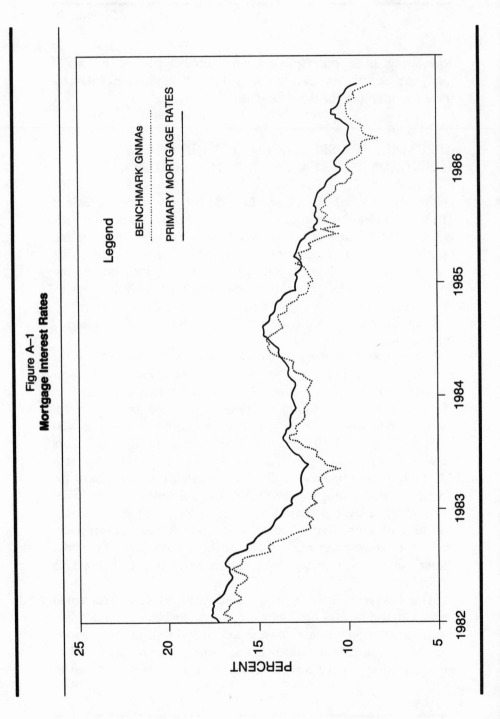

Figure A–1
Mortgage Interest Rates

Legend

BENCHMARK GNMAs

PRIMARY MORTGAGE RATES

Figure A–2
Mortgage–Treasury Yield Spreads

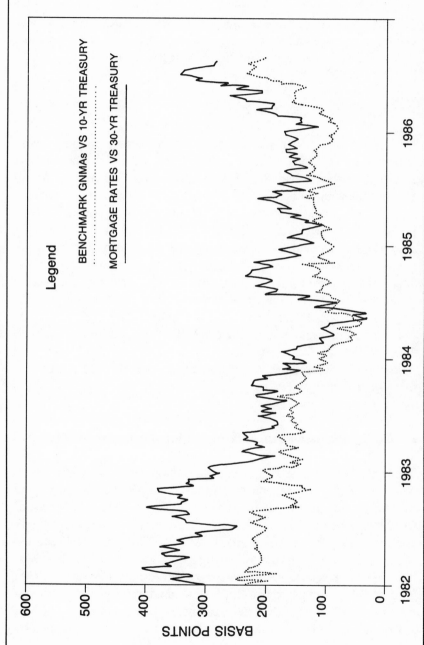

Legend

BENCHMARK GNMAs VS 10-YR TREASURY

MORTGAGE RATES VS 30-YR TREASURY

decline, the lack of price appreciation created much wider spreads between mortgages and Treasuries. Additionally, several other factors influenced yield spreads differently in the two periods.

Demand for Mortgage Credit

During 1985 and 1986, mortgage interest rates have dropped nearly 300 basis points to just under 10 percent. By mid-1986, more than 35 million households had the income necessary to qualify for an 80 percent financing to purchase a median-priced house. In comparison, qualified households averaged only 22 million during the 1982–1984 period. This record level of affordability, along with strong underlying demographic demand for housing, caused the demand for mortgage credit to skyrocket. To finance this demand, a record volume of mortgage loans were originated. Although current data are not readily available as of this writing, originations of one- to four-family mortgages in 1986 have been proceeding at an annual rate of $300 billion. In comparison, originations in the 1982–1984 period averaged less than $200 billion. To fund these originations, yields for mortgages (and mortgage securities in the secondary market) must substantially exceed those of comparable Treasuries.

Declining Originations of Adjustable-Rate Mortgages (ARMs)

The substantial decline in mortgage rates has enabled fixed-rate mortgages (FRMs) to stage a comeback, overtaking ARMs, which were the leading mortgage finance instruments over the 1983–1984 period. (ARMs were available in 1982; however, they became exceedingly popular among home buyers in mid-1983.) This comeback exerted upward pressure on fixed-rate mortgage yields. During 1983–1984, homebuyers selected ARMs because of their lower initial rates. ARMs accounted for as much as two-thirds of total conventional loan originations during that period. Recently, as interest rates plummeted, ARMs' share tumbled to 20 percent. Since ARMs were mostly self-funded by savings institutions (SIs), the small remaining portion of FRMs was easily funded in the capital markets during the 1983–1984 period. In recent months, however, as the bulk of the originations shifted to FRMs, the huge funding needs widened the FRMs' yield spreads to Treasuries.

Savings Institutions as a Funding Source for Mortgages

Since the creation of money market deposit accounts in December 1982, SIs were virtually deregulated, thus greatly enhanced their ability to attract savings at market interest rates. During the 1983–1984 period, these institutions expanded tremendously and attracted about $60 billion net new deposits annually. As a part of the expansion, SIs took down a large portion of newly issued mortgage securities, which helped significantly in reducing mortgage-to-Treasury yield spreads. The "controlled growth" regulation promulgated by the Federal Home Loan Bank Board in the beginning of 1985, however, sharply curtailed this expansion. As a result, savings flows turned negative and SIs became major sellers of mortgage securities. Without the strong presence of SIs as an investor, mortgage yield spreads to Treasuries widened.

Collateralized Mortgage Obligations (CMOs)As a Means of Arbitrage Between Mortgage and Treasuries

CMOs, which were created in mid-1983, not only expanded the investor base for mortgage products but also introduced an opportunity for arbitrage in the mortgage securities market. Market participants, primarily investment bankers, often purchase large amounts of mortgage pass throughs as collateral to issue CMOs. By purchasing the collateral at a wider yield spread to Treasuries and issuing CMOs at a narrower spread, the issuer makes an arbitrage profit. This arbitrage created a significant added demand for mortgage pass throughs in 1983–1984. Coincidentally, during that period, the predominance of ARMs diministed the supply of mortgage securities (which are primarily backed by FRMs). The added demand, combined with the reduced supply, dramatically narrowed the yield spread between mortgage securities and Treasuries. As issuance of CMOs proliferated during 1986, however, even yield spreads between CMOs and Treasuries widened substantially. This proliferation severely reduced CMOs' ability to control mortgage-to-Treasury yield spreads. Nevertheless, the current spreads would have widened even more without CMOs.

Chapter 11

STEVEN J. CARLSON
AND
TIMOTHY D. SEARS

Steven Carlson is Vice President of Mortgage Securities Research for Shearson Lehman Bros. Previously he was Senior Debt Management Analyst with Fannie Mae. Mr. Carlson received a Master of Public Policy from the Kennedy School of Government.

Timothy Sears is Senior Associate with Shearson Lehman Bros. He received his M.S. in economics from Carnegie-Mellon.

Assessing the Duration of Mortgage Securities: A New Approach

STEVEN J. CARLSON AND TIMOTHY D. SEARS

In the Treasury market, the concept of duration has long been valued as a useful indicator of a security's price sensitivity to interest rate changes.* For Treasury securities, duration provides a reasonable approximation of price changes given small yield changes. Duration is therefore useful for traders watching the daily movements of the yield curve, as well as portfolio managers who need some indication about their level of interest rate exposure. Because of its obvious usefulness, mortgage investors have yearned for a similar tool. Unfortunately, the immediate, and most commonly employed adaptation of the duration concept to mortgages is often inadequate for the purposes cited. The reason is that changes in yield levels alter the expected prepayment behavior of a mortgage. Because the standard duration calculation ignores this effect, it is a biased estimate of interest rate sensitivity. Standard duration calculations for mortgages tend to overestimate the interest rate sensitivity of premium coupon mortgages, and underesti-

---

*Academic discussions of duration focus on a number of concepts, each with a slightly different interpretation. In this article we use the term *duration of a Treasury bond* to mean "the percentage price change resulting from a 100 basis point change in its yield." This is often referred to as *modern duration*. Mathematically this is defined as $-(dP/dY)/P$.

mate the interest rate sensitivity of discounts. This report describes an alternative duration formula that attempts to account for the indirect, but instantaneous relationship between market-perceived prepayment rates and mortgage yield levels.

The measure, which we call *mortgage duration,* comes with some advantages and disadvantages. Among the desirable attributes is its ease of calculation, enabling investors to quickly incorporate it in their decision-making process. Additionally, it provides a measure of price volatility for mortgages that better reflects investors' current expectaions. In particular, the measure indicates the observed low price volatility of premium coupon mortgages and admits the possibility of negative duration. As with many mortgage investment decisions, however, it requires that some assumptions be made. In particular, it requires an investor to assess the market's view on the mortgage prepayment rate, as well as the sensitivity of that rate to interest rate changes.

Furthermore, like the duration calculation for Treasury securities, mortgage duration embodies (among others) the implicit assumption that yield changes result only from parallel shifts of the term structure. One implication of these facts is that duration calculations are insensitive to spread relationships between securities, even in the same sector. Despite this potential shortcoming, we believe that mortgage duration provides investors with a convenient means to convert their outlook in the fundamental factors driving mortgage value into a view on mortgage price performance.

THE PRICE/YIELD RELATIONSHIP

Since duration is an approximation of the sensitivity of a security's price to its yield change, it is perhaps worthwhile to begin with a more holistic discussion of prices and yields. The simplest price/yield relationship exists for a noncallable bond, such as a Treasury security. Cash flows for a Treasury are immutable, so that calculating the price of the security at any given yield level is an easy matter. A typical price/yield relationship, that of a 10-year, 7 percent coupon Treasury, is shown in

Figure 11–1. There are several features to notice about the way this relationship is depicted.

The price/yield relationship for this issue is negative, as it is for most instruments traded in the bond market. The sensitivity of price to yield changes is illustrated by the slope of the price/yield curve at a given price and yield. Duration is just the absolute value of the slope at the point divided by its price. Finally, there is some *positive convexity* associated with this bond, that is, the ends of the price/yield curve curl up a bit. This means that if the market yield drops at a constant rate, the 10-year bond rallies at an increasing rate. When yield increases at a constant rate, the bond price falls at a decreasing rate. This convexity is valued positively by market participants because it offers some protection against volatile interest rates.

Discovering the price/yield relationship for a mortgage-backed security is a more complex and somewhat less precise task. A number of assumptions regarding the relationship of prepayments to market yield changes must be employed to convert yield changes into price changes. Because the cash flows on a mortgage pass through are not immutable, they must be projected using the expected prepayment behavior at each particular yield level. In what follows, we have employed a model that deterministically relates the market yield to the prepayment speed of the mortgage. For a 9 percent GNMA priced near par, the model projects an annual prepayment rate of 6.5 percent. If rates drop, prepayments increase rapidly, but cap out near 50 percent. If rates increase, prepayments slow gradually to 4.5 percent CPR. Price is obtained by discounting the projected cash flows at the prevailing yield. Figure 11–2 depicts the resulting price/yield relationship for a 9 percent GNMA. The relationship depicted captures several aspects of the behavior typical of mortgage-backed securities.

As with the Treasury bond, the price/yield relationship is negatively sloped. Another point is a key concern with mortgages, namely negative convexity. In other words, as yield rises, the price of the mortgage falls at an increasing rate and as yield falls, the price increases at a decreasing rate. Mortgages behave like this because cash flows shift adversely when market yields change; effectively the duration of a

Figure 11–1
Price/Yield Curve, 10-Year Treasury Security—7% Coupon

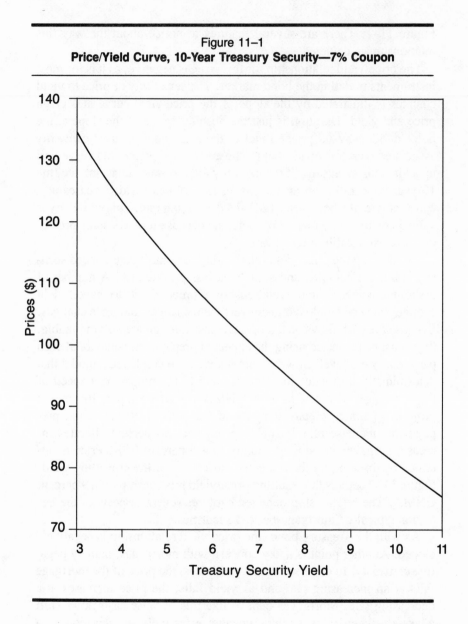

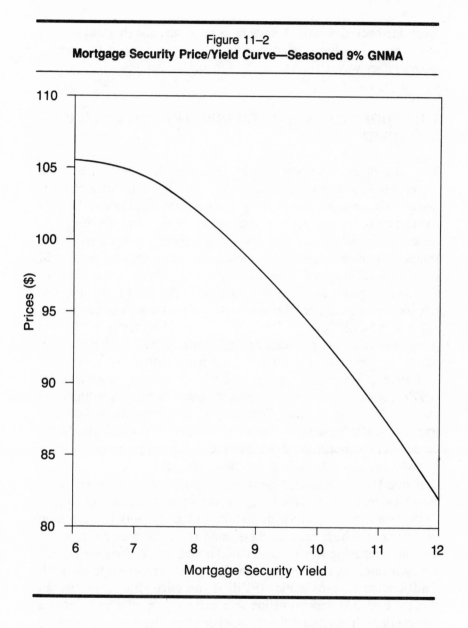

Figure 11–2
Mortgage Security Price/Yield Curve—Seasoned 9% GNMA

mortgage-backed security lengthens as rates rise, and shortens as rates fall. This effect hurts relative price performance when the market moves either way.

WHAT DOES THE STANDARD DURATION CALCULATION MEASURE?

The slope of the mortgage security price/yield relationship shown in Figure 11–3 represents the best first approximation of price changes due to yield changes. However, that is not what the standard duration calculation for mortgages measures. To make the point clearer, let us review the standard duration concept as applied to mortgages. The standard duration calculation is closely related to the cash flow yield calculation. Conceptually, the calculation projects the security's cash flow based upon a prepayment assumption. The yield is the discount rate (or the internal rate of return) that equates the sum of the present value of the cash flows to the security price. One attempt to measure price sensitivity can be made by taking the derivative of price with respect to yield, while holding the mortgage cash flows fixed. This derivative is commonly known as the *price value of a basis point* (*PVBP*), since it measures the absolute change in price resulting from an absolute change in yield. Dividing PVBP by the price of the mortgage and multiplying by -100 is the standard way of calculating the duration of the mortgage; it is expressed in units of percentage change in price due to a 100 basis point change in yield.

Figure 11–4 depicts what the standard duration calculation measures for a 9 percent coupon pass through under different market conditions. In the first case, market yields are low and the security is a premium prepaying at a high rate. In the second case, the pass through is a discount prepaying slowly. Standard duration calculations were made for each case; lines drawn through each point correspond to the standard duration's approximation (PVBP) to the price/yield curve. (Recall that the best first approximation to a curve at a particular point is a tangent line). In each case the standard duration calculation generates a line that cuts the price/yield curve. In fact, it is possible to show that the

Figure 11–3
Mortgage Duration Approximation to the Price/Yield Curve—9% GNMA

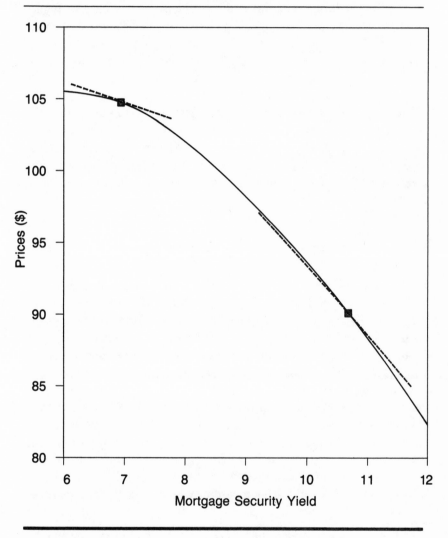

standard duration calculation will generate a tangent line at only one point on the price/yield curve.*

It is also possible to point out the direction of bias for the standard duration calculation. Looking at the premium coupon case in Figure 11–4, we can see that the approximation given by standard duration is too steep. This is the same as saying the duration overstates the sensitivity of price to yield changes (that is, the duration is too long). Similarly, standard duration for a discount coupon underestimates its price sensitivity, but not by very much.

The bias referred to stems directly from the assumption that the prepayment rate (hence cash flow) remains unchanged for infinitessimal changes in yield. However, as soon as one recognizes that the market's perception of prepayment speed is a function of the mortgage level, it immediately follows that mortgage cash flows are also a function of yield.

ACCOUNTING FOR CHANGES IN CASH FLOW

It is possible to address the particular problem of changes in cash flow and their effect on duration without discarding the standard duratoin calculation. The approach taken here is described formally in the mathematical appendix to this chapter and is described intuitively in what follows. A correction factor can be estimated that indicates the direction and magnitude of the bias. The first part captures the sensitivity of price to changes in prepayment speed, holding yield constant. This is just the derivative of the function relating price and CPR when yield is held constant. We call this derivative PVCPR to point out that it represents the change in price resulting from a change in prepayment speed. PVCPR is analogous to PVBP, mentioned earlier.

The second part of the correction factor measures the sensitivity of CPR to changes in yield. This measure, which we call S, needs to be

---

*The price at which this occurs is known as the parity price, which is the same as par when the security has no interest-free payment delay; it is slightly below par for a typical pass through.

Figure 11–4
Standard Duration Approximation to the Price/Yield Curve—9% GNMA

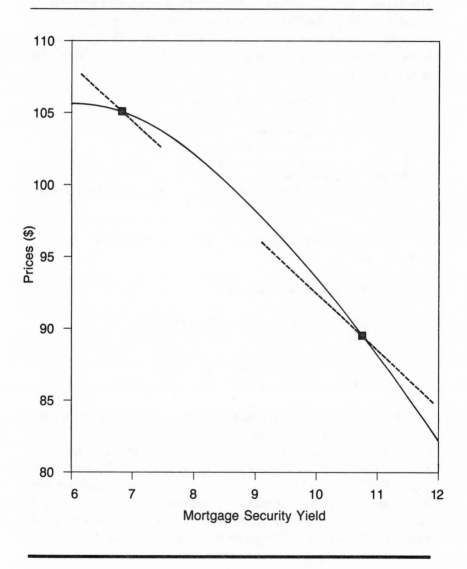

estimated by the analyst. The two terms, S and PVCPR, together gauge the impact of a change in yield that indirectly (yet instantaneously) affects price through changes in the market's perception of prepayment speed. Combining the PVBP with the correction factor produces a new estimate of the change in the price resulting from a change in yield. Mathematically this is known as the total differential of price with respect to yield:

$$dP = PVBP \times dY - (PVCPR \times S) \times dY, \text{ where}$$

dP	= change in price
dY	= change in yield in basis points
PVBP	= price value of a basis point
PVCPR	= price value of a percent of CPR
S	= absolute value of the change in percent CPR per 100 basis point increase or decrease in yield.

Corresponding to this equation is an alternate measure of duration, mortgage duration:

$$\text{Mortgage Duration} = D + (E \times S), \text{ where}$$

$$D = \frac{-PVBP}{P} \times 100, \text{ standard modified duration}$$

$$E = \frac{PVCPR}{P} \times 100, \text{ analogous to duration for CPR.}$$

Both equations can be derived formally using the equations for the price of a mortgage at a given yield and CPR.

Looking at the equation for mortgage duration provides the mathematical analogy to the bias seen in Figure 11–4. For discount mortgages, PVCPR is positive, since prepayments enhance value for that sector, and the converse is true for premium mortgages. S is always positive (see the Mathematical Appendix). Therefore, the correction factor, $E \times S$, is negative for premiums and positive for discounts.

The mathematics allow us to be more specific about where mortgage duration makes a difference. For mortgages with prepayments that are insensitive to market moves, such as deep discounts, S will be small and mortgage duration will be close to the standard calculation. For mortgages close to par, E is small, since prepayments do not have a big impact on price. Mortgage duration for current coupons will also be close to the standard calculation. When applied to premium coupons, the mortgage duration calculation makes the most difference. The value of these mortgages is relatively more sensitive to the prepayment rate; the prepayment rate is also more sensitive to interest rates. The following section shows the difference between the standard calculation and mortgage duration for a premium coupon GNMA.

A SAMPLE CALCULATION

Table 11–1 shows the assumptions necessary to make the calculations.If rates remain unchanged, at the time of this writing Shearson Lehman projections have GNMA 12.5s paying down at a 35 percent CPR. This gives a mortgage yield of 8.38 percent and a standard duration of 1.99. Also, at this prepayment rate, 1 percent CPR is worth − \$.23. To calculate mortgage duration we must estimate the sensitivity of the prepayment rate to changes in interest rates. For this example, Shearson Lehman projects 25 percent and 45 percent annual prepayment rates if yields increase or decrease by 100 basis points, respectively. Therefore S is 10 (= [45 − 25]/2).

PRICE APPRECIATION POTENTIAL OF GNMA SECURITIES

Performing the same exercise for various GNMA coupons provides an interesting view of the potential for price appreciation for each coupon. Table 11–2 incorporates prepayment projections for flat, increasing, and decreasing rate scenarios to compute the mortgage duration of GNMA coupons ranging from 8.0 percent to 13.5 percent.

Table 11–1
Sample Mortgage Duration Calculation for a GNMA 12.5% Security

Price	107–22
Age	38 Months
Mortgage Yield	8.38%
PVCPR	−0.23
PVBP	2.14

Prepayment Assumptions (plus or minus 100 basis points)

Rising Rates	25.00%
Base Case	35.00%
Falling Rates	45.00%
Implied Sensitivity (S)	10.0

Modified Duration	$1.99\ (=2.14/107.6875 \times 100)$
Mortgage Duration	$-0.16\ (=1.990 + -0.23 \times 10.0/107.6875 \times 100)$

Applying the equation gives a mortgage duration of negative .16. Apparently, at current yield levels and prepayment rates, yield changes are slightly more than offset by induced changes in prepayment rates. Very little price volatility should be expected for 12.5 percent GNMAs.

According to the calculations, the price appreciation potential of a GNMA coupon falls into one of three categories:

1. 8.0 percent to 9.5 percent — If the mortgage market rallies by 100 basis points, these coupons will likely increase by 5 to 6 percent in price.
2. 10 percent and 10.5 percent — The up-side potential for these premium coupons is limited somewhat by their potential for increased prepayments. However, the amount of new production in these coupons offers some call protection. These coupons may appreciate by 1.6 percent and 3.9 percent, respectively, with a 100 basis point decrease in mortgage yields.
3. 11.0 percent to 13.5 percent — These coupons actually have the potential to increase a small amount if the mortgage market turns

Table 11–2
Mortgage Duration for Various GNMA Coupons as of September 15, 1986

Coupon	Price	Age	CPR Projection	Mortgage Yield	Standard Duration	Up-Rate % CPR	Down-Rate % CPR	S	Mortgage Duration
13.50%	108–24	42	35.00%	8.79%	1.98	25	45	10.0	−0.42
13.00%	108–00	41	35.00%	8.69%	1.98	25	45	10.0	−0.24
12.50%	107–22	38	35.00%	8.38%	1.99	25	45	10.0	−0.16
12.00%	107–12	27	30.00%	8.58%	2.30	20	45	12.5	−0.50
11.50%	107–06	38	20.00%	9.08%	3.16	10	40	15.0	−0.82
11.00%	107–04	32	10.00%	9.42%	4.77	5	35	15.0	−0.43
10.50%	107–00	13	10.00%	8.99%	4.89	1	20	9.5	1.56
10.00%	104–03	20	10.00%	9.07%	4.85	1	10	4.5	3.88
9.50%	101–08	49	7.00%	9.20%	5.50	3	9	3.0	5.24
9.00%	98–17	41	7.00%	9.20%	5.52	3	8	2.5	5.67
8.50%	96–12	81	7.00%	9.13%	5.31	6	10	2.0	5.65
8.00%	95–05	113	7.00%	8.89%	5.12	6	10	2.0	5.57

bearish by 100 basis points. The appreciation however, would be limited to less than .85 percent.

Mortgage duration calculations in this example appear to offer a view on each GNMA coupon that is more in line with the expectations of many market participants as of mid-1986. In particular, the calculations imply that premium coupons are very unlikely to benefit from a market rally. In fact, the opposite is likely to occur.

CONCLUSION

Mortgage duration offers investors an alternative measure of the sensitivity of mortgage prices to yield changes. This measure is quick and easy to calculate. Investors need only estimate the relationship of changes in market-perceived CPR to changes in mortgage yields. The CPR/yield sensitivity estimate, (S), multiplied by the sensitivity of price with regard to CPR changes (E), adjusts the standard modified duration calculation to reflect the simultaneous nature of yield and CPR changes.

Some caveats on the use of mortgage duration are in order here. First, mortgage duration is subject to many of the criticisms leveled at modified duration calculations for Treasuries in academic literature. Without enumerating on those comments here, suffice it to say that mortgage duration calculations do not escape their application. Also, and perhaps more important, the calculations depend heavily on the analyst's prepayment forecasts. If the market does not share the analyst's view, then the results are less useful. The estimation of mortgage duration also. hinges heavily upon the investor's ability to produce a sound estimate of S. Estimating mortgage duration serves to intensify the debate and efforts to estimate the relationship between yield and prepayment rates. There currently exists three techniques whereby market participants can estimate S. The first is a direct empirical estimation of the relationship between yield and prepayment rate changes; this is commonly accomplished by employing statistical techniques. The second technique is to observe mortgage security price performance to discover the "implied" S. The third is to employ fore-casts and prepayments as we have done in the examples cited.

In spite of its potential shortcomings, mortgage duration can help investors reveal the impact of their own view on the relationship between yields and prepayment rates on the price sensitivity of mortgage-backed securities.

APPENDIX: FORMAL DERIVATION OF MORTGAGE DURATION

The price of a mortgage can be thought of as a function of two variables:

$P = F(Y, CPR)$
where Y = Yield and CPR = Constant prepayment rate

The standard modified duration starts with:

$$\frac{\delta P}{\delta Y} = (F_1(Y_1 CPR),$$

where F_1 (●,●) is the partial derivative with respect to the first term. Modified duration (D) is obtained as follows:

$$D = \frac{-F_1(Y_1, CPR)}{P} \times 100$$

To calculate mortgage duration, begin by recognizing CPR as a function of Y: $CPR = G(Y)$

This makes price a function of yield only: $P = (F(Y, G(Y)))$.

Now we can follow the same procedure to calculate a new duration number. The first step is to take the total derivative of price with respect to yield (with a new result).

$$\frac{dP}{Y} = F_1(Y,G(Y)) + F_2(Y,G(Y)) \times G'(Y) = PVBP - PVCPR \times S, \text{ where}$$

$$PVBP = F_1(Y,G(Y)); \; PVCPR = F_2(Y,G(Y)); \; S = -G'(Y).$$

Using this derivative to calculate a new duration measure gives:

$$\text{Mortgage Duration} \quad = \frac{-dP/dY}{P} \times 100$$

$$= \frac{-PVBP + PVCPR \times S}{P} \times 100$$

$$= D + E \times S, \text{ where}$$

$$D = \frac{-PVBP}{P} \times 100, \quad E = \frac{PVCPR}{P} \times 100, \text{ and S is as defined above.}$$

Chapter 12

BLAINE E. ROBERTS
AND
RICHARD ELLSON

Blaine Roberts is Director of Government Bond Research for Bear Stearns & Co., Inc. Previously he was Director of MBS Research for Merrill Lynch. Mr. Roberts received his Ph.D. in economics from Iowa State University, and has been a professor of economics with the Universities of Florida and South Carolina.

Richard Ellson is Associate Professor with the University of South Carolina.

How to Use Regional Economic Data to Increase the Yield on Mortgage-Backed Securities

BLAINE ROBERTS AND RICHARD ELLSON

INTRODUCTION

This chapter shows how to use regional economic data to increase the value of mortgage-backed security portfolios through a better understanding of prepayment probabilities. Prepayments are a crucial element in valuing mortgage-backed securities, especially for premium and discount securities. While economic activity is important in the aggregate, it is even more important on a regional basis because economic activity generally varies enormously from one region of the country to another. Using regional economic data can unmask important regional differences in prepayment probabilities and thus important differences in the value of mortage-backed securities with regionally concentrated collateral.

Analysis shows a very high correlation between specific measures of regional economic activity and prepayment rates of specified pools. Some important features of this relation are:

1. Regional economies based on extractive industries or basic manufacturing tend to be quite volatile and have high prepayments.

2. When a region experiences an economic "shock," there is a substantial lag between the shock and changes in the prepayment rate.
3. Many regions of the country are currently undergoing fundamental economic shifts that will have dramatic effects on prepayments.

THE GENERAL DETERMINANTS OF PREPAYMENTS

The general factors that affect prepayments compose the following major categories:

Financial incentives
Economic activity
Seasonality
Aging

Financial Incentives: Interest Rate Differentials Alone Do Not Explain Prepayments

The financial incentive to refinance a home when interest rates fall below the coupon on the mortgage is often given the greatest emphasis by investors. The financial effect, in part, derives from the right that mortgagors have to prepay their mortgages at any time. This option is like an option to call debt that some corporate bond issuers have, or like a stock option. However, unlike corporate bonds or stocks, there are high transaction costs associated with a mortgage. In some instances, penalties must be paid if the homeowner prepays the mortgage. New mortgages require origination fees, lawyers' fees, and, perhaps, taxes paid at closing. Evaluating alternative mortgages involves the additional costs of time and effort. Because of these high transaction costs, interest rate differentials alone do not explain prepayment rates very well. Furthermore, the use of traditional optional pricing models such as Black-Scholes or Cox-Ross-Rubenstein often do not work well with mortgage prepayments, primarily because these models are based on the assumption of zero transaction costs and have other theoretical limitations.

Even if there were no transactions costs, the financial effect alone would not fully explain prepayment rates. Lenders can demand the full repayment of many mortgage loans when the house is sold. This due-on-sale clause gives the lender a valuable option that is typically only good at the time the homeowner moves or othewise needs the equity in the house. Consequently, economic activity and demographic processes enhance the explanatory power of interest rate differentials on prepayment rates, even when transaction costs are insignificant. This is because changes in economic activity and changes in peoples' lifestyles or needs cause people to move into bigger homes, to move to new regions, to change jobs, and so forth. A focus limited solely on interest rate differentials ignores all of these other factors.

Lock-In Effects. The lock-in effect is a measure of the financial incentive to prepay a mortgage that takes into account the significant transaction costs of refinancing. Specifically, the *lock-in effect* is the ratio of the asset value of the mortgage to the value of the house. It measures how locked in to a mortgage a homeowner is. The *asset value* of a mortgage is the difference between the current face value and the market value of a mortgage. For example, if a mortgage has a $50,000 balance and an 8 percent coupon and market interest rates are 12 percent, the market value of the mortgage might be $35,000. The difference is the asset value of the mortgage, or $15,000.

The asset value of a mortgage is also equal to the net present value (NPV) of the change in monthly payments if the mortgage were refinanced. Refinancing an 8 percent coupon mortgage with a $50,000 balance in a 12 percent market would result in an increase in the monthly payment. The NPV of this payment increase would be approximately $15,000.

The significance of that $15,000 asset value in reducing the incentive to refinance depends greatly on the value of the home. If the house has a market value of $70,000, there is a strong incentive for the homeowner not to refinance the mortgage or for a new homeowner buying the home to assume the mortgage. However, if the market value of the home were $350,000, the strength of the $15,000 asset value is reduced substantially. In fact, a new owner may find it uneconomical to assume an 8 percent mortgage in a 12 percent environment if it means taking out a large second mortgage at 1 or 2 percentage points above the market rate for first mortgages.

Among other things, the value of a house depends on housing inflation. The higher the rate of inflation, the higher the value of the house and the lower the lock-in effect for discount mortgages. The lower the lock-in effect, the higher the rate of prepayment.

The value of the house also influences the prepayment rate on premium mortgags. For example, suppose a $50,000 mortgage has an 8 percent coupon, market rates are 7 percent, and the market value of the mortgage is $55,000. The homeowner could save $5,000 in NPV of future payments if the mortgage were refinanced. If the market value of the home is $70,000, the incentive to refinance is strong. If the value of the home is $350,000, the $5,000 savings is relatively less, and correspondingly, the probability of prepayment is relatively less.

Expectations enter into the lock-in effect. Because of the high transaction costs of mortgages, expectations about future moves and future interest rates influence the homeowner's decision to refinance a mortgage. If an individual is holding a 17 percent mortgage in a 12 percent rate environment, the financial incentive to refinance would appear to be quite strong. However, if the mortgagor expected interest rates to fall quickly to 10 percent, it might not be advantageous to refinance. Likewise, if the individual expected to move in six months, it might not pay to refinance. While these expectations and their effects on the lock-in effect are difficult, if not impossible, to measure empirically, they do affect prepayment patterns. Particularly when interest rates are falling, prepayment rates tend not to be as strong as they would be if interest rates were to stabilize.

How Economic Activity Impacts Prepayments

Transfer Effects. Economic growth influences prepayments in several ways, one of which is termed the *transfer effect*. This is the effect on prepayments of individuals moving around because of economic growth. The higher the rate of economic growth, the greater the prepayment rate. Economic growth tends to occur in new technological areas or more recently developed regions of the country. In either case, new skills and additional labor are required, and workers migrate to a specific region. Often existing workers are displaced and moved elsewhere. Thus, economic growth results in a number of individuals moving and, consequently, in mortgage prepayments.

A good due-on-sale clause is an important component of the transfer effect on prepayments. Suppose an individual sells a house and moves because of changes in economic opportunities. If the mortgage coupon rate is lower than current market rates, the new homeowner would want to assume the old mortgage loan, rather than borrow at the higher rate for a new mortgage. A good due-on-sale clause would preclude that event. This explains why economic growth often causes a greater change in prepayments on discount FHLMC and FNMA securities than on discount GNMAs. Most FHLMC and FNMA securities are backed by conventional mortgages having a good due-on-sale clause. GNMAs are backed by FHA, VA, and FHMA mortgages, all of which are assumable.

Income Effects. Economic growth also affects prepayments through the *income effect*. The greater the rate of economic growth, the greater the increase in personal income. Over the long term, there is close to a one-to-one relation between the increases in real income and expenditures on housing. Each percent that real personal incomes increases causes about a 3 percent increase in real housing expenditures.

Seasonality

An aside, but a very important, practical one, are *seasonal effects*. Prepayment patterns are seasonal because moving patterns are seasonal. More people move in the summer than they do in the winter. Consequently, prepayment rates are higher in the summer than in the winter. Prepayment rates in the spring and fall are about equal and lie between the summer and winter rates.

The Pure Aging Effects

The *pure aging effect* comprises deomographic regularities that capture everything else that happens with regularity in society that affects prepayment rates. For example, a typical young couple get married and buy their first home shortly thereafter. A few years and children later, the first home becomes too small, and they move. Later on, the children grow up, move away, the house becomes too large, and they move into a smaller house. They retire and move once again. Some individuals move every three or four years regardless of economic activity. Some people get divorced every few years.

Several studies have provided evidence of the pure aging effect and its magnitude. In a previous study*, I reported estimates for annual prepayment rates solely because of the pure aging effect for GNMA mortgage-backed securities. Prepayment rates start out very low, around 1 percent in the first year, increase to a peak of over 8.5 percent late in the fifth year, then decline to about 7.5 percent in the 15th year, and increase to about 15 percent in the 30th year.

REGIONAL ECONOMIC ANALYSIS

Of all the general determinants of prepayments, only interest rate differentials are roughly homogeneous across the country. The rest of the determinants of prepayments depend upon regional economic activity. To understand the relation between regional economic activity and regional prepayment rates, one must be familiar with the underpinnings of a regional economy. The traditional approach is to categorize all economic sectors as either basic or nonbasic industries.

---

*Blaine Roberts, "The Consequences of the Pure Aging Effect on the Yields of Mortgage-backed Securities," December 8, 1984, pp. 10–11.

Basic industries are those that "export" their goods and services to other regions. This is easy to see with manufacturing and extractive industries. For example, the Carolinas export textiles; Michigan, cars; Arizona, copper; and Alaska, oil. However, export industries extend beyond these sectors. Miami "exports" tourism, and the Boston region "exports" education. Therefore, basic industries represent those that draw income into the region from outside of it.

Nonbasic industries are divided into two categories: business-serving and household-serving. The former refers to local firms that provide goods and services to the region's basic industries, often referred to as *ancillary industries*. Household-serving industries provide goods and services to households. Therefore, this approach leads to the result that regional economic growth or decline is directly related to trends in a region's export industires.

The situation in the Silicon Valley of California is an excellent example of regional economic activity and prepayments. For a long period of time, this region grew extremely rapidly as the computer and related products industries prospered. Service industries for both business and households blossomed as well. It was generally thought that the industry—and hence, the region—were recession-proof. When the industry slumped in 1986, this open-ended optimism was shattered. Although the Silicon Valley economy is not going to collapse, a return to its prior growth rate is probably unlikely.

More dramatic examples of declining basic industries are: steel (Pittsburgh and the Ohio Valley), agriculture (Iowa, to cite on area), heavy equipment manufacturing (various Midwest regions, particularly in Illinois), textiles (Georgia and the Carolinas), and several others. Clearly, when the basic industries of a region are in trouble, the nonbasic sectors are vulnerable as well. A regional economy is not static; rather, it is always evolving. As the steel mills were shutting down throughout the Pittsburgh region, there was an upsurge in central office and financial services activities. A fundamental economic shift is taking place that will have significant effects on economic activity, and accordingly, prepayment rates.

Therefore, trends in regional economic activity are largely determined by trends in basic, export industries. Growth in these industries will translate to growth in ancillary or nonbasic sectors. Erosion in the basic industries will have the opposite effect. However, the composition of basic industries will change over time, and as is normally the case, there are gainers and losers among regions and households.

REGIONAL PREPAYMENT DIFFERENCES

Changes in regional economic activity cause households to move. When a regional economy is declining, prepayment rates increase as people move to new jobs or because defaults occur. When a regional economy is growing, households trade up in response to gains in personal income and wealth. Inmigration in response to economic growth generally spurs this activity. Moreover, studies of household migration have shown that inmigration is highly correlated with out-migration. Some houesholds are displaced, and others may move in, decide they do not like it, and move out.

Given these factors, there are several regional economic statistics that are highly correlated with regional prepayment rates. Some examples include basic employment such as manufacturing, total employment, housing starts, retail sales, personal income, and migration. Unfortunately, at the level of an MSA (metropolitan statistical area), migration data is unavailable or extremely unreliable, and personal income data is not timely. Thus, for an initial analysis basic employment, total employment, and the housing sector are the primary statistics to be used. Population and personal income data can also be evaluated, but the data are not current.

These regional statistics should be evaluated on the basis of short- and long-term trends relative to national averages and conformity to the national business cycle. In other words, it is important to know whether the region is growing in a relative and an absolute sense, and whether it conforms to the national business cycle (cyclical), is more volatile than the national cycle (procyclical), moves opposite the national cycle (countercyclical), or is independent of the national cycle (acyclical).

To illustrate this analysis, two urban areas with high prepayment rates were selected: Albuquerque and Pittsburgh. The relevant data for each are provided in Table 12–1. For total employment, manufacturing employment, and single-family housing starts, there are two sets of characteristics (trend and elasticity) over three time periods (1980–82, 1980–83, and 1980–84). Similar statistics are calculated for personal income. Although this data is several years old, it will suffice for this example.

Starting with the trends, each of the values represent the ratio of the compounded annual growth rate of the MSA relative to the national rate. For example, bewteen 1980 and 1982, national total nonfarm employment declined at a 0.5 percent compounded annual rate. In contrast, Albuquerque, NM had a growth rate of 0.9% over this period. The resulting ratio (− 1.8) implies that Albuqurque continued to grow while the national economy declined. By the 1980–84 period national total nonfarm employment had a growth rate of 1.0 percent. The ratio of 3.3 indicates that the Albuquerque economy was much stronger at 3.3 times the national rate.

The elasticity values have a somewhat different interpretation. An asterisk (*) in Table 12–1 indicates an insignificant relation between the MSA and the national rate. In other words, the MSA's economy is acyclical, or independent of the national business cycle. If the elasticity value is negative, the MSA is countercyclical, which means that it moved in the opposite direction relative to the national economy. When the MSA value is less (greater) than one, then the region's economy moves in the same direction but is less (more) volatile than the national economy.

A comparison of the results in Table 12–1 shows striking differences between economic activity in a growing sun-belt region and a declining basic manufacturing region. During the recession, the Albuquerque MSA expanded countercyclically and outperformed the national economy in the recovery. This generated high prepayments because of trading up and migration flows. In contrast, the Pittsburgh MSA was very procyclical during the recession and countercyclical in the expansion reflecting the weakness of basic manufacturing. In addition to growth in the trade and service sectors, high prepayments were the result of considerable migration out of the region because of the substantial losses in the manufacturing sector.

Table 12-1
Comparison of Regional Economic Data to National MSA* Mean and Standard Deviation

Total Employment Trend

Time Span	Pittsburgh, PA	Albuquerque, NM	National MSA Mean/ Standard Deviation
1980–82	5.6	−1.8	0.80/ 6.10
1980–83	28.0	−21.0	2.84/28.13
1980–84	−2.1	3.3	0.73/ 2.57

Manufacturing Employment Trend

Time Span	Pittsburgh, PA	Albuquerque, NM	National MSA Mean/ Standard Deviation
1980–82	2.47	−0.08	0.87/1.17
1980–83	3.43	−0.37	1.06/1.42
1980–84	9.78	−2.89	0.73/6.06

Single-Family Housing Trend

Time Span	Pittsburgh, PA	Albuquerque, NM	National MSA Mean/ Standard Deviation
1080–82	0.39	1.02	1.12/0.86
1980–83	0.37	0.37	1.12/0.85
1980–84	0.39	1.27	1.16/0.85

Income Trend

Time Span	Pittsburgh, PA	Albuquerque, NM	National MSA Mean/ Standard Deviation
1978–83	0.81	1.11	1.08/0.23

* Note: The MSA value represents a ratio between the MSA and national growth rate. A number greater than one means that the MSA is growing (declining)

Total Employment Elasticity

Time Span	Pittsburgh, PA	Albuquerque, NM	National MSA Mean/ Standard Deviation
1980–82	2.58	−0.52	1.66/1.95
1980–83	1.98	−0.01*	1.69/1.35
1980–84	−0.42*	1.96	1.21/2.11

Manufacturing Elasticity

Time Span	Pittsburgh, PA	Albuquerque, NM	National MSA Mean/ Standard Deviation
1980–82	2.38	0.02*	1.05/0.95
1980–83	2.82	−0.12	1.11/1.06
1980–84	2.56	−0.02*	1.11/0.96

Single Family Housing Elasticity

Time Span	Pittsburgh, PA	Albuquerque, NM	National MSA Mean/ Standard Deviation
1980–82	1.12	1.63	1.40/0.64
1980–83	1.07	1.64	1.35/0.60
1980–84	1.02	1.64	1.30/0.56

Income Trend

Time Span	Pittsburgh, PA	Albuquerque, NM	National MSA Mean/ Standard Deviation
1978–83	0.88	1.09	1.01/0.24

† Note: An asterisk (*) indicates that the MSA is acyclical. An elasticity greater (less) than one means that the MSA is more (less) volatile than the national economy. A negative number implies that the MSA is countercyclical.

There are numerous ways to evaluate a regional economy. The examples provided in Table 12–1 illustrate the diversity across regions and how various economic measures can be used to evaluate prepayments. A regional analysis system that is updated and enhanced regularly can take advantage of regional value among mortgage-backed securities.

GENERAL CONCLUSIONS BASED ON REGIONAL ANALYSIS

Regional economies dependent on extractive industries and traditional basic manufacturing sectors tend to be volatile, and volatility produces higher prepayments during good and bad times for several reasons. Commodity prices often have wide swings that exaggerate boom and bust cycles. One example is oil prices. Many regions that experienced rapid inmigration when oil prices rose experienced the opposite when oil prices fell dramatically.

Durable goods manufacturing sectors, such as appliances, cars, and heavy equipment, are quite sensitive to the business cycle because household consumption of these goods and business investments vary sharply. This situation becomes even more volatile as the trade position erodes, and numerous plants shut down in the midst of general prosperity.

There is a substantial lag between economic shocks to a region and changes in prepayment rates. When a regional economy experiences an economic shock, the immediate effect will be to *lower* prepayments. This results from several factors:

- Households cease "trading up," even if their own positions are relatively safe.
- Defaults generally do not occur until the situation between the mortgagee and mortgagor becomes drastic.
- People do not move out of the region until a significant time period has elapsed; three to six months is usually the minimum.

The first factor refers to the general observation that the perception of rising unemployment will restrain household consumption of durable goods, with housing the most obvious example. Although some astute investors may regard this type of situation as a rare opportunity to trade up in a buyers' market, most people will simply not take the risk, whether real or perceived.

The second factor causing initially lower prepayments results from the fact that households normally do anything possible to protect their home from foreclosure. In recent years, some homeowners with little or no equity have simply "walked away" from their homes, but this is still the exception. Furthermore, lending institutions have recently become somewhat more flexible toward problem loans, realizing that foreclosures in a distressed market are often a continuing drain rather than a solution.

The third factor refers to the perception that despite an actual or threatened layoff, an individual's best job prospects are in the region that he or she knows best. This is where the individual's job network is, and job search costs are relatively low. Two exceptions to this rule are: when the regional economy is highly dependent on one industry, and the situation where one's skills are easily transferable—the job search outside of the region begins immediately. In general, however, laid-off workers tend to wait things out in the hope that the economic shock is short-lived.

Once the process of outmigration begins (usually after a period of six months), it can continue for a considerable period of time. It is reasonable to say that in the case of a declining regional economy, one could expect prepayments to remain higher for several years, *ignoring all other determinants of prepayments*. This is extremely important because it implies that we can forecast prepayments on a relative basis at least by evaluating recent and current regional economic trends, such as those just discussed.

Many regions of the country are undergoing a fundamental economic transition comparable to the change from an agrarian to an industrial society. Some regions have permanently lost their economic base, primarily in manufacturing, and have little to fall back on unless new manufacturers can be attracted.

Other areas, such as Pittsburgh, can absorb the loss of much of their manufacturing base while their economy expands substantially in the trade and service sectors. There are numerous other examples. Portland, Oregon is attracting high-tech firms while its traditional forest products orientation declines. New England has evolved from textiles and shoe manufacturing to high-tech and services.

For regions that experience a continual erosion of their economic base, outmigration and higher-than-average prepayments can occur for years. Regional economies that are in transition experience both outmigration and inmigration, resulting in trading up if new industries prosper.

As one should expect, there are certainly exceptions to these general cases. Regional economies dominated by government typically are more stable (prepay slower) than would otherwise be expected. Retirees can have a similar effect on otherwise fast-growing regions. Some areas retain their populations almost regardless of economic conditions.

SUMMARY

In addition to seasonality, the pure aging effect, and interest rate incentives to prepay, regional economic fundamentals drive the prepayments of mortgage-backed securities. Rigorous analysis can produce excellent investment opportunities in situations where the "consensus" viewpoint would be extremely negative. For example, there is no question that oil-related industries face severe problems when oil prices fall significantly, and the negative economic consequences will be far-reaching. However, there are tremendous economic differences between regions in oil producing states, and one should not be deterred from investigating the possibilities.

This overview demonstrates that regional economic data can show what a region's prepayment rate should be based strictly on its economic trends. We have found a strong relation between what prepayments should be, using this approach, and what they turn out to be. A regional economic data evaluation system to assess prepayment potential of mortgage related securities can significantly enhance the yield performance of a portfolio.

Chapter 13

HENRY J. CASSIDY
AND
PATRICIA M. DODSON

Henry Cassidy was appointed Vice President of Financial Research of the Federal Home Loan Mortgage Corporation (Freddie Mac) in December 1985. He is responsible for the formulation of financial policies and strategies, and for performing research activiites for the corporation in the areas of pricing and risk management.

Cassidy joined Freddie Mac in August 1984 as Director of Financial Research and was responsible for directing the writing and preparing of financial issues papers and briefings, and supervising research projects in the areas of hedging, pricing, and financing strategies.

Prior to joining Freddie Mac, Cassidy was Director of the General Research Division at the Federal Home Loan Bank Board from 1971–1984. Concurrently he taught economics at George Washington, George Mason and Virginia Polytechnic Institute and State Universities. Cassidy was also senior associate at Planning Research Corporation from 1968–71 and a research fellow at the Brookings Institution from 1967–68.

Cassidy holds a Ph.D. in Economics and an M.A. in Mathematical Statistics from the University of Illinois, and a B.S. from Carroll College in economics and mathematics. He has also authored a book and many articles on economics and housing finance in academic and popular journals.

Patricia Dodson is a Security Sales Representative with Freddie Mac's Security Sales and Trading Group. Since joining Freddie Mac in 1983, Patricia has also worked in the Product Development Analysis and Marketing and Sales Research departments. She is currently a graduate student in economics at the George Washington University.

The Uses of Freddie Mac PCs

HENRY J. CASSIDY AND PATRICIA M. DODSON

INTRODUCTION TO PARTICIPATION CERTIFICATES

Freddie Mac PCs (participation certificates) are mortgage-backed securities (MBSs) that have cash flow characteristics based on the cash flow generated by a specified pool of mortgages. For example, the underlying mortgages may be fixed-rate or adjustable-rate, 30-year or 15-year mortgages, and the associated PC will have many of the same cash flow features, including the amortization schedule of the underlying mortgages. As of mid-1986, Freddie Mac issued PCs backed by (conventional and government-underwritten) single-family, 30-year fixed-rate mortgages, 15-year fixed-rate mortgages, 30-year adjustable-rate mortgages, and multifamily fixed-rate 15-year balloon (Plan B) mortgages. Freddie Mac has plans for second-mortgage PCs and multifamily and adjustable-rate guarantor PCs. Guarantor PCs are obtained by "swapping" mortgages for PCs. Prior to 1981, PCs were obtained only by purchasing them with cash. Since then, mortgage holders have been able to obtain PCs without cash by turning over ownership in mortgages to Freddie Mac and receiving PCs in return. This process is referred to as the *securitization* of the mortgages. For accounting purposes, the swap is not a sale of the mortgage assets, but an exchange of like securities.

In fact, we maintain that it is an exchange for acquiring higher-quality securities, securities that have many valuable uses. PCs are one of the best investment values that savings institutions and others can purchase. This chapter focuses on the uses of PCs once they are obtained, and primarily on the uses of the guarantor PC.

The principal advantage of owning PCs instead of unsecuritized mortgages is that Freddie Mac guarantees the ultimate repayment and, if requested, the timely payment of principal. Consequently, if the mortgagor defaults, the PC investor suffers no capital loss. In addition to the superior credit quality of mortgages securitized and guaranteed by Freddie Mac, PCs are much more liquid than unsecuritized mortgages. Primarily because of this improvement in credit quality and liquidity, the PC is better collateral for a number of uses, such as in structured financings.

This chapter is addressed mainly to financial institutions that own PCs or who own mortgages that can be swapped for PCs. We explore some of the major uses of Freddie Mac PCs in various financing strategies. The ones we emphasize involve use of PCs as collateral for: repurchase agreements, dollar rolls, Federal Home Loan Bank advances, Federal Reserve discount window borrowings, mortgage-backed bonds, CMOs, preferred stock issuances, and public unit deposits. Each of these transactions represents a way for financial institutions to expand their financing opportunities and, in many cases, take advantage of arbitrage opportunities to enhance profitability. (For example, in the "swap and sell" strategy, mortgages are first enhanced by a swap for PCs, and then the PCs are sold in the secondary market.) These opportunities now are available for both current-coupon and discount mortgages, and for both mortgage bankers and portfolio lenders.

Figure 13–1 shows the two basic steps in this process. The first step is always to swap the mortgages with Freddie Mac for PCs. Then the second step is to use the PCs as collateral for various types of financings, such as mortgage-backed bonds. No cash exchanges hands in the swap with Freddie Mac unless the buy-up or buy-down features are used. In the former, Freddie Mac pays cash for an increase in the guarantee fee. In the latter, the seller pays cash up front for a decrease in the guarantee fee. At the second step, when the savings institution or

Figure 13–1
**Two Basic Steps in Raising Funds
Using Portfolio Mortgages**

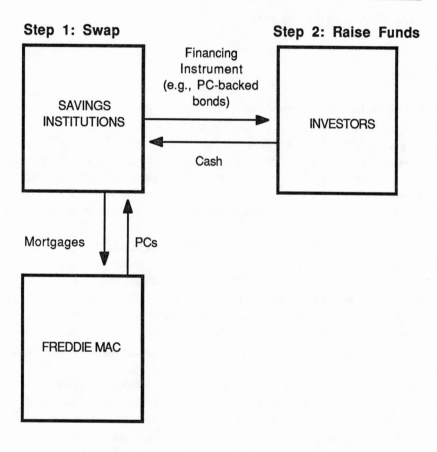

Step 1: Swap   Step 2: Raise Funds

SAVINGS
INSTITUTIONS

Financing
Instrument
(e.g., PC-backed
bonds)

INVESTORS

Cash

Mortgages   PCs

FREDDIE MAC

other holder of the PC issues a financing instrument backed by the PCs, it receives cash in return.

TYPES OF USES FOR PCs

Repos

The *repurchase agreement* ("repo") is a major form of borrowing using Freddie Mac PCs. Under a repurchase agreement, one party sells a security to another party with a simultaneous agreement to repurchase the identical security at a future date, at an agreed upon price. Hence, the name *repurchase agreement*. From the opposite perspective, the party initially purchasing the security with the agreement to later resell the same security is said to be performing a *reverse repurchase agreement*. The repos is, in essence, a borrowing collateralized by securities, with the repurchase price set to reflect the required rate of interest. (In a repo on mortgage-backed securities, the seller remains entitled to all principal and interest payments on the securities.) The PCs serve as security for the funds disbursed by the purchaser. The purchaser of the PC commonly funds only a portion of its market value. The difference between its market value and the amount of funds disbursed is known as "the haircut" and can be thought of, quite simply, as over-collateralization. Haircuts of 3 to 5 percent are typical on repos on MBSs, depending on the term of the repo. Maturities generally range from 1 to 90 days. Because the repo haircut represents over-collateralization, it exposes the repo originator to credit risk. If the repo partner fails to execute the repurchase, the partner retains the PCs, which, because of the haircut, are of greater value than the amount of cash received. Consequently, it is important to enter into repurchase agreements with creditworthy partners.

Although the mechanics of a repo involve the actual sale and purchase of a security, it can usually be accounted for as a financing. This is a key feature, because by using repos on MBSs, portfolio lenders can raise cash with portfolio mortgages without recognizing any accounting gains or losses.

The major advantage of repos is that they are a consistent, low-cost source of financing. Many times, funds can be reinvested into other short-term instruments as a positive spread; that is, arbitrage opportunities become available. These opportunities are typically short-lived, so it is important to be ready to execute the transactions quickly. A portfolio of Freddie Mac PCs can represent an instant source of liquidity for savings institutions. Once PCs are obtained through a swap, they can be mobilized very quickly. Repurchase agreements also represent a widely used source of short-term financing for mortgage bankers. Prior to settlement on a forward trade, they swap the mortgages for PCs, then use the PCs as collateral for repos. In this way, mortgage bankers can often use repos as an alternative to borrowing from their warehouse lenders.

The bulk of repo activity is transacted through Wall Street dealers. Recently, however, Freddie Mac has introduced a limited program whereby selected federally insured savings institutions can execute repurchase agreements with Freddie Mac using PCs.

Dollar Rolls

An extremely popular use for Freddie Mac PCs is the *dollar roll,* which is quite similar to the repurchase agreement. In fact, in some formal circles, the dollar roll is known as a "dollar repurchase agreement." In a dollar roll, as in a repo, a security is sold with an agreement that a security will be repurchased at a later date at a given price. Like the repo, the dollar roll can be thought of as a loan secured by MBSs.

There are, however, some very important differences between repos and dollar rolls on MBSs. First, in a dollar roll the purchaser agrees to return to the seller a security that is *substantially similar* to the security originally sold. There is absolutely no agreement that the security be the same security that was originally sold, as is the case in a repo. Minimal qualifications for securities to be considered substantially similar would include that they be of the same type (for example, a

GNMA) and have similar coupons and original maturities. However, it is possible and not uncommon for those engaging in dollar rolls to put other limitations on the characteristics of securities that can be delivered at maturity. Because the seller of the security is likely to receive a different security than that sold, dollar rolls are generally done on very generic types of securities; for example, current coupon Freddie Mac PCs.

Another very important difference between the repo and the dollar roll is that under a dollar roll, the purchaser of the PC is entitled to all principal and interest payments due to the holder of the security during the term of the dollar roll. Thus, the repurchase price of the security must reflect not only a rate of interest, but also the expected benefits of receiving the payments on the security. This is a related reason that dollar rolls are generally done on generic securities—those having relatively predictable cash flows.

Because there is no haircut, the dollar roll can be considered a more efficient transaction than the repo. When the security is initially sold, the seller receives the full market value of the security. The absence of over-collateralization makes the dollar roll less risky from the seller's point of view.

Many of the differences between dollar rolls and repos exist because the repo is primarily a vehicle for intermediation of funds (getting persons needing funds together with persons having funds), whereas a dealer uses a dollar roll to obtain a particular type of security. In effect, the dollar roll allows MBS dealers to "buy time" to come up with securities they have committed to deliver. For example, if a dealer has sold Freddie Mac 9s (9 percent coupon PCs) for delivery in the current month, but has been unable to purchase the desired amount of Freddie Mac PC 9s at a target price, it may turn to the dollar roll market for help. The dealer will seek to buy PC 9s in the current month, agreeing to resell the same amount of PC 9s later. In the meantime, the dealer attempts to purchase the amount needed for permanent delivery. For holders of PC 9s, the dealer's need represents an opportunity. Institutions with PC 9s in their portfolios can mobilize them instantly to take advantage of an arbitrage opportunity, and the pricing of the dollar roll may imply an attractive lending rate.

Accounting for dollar rolls is more complicated than accounting for repos. For most straightforward dollar roll transactions, however, it is usually possible to account for the dollar roll as a financing, as is the case for the repo.

Federal Home Loan Bank Advances

Freddie Mac securities can collateralize advances from the Federal Home Loan Banks, a major source of both short- and long-term financing by savings institutions across the nation. Freddie Mac PCs are particularly suitable collateral for such borrowing because the collateral is easily identified; in many cases, the Federal Home Loan Banks advance a greater dollar amount against PCs than against unsecuritized mortgages (require less over-collaterlization). Several of the Federal Home Loan Banks use net present value formulas to calculate the collateral value of mortgages, but use dealer quotes for PCs. Table 13–1 shows the dramatic difference that can sometimes result from the different valuation methods.

Discount Window Borrowings

Both banks and savings institutions can use PCs as collateral for borrowing from the Federal Reserve discount window. Paperwork and documentation may be greatly reduced by offering PCs as collateral rather than unsecuritized mortgages, because collateral must be specifically identified.

CMOs

An extremely efficient form of borrowing backed by MBSs is the *collateralized mortgage obligation (CMO)*. A CMO is a type of bond for which cash flows generated by a specific pool of collateral are dedicated to repay the obligation. Under a standard CMO design,

Table 13–1
An Example of the Use of PCs as
Collateral for Federal Home Loan Bank Advances

	Assumptions	
	PC	*Mortgage*
WAC	8.5%	8.5%
WAM	233	233
UPB	$87,592.09	$87,592.09
PMT	$768.91	$768.91
Certificate rate	8.0%	N/A
Price	78–26/32	N/A
Discount rate	N/A	13%

Note: In this case, the discount rate was based on the average Freddie Mac required net yields for the past three weeks.

Collateral Value of Mortgages Versus
PCs—FHLB of Atlanta Example

$$PV = \sum_{t=1}^{233} \frac{768.91}{(1+.13/12)^t} = 65,211.60$$

$$\text{Calculated price} = \frac{\text{Present Value}}{\text{Unpaid balance}} = \frac{65,211.90}{87,592.09} = 74\text{–}14/32$$

PCs

Dealer quoted price = 78–26/32

PC advantage as collateral = 4–12/32

Conclusion: It is clear in this case that PC's would represent more efficient collateral (that is, less over-collateralization) than the unsecuritized mortgages.

payments on the underlying collateral are partitioned to provide for different maturity classes, called *tranches*. Payments of principal on each class do not begin until all previous classes have been retired. It is common for interest to accrue (that is, not be paid out in cash) on the last class until all previous classes have been retired. By dividing the cash flows into maturity classes, the CMO offers issuers a blended financing rate based on pricing along different segments of the Treasury yield curve. This blended rate can be very attractive to issuers. Indeed, the CMO structure with different maturity classes often provides a higher price overall than would the outright sale of the mortgages. The price obtained can vary considerably over time, so it pays to have the deal ready (the PCs in hand and the CMO structure established) so that the CMO can be issued at the most favorable time. In this way, the CMO can be used both to borrow against a portfolio of mortgages and to engage in arbitrage.

Most CMOs are issued with MBSs such as PCs instead of the mortgages themselves as the collateral for the CMO. In other words, the first step is to swap for PCs, just as in Figure 13–1, but in this case, the PCs are used to back a CMO. Both thrifts and dealers have purchased MBSs and issued CMOs to take advantage of arbitrage opportunities.

The expected cash flow from the PC collateral and the reinvestment income from it are the base for projecting the CMO payments. CMOs are rated by independent rating agencies, and the reliability of cash flows is the primary concern. The higher the rating, the lower the required interest payments on the CMO, other things being the same. The rating agencies regard the cash flow on Freddie Mac PCs as highly reliable, and top ratings can be obtained when PCs are the CMO collateral.

Because of the way collateral is valued, however, the overall proceeds of the CMO issue fall short of the value of the collateral, thus creating the need to finance the shortfall. Many thrift issuers simply finance the shortfall internally. Investment bankers, however, have been very creative in developing ways to finance the initial over-collateralization. For example, residual cash flows produced by CMOs have been packaged and sold to investors.

Freddie Mac has been extremely responsive to the needs of CMO issuers by adapting the PC to minimize the need for over-collateralization. Freddie Mac's standard guarantee is that principal will ultimately be paid, but Freddie Mac also offers a guarantee of timely payment of principal to sellers swapping mortgages for PCs, and to those servicing PCs for which they previously swapped. The guarantee of timely principal enhances the collateral value of the PC because principal payments may be included without lags when projecting the collateral cash flows that will service the debt. Other enhancements to the Guarantor Program include the ability of sellers to create PCs with coupon rates out to three decimal places (for exmple, 10.125 percent). This feature maximizes collateral value by minimizing excess servicing. Another recently announced program enhancement is the ability to swap for PCs having pool balances as low as $250,000. This feature allows CMO issuers to aggregate securitized mortgages more quickly than they could with the previous $1 million minimum pool balance.

Rather than issue the CMO itself, a thrift may prefer to dedicate the PCs to a finance subsidiary that will issue a CMO backed by these PCs. This removes the PCs from the parent's balance sheet for purposes of the FSLIC calculation of net worth. Because the CMO has the same duration (or effective maturity) as the PCs, the parent has a reduced net worth requirement but does not lose control of the assets.

Preferred Stock

An extremely innovative use thrifts make of Freddie Mac securities is to back issues of *preferred stock*. Preferred stock offerings can be structured to produce the favorable ratings and lower costs of collateralizing stock with specific assets. Most recent issues of preferred stock provide dividend payments that are not constant but that change periodically. In general, dividend payments on adjustable preferred stock float according to a dividend reset formula; for auction preferred stock, they float according to the results of a periodic auction.

A popular way to issue the stock is as follows: A thrift establishes a subsidiary and transfers PCs to the subsidiary in exchange for common stock. The subsidiary then issues a single class of preferred stock. Because the preferred stockholders have first claim to the assets of the subsidiary corporation, the effect of collateralization is achieved. Moreover, if the assets of the subsidiary are limited to high-quality securities such as Freddie Mac PCs, rating services generally confer top ratings on the stock, provided that the market value of the securities is maintained at a specified level relative to the outstanding amount of preferred stock. Top ratings translate into low financing rates for issuers.

An advantage of the subsidiary arrangement is that the dedicated PCs come off the books of FSLIC-insured thrifts, reducing the net worth requirement. However, in order to realize this benefit, the PCs dedicated to the subsidiary must have nearly the same duration, or effective maturity, as the financing vehicle. Consequently, to comply with this restriction, adjustable-rate PCs would be needed to back adjustable preferred stock. A thrift having fixed-rate PCs and seeking to reduce required a net worth would be better off having the subsidiary issue a CMO or a mortgage-backed bond.

Because dividend income is largely exempt from corporate taxation, issuers of preferred stock can issue a debt-like instrument at tax-advantaged rates. Although the dividend payments on the preferred stock are not tax-deductible as are interest payments on debt, if the issuer's parent has sufficient tax loss carryforwards, the usual advantage to issuing debt is overcome. The need for tax loss carryforwards limits the applicability of this financing technique, but where the issuer's tax situation permits, preferred stock issues backed by PCs can be highly attractive to both the issuer and the investors.

Public Unit Deposits

Freddie Mac securities are widely used as collateral for Treasury tax and loan accounts, as well as for deposits by federal, state, and local agencies. Such deposits represent an attractive source of funds for many banks and savings institutions across the country, but they usually must be collateralized by qualifying assets. The eligibility of PCs to serve as collateral for state and local public unit deposits varies by jurisdiction, but PCs are always eligible for federal Treasury tax and loan accounts.

CONCLUSION

This chapter outlined some of the most common uses for Freddie Mac PCs. The uses described all have one common theme: mortgages are not sold for accounting purposes; instead, (1) the mortgages are swapped for Freddie Mac PCs, and then (2) the PCs are used as collateral for various kinds of financing, including repos, dollar rolls, Federal Home Loan Bank advances and Federal Reserve borrowings, CMOs, preferred stock, and public unit deposits. Because there are so many uses, and some market opportunities for arbitrage arise and disappear quickly, financial institutions holding mortgage assets should consider swapping the mortgages for PCs to be ready to take advantage of fleeting opportunities. Freddie Mac and investment bankers can assist in both this step and the second—the use of the PC collateral for financing and arbitrage opportunities.

This by no means covers all of the current and potential uses for high-quality mortgage-backed securities. Freddie Mac PCs have also been used to collateralize commercial paper, interest rate swaps, and private certificates of deposit, to name a few. Moreover, new uses for Freddie Mac securities will continue to be developed, because the superior credit quality and liquidity of Freddie Mac securities make them a much more efficient funding vehcile than unsecuritized mortgages.

Chapter 14

JAYNE J. SHONTELL

Jayne Shontell is Vice President with the Federal National Mortgage Association. Previously she was Chief Economist for Freddie Mac. Ms. Shontell received a B.A. and an M.B.A. in economics from Georgetown University.

The Fannie Mae Mortgage-Backed Security

JAYNE J. SHONTELL

Mortgage-backed securities are the most effective tool lenders have for managing residential mortgage loan programs and portfolios. The efficiencies mortgage-backed securities add to the execution of mortgage sales and collateralized borrowings are a function of the structural and programmatic elements of the securities program. Fannie Mae developed its mortgage-backed securities program in 1981 in response to the changing environment for mortgage lending. The program was patterned after and improved upon the features of the successful GNMA program.

In this chapter, you will be introduced to the fundamental elements of a successful pass-through program. The cash flow structure will be explained in terms of who holds the payments, how long they are held, and who benefits from the interest earned on the carry. The value added to the pool of mortgages will be examined, and the process required to achieve that added value will be outlined. These discussions will be help you understand why the Fannie Mae MBS has become the leading conventional pass-through security for most of the mortgage industry's needs.

THE FANNIE MAE MBS

In developing the MBS program, Fannie Mae sought the most efficient structure for both the lender who was swapping loans and the investor who was buying the security. By 1981, the GNMA program had become the most widely used securitization program, and the mortgage lending industry had developed practices to conform to its requirements. Fannie Mae modeled its MBS business after the GNMA pass-through structure, adding new features to meet lender and investor needs.

The most significant aspect of a pass-through security is the cash flow of payments from homeowner to investor. Fannie Mae designed its MBS to provide as direct a pass through as possible, with Fannie Mae holding the payments for as short a period as practical, given its responsibilities to the investors. With very little Fannie Mae involvement, market pricing is unobstructed, and lenders and investors can directly value the program features.

Fannie Mae provides lenders with a very efficient remittance cycle. Principal and interest payments due on the 1st of the month, as well as any loan payoffs of the previous month, are payable on the 18th of each month. This provides lenders with a reasonable period to collect payments, during which time they can reinvest collections prior to remittance. The schedule also allows Fannie Mae to pay investors on the 25th of the month. The pass-through delay on Fannie Mae MBSs is thus 20 days shorter than the delay on Freddie Mac PCs; as a result, investors have been willing to pay a higher price for the MBS. The payment to investors in the month of mortgage collection also allows for advantageous structuring of financings collateralized by the MBS, including collaterized mortgage obligations (CMOs).

The shorter payment delay of the MBS is its most widely recognized advantage, producing a price spread versus a Freddie Mac PC of a quarter to half a point. Fannie Mae also has developed other features that provide concrete advantages, including the fastest process for securities issuance following document submission. These features will be discussed in more detail later in the chapter.

In the development of its MBS business, Fannie Mae has addressed the needs arising from the various uses of securities. Mortgage lenders and investors may securitize mortgages to get a higher price on sale, to improve the value of collateral for short-term or long-term borrowings, or to obtain the most liquid and easily transacted form of the asset for portfolio flexibility. The following discussion will identify the program features specific to each of these objectives and will explain how the efficiencies of the Fannie Mae MBS program affect the execution for each objective.

A LARGE AND GROWING MARKET

Understanding how and why Fannie Mae's MBS program works so well requires an understanding of why securitization of loans adds value. Lenders who swap loans for securities must receive a higher-valued asset in order to be willing to pay the guaranty fee required to obtain that security. The value added generally falls into two categories: the reduction of uncertainties from the guaranty of pass through of principal and interest, and the reduction of transaction costs and risks due to the organized and efficient markets for the securities.

The market for mortgages and mortgage-backed securities comprises investors offering prices for expected cash flow streams off of a group of mortgages. Investors base the valuation of those cash flows upon forecasts of the consistency and certainty of the monthly payment. Residential mortgages represent a borrower's promise to pay a given amount per month and an option to prepay the remaining balance at any time. Investors estimate the probability that the payment will be made every month and the likelihood the borrower will exercise the option to prepay.

The MBS program reduces these uncertainties by guaranteeing that the principal and interest will be paid every month and by underwriting each loan against an established set of criteria. Fannie Mae guarantees the timely payment of principal and interest on all its MBSs–in contrast to the Freddie Mac PC, which generally guarantees timely payment of interest and the eventual distribution of principal. The underwriting of the loan in MBS pools provides the investor with knowlege about the loans represented by the MBS, and therefore better data on which to make estimates. Fannie Mae's underwriting requirements are recognized by the mortgage lending and investing industries as the standard against which all others are evaluated. Fannie Mae's MBS program further reduces investor uncertainties with disclosure of detailed pool statistics from which to analyze projected cash flow. The guaranty of timely principal and interest, and the detailed disclosure of pool statistics on all pools, distinguish the Fannie Mae MBS from other securities and improve its value to investors—particularly in collateralized financing structures.

The market for the MBS represents one of the most efficient financial markets in the world. With a face amount of $500 billion in securities issued, it is one of the world's largest markets. Fannie Mae alone recently passed the $100 billion mark in MBSs issued. The sheer volumes involved in mortgage pass-through trading have created the need for ever-increasing efficiencies and a concomitant rise in resources allocated to this market place.

The aggregate amount of securities is composed of specific mortgage types, which are each pooled and valued separately. For example, the Fannie Mae MBS program represents over $5 billion in 15-year MBSs, $5 billion in adjustable-rate MBSs, $6.5 billion in variable-rate MBSs, and $1 billion in multifamily MBSs, in addition to more than $80 billion in 30-year MBSs. Each of these MBS types has been analyzed and traded in such volume that buyers and sellers can quickly and effectively come to agreement on value and price.

Investment bankers and dealers on Wall Street and around the country make active markets, offering to buy and sell the MBS. These participants have developed standards for transacting in mortgage-backed securities—standards that reduce costs and risks in transferring ownership on large volumes of securities in a timely and consistent manner.

The considerations of reduced uncertainty and enhanced marketability specifically add value to MBSs for lenders seeking immediate sales. The prices available on the MBS are improved by Fannie Mae's guaranty and provision of information, and the active market for all types of MBS allows flexibility in delivery terms and volume. These considerations also add value to the MBS as collateral for borrowings, both short and long term. The guaranty of timely principal and interest payments improves the use of the securities as collateral for structured financings, such as CMOs, while their marketability increases investors' willingness to take MBS as collateral for repuchase agreements and other short-term borrowings.

The management of mortgage portfolios is enhanced through securitization of assets, which increases lenders' flexibility in marketing the securities quickly and efficiently. MBS portfolios can be adjusted to reflect changing market conditions and expectations without examining each loan and then pulling together documents and loan histories.

Fannie Mae has supported the development of these markets and standards through active work with the major securities dealers and through the provision of information and services that enhance the market. Fannie Mae converted all of its MBS issues to the Federal Reserve book-entry system, reducing the paperwork required and the delays inherent in the sale of securities. Fannie Mae has also provided the market with information and program parameters that allow securities to be evaluated and priced consistently.

THE ADDED VALUE OF PASS-THROUGH SECURITIES

The value added by securitization is similar for all available securitization programs, but the relative value of each program is determined by a number of factors. The most significant factor is the nature of the guaranty and the market's evaluation of the guarantor.

The strongest guaranty of any mortgage-backed security is that of the GNMA program, carrying the full faith and credit of the U.S. government. The guaranties of the two federal agencies—Fannie Mae and Freddie Mac—are viewed by the market as carrying a moral obligation of the government and are specifically backed up by a formal relationship between the agencies and the U.S. Treasury. Privately guaranteed and insured securities are rated and valued on the basis of the structure of the security and the financial strength of the guarantor.

The additional factors affecting value relate to the specific features of each securitization program, principally the cash flows from the lender to the investor and the procedures the lender and investor must manage. As was discussed earlier, the feature with the most direct impact is the pass-through process and timing of remittances and receipt by each party.

The timing of payments to the investor determines the return realized on the investment; it is therefore a deciding factor in market pricing. The Fannie Mae MBS pays the investor scheduled principal and interest for a given month on the 25th of that month. This payment reflects interest one month in arrears—the standard mortgage convention—and therefore represents a 55-day interest delay (30 days interst in arears plus a 25-day interest-free period). An investor calculates this cash flow in relation to the required yield and determines a price.

The payment date for the GNMA security is the 15th of the month for the original GNMA I program and the 20th of the month for the GNMA II program. GNMA securities command a higher price than the Fannie Mae MBS to achieve the same yield for the same security interest rate. For example, an MBS with a 9.50 percent security rate Fannie Mae MBS is priced at 97.6875 to yield 9.75 percent, while the GNMA is priced at 97.90625 for the same yield—using the industry standard of loans prepaying in 12 years.

Actual market prices reflect many considerations, such as the value of the guaranty, conditions of supply and demand, and differences in payment characteristics. A clearer picture of the value of the pass-through delay is seen in the price difference between the Fannie Mae MBS and the Freddie Mac PC. The guaranty and the underlying collateral are substantially similar. However, the MBS pays investors on the 25th of the month of homeowner payment, while Freddie Mac pays investors on the 15th of the month following the homeowner's scheduled payment. This 20-day faster remittance for the MBS has a price value ranging from .50% (16/32) for 8.50% security rates to .75% (24/32) for 13.00% security rates. Investors are therefore willing to pay a higher price for the Fannie Mae MBS than the Freddie Mac PC, for a given required return. The actual price difference varies from security rate to security rate because of the supply and demand considerations at each rate.

The structural efficiency of paying the investor as soon as practical is fully appreciated by investors and lenders who use the MBS as collateral for structured financings, such as CMOs. Receipt of payment on the MBS within the month of homeowner remittance provides the issuer of the CMO with the principal and interest for payment to bondholders as early as possible. CMOs backed by Freddie Mac PCs generally are required to advance one month's interest into the CMO trust to make up for the delayed remittance to investors, in order to be structured the same as an MBS-backed issue. This cost advantage, which produces greater net proceeds on issue, has been recognized by the market and became a deciding factor in determination of collateral choice for CMO issuers.

FANNIE MAE VERSUS FREDDIE MAC

The true nature of the pass-through process and the cash flows to and from each party is most clearly understood by examining the cash flow when the lender swapping loans for securities holds those securities as an investment or for use as collateral. Up to this point the discussion of cash flow has concentrated on the remittance delays to investors and the valuation of those delays. The next issue discussed will be the structure of the remittance from the servicing institution to the guarantor, such as Fannie Mae, and then distribution to the investor.

As described earlier, Fannie Mae has designed the MBS cash flow for as little diversion of the pass-through as possible. On the 18th of each month the lender servicing a pool remits the payoffs of the previous month and the scheduled payments of the current month. The amounts of the payoffs and the scheduled payments are reported to Fannie Mae by the second business day of the month, and a paydown factor on the pool is generally announced by the fifth business day. The paydown factor for the pool tells the investors in that pool how much the remittance due on the 25th of that month will be. Fannie Mae therefore will collect the remittance due it on the 18th and will pass through exactly that amount to the investor on the 25th—a 7-day delay. This process is especially significant for the lender who is both servicing the loans and holding the securities, because the cash will be out of his hands for only 7 days. He will also know that the exact amount collected and passed through to Fannie Mae will be remitted back. Fannie Mae collects its guaranty fee in a separate payment due at the time the accounting report is submitted, on the seventh day of the month.

The value in the simplicity and straightforward nature of the pass through of the MBS is fully appreciated when it is compared with the cash flow modifications of the Freddie Mac PC. The Freddie Mac PC program requires all loan payoffs to be remitted within five business days of receipt. Scheduled principal, if collected, and scheduled interest, whether collected or not, are remitted on the first Tuesday of the month following the month of collection. The reporting cycle is structured from the fifteenth of one month to the fifteenth of the next month; therefore, the reductions reported would represent payoffs from the fifteenth to the fifteenth and scheduled payments due on the first. The paydown factor for each pool is based on the most recent reporting cycle, and is published on the first of every month, representing the balance on the fifteenth of the previous month. The paydown to the investor, based on that published factor, occurs 60 days after the balances are reported to Freddie Mac. The payoffs reflected in the reporting to Freddie Mac may have occurred up to 30 days prior to the report; therefore, the investor receives the remittance on payoffs a minimum of 60 days, and up to 90 days, after the homeowner's payment. Scheduled payments reflected in the reporting are due on the first of that month, and are therefore received by investors up to 75 days after the homeowner's payment.

The servicing institution holds the homeowner's payments for five business days (seven calendar days) on payoffs, and approximately 33 days on scheduled payments. For the servicing institution that also is the investor, the period over which collected payments are out of its hands ranges from 53 to 83 days on loan payoffs and approximately 50 days on scheduled payments.

In all cases, the investor receives interest at the security rate on the outstanding balance up through 45 days prior to the investor's payment; so that while funds may be out of the investor's hands for up to 83 days, the "interest free" period will be 45 days on payoffs and approximately 40 days on scheduled payments.

An institution that swaps loans for use as collateral—for example, in repurchase agreements or structured financings, loses control of its funds for up to 76 days more when using the Freddie Mac PC than when using the Fannie Mae MBS program; it experiences an interest-free period of 33 to 38 days longer.

Of special note, when considering the impact of the lost use of funds on securities held as collateral, is the added effect of the shorter delay to investors. The market price of the collateral, which determines the amount that can be borrowed against that collateral, will reflect the investors' willingness to pay a higher price for the MBS than the alternative Freddie Mac PC. Therefore, the MBS program will provide a higher-priced collateral, allow greater borrowing, and will give the significant cash flow advantages outlined above.

THE SECURITIZATION DECISION

The pass-through mechanisms are by far the most significant differences between the two agency pass-through programs. In order to access these programs, however, the appropriate mortgage loans must be identified and processed according to the program's requirements. Although the pass-through and remittance processes are important, the price effects of choosing the proper loans, achieving the proper marketing and executing the transactioin can overwhelm the pass-through costs and price effects.

Choosing the appropriate program for loan production or portfolio securitization is the first consideration. The type of loan, its payment terms, or adjustment characteristics, must be eligible for the targeted securities programs. Fannie Mae has extended to the MBS program its traditional position of accommodating, rather than restricting, the creativity of the lending industry. This is evidenced by Fannie Mae's flexibility in securitizing a wide range of loan products; these include a number of ARM products, the California Variable Rate Mortgage, Growing Equity Mortgages, FHA/VA loans, 15-year fixed-rate loans, and multifamily loans. The company's five regional offices evaluate the characteristics of these individual loan types and negotiate price accordingly with lenders. All loans must meet the standard underwriting guidelines and statutory loan amount limits.

The next consideration after eligibility is the market for the product being securitized. The value added by the security program relies heavily on the ability to efficiently market the security. For all its major securities products, Fannie Mae has worked to ensure an active and consistent market through the major mortgage-backed securities dealers. The Fannie Mae ARM and VRM programs have redefined the valuation of those products and have provided significant value additions to the loans securitized. The consistency of the 15-year fixed-rate program has generated enough investor acceptance to provide the widest price spread to alternative programs.

After determining the most appropriate program, based on eligibility and market, lenders must consider the processing of the loans into securities. Fannie Mae recognized the importance of processing considerations in the initial design of the MBS and built in streamlined processing to effect the fastest securities issuance. The process begins with approval as an eligible lender, which already is embodied in the approval as a Fannie Mae seller. The appropriate accounts must then be established to hold the principal and interest and tax and insurance balances on the pools. Only one account is necessary for all the pools. A custodial account for holding the mortgage notes and certifying the documents must be established with an eligible institution. Lenders who are federally insured may act as their own document custodian, through proper segregation of responsibilities. When a lender does create a pool, the mortgage notes and assignments are delivered to the custodian and certified on a schedule. The schedule is delivered to Fannie Mae—with instructions on delivery of the securities—and Fannie Mae issues the securities to the Federal Reserve Book-Entry account directly.

Before the pool can be created, the lender must obtain a commitment from Fannie Mae. At the time of commitment, the lender also chooses the servicing option—either servicing with or without recourse on foreclosures. A lender can choose to service *with recourse* on foreclosure, where Fannie Mae will look to the lender to bear the foreclosure costs. Alternatively, the lender can choose to service *without recourse*, where Fannie Mae will cover all costs of any foreclosures. Fannie Mae terms its with-recourse servicing as its regular servicing option and the without-recourse servicing as the special servicing option. Fannie Mae will charge a higher guaranty fee for without-recourse servicing (approximately 5 basis points more than on its standards program).

Commitments can be obtained by either calling Fannie Mae's "open window" commitment line or by negotiating special considerations through the company's regional negotiators. In either case, a fixed commitment dollar amount will be set, with a given period under which to deliver. For negotiated commitments, the amount may be delivered in multiple pools at any point during the commitment period. The standard program offers a six-month optional delivery commitment, for which a commitment fee of .01 percent or $1,000, is charged. Lenders therefore have the flexibility to take down commitments in advance and delivery pools as loans are received.

The process of delivering against the commitment and effecting the security issuance incorporates the most valuable aspect of the Fannie Mae processing enhancements. Fannie Mae has established a centralized processing division, which edits the loan summaries and securities issuance instructions, and, if the pools are clean, sets up the securities for Federal Reserve book entry issuance in eight business days.

The value of this turnaround of mortgage documents to security issuance lies in the ability of mortgage lenders to sell their securities for earlier settlement dates than is otherwise available. The market price for a given security varies with the date of settlement because of the difference between short-term costs of funds and the yield on the security. This difference in price is termed the *cost of carry* for the security between different dates. The cost of carry is generally determined by the market between given settlement dates each month, which are determined by the Public Securities Association as the most convenient date for securities transfer. The cost of carry between one monthly settlement date and the next can be positive or negative. When short-term rates are below long-term rates, the price for the forward month will be lower than the price for the current month. The monthly cost of carry on the MBS ranged from $\frac{1}{4}$ ($\frac{8}{32}$) to $\frac{5}{8}$ ($\frac{20}{32}$) of a point during the first half of 1986.

Sellers of securities who are able to settle earlier—and particularly by the regular settlement of one month versus the next—will realize a higher price than by settling later. The market cost of carry reflects the difference between the short and long term borrowing costs of large dealers and investors. It represents a greater price advantage than most lenders will realize by holding the securities at their own cost of funds. In addition, lenders that originate loans for immediate MBS securitization and sale are able to close the loans and get securities issued quickly, freeing up funds for additional lending and fee generation. Lenders that are using the securities as collateral for borrowing can initiate their borrowing or structured financings more quickly to meet changing market demands.

THE FANNIE MAE ADVANTAGES

As part of the continuing process to streamline and enhance the processing of securities issuance, Fannie Mae has developed a data processing network to improve the quality and delivery of mortgage documents. The network—called MORNET—serves as an electronic message system for Fannie Mae and the mortgage industry. MORNET allows electronic transmission of the data on the Schedule of Mortgages, which is delivered directly to Fannie Mae without any manual processing. The MORNET software for pool submission also offers the lender the opportunity to edit the data in-house prior to transmission, to clear up most of the common data problems that can delay pool issuance. Lenders can also use MORNET to communicate other information to Fannie Mae (such as monthly call-ins of pool balances), communicate with other lenders, or transmit information within their own organization.

The reason for undertaking the process of determining eligibility, obtaining a commitment, and processing loans for securitization is to prepare to sell the securities or pledge them as collateral. Arrangements for disposition of the securities should be a concurrent process with the

creation of the security. Sales of securities can be arranged and executed in advance of settlement, at prices actively quoted and maintained
by the numerous securities dealers involved in the market.

The seller of the security must establish a relationship with a security
dealer, broker, or investor in order to establish the process and limitations under which the security will be sold. Relationships with more
than one dealer expand the opportunities to obtain the best pricing on
various types of securities and in different market conditions. Fannie
Mae assists lenders seeking to sell their MBS in two ways. First, Fannie
Mae has established an 18-member dealer group, composed of securities dealers with proven capabiliteis in the area of mortgage-backed
securities. These dealers are provided information on the program and
allowed to participate in organized sales of securities from Fannie
Mae's portfolio. This support helps the dealers maintain consistent
investor interest in the securities.

Second, Fannie Mae assists sellers directly through its Customer
Service Trading Desk, which buys securities from the seller for resale
to the 18-member selling group. The CSTD acts as a broker to obtain
the best pricing for the seller. Through regular contact and transactions,
it is able to determine which dealers will provide the highest prices.

The program described, from the initial design to current enhancements and operations, is a product of Fannie Mae's overall commitment to, and support of, the market for residential mortgages. Fannie
Mae has been a sustaining force in the market and has pioneered
numerous products and systems that have become industry standards.
Fannie Mae's MBS program is an integral part of offering lenders the
range of options that best suit their needs. Together with Fannie Mae's
ability to purchase a full range of loan products for its own portfolio,
the MBS program allows lenders to build their operations for all their
products around one consistent system. Fannie Mae will continue to
incorporate the accommodation of lender-driven product needs, while
addressing investor concerns. This allows the mortgage industry to
continue reaping the benefits provided by securitization as market
conditions change.

Chapter 15

JOHN B. CROSBY, JR.

John Crosby joined Salomon Brothers as a Vice President in 1982. He has extensive experience in development financing as well as structuring and marketing equity and negotiated debt financings. Prior to joining Salomon, Mr. Crosby worked for Chase Manhattan Bank. He is a graduate of Brown University.

The Securitization of Commercial Mortgages

JOHN B. CROSBY, JR.

The secondary market for residential mortgages is as liquid and efficient as any market for securities traded in the capital markets. At $400 billion, this market compares favorably in size, for example, with corporate and municipal bonds.

A decade ago, however, the market hardly existed. Residential mortgages were originated for institutional portfolios and held there until they matured, prepaid, or defaulted.

In its evolutionary stages, the secondary mortgage market was a misunderstood entity, drawing considerable confusion and skepticism from the investing public. It was the case of a new type of product being offered with no performance history. Investor concern translated into price: Securities backed by the Government National Mortgage Association (better known as Ginne Mae), for example, initially sold at yields about 2½ percentage points higher than comparable term Treasury bonds—despite their government guarantees of timely payment of interest and principal.

Now, the yields on these securities are solely a function of market forces, rather than investor unfamiliarity. After a decade and a half, the secondary residential mortgage market enjoys widespread credibility, and about half of all newly originated fixed-rate mortgages are traded as securities.

To be sure, some thrift institutions, as well as commercial banks, continue to hold fixed-rate residential mortgages. But, for the most part, they pool, securitize, and sell them into the capital markets. They have learned the benefits of maximizing up-front fees and retaining servicing. In essence, they have followed the cue of mortgage bankers who originate for sale.

Today the mortgage markets are again in the developmental stages. This time the goal is to introduce secondary market liquidity to the $600 billion commercial mortgage debt market.

Upon initial observation, the securitization of commercial mortgages might seem implausible. After all, every property is different. There are variances in credit, terms, and location. Commercial mortgages are heterogeneous products in contrast to the homogeneous nature of residential mortgages.

Yet in less than three years, securitized commercial real estate debt has become a market estimated conservatively at $12 billion, with most of the growth occurring over the last 12 to 18 months. Still, in a market that is about the size of the corporate and tax-exempt bond markets, only about three percent of commercial mortgage debt has thus far found its way into the secondary market.

The commercial mortgage market is best viewed along two broad fronts: the issuance of *new debt in securitized form* and the *liquidizing of seasoned commercial loans held in institutional portfolios.*

In the former case, the most important event fueling the market's development has been the issuance of criteria by Standard & Poor's for granting double-A ratings on the financing of high-quality office buildings based solely on the cash flow from those properties. (Criteria have also been established for multifamily properties, although no ratings have been issued.)

S&P ratings represent a major breakthrough because they simultaneously cut financing costs while permitting owners to tap a broader universe of lenders—some of whom would not or could not consider the financing without the assurance of quality that the rating provides.

CHANGES IN TRADITIONAL FUNDING

The advent of ratings, however, is only a catalyst spurring the development of this market. In a broader sense, it is first important to consider the fundamental changes affecting the financing of high-quality commercial real estate and the new advantages the capital markets are offering developers and investors.

In the traditional lending process, commercial banks generally fund construction loans, while savings and loans and insurance companies offer permanent financing. As with residential mortgages a decade ago, it's been primarily a local market activity with loans relegated to portfolios.

In the early 1980s these traditional lenders began confronting volatile interest rates that played havoc with asset-liability management. Even the insurance companies found their largest source of cheap funds, the whole life policy, disappearing as policyholders shifted to universal life and borrowed against their policies and began investing in money market funds at higher rates.

Life insurance companies now depend on selling guaranteed investment contracts (GICs) to pension funds. The process involves "spread banking" the proceeds from these contracts by investing in "bullet" commercial loans at higher rates.

This new source of funds from GICs does not, however, offset other fundamental shifts in the market. One important development is the size of transactions. Inflation in the late 1970s and early 1980s dramatically increased the value of many properties, especially office buildings located in strong markets. As owners have sought to finance or refinance their properties, they have been hindered by single-lender limitations.

The capital markets are better able to address rising values by establishing a multilender system, in which a borrower taps not a single lender, but institutional funds from a wide range of sources. In the process, it is often possible to achieve more favorable costs of financing.

In early 1984, for example, Olympia & York came to Salomon

Brothers to refinance three prime Manhattan office buildings. The solution was to structure and securitize a blanket $970 million first mortgage, cross-collateralized by the three buildings.

This transaction, which has no recourse to the developer, is widely regarded as the beginning of commercial mortgage securitization. However, unlike many of the deals coming to market today, it carries no rating.

No single lender could have financed this nearly $1 billion transaction. Even if the capital were available, no single instituion could have taken that risk.

Olympia & York might have tried to finance each building individually, but even three separate deals of approximately $350 million each would have been a significant strain on the traditional market.

Through the capital markets, the $970 million mortgage was placed originally with over 40 institutions, including thrifts, life insurance companies, commercial banks, real estate investment trusts (REITs), pension funds, and foreign investors. Today, some 70 institutional investors hold participations in these notes that are collateralized by high-quality office buildings.

From the borrower's perspective, the ability, first, to secure large financings, and second, to do so at favorable rates, are two important advantages the capital markets can provide.

Another benefit is the flexibility the capital markets offer in the terms of structuring and placing financing. This has been especially true for the handful of transactions that have earned S&P ratings. Depending on rates, there is the flexibility to launch these issues either domestically or in the Euromarkets.

One rated transaction was a dual Eurobond and domestic private placement, and in two transactions the issuers were able to secure 15-year financing in a market where a traditional single lender would have resisted fixed-rate financing for more than 10 or 12 years.

ADVANTAGES TO LENDERS

On the other side of the equation, institutional investors (many of whom are traditional mortgage lenders) are viewing commercial mortgage-backed bonds as a way of making strong real estate investments at favorable spreads.

Investors have begun to view these securities as an alternative to stocks and corporate and government bonds, as they can be used to restructure portfolios to meet changing conditions.

Commercial mortgage-backed bonds tend to offer high yields (partly as a function of the newness of the instrument), call protection, marketability, and quality.

In the case of double-A rated mortgage-backed bonds, the initial pricing has been 40 to 50 basis points above similarly rated corporates, but substantially below traditional financing costs for less liquid real estate investments. Developers can cut their costs of financing, while investors enjoy higher returns than they can obtain from fixed-income investments of similar credit quality.

At the same time, these securities offer significant call protection. Where corporations can refinance through the sale of equity and residential mortgage securities are subject to prepayment risk, commercial mortgage-backed bonds usually cannot be refinanced at lower interest rates.

In terms of quality, capital markets transacions can offer many originators the opportunity to finance properties with lower credit risk than those usually available for financing in their local markets—and rarely with any loss of yield.

Finally, the capital markets ensure liquidity. An active trading market permits lenders to invest confidently in real estate, knowing that the investment is not relegated to a single portfolio for the life of the loan.

LIQUIDIZING PORTFOLIOS

Commercial mortgage securitization is not limited to the financing of multimillion dollar office buildings. Capital markets technology is also being applied innovatively to pools of seasoned loans, smaller properties, and real estate equity.

Seasoned, high-quality commercial loans can be securitized out of institutional portfolios and sold into the secondary markets. Unlike new debt originations, these so-called "liquification transactions" have their ratings tied directly to the quality of the issuers rather than to the asset.

Most of the issuers have been triple-A rated mutual insurance companies. They have a large supply of loans (some of which remain below market) and the pressing need for asset-liability managment. Their knowledge of real estate makes these issuers quite comfortable about taking the credit risk. In a liquidizing transaction, most often the issuer agrees to replace a nonperforming loan with another in its portfolio that has similar terms and coupon.

The first portfolio securitization for commercial mortgages was a domestic private placement for Penn Mutual Life Insurance Company in late 1984. That was followed by a $1.3 billion transaction in January 1985 for Prudential Insurance Company, which may still be the largest Eurobond offering in history.

Other liquidizing transactions have subsequently been structured for companies such as Massachusetts Mutual, Travelers, and Equitable. For some insurers, the transactions have resulted in planned tax losses. However, the use of current-coupon debt can permit other insurers to book a profit while they use the proceeds to issue new loans.

As of mid-1986, about $8 billion of such transactions have been completed.

SECONDARY MARKET FOR WHOLE LOANS

Portfolio liquidizing is a realistic asset-liability management tool even if the originator's credit quality is below investment grade. Wall Street has begun to liquify pools of loans originated by thrifts and other financial institutions—with recourse only to the assets. While there has always been some trading of whole loans between financial institutions, the establishment of a secondary commercial mortgage market now enables a more systematic approach to liquifying these assets.

A strong secondary market permits the trading and retrading of loans at prices the market establishes based upon an evaluation of mortgage coupons, current mortgage yields, other mortgage terms, and the quality of the mortgage underwriting and the underlying properties. In this case, the due diligence process and loan documentation are paramount, because the commercial mortgages being sold by institutions have neither high credit ratings nor can they be replaced in the event of delinquencies.

The continued expansion of this new market should be enhanced by three important initiatives:

First, there is an effort to develop uniform underwriting criteria to evaluate loans and speed their acceptance in the secondary market. These criteria would be used in underwriting new commercial mortgages.

Second, an advance purchase program is being developed for institutions that are able to originate a larger loan volume than they wish to hold in portfolio. These institutions can originate and close loans according to an investment banker's general specifications, increasing the probability that they will be bought for distribution in the secondary market.

Finally, the rating agencies are working to develop practical standards to rate pools of seasoned commercial mortgages. Various credit enhancement structures are also being designed to secure ratings for individual loans and pools of newly originated commercial mortgages.

APPLYING CAPITAL MARKETS TECHNOLOGY

Beyond the financings already described, securitization can be applied to commercial properties using capital markets tools that were originally developed for stocks and bonds other than real estate. Several of these unique financings have involved smaller properties or even groups of properties.

For example, in 1985 VMS, a large national syndication firm, asked Salomon Brothers to finance an asset VMS had acquired, a $135 million office building leased to the life insurance giant, Cigna. Using capital markets technology, the financing was completed by bifurcating the loan so that it became both a credit transaction and a real estate transaction.

Essentially, Salomon Brothers created two securities for this transaction. The first was a private debt offering in which the Cigna lease payments were passed through to the investors. This note was divided into two pieces (or tranches) with different maturities, hence different coupons, and was priced very close to Cigna's double-A corporate borrowing rate.

To raise the balance of the funds, Salomon Brothers used a zero coupon bond backed only by a first mortgage lien on the property. Zero coupon bonds are sold at a discount, and lenders are repaid interest and principal at the end of a fixed time period.

In this case, the beginning balance of the loan was to grow over 10 years, with the investor being repaid when the property is refinanced or sold at maturity. The risk to the zero coupon investor is minimal, because very low loan to values (both initial and final) were maintained under the most conservative assumptions.

The zero was priced 250 basis points over the comparable term Treasury and was sold to a savings and loan association. Total loan to value for VMS approximated 90 percent, with a coupon 25 basis points better than available bullets at the time. The S&L, in turn, did its own capital markets financing on the zero, creating the zero coupon CD, and then pocketed an attractive spread in the process.

Salomon Brothers also structured the transaction to allow VMS to sell another zero and subordinate to the first, resulting in 100 percent financing. Under conventional methods VMS might have raised $100 to $110 million at most. Instead, this transaction raised $120 million and ultimately allowed for the total $135 million purchase price to be financed.

Several securitized debt transactions executed during the past year or so in the capital markets have involved pooling and cross-collateralizing a number of small properties. This pooling is necessary to create a large enough dollar volume to create liquid secondary "aftermarkets" in which to trade the mortgages.

To finance a portfolio of motels for American Motor Inns, a wholly owned subsidiary of Prime Motor Inns, Salomon Brothers packaged 43 Holiday Inns into one $175 million financing. Individually, the properites might have been too small to finance effectively, or they may have been below credit standards or perhaps in the wrong town. Together the risk profile became much different, spread over a number of properties, cash flows, cities, and states. Investors who would not usually invest in a single hotel could now comfortably invest in 43 diverse assets. For AMI and for the investors, financing costs and yields proved better by selling securities collateralized by the properties than by using traditional executions.

Other similar transactions included the cross-collateralization of 11 Woodward and Lothrop department stores in the Washington, D.C./ Baltimore area, and six neighborhood and community shopping centers in Texas.

Finally, in a unique application of capital markets technology, Salomon Brothers used commercial paper and forward interest rate swaps to help a developer lock in low, fixed-rate financing for the $75 million expansion of a large, successful California shopping center.

By combining the two capital markets tools, the developer was able to obtain construction and permanent financing early in the expansion process. In this instance, the traditional financing alternative, a forward commitment from an insurance company, had dried up. Even if the commitment had been available, the capital markets would have offered lower costs as well as greater flexibility to take advantage of any future downward shift in interest rates. It is expected that the use of these techniques will result in Wall Street's greater involvement in development financing.

APPLICATIONS TO EQUITY

Securitization of commercial real estate is not limited to debt. On the equity side, the formation of REITs in the 1960s served as a vehicle for small investors to own participations in commercial property. From 1969 to 1974, REIT assets grew from $1 billion to $21 billion. Unfortunately, many of those assets were channeled into risky construction loans. When the recession of 1974–75 occurred, many construction projects failed, and many REITs lost most or all of their value. The REITs that survived tended to be of higher quality, focusing on less risky, high-quality equity participations.

During the past two to three years, REIT activity has been revived by a high degree of participation from institutional investors. Changes in the law that favor cash flow and capital appreciation over tax advantages have helped to encourage new investment.

An important change in the equity REIT format has been the development of the finite term REIT, or FRIET as it is sometimes called. With finite term REITs, the properties in the trust must be sold within a specific timeframe, usually 8 to 12 years. This ensures that future shares will trade at a market value based on expected yield to maturity or internal rate of return.

Again, applying capital markets technology can make these investments even more attractive. In some cases, low loan-to-value zero coupon mortgages have been placed on the properties in REIT portfolios.

From the zero investor's standpoint, there is usually high yield and the elimination of prepayment and reinvestment concerns. From the REIT investor's perspective, the zero provides positive leverage and higher current yield based upon the cash flow from the properties because none of the interest on the zero is payable until maturity.

A more recent approach to securitizing real estate equity is the use of *master limited partnerships (MLPs)*, which can offer even higher returns than REITs. They are structured with shorter depreciation schedules. With MLPs, depreciation can be passed through to the investor as a tax-free return of capital.

CONCLUSION

In many respects, the commercial real estate market is, for the most part, where the secondary residential mortgage market was 10 to 15 years ago: highly negotiated; limited access to high-quality properties; and a market characterized by illiquidity, inconsistent documentation, and an absence of standardization and diligent underwriting.

While there will never be the equivalent of government guarantees for mortgages on commercial real estate, the market is beginning to evolve to a degree where developers with high quality properties can find a welcome reception, available funds, and greater flexibility through the capital markets.

At the same time, investors in commercial mortgage-backed instruments are finding that they own securities offering strong yields, diversification, and liquidity—all with no additional credit risk.

As the industry becomes more competitive and the need for financial options continues to rise, Wall Street's ability to marry a borrower with a multitude of lenders in a variety of formats is becoming increasingly important.

In the case of the most exciting new growth area, rated commercial mortgage-backed bonds, the number of transactions will grow as S&P criteria are applied to other property types, as the market expands nationally, as a broader range of ratings are developed, and as other rating agencies come on board. Overall, the potential growth of this market will be limited only by the time it takes new developers and investors to discover and enter it.

Chapter 16

JAMES A. HORNIG

James Hornig is Managing Director with Hunter, Keith, Marshall & Co. He is the founder and director of HKM's mortgage group, which focuses on private placements of fixed rate mortgage assets for thrifts and other financial institutions. Mr. Hornig practiced law for 10 years with a Minneapolis law firm. He is a graduate of Harvard College and received his law degree from the University of Wisconsin.

The Private versus the Public Market for CMOs

JAMES A. HORNIG

The private placement of mortgage debt, including collateralized mortgage obligations (CMOs), mortgage-backed bonds, and pay throughs, represents an attractive alternative to the public market. The private market allows portfolio lenders (thrifts, savings and commercial banks, and insurance companies) with $10–$100 million of mortgage collateral to access the capital markets as their own issuer rather than as part of a multi-issuer conduit. Typically, the cost of a public transaction requires a minimum size of $100 million, thus creating the need to aggregate multiple issuers. Institutions are increasingly using the private market, due to the following benefits:

- Smaller size (typically $10–$100 million);
- Significant cost savings (particularly on an ongoing basis);
- Increased flexibility in terms of both collateral and structure;
- Control over market timing;
- Control over the bond terms.

The private market's primary disadvantage is that investors typically require a slightly higher yield (about 15–25 basis points). This premium has declined significantly as market liquidity has improved. As a result, the premium is often outweighed by cost savings and the other advantages of a private placement.

Probably the most compelling reason for using the private placement market is the significant up-front *and* ongoing cost savings. An example will illustrate this point. Assume a thrift has $45 million of discount collateral and wants to issue a $40 million CMO. Because a $40 million single-issue public offering is uneconomical, the issuer's choice is between a private placement or a public conduit. The example given here in Table 16–1 illustrates the dramatic savings of a private placement. Although costs vary for different conduits, Table 16–1 uses an average cost for comparison.

Although up-front costs appear equal, the issuer should determine if these fees are based on a "discount bond" or a "par bond." Since investment banking fees are based on the bond size and not the money raised, a discount structure effectively increases the fee on the money actually raised. A 10 percent discount, for example, means that an issuance cost for the dollars raised increases 10 percent compared to a par structure. Also, the issuer should focus on what we have termed the "discount adjustment." In a discount structure an institution must amortize the discount over the "expected" life of the bond. Expected life requires the issuer to make a prepayment assumption. If prepayments are greater than assumed, the discount must be amortized earlier, increasing the bond cost.

Ongoing expenses—administrative fees, trustee fees, legal and accounting expenses—are significantly higher because a public conduit involves multiple issuers and investors and is significantly more complex to administer. Administrative costs reflect this difference—the public is typically .08 percent to .125 percent versus .03 percent to .04 percent for the private, a difference of .065 percent per year.

Structural costs are the most significant cost category an issuer should review. Although structural costs are the most significant, they are the most difficulty to analyze.

Typical structural costs are loss of float, a slower bond amortization, and higher reserve requirements. These costs are imposed as a result of different bond payment periods—monthly, quarterly, or semiannually.

Although the issuer remits all principal and interest monthly to the trustee, the trustee may accumulate funds and remit to the investor either quarterly or semiannually. This timing difference between collection and payment creates the higher structural costs.

Lost float is one of the major structural costs in a conduit. Some conduits keep all float, while others return a small part of the earnings, commonly 3 percent. The conduit benefits from the earnings on your money (the ultimate arbitrage). The longer the payment lag, the greater the conduit's gain.

In addition to the lost float, the payment delay increases the bond amortization and therefore increases financing costs. The faster the payment to the investor, the faster the debt will amortize. Just as a biweekly mortgage amortizes more quickly than a monthly pay, a monthly pay bond amortizes more quickly than a semiannual pay bond. Also, elementary finance and common sense dictate that a borrower, faced with the choice of paying off 9.50 percent debt or earning 3 percent interest, would pay off the debt as quickly as possible.

Another structural cost is the higher reserves required by the rating agencies. Since the rating agencies look at worst case scenarios, reserves equal to one full interest payment must be established in order to protect against total prepayments. Since a monthly pay bond does not have this risk, the cost associated with additional reserves is elimimated.

Therefore, the issuer derives a great benefit by minimizing its lag between payments to the trustee and the lender. Taken together, the structural costs between a monthly versus quarterly bond is about 20 basis points, (.20 percent) *on an ongoing basis.* This translates into about 1 full percentage point in price, more than the entire up-front issuance costs.

In addition to significant cost savings, the private placement offers several other advantages:

- Control of market timing
- Control of bond terms and structure
- Greater collateral flexibility

Table 16–1
Cost Comparison for $40 Million CMO
Public Conduit versus Private Placement

1. Upfront Expenses

	Public	Private	Difference
Issuance Costs:	$100,000 (.25)	$100,000 (.25)	– 0 –
Investment Banking Fee:	$270,000 (.675)	$260,000 (.65)	$ 10,000 (.025)
	$370,000 (.925)	$360,000 (.90)	$ 10,000 (.025)
Discount Adjustment	$ 65,200 (.163)	– 0 –	$ 65,200 (.163)
Total	$435,200 (1.088)	$360,000 (.90)	$ 75,200 (.188)

2. Ongoing Expenses (Annual)

	Public	Private	Difference
Administrative Fee:	$ 50,000 (.105)	$ 24,000 (.04)	$ 26,000 (.065)
Structural Costs (Note a):	$ 80,000 (.20)	– 0 –	$ 80,000 (.20)
Total	$130,000 (.305)	$ 24,000 (.04)	$106,000 (.265)
Present Value of the Ongoing Annual Expenses (Note b):	$535,000	$115,000	$420,000

3. Summary

	Public	Private	Difference
Upfront Expenses:	$435,200	$360,000	$ 75,200
Ongoing Expenses:	$595,077	$109,860	$485,217
Total Cost	$1,030,277	$469,860	$560,417
Overall Cost	2.57%	1.17%	1.40%

Notes:

a. The structure of the public conduit imposes an ongoing expense of about 20 basis points on the participants. These structural costs stem from three factors:

(1) Interest rate differential—The public conduits structure their CMO bonds to pay principal and interest quarterly. Hunter, Keith structures its CMO bonds to pay monthly so that the issuer can save the interest rate adjustment. Assuming an average bond equivalent interest rate of 9% on the CMO bonds, the quarterly equivalent interest rate would be 8.901% and the monthly equivalent rate would be 8.836%. Hence, quarterly payments versus monthly payments cost the issuer 6.5 basis points annually.

(2) Lost float—The public conduits retain some or all of the float income that results from receiving payment on the collateral monthly and paying the bondholders quarterly or semiannually.

(3) Efficiency—The monthly payment structure is more efficient than the quarterly payment structure—it raises more dollars from the same collateral pool.

b. Assumes a present value factor of 10% and that the CMO bonds will be retired over 14 years.

Table 16-2
Summary Comparison

	Private Placement	Public Conduit	Public Issue
Number of Issuers	1	Multiple	1
Required Collateral Amount	$10–$100 Million	$5 million per participant $100 million + total	$100 million +
Collateral Type	Mortgage backed securities, whole loans, conforming and nonconforming, commercial, multifamily, vacation properties.	Mortgage backed securities.	Mortgage backed securities, whole loans, conforming and nonconforming, commercial, multifamily, vacation properties.
Control of Market Timing	Issuer	Conduit	Issuer
Control of Structure	Issuer	Conduit	Issuer

Table 16–2 presents a summary comparison of the noncash differences.

As significant as the cost savings may be, the ability to control market timing is an equally compelling reason to consider the private market. The private market allows the issuer to place the bond as soon as the collateral has been reviewed. A public conduit must wait until all collateral is securitized, legal and accounting documents are complete, the rating agencies have reviewed the issue, and the conduit has accumulated sufficient colateral (at least $100 million). Such delays can cause an issuer to miss a favorable market. In volatile markets, any delay can severely penalize an issuer who does not control timing.

Reinvestment timing is tied to issuance timing. Private placements allow the issuers to pick a time when a favorable spread can be achieved. If one uses a conduit, one has limited control over timing. As a result, an issuer may lose attractive reinvestment opportunities while waiting for the conduit to go to market.

Another advantage of the private market is the ability to control the terms of the issue. The importance of the appropriate structure, monthly pay versus quarterly, par versus discount, or matched or mismatched duration, can greatly affect financing costs. As a single issuer, you can tailor bond terms to your collateral pool and your investment and accounting objectives. This capability can reduce financing costs and increase reinvestment profitability.

Finally, the private market allows institutions to use otherwise "unusable" collateral. Most conduits only deal with conforming loans that can be securitized. The private placement market is particularly adapted to utilizing nonconforming products such as second mortgages, jumbo loans, vacation properties, multifamily loans and other nonconforming loans.

For issuers considering a mortgage-backed financing, the private market represents a realistic and flexibile alternative to the public market. Cost, control over timing and terms, and broader collateral choice are the reasons large and small institutions are using the private market. It is a powerful tool that should be understood.

Chapter 17

MARKO ISSEVER
AND
CAROL R. KALIN

Marko Issever is an Associate in the Financial Strategies Group with Prudential Bache Securities. Previously he has held positions with the United Nations in Geneva and with the Investment Department of the World Bank.

Carol Kalin is an Associate with Prudential Global Funding.

The authors gratefully acknowledge the lengthy discussions and editing sessions with Glen Culbertson. They also thank Eve Sladowsky for creating the graphs included in this chapter. The analysis is for illustrative purposes only and should not be relied upon to meet the specific needs of an institution in particular circumstances. Results will differ if different assumptions are made.

Synthetic CMOs via Interest Rate Swaps

MARKO ISSEVER AND CAROL R. KALIN

INTRODUCTION

This analysis demonstrates how a financial institution can use the interest rate swap market to arbitrage mortgage-backed securities and thereby create a "synthetic CMO." The proposed structure would lock in handsome profits for the short and medium term if interest rates rise, as many analysts expect them to do. But a positive arbitrage can be obtained under many other interest rate scenarios, including constant or even moderately declining rates.

In this paper we quantify the expected dollar amount of the arbitrage for variations on the proposed swap structure and for various interest rate scenarios.

Our analysis is particularly useful because it includes the following elements:

- Methodology for the quick and easy creation of a synthetic CMO
- Relation of prepayment behavior to the interest rate environment
- Estimation of a statistical relationship between LIBOR and REPO rates
- Analysis of the effect on the income statement for the first 10 years

- Translation of profits into net interest margin
- Illustration of the duration match/mismatch of maturing swaps and assets by year

Two kinds of investor might be interested in employing this type of structure: one is an institution that already owns mortgage-backed securities and would like to raise funds at attractive rates; the other is an investor who wishes to exploit an arbitrage in the market with controlled risk.

The first type of investor might well be a thrift, seeking funds with which to originate new mortgages. The thrift might consider a CMO, but such an issue involves considerable time and expense, and requires ongoing administration. The synthetic CMO is a straightforward, low-cost alternative.

The second type of investor, the arbitrageur, could be almost any institution with a good understanding of the mortgage-backed securities and swaps markets.

THE BASIC SYNTHETIC CMO STRUCTURE

Like a true collateralized mortgage obligation (CMO), the "synthetic CMO" structure exploits the arbitrage in a positively sloping yield curve. "Plain vanilla" interest rate swaps are put on with different notional principal amounts and maturities, such that at any given time during the life of the synthetic CMO, the sum of remaining notional principal amounts approximates the expected remaining balance of the mortgage-backed securities (MBS). The individual swaps, with their separate principal amounts, maturities and rates, are much like the tranches of a CMO.

The transaction is structured as a classic asset-based swap. The institution purchases an MBS funded by 3-month MBS repurchase agreements (repo) until the MBS either matures or is sold. The cost of funds is therefore the repo rate for the MBS.

If left unhedged, the institution would face serious interest rate risk because rising rates would increase its cost of funds. An interest rate

Figure 17-1

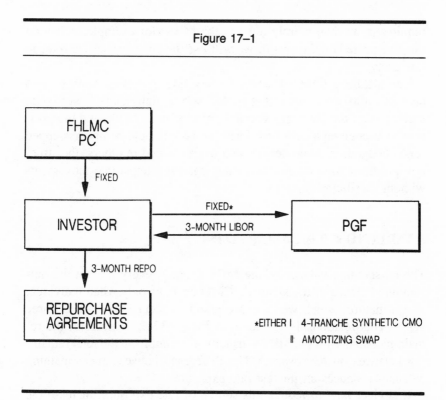

swap can help to reduce this risk. Prudential Global Funding, Inc. (PGF) would pay the 3-month London Interbank Offering Rate (LIBOR) to the institution, and the institution would pay a fixed rate to PGF. The decision choice is diagramed in Figure 17-1.

The synthetic CMO for a generic MBS with an average life of about 7 years could combine, for example, a 3-year, a 5-year, a 7-year and a 10-year swap. Notional principal amounts could be allocated to the four tranches to approximate a cash flow match while maintaining a duration match. This would afford the maximum possible protection against interest rate movements.

For a synthetic CMO, the party who repos the MBS is analogous to the issuer of a true CMO. Although "issuing" the synthetic CMO requires more than merely repoing the MBS (for example, collateral must be posted on the swap), we will use the term "issuer" to refer to this party.

The synthetic CMO structure is very liquid. Should interest rates take an unfavorable turn (that is, fall substantially), the issuer could easily assign the swap or execute a reverse swap to unwind the position. Although on a cash flow basis the issuer could be underswapped (underhedged) in some periods and overswapped in others, the structure provides good overall protection against interest rate movements without sacrificing liquidity.

A VARIATION: THE AMORTIZING SWAP

The outstanding balance of the MBS declines every month; the outstanding balance of the synthetic CMO declines only when individual swaps mature, which we have presumed to occur every two or three years. This relationship is shown in Figure 17–2. Therefore, the remaining balance on the MBS is usually different from the total remaining balances on the swaps.* The difference between the remaining balances produces an interest rate exposure.

It is clear how to reduce this source of rate exposure: increase the number of tranches. If a separate swap is put on for each of the 120 months of a 10-year period such that for any given month the scheduled principal paydown plus the unscheduled (but expected) principal prepayment for the MBS matches the motional principal due for the swap, then the differences in the remaining balances will be eliminated.

As a practical matter, setting up 120 different swaps is probably unworkable. But the effective interest rate on the various notional principals can be expressed on an internal rate of return basis by a single rate applied to a declining monthly balance. Because PGF as a swap counterparty can accommodate either type of payment, the equiv-

---

*In Figure 17–2 the sum of remaining balances in the synthetic CMO is always less than the expected principal outstanding of the MBS. This happens because the notional principal on the fourth tranche is intentionally reduced to achieve a duration match at the beginning.

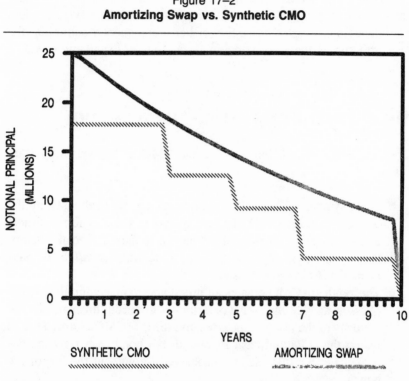

Figure 17–2
Amortizing Swap vs. Synthetic CMO

alent, single-rate strategy can be put into place instead of the 120-rate strategy. This amortizing swap is really a synthetic CMO with the maximum possible number of tranches and a single-rate structure on a declining balance that substitutes for the series of individual swaps.

Because the amortizing swap agreement would be highly illiquid, the institution would pay a premium. This would raise the all in cost of funding, but the result may still be cheaper than a three- or four-tranche structure, depending on the specifics of the deal.

If the prepayment assumptions turn out to be accurate, then the amoritizing swap would better control interest rate risk than would a synthetic CMO with only a few tranches. This advantage may more than offset the higher fixed-rate swap payments. However, the less confidence the investor has in his or her prepayment assumption, the less attractive is the amortizing swap relative to a synthetic CMO.

THE SYNTHETIC CMO VERSUS THE TRUE CMO

The synthetic CMO differs from a true CMO in two very important ways:

- For a synthetic CMO, the prepayment risk is warehoused by the issuer. For a true CMO, the prepayment risk is transferred almost entirely to the purchasers of the bonds. In fact, if special redemption is allowed at any time, the true CMO transfers *all* the prepayment risk to the bondholders.
- The synthetic CMO creates an initial approximate duration match of assets and liabilities that deteriorates to serious mismatch by the maturity of the last tranche. Because the true CMO is structured to match the collateral cash flow with the bond cash flow, an approximate duration match is achieved throughout the life of the bonds.

In a true CMO, an option against the prepayment risk is paid for by an acceptance of proceeds in general, substantially below the market value of the collateral—at least three points, and usually more. The residuals repay the issuer for the option, with a premium if rates behave reasonably. If rates are mildly unfavorable, the residuals will still probably return the cost of the option, if not some excess. If rates are very unfavorable, the residuals will still return most of the cost of the option.

In general, therefore, the synthetic CMO is a more risky method of financing than is the true CMO because the warehousing of the prepayment risk creates an exposure to a decline in interest rates.

THE CASE STUDY

The Mortgage-Backed Security

An investor buys a generic FHLMC PC with a coupon of 9.5 percent that was trading at 99⅞ on February 28, 1986. This security has a quoted yield of 9.35 percent based on a 12-year prepaid life, and a cash flow yield of 9.28 percent based on the last three months' constant prepayment rate (CPR) of 9.1 percent. The weighted average maturity, average life, and duration of this generic FHLMC PC is 22 years, 9 months; 7 years, 7 months; and 4 years, 10 months, respectively. Figure 17–3 tracks the expected amortization schedule for this FHLMC.

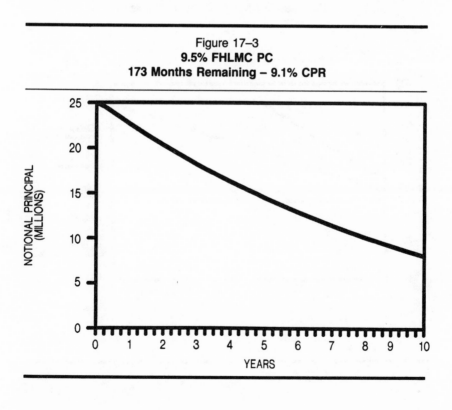

Figure 17–3
9.5% FHLMC PC
173 Months Remaining – 9.1% CPR

Interest Rate Scenarios

We consider seven different interest rate scenarios: one constant, three rising, and three falling. Rates are assumed to fall no more than 300 basis points or to rise no more than 500 basis points from a starting level of 7⅜ percent. The various rising (falling) scenarios differ in how fast rates rise (fall) over a 10-year period. These scenarios are given in Figure 17–4.

Figure 17–4
Rate Scenarios
Cumulative Change in Basis Points

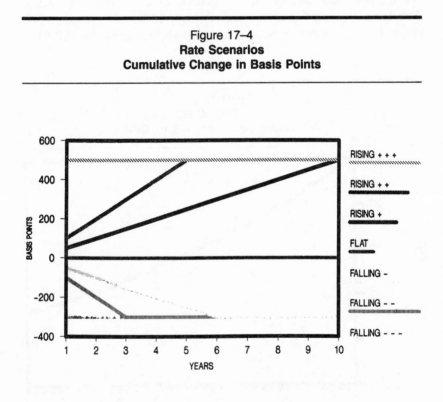

We assume that short-term rates and long-term rates fluctuate in parallel shifts: for example, a 100 basis point drop in 3-month LIBOR is accompanied by a 100 basis point drop in long-term rates, including mortgage origination rates.

Relationship of Interest Rates to Prepayments

Whatever the rate scenario, the crux of the problem is the relation of interest rate scenarios to prepayment rates. Figure 17–5 shows the probability distribution for five prepayment rates (2 percent CPR to 40 percent CPR) under each interest rate scenario. These assumptions are arbitrary and are based solely on a subjective evaluation of historical mortgage prepayment rates.

LIBOR versus Repo

The investor's cost of funds is assumed to be the FHLMC repo rate. We used instead the GNMA repo rates from the Data Resources, Inc. database. The spread between the FHLMC repo Rate and the GNMA repo rate is negligible.

Figure 17–6 displays the quarterly average for both repo and LIBOR rates from the second quarter of 1981 to the last quarter of 1985. LIBOR was always above repo during this time, with spreads usually between 10 and 30 basis points. Because the investor will be funding at repo and receiving LIBOR, there is an almost certain positive spread to be earned on the floating rate side of the interest rate swap. This is in addition to the yield pickup on the high-coupon FHLMC PCs (relative to the fixed-rate swap payments). Future repo rates were estimated by fitting a regression line between repo and LIBOR rates for the historical data in Figure 17–6 and applying the resulting equation to forward LIBOR rates.

Figure 17-5

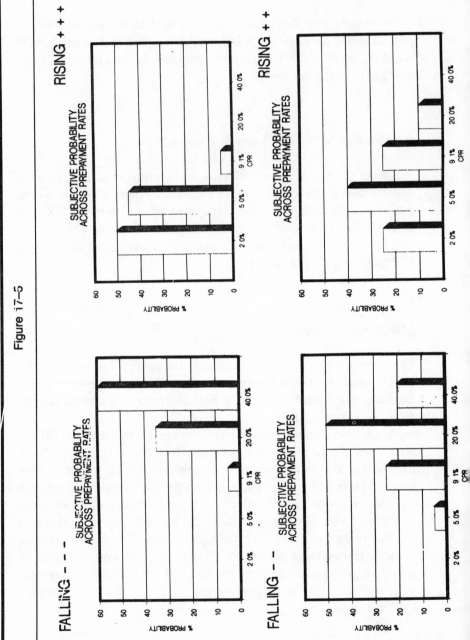

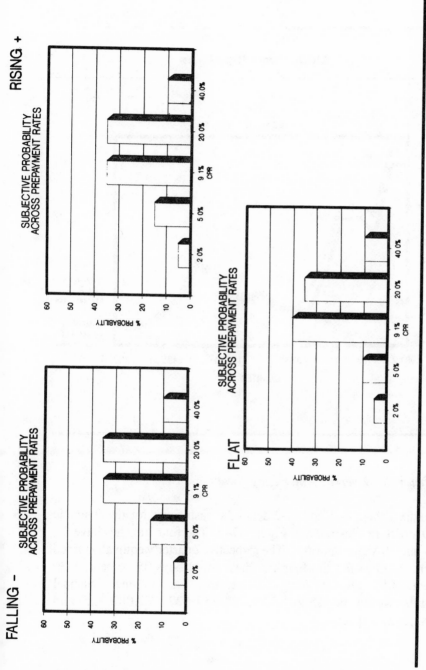

Figure 17–6
LIBOR verses Repo Rates

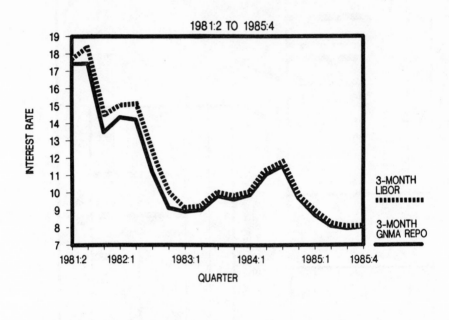

Synthetic CMO versus Amortizing Swap

Appendix Tables A–1 and A–2 detail the cash flows for the synthetic CMO structure illustrated in Figure 17–2. The four tranches have 3-, 5-, 7- and 10-year maturities. The respective quarterly equivalent fixed percentage rates for the four tranches would be 8.05 percent, 8.30 percent, 8.55 percent, and 8.69 percent. The notional principal amounts would be $5,201,718, $3,359,527, $5,082,335 and $4,082,502, respectively:

Maturity (Years)	Notional Principal ($)	Rate (%)
3	5,201,718	8.05
5	3,359,527	8.30
7	5,082,335	8.55
10	4,082,502	8.69

Had the four-tranche swap been done on a straight cash flow matched basis, the issuer would be underswapped part of the time and overswapped at other times. However, the notional principal for the fourth tranche was reduced from the cash flow matched amount in order to maintain a duration match. Therefore, the total remaining swap notionals for the synthetic CMO are always lower than the remaining notionals for the amortizing swap.

If an amortizing swap is structured with an 8.65 percent fixed rate, then the investor would be "precisely" swapped throughout all 10 years. If the expected prepayment rate that serves as the basis for the deal is confirmed by subsequent experience, then this structure would turn higher arbitrage profits than would the synthetic CMO.

RESULTS

Overall Arbitrage Analysis

The expected value of a deal done at 9.1 percent CPR (the last three months' CPR of the FHLMC PC) is the summation of the investor's profit/(loss) if each of the five CPR rates were to actually be observed, multiplied by the assigned probabilities for each CPR rate.

Table 17–1 shows the investor's expected profit/(loss) across the seven rate scenarios for a 4-tranche synthetic CMO versus no swap (pure speculation) for each of two strategies: holding the MBS to maturity or selling the MBS at the expiration of the swaps.

The 4-tranche synthetic CMO, coupled with continued holding of

Table 17–1
Overall Expected Arbitrage Value

Rate Scenarios	MBS Held to Maturity		MBS Sold at Expiration of Swaps	
	Synthetic CMO ($)	No Swap ($)	Synthetic CMO ($)	No Swap ($)
Falling – – –	(554,718)	2,647,550	(623,349)	2,578,918
Falling – –	1,192,951	3,855,312	955,997	3,618,357
Falling –	2,434,036	4,527,755	2,020,457	4,114,176
Flat	1,578,272	2,493,249	1,309,087	2,224,063
Rising +	878,485	693,738	821,900	637,154
Rising + +	361,999	(607,401)	206,109	(763,290)
Rising + + +	(225,544)	(2,375,427)	(473,571)	(92,623,454)

the MBS after expiration of the swaps, results in a $0.4 million profit for the "rising + +" rate scenario (100 basis points over five years). The naked, no-swap position results in a $0.6 million loss. In fact, the swap results in profits for all rate scenarios except for the two extreme cases. The expected losses in a dramatically increasing rate scenario are $0.2 million versus $2.4 million.

While we do not take a view on the future course of interest rates, as of mid-1986 many economists believe rates will either stay moderately flat or rise. The synthetic CMO is most advantageous in such an environment.

Expected Net Interest Margins

Finally, we analyze the effect of rate fluctuations on the expected net interest margins for the first 10 years.

The effects discussed in relation to Table 17–1 are shown again in Table 17–2. Rising rates are devastating for the naked, no swap position.

Table 17-2
Expected Net Interest Margins
(In Basis Points)

| | Synthetic CMO Rate Scenario | | | | | | | No Swap Rate Scenario | | | | | | |
| | Rising | | | Flat | | Falling | | Rising | | | Flat | | Falling | |
Years	+++	++	+	0	−	−−	−−−	+++	++	+	0	−	−−	−−−
1	87	83	70	70	70	62	44	152	148	135	135	135	127	110
2	65	134	126	128	131	111	22	(231)	135	168	212	257	290	430
3	81	125	124	114	106	45	(154)	(231)	44	126	214	303	379	435
4	(7)	69	110	121	135	67	(169)	(231)	(48)	82	215	349	469	440
5	5	56	117	108	102	(19)	(398)	(231)	(139)	38	216	396	472	444
6	(52)	(26)	92	119	149	31	(403)	(231)	(230)	(6)	217	441	474	449
7	(41)	(9)	107	105	109	(56)	(681)	(231)	(230)	(51)	217	487	475	452
8	(143)	(126)	3	157	292	189	(219)	(231)	(230)	(96)	218	488	476	455
9	(137)	(117)	(2)	148	266	136	(415)	(231)	(230)	(140)	218	488	477	458
10	(131)	(107)	1	139	236	73	(659)	(231)	(230)	(185)	218	488	477	459

For the 4-tranche synthetic CMO under the moderate "rising + +" rate scenario (100 basis points over five years), Table 17–2 shows that an initial 83 basis point net profit with the swap will drop over 10 years to a loss of 107 basis points. Without a swap, the 148 basis point advantage in the beginnning erodes to a loss of 230 basis points.

Duration Considerations

Appendix Tables A–8 through A–21 show the expected dynamic durations for ten years. Because the mortgage is a long-term asset, the duration gap widens as the swaps mature. Rebalancing is necessary in order to be relatively matched throughout. Rebalancing could involve entering into appropriate new swaps or taking futures positions during the term of the initial swaps.

APPENDIX

Tables A–3 through A–7 and Figures A–1 through A–6 show the arbitrage profit/(loss) in dollars for the 4-tranche synthetic CMO, the amoritizing swap, and no swap (pure speculation). For each of these structures, results are given first for an MBS held to maturity, followed by an MBS sold at the expiration of the swap(s).

The swap structures are chosen based on an expected prepayment rate of 9.1 percent CPR. The cost of funds or repo rate is calculated from an initial LIBOR rate of 7⅜ percent as:

$$REPO = .16\% + 94.8\% \times LIBOR$$

The first column of each table labels the interest rate scenario. The next five columns show the net present value of the structure across five prepayment rates ranging from 2 percent CPR to 40 percent CPR. For example, in Table A–3, a profit of $7,882,455 results if the MBS prepays at only 2 percent CPR under the "falling − − −" interest rate scenario, and a loss of $1,560,110 if the MBS prepayment increases to 40 percent CPR.

The statistical analysis of these results begins with the column marked Expected Value. In Table A–3, a loss of $554,718 under the falling – – – " interest rate scenario was calculated using the probabilities assigned in Figure A–5 to the results across the five prepayment rates:

$$7,882,455 \times 0\% + \ldots + 1,560,110 \times 60\% = (554,718)$$

Finally, column 7 gives the standard deviation for the expected value in column 6, while the last four columns give the dollar profit (loss) at the lower and upper bounds for one standard deviation (a 68% confidence interval) and two standard deviations (a 95% confidence interval). The statistical analysis is also presented in graphic form following each table.

Table A–1
Cumulative Effect of 4-Tranche Synthetic CMO

3 Year		8.05%	
5 Year		8.30%	
7 Year		8.55%	
10 Year		8.69%	

Date	Principal Balance	Principal Cash Flow	Interest Cash Flow	Total Cash Flow
01–Apr–86	(17,726,082)	17,726,082	0	17,726,082
01–Jul–86	(17,726,082)	0	(246,956)	(246,956)
01–Oct–86	(17,726,082)	0	(371,722)	(371,722)
01–Jan–87	(17,726,082)	0	(371,722)	(371,722)
01–Apr–87	(17,726,082)	0	(371,722)	(371,722)
01–Jul–87	(17,726,082)	0	(371,722)	(371,722)
01–Oct–87	(17,726,082)	0	(371,722)	(371,722)
01–Jan–88	(17,726,082)	0	(371,722)	(371,722)
01–Apr–88	(17,726,082)	0	(371,722)	(371,722)
01–Jul–88	(17,726,082)	0	(371,722)	(371,722)
01–Oct–88	(17,726,082)	0	(371,722)	(371,722)
01–Jan–89	(17,726,082)	0	(371,722)	(371,722)
01–Apr–89	(12,524,364)	(5,201,718)	(371,722)	(5,573,440)
01–Jul–89	(12,524,364)	0	(267,037)	(267,037)
01–Oct–89	(12,524,364)	0	(267,037)	(267,037)
01–Jan–90	(12,524,364)	0	(267,037)	(267,037)
01–Apr–90	(12,524,364)	0	(267,037)	(267,037)
01–Jul–90	(12,524,364)	0	(267,037)	(267,037)
01–Oct–90	(12,524,364)	0	(267,037)	(267,037)
01–Jan–91	(12,524,364)	0	(267,037)	(267,037)
01–Apr–91	(9,164,837)	(3,359,527)	(267,037)	(3,626,564)
01–Jul–91	(9,164,837)	0	(197,327)	(197,327)
01–Oct–91	(9,164,837)	0	(197,327)	(197,327)
01–Jan–92	(9,164,837)	0	(197,327)	(197,327)
01–Apr–92	(9,164,837)	0	(197,327)	(197,327)
01–Jul–92	(9,164,837)	0	(197,327)	(197,327)
01–Oct–92	(9,164,837)	0	(197,327)	(197,327)
01–Jan–93	(9,164,837)	0	(197,327)	(197,327)

Table A–1 (continued)
Cumulative Effect of 4-Tranche Synthetic CMO

Date	Principal Balance	Principal Cash Flow	Interest Cash Flow	Total Cash Flow
01–Apr–93	(4,082,502)	(5,082,335)	(197,327)	(5,279,662)
01–Jul–93	(4,082,502)	0	(88,692)	(88,692)
01–Oct–93	(4,082,502)	0	(88,692)	(88,692)
01–Jan–94	(4,082,502)	0	(88,692)	(88,692)
01–Apr–94	(4,082,502)	0	(88,692)	(88,692)
01–Jul–94	(4,082,502)	0	(88,692)	(88,692)
01–Oct–94	(4,082,502)	0	(88,692)	(88,692)
01–Jan–95	(4,082,502)	0	(88,692)	(88,692)
01–Apr–95	(4,082,502)	0	(88,692)	(88,692)
01–Jul–95	(4,082,502)	0	(88,692)	(88,692)
01–Oct–95	(4,082,502)	0	(88,692)	(88,692)
01–Jan–96	(4,082,502)	0	(88,692)	(88,692)
01–Apr–96	0	(4,082,502)	(88,692)	(4,171,194)

Table A–2
Effect of Amortizing Swap at 8.65%

Year	Date	Principal Balance	Principal Cash Flow	Interest Cash Flow	Total Cash Flow
0.00	01–Apr–86	(25,000,000)	25,000,000	0	25,000,000
0.25	01–Jul–86	(24,557,921)	(442,079)	(359,198)	(801,277)
0.50	01–Oct–86	(23,907,782)	(650,139)	(526,441)	(1,176,580)
0.75	01–Jan–87	(23,272,893)	(634,889)	(512,490)	(1,147,379)
1.00	01–Apr–87	(22,652,894)	(619,999)	(498,866)	(1,118,865)
1.25	01–Jul–87	(22,047,434)	(605,460)	(485,562)	(1,091,022)
1.50	01–Oct–87	(21,456,170)	(591,264)	(472,569)	(1,063,833)
1.75	01–Jan–88	(20,878,768)	(577,402)	(459,882)	(1,037,284)
2.00	01–Apr–88	(20,314,900)	(563,868)	(447,491)	(1,011,359)
2.25	01–Jul–88	(19,764,248)	(550,652)	(435,391)	(986,043)
2.50	01–Oct–88	(19,226,500)	(537,748)	(423,575)	(961,323)

Table A–2 (continued)
Effect of Amortizing Swap at 8.65%

Year	Date	Principal Balance	Principal Cash Flow	Interest Cash Flow	Total Cash Flow
2.75	01–Jan–89	(18,701,352)	(525,148)	(412,036)	(937,184)
3.00	01–Apr–89	(18,188,506)	(512,846)	(400,767)	(913,612)
3.25	01–Jul–89	(17,687,673)	(500,833)	(389,761)	(890,594)
3.50	01–Oct–89	(17,198,570)	(489,103)	(379,014)	(868,117)
3.75	01–Jan–90	(16,720,920)	(477,650)	(368,519)	(846,169)
4.00	01–Apr–90	(16,254,452)	(466,468)	(358,269)	(824,736)
4.25	01–Jul–90	(15,798,904)	(455,548)	(348,259)	(803,807)
4.50	01–Oct–90	(15,354,017)	(444,887)	(338,483)	(783,370)
4.75	01–Jan–91	(14,919,541)	(434,476)	(328,936)	(763,412)
5.00	01–Apr–91	(14,495,230)	(424,311)	(319,613)	(743,924)
5.25	01–Jul–91	(14,080,844)	(414,386)	(310,507)	(724,893)
5.50	01–Oct–91	(13,676,149)	(404,695)	(301,615)	(706,310)
5.75	01–Jan–92	(13,280,917)	(395,232)	(292,931)	(688,163)
6.00	01–Apr–92	(12,894,925)	(385,992)	(284,449)	(670,442)
6.25	01–Jul–92	(12,517,955)	(376,971)	(276,166)	(653,137)
6.50	01–Oct–92	(12,149,793)	(368,161)	(268,977)	(636,238)
6.75	01–Jan–93	(11,790,233)	(359,560)	(260,176)	(619,736)
7.00	01–Apr–93	(11,439,071)	(351,162)	(252,460)	(603,622)
7.25	01–Jul–93	(11,096,110)	(342,961)	(244,925)	(587,886)
7.50	01–Oct–93	(10,761,156)	(334,954)	(237,565)	(572,519)
7.75	01–Jan–94	(10,434,020)	(327,136)	(230,377)	(557,513)
8.00	01–Apr–94	(10,114,518)	(319,502)	(223,357)	(542,859)
8.25	01–Jul–94	(9,802,471)	(312,048)	(216,500)	(528,548)
8.50	01–Oct–94	(9,497,701)	(304,770)	(209,804)	(514,574)
8.75	01–Jan–95	(9,200,038)	(297,663)	(203,264)	(500,927)
9.00	01–Apr–95	(8,909,313)	(290,724)	(196,876)	(487,600)
9.25	01–Jul–95	(8,625,364)	(283,949)	(190,637)	(474,586)
9.50	01–Oct–95	(8,348,031)	(277,333)	(184,544)	(461,877)
9.75	01–Jan–96	(8,077,157)	(270,874)	(178,592)	(449,446)
10.00	01–Apr–96	0	(8,077,157)	(172,779)	(8,249,936)

Table A–3
Detailed Arbitrage Analysis
Profit/Loss in $
4-Tranche Synthetic CMO
MBS Held to Maturity

Table B1

SWAP RATES:	3 YEAR 8.05%	5 YEAR 8.3%	7 YEAR 8.55%	10 YEAR 8.69%

CPR	2.00%	5.00%	9.10%	20.00%	40.00%	EXPECTED VALUE	STANDARD DEVIATION	68.00% CONFIDENCE INTERVAL LO	68.00% CONFIDENCE INTERVAL HI	95.00% CONFIDENCE INTERVAL LO	95.00% CONFIDENCE INTERVAL HI
RATE SCENARIOS											
FALLING ---	7,882,455	5,736,918	3,634,381	570,370	(1,560,110)	(554,718)	1,388,148	(1,942,865)	833,430	(3,331,013)	2,221,577
FALLING --	7,560,776	5,503,383	3,497,074	611,994	(1,312,417)	1,192,951	1,918,428	(725,477)	3,111,380	(2,643,905)	5,029,808
FALLING -	7,051,516	5,144,601	3,302,051	708,870	(940,522)	2,434,036	2,147,620	286,416	4,581,656	(1,861,204)	6,729,276
FLAT	3,573,245	2,811,355	2,044,273	867,617	(29,006)	1,578,272	934,346	643,926	2,512,618	(290,420)	3,446,964
RISING+	466,368	705,980	896,120	1,011,426	816,280	878,485	140,133	738,352	1,018,617	598,219	1,158,750
RISING++	(136,387)	273,653	669,486	1,192,625	1,380,618	361,999	397,303	(35,305)	759,302	(432,608)	1,156,606
RISING+++	(492,846)	(8,528)	494,335	1,302,112	1,930,807	(225,544)	287,802	(513,346)	62,258	(801,147)	350,060

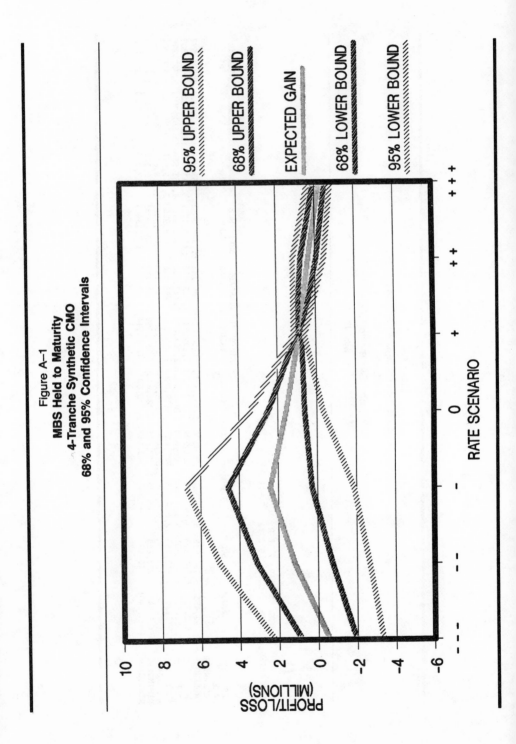

Figure A–1
MBS Held to Maturity
4-Tranche Synthetic CMO
68% and 95% Confidence Intervals

Table A-4
Detailed Arbitrage Analysis
Profit/Loss in $
4-Tranche Synthetic CMO
MBS Sold at Expiration of Swap

Table B2

| SWAP RATES: | 3 YEAR 8.05% | 5 YEAR 8.3% | 7 YEAR 8.55% | 10 YEAR 8.69% |

CPR RATE SCENARIOS	2.00%	5.00%	9.10%	20.00%	40.00%	EXPECTED VALUE	STANDARD DEVIATION	68.00% CONFIDENCE INTERVAL LO	68.00% CONFIDENCE INTERVAL HI	95.00% CONFIDENCE INTERVAL LO	95.00% CONFIDENCE INTERVAL HI
FALLING ---	6,258,884	4,686,862	3,060,466	462,116	(1,563,521)	(623,349)	1,273,287	(1,896,636)	649,938	(3,169,924)	1,923,226
FALLING --	6,025,575	4,510,763	2,954,757	509,792	(1,315,633)	955,997	1,661,983	(705,987)	2,617,980	(2,367,970)	4,279,963
FALLING -	5,644,262	4,235,140	2,805,480	615,431	(943,457)	2,020,457	1,782,534	237,924	3,802,991	(1,544,610)	5,585,524
FLAT	2,631,854	2,195,182	1,702,173	800,654	(31,220)	1,309,087	705,640	603,447	2,014,727	(102,193)	2,720,366
RISING+	289,855	586,100	826,368	996,264	815,709	821,900	182,059	639,840	1,003,959	457,781	1,186,019
RISING++	(385,719)	105,533	572,527	1,171,938	1,379,856	206,109	467,397	(261,287)	673,506	(728,684)	1,140,902
RISING+++	(794,651)	(211,409)	377,772	1,277,444	1,929,906	(473,571)	344,548	(818,119)	(129,022)	(1,162,667)	215,526

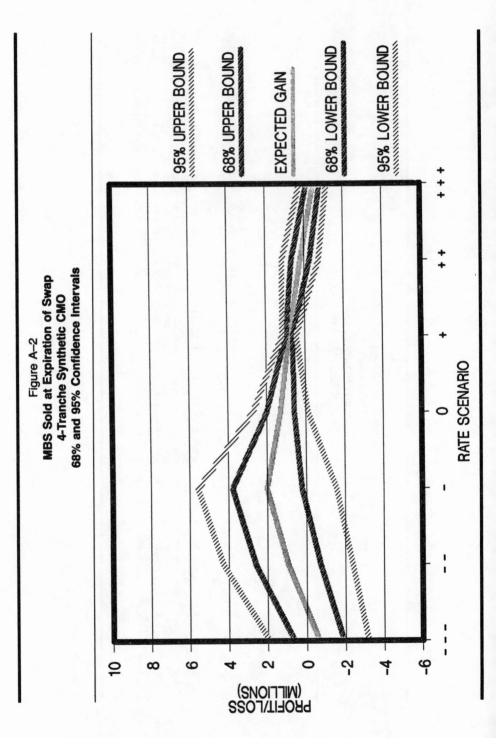

Figure A–2
MBS Sold at Expiration of Swap
4-Tranche Synthetic CMO
68% and 95% Confidence Intervals

95% UPPER BOUND

68% UPPER BOUND

EXPECTED GAIN

68% LOWER BOUND

95% LOWER BOUND

PROFIT/LOSS (MILLIONS)

RATE SCENARIO

Table A-5
Detailed Arbitrage Analysis
Profit/Loss in $
Amortizing Swap
MBS Held to Maturity

Table B3   PROFIT/LOSS

SWAP RATE: 8.65%

CPR RATE SCENARIOS	2.00%	5.00%	9.10%	20.00%	40.00%	EXPECTED VALUE	STANDARD DEVIATION	68.00% CONFIDENCE INTERVAL LO	68.00% CONFIDENCE INTERVAL HI	95.00% CONFIDENCE INTERVAL LO	95.00% CONFIDENCE INTERVAL HI
FALLING ---	6,460,996	4,315,459	2,212,921	(851,089)	(2,981,570)	(1,976,177)	1,388,148	(3,364,324)	(588,029)	(4,752,472)	800,118
FALLING --	6,254,626	4,197,233	2,190,924	(694,156)	(2,618,567)	(113,199)	1,918,428	(2,031,627)	1,805,229	(3,950,055)	3,723,658
FALLING -	5,908,387	4,001,472	2,158,922	(434,259)	(2,083,651)	1,290,907	2,147,620	(856,713)	3,438,527	(3,004,333)	5,586,147
FLAT	3,043,563	2,281,673	1,514,591	337,935	(558,687)	1,048,591	934,346	114,245	1,982,937	(820,102)	2,917,283
RISING+	515,691	755,302	945,443	1,060,748	865,602	927,807	140,133	787,674	1,067,940	647,542	1,208,072
RISING++	190,054	600,094	995,927	1,519,065	1,707,059	688,439	397,303	291,136	1,085,743	(106,168)	1,483,046
RISING+++	45,989	530,308	1,033,171	1,840,947	2,469,642	313,291	287,802	25,490	601,093	(262,312)	888,895

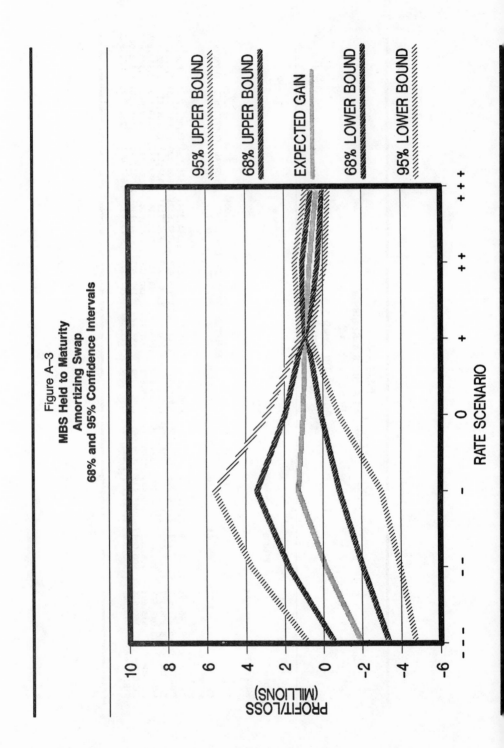

Figure A–3
MBS Held to Maturity
Amortizing Swap
68% and 95% Confidence Intervals

95% UPPER BOUND

68% UPPER BOUND

EXPECTED GAIN

68% LOWER BOUND

95% LOWER BOUND

RATE SCENARIO

PROFIT/LOSS
(MILLIONS)

Table A-6
Detailed Arbitrage Analysis
Profit/Loss in $
Amortizing Swap
MBS Sold at Expiration of Swap

Table B4   PROFIT/LOSS

SWAP RATE :   8.65%

CPR RATE SCENARIOS	2.00%	5.00%	9.10%	20.00%	40.00%	EXPECTED VALUE	STANDARD DEVIATION	68.00% CONFIDENCE LO	INTERVAL HI	95.00% CONFIDENCE LO	INTERVAL HI
FALLING ---	4,837,425	3,265,402	1,639,007	(959,344)	(2,984,981)	(2,044,808)	1,273,287	(3,318,096)	(771,521)	(4,591,383)	501,766
FALLING --	4,719,425	3,204,613	1,648,607	(796,358)	(2,621,783)	(350,154)	1,661,983	(2,012,137)	1,311,830	(3,674,120)	2,973,813
FALLING -	4,501,132	3,092,011	1,662,351	(527,699)	(2,086,586)	877,328	1,782,534	(905,206)	2,659,861	(2,687,739)	4,442,395
FLAT	2,102,173	1,665,500	1,172,491	270,972	(560,902)	779,405	705,640	73,765	1,485,045	(631,874)	2,190,685
RISING+	339,177	635,423	875,690	1,045,586	865,031	871,222	182,059	689,163	1,053,282	507,103	1,235,341
RISING++	(59,278)	431,974	898,968	1,498,379	1,706,296	532,550	467,397	65,153	999,946	(402,243)	1,467,343
RISING+++	(255,816)	327,427	916,607	1,816,280	2,468,741	65,265	344,548	(279,284)	409,813	(623,832)	754,361

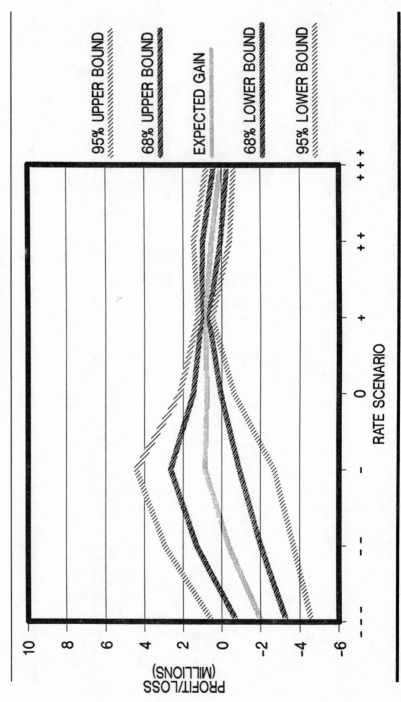

Figure A–4
MBS Sold at Expiration of Swap
Amortizing Swap
68% and 95% Confidence Intervals

95% UPPER BOUND

68% UPPER BOUND

EXPECTED GAIN

68% LOWER BOUND

95% LOWER BOUND

PROFIT/LOSS
(MILLIONS)

10
8
6
4
2
0
-2
-4
-6

RATE SCENARIO

- - -   - -   -   0   +   + +   + + +

Table B5

Table A-7
Detailed Arbitrage Analysis
Profit/Loss in $
No Swap, Pure Speculation
MBS Held to Maturity

CPR RATE SCENARIOS	2.00%	5.00%	9.10%	20.00%	40.00%	EXPECTED VALUE	STANDARD DEVIATION	68.00% CONFIDENCE INTERVAL LO	INTERVAL HI	95.00% CONFIDENCE INTERVAL LO	INTERVAL HI
FALLING ---	11,084,723	8,939,185	6,836,648	3,772,637	1,642,157	2,647,550	1,388,148	1,259,402	4,035,697	(128,745)	5,423,845
FALLING --	10,223,136	8,165,743	6,159,435	3,274,354	1,349,943	3,855,312	1,918,428	1,936,883	5,773,740	18,455	7,692,168
FALLING -	9,145,234	7,238,320	5,395,769	2,802,588	1,153,196	4,527,755	2,147,620	2,380,135	6,675,375	232,515	8,822,995
FLAT	4,488,221	3,726,331	2,959,249	1,782,593	885,971	2,493,249	934,346	1,558,902	3,427,595	624,556	4,361,941
RISING+	281,622	521,234	711,374	826,680	631,534	693,738	140,133	553,606	833,871	413,473	974,004
RISING++	(1,105,786)	(695,746)	(299,913)	223,225	411,219	(607,401)	397,303	(1,004,704)	(210,097)	(1,402,008)	187,206
RISING+++	(2,642,730)	(2,158,411)	(1,655,548)	(847,772)	(219,077)	(2,375,427)	287,802	(2,663,229)	(2,087,626)	(2,951,031)	(1,799,824)

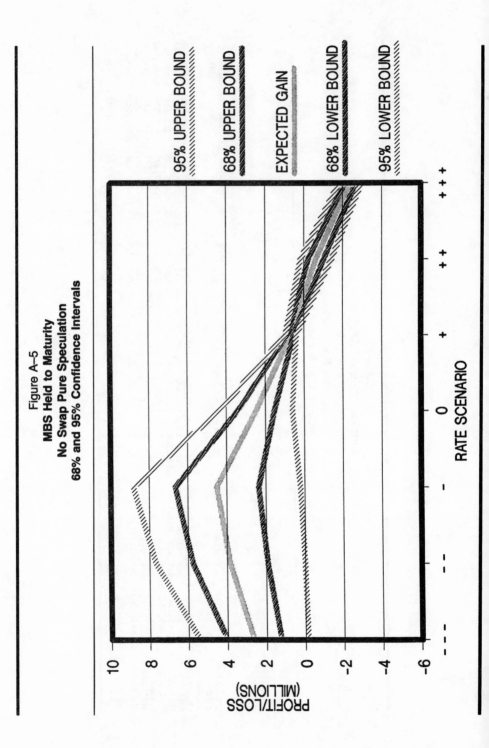

Figure A-5
MBS Held to Maturity
No Swap Pure Speculation
68% and 95% Confidence Intervals

95% UPPER BOUND

68% UPPER BOUND

EXPECTED GAIN

68% LOWER BOUND

95% LOWER BOUND

RATE SCENARIO

PROFIT/LOSS
(MILLIONS)

Table A–8
Detailed Arbitrage Analysis
Profit/Loss in $
No Swap, Pure Speculation
MBS Sold at the Expiration of Swap

Table B6

CPR RATE SCENARIOS	2.00%	5.00%	9.10%	20.00%	40.00%	EXPECTED VALUE	STANDARD DEVIATION	68.00% CONFIDENCE LO	INTERVAL HI	95.00% CONFIDENCE LO	INTERVAL HI
FALLING ---	9,461,151	7,889,129	6,262,733	3,664,383	1,638,746	2,578,918	1,273,287	1,305,631	3,852,206	32,344	5,125,493
FALLING --	8,687,936	7,173,124	5,617,117	3,172,152	1,346,727	3,618,357	1,661,983	1,956,373	5,280,340	294,390	6,942,323
FALLING -	7,737,980	6,328,859	4,899,198	2,709,149	1,150,261	4,114,176	1,782,534	2,331,642	5,896,709	549,108	7,679,243
FLAT	3,546,831	3,110,158	2,617,149	1,715,630	883,756	2,224,063	705,640	1,518,423	2,929,703	812,784	3,635,343
RISING+	105,109	401,354	641,622	811,518	630,963	637,154	182,059	455,094	819,213	273,035	1,001,273
RISING++	(1,355,118)	(863,866)	(396,872)	202,539	410,456	(763,290)	467,397	(1,230,687)	(295,894)	(1,698,083)	171,503
RISING+++	(2,944,534)	(2,361,292)	(1,772,111)	(872,439)	(219,978)	(2,623,454)	344,548	(2,968,002)	(2,278,906)	(3,312,551)	(1,934,358)

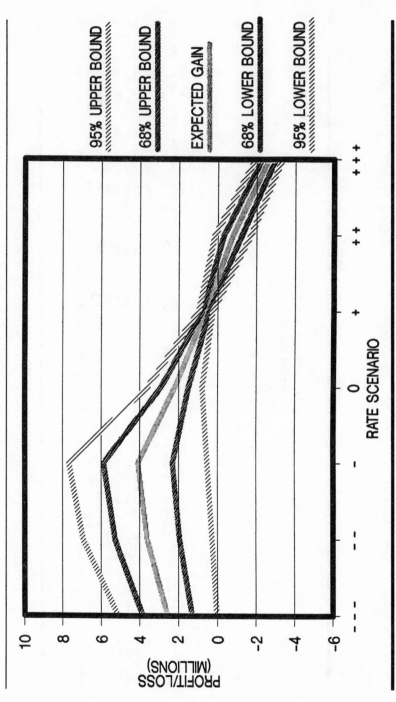

Figure A–6
MBS Sold at Expiration of Swap
No Swap, Pure Speculation
68% and 95% Confidence Intervals

95% UPPER BOUND

68% UPPER BOUND

EXPECTED GAIN

68% LOWER BOUND

95% LOWER BOUND

PROFIT/LOSS (MILLIONS)

RATE SCENARIO

Table A–9
Expected Income Statement and Margins
4-Tranch Synthetic CMO

					Years					
INCOME	1	2	3	4	5	6	7	8	9	10
FHLMC INCOME	1,864,414	1,409,717	984,323	703,048	513,040	381,728	288,851	221,654	171,995	134,587
FLOAT SWAP INC	1,199,027	775,516	775,516	547,941	547,941	400,962	400,962	178,609	178,609	178,609
EXPENSE										
FIX SWAP PMT	(1,362,122)	(1,486,888)	(1,486,888)	(1,068,150)	(1,068,150)	(789,309)	(789,309)	(354,769)	(354,769)	(354,769)
REPO PMTS	(1,590,290)	(659,125)	(459,321)	(327,440)	(238,522)	(177,193)	(133,902)	(102,639)	(79,577)	(62,231)
NET PROFIT W/ SWAP	111,029	39,220	(186,371)	(144,602)	(245,691)	(183,812)	(233,398)	(57,145)	(83,742)	(103,804)
NET PROFIT W/O SWAP	274,124	750,592	525,001	375,607	274,518	204,535	154,949	119,015	92,418	72,356
NET INTEREST MARGIN IN bp W/ SWAP	44	22	(154)	(169)	(398)	(403)	(681)	(219)	(415)	(659)
NET INTEREST MARGIN IN bp W/O SWAP	110	430	435	440	444	449	452	455	458	459
DURATION OF MORTGAGE IN YEARS	2.627	2.762	2.889	3.003	3.097	3.167	3.211	3.229	3.220	3.185
DURATION OF SWAP IN YEARS	4.238	3.517	3.754	3.004	2.933	2.124	2.688	1.862	0.969	0.000
DURATION GAP IN YEARS	-1.611	-0.755	-0.865	-0.001	0.163	1.042	0.523	1.367	2.251	3.185
MARKET VALUE OF MORTGAGE	18,925,109	13,136,650	9,328,074	6,769,088	5,010,526	3,773,677	2,883,669	2,229,274	1,738,590	1,364,258
PRICE OF MORTGAGE	108.31%	108.75%	109.17%	109.55%	109.87%	110.12%	110.29%	110.37%	110.36%	110.26%

*Rate Scenario: Falling – – – (300 basis points beginning of second year).

Table A-10
Expected Income Statement and Margins
Amortizing Swap

	Years									
	1	2	3	4	5	6	7	8	9	10
INCOME										
FHLMC INCOME	1,864,414	1,409,717	984,323	703,048	513,040	381,728	288,851	221,654	171,995	134,587
FLOAT SWAP INC	1,619,116	943,357	845,388	756,283	675,236	601,513	534,448	473,434	417,920	367,406
EXPENSE										
FIX SWAP PMT	(1,896,995)	(1,865,504)	(1,671,769)	(1,495,563)	(1,335,291)	(1,189,503)	(1,056,879)	(936,223)	(826,444)	(726,552)
REPO PMTS	(1,590,290)	(659,125)	(459,321)	(327,440)	(238,522)	(177,193)	(133,902)	(102,639)	(79,577)	(62,231)
NET PROFIT W/ SWAP	(3,755)	(171,555)	(301,380)	(363,673)	(385,537)	(383,454)	(367,482)	(343,775)	(316,106)	(286,790)
NET PROFIT W/O SWAP	274,124	750,592	525,001	375,607	274,518	204,535	154,949	119,015	92,418	72,356
NET INTEREST MARGIN IN bp W/ SWAP	(2)	(98)	(249)	(426)	(624)	(841)	(1,072)	(1,315)	(1,565)	(1,820)
NET INTEREST MARGIN IN bp W/O SWAP	110	430	435	440	444	449	452	455	458	459
DURATION OF MORTGAGE IN YEARS	2.627	2.762	2.889	3.003	3.097	3.167	3.211	3.229	3.220	3.185
DURATION OF SWAP IN YEARS	4.533	4.277	3.985	3.650	3.263	2.815	2.288	1.665	0.915	0.000
DURATION GAP IN YEARS	-1.905	-1.515	-1.095	-0.647	-0.167	0.352	0.923	1.564	2.304	3.185
MARKET VALUE OF MORTGAGE	18,925,109	13,136,650	9,328,074	6,769,088	5,010,526	3,773,677	2,883,669	2,229,274	1,738,590	1,364,258
PRICE OF MORTGAGE	108.31%	108.75%	109.17%	109.55%	109.87%	110.12%	110.29%	110.37%	110.36%	110.26%

Table A–11
Expected Income Statement and Margins
4-Tranche Synthetic CMO

INCOME	Years									
	1	2	3	4	5	6	7	8	9	10
FHLMC INCOME	1,978,198	1,723,148	1,383,084	1,125,239	926,288	769,149	642,977	540,218	455,488	384,863
FLOAT SWAP INC	1,199,027	1,130,038	952,777	547,941	547,941	400,962	400,962	178,609	178,609	178,609
EXPENSE										
FIX SWAP PMT	(1,362,122)	(1,486,888)	(1,486,888)	(1,068,150)	(1,068,150)	(789,309)	(789,309)	(354,769)	(354,769)	(354,769)
REPO PMTS	(1,660,954)	(1,143,485)	(777,360)	(518,395)	(426,377)	(353,809)	(295,619)	(248,282)	(209,288)	(176,815)
NET PROFIT W/ SWAP	154,149	222,813	71,613	86,635	(20,298)	26,993	(40,989)	115,777	70,040	31,888
NET PROFIT W/O SWAP	317,244	579,663	605,724	606,844	499,911	415,340	347,358	291,937	246,200	208,048
NET INTEREST MARGIN IN bp W/SWAP	62	111	45	67	(19)	31	(56)	189	136	73
NET INTEREST MARGIN IN bp W/O SWAP	127	290	379	469	472	474	475	476	477	477
DURATION OF MORTGAGE IN YEARS	3.578	3.818	4.038	4.084	4.102	4.095	4.062	4.004	3.923	3.816
DURATION OF SWAP IN YEARS	4.109	3.457	3.754	3.004	2.933	2.124	2.688	1.862	0.969	0.000
DURATION GAP IN YEARS	-0.531	0.360	0.284	1.080	1.169	1.971	1.374	2.142	2.954	3.816
MARKET VALUE OF MORTGAGE	20,873,938	17,308,234	14,603,361	11,987,009	9,926,506	8,276,064	6,934,697	5,830,813	4,912,508	4,141,343
PRICE OF MORTGAGE	104.30%	108.39%	112.94%	113.12%	113.22%	113.22%	113.14%	112.98%	112.74%	112.41%

*Rate Scenario: Falling – – (100 basis points over first three years).

Table A-12
Expected Income Statement and Margins
Amortizing Swap

	1	2	3	4	Years 5	6	7	8	9	10
INCOME										
FHLMC INCOME	1,978,198	1,723,148	1,383,084	1,125,239	926,288	769,149	642,977	540,218	455,488	384,863
FLOAT SWAP INC	1,619,116	1,374,606	1,038,619	756,283	675,236	601,513	534,448	473,434	417,920	367,406
EXPENSE										
FIX SWAP PMT	(1,896,995)	(1,865,504)	(1,671,769)	(1,495,563)	(1,335,291)	(1,189,503)	(1,056,879)	(936,223)	(826,444)	(726,552)
REPO PMTS	(1,660,954)	(1,143,485)	(777,360)	(518,395)	(426,377)	(353,809)	(295,619)	(248,282)	(209,288)	(176,815)
NET PROFIT W/ SWAP	39,365	88,765	(27,425)	(132,436)	(160,144)	(172,649)	(175,074)	(170,853)	(162,324)	(151,098)
NET PROFIT W/O SWAP	317,244	579,663	605,724	606,844	499,911	415,340	347,358	291,937	246,200	208,048
NET INTEREST MARGIN IN bp W/ SWAP	16	44	(17)	(102)	(151)	(197)	(240)	(279)	(315)	(347)
NET INTEREST MARGIN IN bp W/O SWAP	127	290	379	469	472	474	475	476	477	477
DURATION OF MORTGAGE IN YEARS	3.578	3.818	4.038	4.084	4.102	4.095	4.062	4.004	3.923	3.816
DURATION OF SWAP IN YEARS	4.349	4.201	3.985	3.650	3.263	2.815	2.288	1.665	0.915	0.000
DURATION GAP IN YEARS	-0.770	-0.383	0.054	0.434	0.839	1.280	1.774	2.340	3.007	3.816
MARKET VALUE OF MORTGAGE	20,873,938	17,308,234	14,603,361	11,987,009	9,926,506	8,276,064	6,934,697	5,830,813	4,912,508	4,141,343
PRICE OF MORTGAGE	104.30%	108.39%	112.94%	113.12%	113.22%	113.22%	113.14%	112.98%	112.74%	112.41%

Table A–13
Expected Income Statement and Margins
4-Tranche Synthetic CMO

					Years					
INCOME	1	2	3	4	5	6	7	8	9	10
FHLMC INCOME	2,033,315	1,885,878	1,609,796	1,387,334	1,204,479	1,051,578	921,821	810,617	713,895	628,907
FLOAT SWAP INC	1,199,027	1,218,668	1,130,038	735,806	673,185	446,786	400,962	178,609	178,609	178,609
EXPENSE										
FIX SWAP PMT	(1,362,122)	(1,486,888)	(1,486,888)	(1,068,150)	(1,068,150)	(789,309)	(789,309)	(354,769)	(354,769)	(354,769)
REPO PMTS	(1,694,992)	(1,339,069)	(1,061,426)	(844,661)	(672,640)	(534,357)	(422,105)	(371,116)	(326,809)	(287,909)
NET PROFIT W/ SWAP	175,227	278,590	191,520	210,330	136,874	174,698	111,368	263,341	210,927	164,838
NET PROFIT W/O SWAP	338,322	546,809	548,370	542,673	531,839	517,221	499,716	439,501	387,087	340,998
NET INTEREST MARGIN IN bp W/ SWAP	70	131	106	135	102	149	109	292	266	236
NET INTEREST MARGIN IN bp W/O SWAP	135	257	303	349	396	441	487	488	488	488
DURATION OF MORTGAGE IN YEARS	4.305	4.467	4.596	4.692	4.752	4.777	4.689	4.576	4.439	4.278
DURATION OF SWAP IN YEARS	4.078	3.399	3.693	2.968	2.922	2.124	2.688	1.862	0.969	0.000
DURATION GAP IN YEARS	0.227	1.068	0.903	1.723	1.830	2.652	2.001	2.714	3.470	4.278
MARKET VALUE OF MORTGAGE	21,929,938	19,057,893	16,750,283	14,847,600	13,241,499	11,856,730	10,392,616	9,120,829	8,005,337	7,018,460
PRICE OF MORTGAGE	103.05%	105.40%	107.87%	110.41%	112.99%	115.56%	115.30%	114.96%	114.52%	114.01%

*Rate Scenario: Falling – (50 basis points over first six years).

Table A-14
Expected Income Statement and Margins
Amortizing Swap

	Years									
	1	2	3	4	5	6	7	8	9	10
INCOME										
FHLMC INCOME	2,033,315	1,885,878	1,609,796	1,387,334	1,204,479	1,051,578	921,821	810,617	713,895	628,907
FLOAT SWAP INC	1,619,116	1,482,418	1,231,851	1,015,580	829,576	670,258	534,448	473,434	417,920	367,406
EXPENSE										
FIX SWAP PMT	(1,896,995)	(1,865,504)	(1,671,769)	(1,495,563)	(1,335,291)	(1,189,503)	(1,056,879)	(936,223)	(826,444)	(726,552)
REPO PMTS	(1,694,992)	(1,339,069)	(1,061,426)	(844,661)	(672,640)	(534,357)	(422,105)	(371,116)	(326,809)	(287,909)
NET PROFIT W/ SWAP	60,443	163,723	108,453	62,691	26,124	(2,024)	(22,716)	(23,289)	(21,437)	(18,148)
NET PROFIT W/O SWAP	338,322	546,809	548,370	542,673	531,839	517,221	499,716	439,501	387,087	340,998
NET INTEREST MARGIN IN bp W/ SWAP	24	77	60	40	19	(2)	(22)	(26)	(27)	(26)
NET INTEREST MARGIN IN bp W/O SWAP	135	257	303	349	396	441	487	488	488	488
DURATION OF MORTGAGE IN YEARS	4.305	4.467	4.596	4.692	4.752	4.777	4.689	4.576	4.439	4.278
DURATION OF SWAP IN YEARS	4.303	4.126	3.896	3.606	3.248	2.815	2.288	1.665	0.915	0.000
DURATION GAP IN YEARS	0.001	0.341	0.701	1.086	1.504	1.962	2.401	2.912	3.524	4.278
MARKET VALUE OF MORTGAGE	21,929,938	19,057,893	16,750,283	14,847,600	13,241,499	11,856,730	10,392,616	9,120,829	8,005,337	7,018,460
PRICE OF MORTGAGE	103.05%	105.40%	107.87%	110.41%	112.99%	115.56%	115.30%	114.96%	114.52%	114.01%

*Rate Scenario: Falling – (50 basis points over first six years).

Table A–15
Expected Income Statement and Margins
4-Tranche Synthetic CMO

INCOME	Years									
	1	2	3	4	5	6	7	8	9	10
FHLMC INCOME	2,031,382	1,880,234	1,600,950	1,375,818	1,190,796	1,036,200	905,180	792,773	695,292	609,939
FLOAT SWAP INC	1,199,027	1,307,299	1,307,299	923,672	923,672	675,907	675,907	301,085	301,085	301,085
EXPENSE										
FIX SWAP PMT	(1,362,122)	(1,486,888)	(1,486,888)	(1,068,150)	(1,068,150)	(789,309)	(789,309)	(354,769)	(354,769)	(354,769)
REPO PMTS	(1,693,811)	(1,429,477)	(1,216,039)	(1,044,296)	(903,370)	(785,774)	(686,226)	(600,905)	(526,979)	(462,301)
NET PROFIT W/ SWAP	174,476	271,167	205,321	187,044	142,948	137,023	105,552	138,183	114,629	93,954
NET PROFIT W/O SWAP	337,571	450,756	384,911	331,522	287,426	250,426	218,954	191,868	168,314	147,638
NET INTEREST MARGIN IN bp W/ SWAP	70	128	114	121	108	119	105	157	148	139
NET INTEREST MARGIN IN bp W/O SWAP	135	212	214	215	216	217	217	218	218	218
DURATION OF MORTGAGE IN YEARS	4.159	4.231	4.275	4.292	4.285	4.255	4.202	4.126	4.029	3.909
DURATION OF SWAP IN YEARS	4.047	3.342	3.634	2.899	2.864	2.064	2.673	1.857	0.969	0.000
DURATION GAP IN YEARS	0.113	0.889	0.641	1.393	1.421	2.191	1.529	2.269	3.060	3.909
MARKET VALUE OF MORTGAGE	21,421,078	18,154,012	15,543,857	13,415,195	11,648,262	10,159,257	8,888,062	7,790,482	6,833,273	5,990,902
PRICE OF MORTGAGE	100.88%	100.90%	100.91%	100.91%	100.91%	100.90%	100.89%	100.88%	100.85%	100.83%

*Rate Scenario: Flat (for 10 years)

Table A–16
Expected Income Statement and Margins
Amortizing Swap

					Years					
	1	2	3	4	5	6	7	8	9	10
INCOME										
FHLMC INCOME	2,031,382	1,880,234	1,600,950	1,375,818	1,190,796	1,036,200	905,180	792,773	695,292	609,939
FLOAT SWAP INC	1,619,116	1,590,230	1,425,082	1,274,877	1,138,255	1,013,979	900,926	798,074	704,494	619,342
EXPENSE										
FIX SWAP PMT	(1,896,995)	(1,865,504)	(1,671,769)	(1,495,563)	(1,335,291)	(1,189,503)	(1,056,879)	(936,223)	(826,444)	(726,552)
REPO PMTS	(1,693,811)	(1,429,477)	(1,216,039)	(1,044,296)	(903,370)	(785,774)	(686,226)	(600,905)	(526,979)	(462,301)
NET PROFIT W/ SWAP	59,692	175,482	138,224	110,837	90,391	74,902	63,001	53,719	46,364	40,428
NET PROFIT W/O SWAP	337,571	450,756	384,911	331,522	287,426	250,426	218,954	191,868	168,314	147,638
NET INTEREST MARGIN IN bp W/ SWAP	24	83	77	72	68	65	63	61	60	60
NET INTEREST MARGIN IN bp W/O SWAP	135	212	214	215	216	217	217	218	218	218
DURATION OF MORTGAGE IN YEARS	4.159	4.231	4.275	4.292	4.285	4.255	4.202	4.126	4.029	3.909
DURATION OF SWAP IN YEARS	4.258	4.051	3.807	3.518	3.173	2.759	2.260	1.655	0.914	0.000
DURATION GAP IN YEARS	-0.099	0.180	0.467	0.774	1.112	1.495	1.941	2.472	3.115	3.909
MARKET VALUE OF MORTGAGE	21,421,078	18,154,012	15,543,857	13,415,195	11,648,262	10,159,257	8,888,062	7,790,482	6,833,273	5,990,902
PRICE OF MORTGAGE	100.88%	100.90%	100.91%	100.91%	100.91%	100.90%	100.89%	100.88%	100.85%	100.83%

Table A-17
Expected Income Statement and Margins
4-Tranche Synthetic CMO

	Years									
	1	2	3	4	5	6	7	8	9	10
INCOME										
FHLMC INCOME	2,033,315	1,887,442	1,612,466	1,390,785	1,208,474	1,055,939	926,409	814,986	718,038	632,816
FLOAT SWAP INC	1,199,027	1,395,929	1,484,559	1,111,537	1,174,159	905,028	950,852	443,972	464,385	484,797
EXPENSE										
FIX SWAP PMT	(1,362,122)	(1,486,888)	(1,486,888)	(1,068,150)	(1,068,150)	(789,309)	(789,309)	(354,769)	(354,769)	(354,769)
REPO PMTS	(1,694,992)	(1,528,975)	(1,385,465)	(1,263,417)	(1,157,319)	(1,063,297)	(978,579)	(901,140)	(829,458)	(762,359)
NET PROFIT W/ SWAP	175,227	267,508	224,672	170,755	157,164	108,361	109,373	3,048	(1,804)	485
NET PROFIT W/O SWAP	338,322	358,467	227,001	127,368	51,155	(7,358)	(52,170)	(86,154)	(111,420)	(129,543)
NET INTEREST MARGIN IN bp W/ SWAP	70	126	124	110	117	92	107	3	(2)	1
NET INTEREST MARGIN IN bp W/O SWAP	135	168	126	82	38	(6)	(51)	(96)	(140)	(185)
DURATION OF MORTGAGE IN YEARS	4.135	4.132	4.106	4.060	3.998	3.921	3.832	3.731	3.618	3.493
DURATION OF SWAP IN YEARS	4.016	3.286	3.575	2.831	2.808	2.005	2.654	1.851	0.968	0.000
DURATION GAP IN YEARS	0.120	0.847	0.531	1.229	1.190	1.916	1.178	1.880	2.650	3.493
MARKET VALUE OF MORTGAGE	21,030,746	17,500,228	14,718,175	12,485,525	10,665,510	9,161,848	7,905,100	6,844,011	5,939,918	5,163,065
PRICE OF MORTGAGE	98.83%	96.78%	94.78%	92.85%	91.01%	89.29%	87.70%	86.26%	84.98%	83.87%

*Rate Scenario: Rising + (50 basis points over ten years).

Table A–18
Expected Income Statement and Margins
Amortizing Swap

	Years									
INCOME	1	2	3	4	5	6	7	8	9	10
FHLMC INCOME	2,033,315	1,887,442	1,612,466	1,390,785	1,208,474	1,055,939	926,409	814,986	718,038	632,816
FLOAT SWAP INC	1,619,116	1,698,042	1,618,314	1,534,174	1,446,935	1,357,701	1,267,405	1,176,821	1,086,592	997,245
EXPENSE										
FIX SWAP PMT	(1,896,995)	(1,865,504)	(1,671,769)	(1,495,563)	(1,335,291)	(1,189,503)	(1,056,879)	(936,223)	(826,444)	(726,552)
REPO PMTS	(1,694,992)	(1,528,975)	(1,385,465)	(1,263,417)	(1,157,319)	(1,063,297)	(978,579)	(901,140)	(829,458)	(762,359)
NET PROFIT W/ SWAP	60,443	191,005	173,546	165,979	162,798	160,841	158,355	154,443	148,728	141,150
NET PROFIT W/O SWAP	338,322	358,467	227,001	127,368	51,155	(7,358)	(52,170)	(86,154)	(111,420)	(129,543)
NET INTEREST MARGIN IN bp W/ SWAP	24	90	96	107	121	137	154	171	187	202
NET INTEREST MARGIN IN bp W/O SWAP	135	168	126	82	38	(6)	(51)	(96)	(140)	(185)
DURATION OF MORTGAGE IN YEARS	4.135	4.132	4.106	4.060	3.998	3.921	3.832	3.731	3.618	3.493
DURATION OF SWAP IN YEARS	4.213	3.978	3.720	3.430	3.097	2.703	2.227	1.641	0.912	0.000
DURATION GAP IN YEARS	-0.078	0.155	0.386	0.630	0.901	1.218	1.605	2.089	2.706	3.493
MARKET VALUE OF MORTGAGE	21,030,746	17,500,228	14,718,175	12,485,525	10,665,510	9,161,848	7,905,100	6,844,011	5,939,918	5,163,065
PRICE OF MORTGAGE	98.83%	96.78%	94.78%	92.85%	91.01%	89.29%	87.70%	86.26%	84.98%	83.87%

*Rate Scenario: Rising + (50 basis points over ten years).

Table A–19
Expected Income Statement and Margins
4-Tranche Synthetic CMO

	1	2	3	4	5	6	7	8	9	10
					Years					
INCOME										
FHLMC INCOME	2,114,848	2,136,356	1,972,903	1,823,520	1,686,073	1,558,775	1,438,943	1,326,659	1,220,813	1,120,450
FLOAT SWAP INC	1,199,027	1,484,559	1,661,820	1,299,403	1,424,646	1,134,149	1,134,149	505,210	505,210	505,210
EXPENSE										
FIX SWAP PMT	(1,362,122)	(1,486,888)	(1,486,888)	(1,068,150)	(1,068,150)	(789,309)	(789,309)	(354,769)	(354,769)	(354,769)
REPO PMTS	(1,745,211)	(1,824,188)	(1,879,894)	(1,917,792)	(1,939,687)	(1,946,955)	(1,797,428)	(1,657,394)	(1,525,458)	(1,400,418)
NET PROFIT W/ SWAP	206,542	309,840	267,942	136,981	102,883	(43,341)	(13,646)	(180,295)	(154,204)	(129,528)
NET PROFIT W/O SWAP	369,637	312,169	93,010	(94,272)	(253,613)	(388,180)	(358,485)	(330,735)	(304,645)	(279,968)
NET INTEREST MARGIN IN bp W/ SWAP	83	134	125	69	56	(26)	(9)	(126)	(117)	(107)
NET INTEREST MARGIN IN bp W/O SWAP	148	135	44	(48)	(139)	(230)	(230)	(230)	(230)	(230)
DURATION OF MORTGAGE IN YEARS	5.291	5.042	4.808	4.586	4.376	4.312	4.232	4.137	4.025	3.895
DURATION OF SWAP IN YEARS	3.985	3.230	3.517	2.765	2.753	1.967	2.646	1.849	0.968	0.000
DURATION GAP IN YEARS	1.306	1.811	1.290	1.822	1.623	2.345	1.586	2.288	3.057	3.895
MARKET VALUE OF MORTGAGE	22,231,508	19,490,919	17,159,975	15,164,933	13,446,959	12,470,725	11,562,852	10,712,496	9,910,219	9,147,683
PRICE OF MORTGAGE	95.91%	91.17%	86.94%	83.17%	79.83%	80.17%	80.57%	81.03%	81.57%	82.18%

*Rate Scenario: Rising + (100 basis points over five years)

Table A-20
Expected Income Statement and Margins
Amortizing Swap

					Years					
INCOME	1	2	3	4	5	6	7	8	9	10
PHLMC INCOME	2,114,848	2,136,356	1,972,903	1,823,520	1,686,073	1,558,775	1,438,943	1,326,659	1,220,813	1,120,450
FLOAT SWAP INC	1,619,116	1,805,854	1,811,545	1,793,471	1,755,614	1,701,423	1,511,724	1,339,141	1,182,117	1,039,234
EXPENSE										
FIX SWAP PMT	(1,896,995)	(1,865,504)	(1,671,769)	(1,495,563)	(1,335,291)	(1,189,503)	(1,056,879)	(936,223)	(826,444)	(726,552)
REPO PMTS	(1,745,211)	(1,824,188)	(1,879,894)	(1,917,792)	(1,939,687)	(1,946,955)	(1,797,428)	(1,657,394)	(1,525,458)	(1,400,418)
NET PROFIT W/ SWAP	91,758	252,519	232,786	203,637	166,710	123,740	96,359	72,182	51,028	32,714
NET PROFIT W/O SWAP	369,637	312,169	93,010	(94,272)	(253,613)	(388,180)	(358,485)	(330,735)	(304,645)	(279,968)
NET INTEREST MARGIN IN bp W/ SWAP	37	109	109	103	91	73	62	50	39	27
NET INTEREST MARGIN IN bp W/O SWAP	148	135	44	(48)	(139)	(230)	(230)	(230)	(230)	(230)
DURATION OF MORTGAGE IN YEARS	5.291	5.042	4.808	4.586	4.376	4.312	4.232	4.137	4.025	3.895
DURATION OF SWAP IN YEARS	4.169	3.904	3.633	3.343	3.021	2.665	2.213	1.638	0.912	0.000
DURATION GAP IN YEARS	1.122	1.138	1.175	1.244	1.356	1.646	2.019	2.499	3.113	3.895
MARKET VALUE OF MORTGAGE	22,231,508	19,490,919	17,159,975	15,164,933	13,446,959	12,470,725	11,562,852	10,712,496	9,910,219	9,147,683
PRICE OF MORTGAGE	95.91%	91.17%	86.94%	83.17%	79.83%	80.17%	80.57%	81.03%	81.57%	82.18%

*Rate Scenario: Rising ++ (100 basis points over five years).

Table A-21
Expected Income Statement and Margins
4-Tranche Synthetic CMO

					Years					
	1	2	3	4	5	6	7	8	9	10
INCOME										
FHLMC INCOME	2,144,049	2,239,174	2,126,849	2,017,437	1,910,596	1,805,991	1,703,292	1,602,171	1,502,306	1,403,373
FLOAT SWAP INC	1,199,027	2,193,603	2,193,603	1,549,890	1,549,890	1,134,149	1,134,149	505,210	505,210	505,210
EXPENSE										
FIX SWAP PMT	(1,362,122)	(1,486,888)	(1,486,888)	(1,068,150)	(1,068,150)	(789,309)	(789,309)	(354,769)	(354,769)	(354,769)
REPO PMTS	(1,763,089)	(2,789,827)	(2,650,162)	(2,514,149)	(2,381,362)	(2,251,384)	(2,123,805)	(1,998,220)	(1,874,227)	(1,751,424)
NET PROFIT W/ SWAP	217,865	156,062	183,401	(14,972)	10,975	(100,553)	(75,673)	(245,608)	(221,480)	(197,611)
NET PROFIT W/O SWAP	380,961	(550,653)	(523,314)	(496,712)	(470,766)	(445,393)	(420,513)	(396,048)	(371,920)	(348,051)
NET INTEREST MARGIN IN bp W/ SWAP	87	65	81	(7)	5	(52)	(41)	(143)	(137)	(131)
NET INTEREST MARGIN IN bp W/O SWAP	152	(231)	(231)	(231)	(231)	(231)	(231)	(231)	(231)	(231)
DURATION OF MORTGAGE IN YEARS	5.045	4.983	4.913	4.833	4.743	4.641	4.527	4.399	4.257	4.098
DURATION OF SWAP IN YEARS	3.749	3.071	3.442	2.732	2.753	1.967	2.646	1.849	0.968	0.000
DURATION GAP IN YEARS	1.295	1.912	1.470	2.100	1.989	2.674	1.881	2.550	3.289	4.098
MARKET VALUE OF MORTGAGE	18,342,356	17,504,590	16,692,106	15,901,816	15,130,613	14,375,341	13,632,765	12,899,533	12,172,138	11,446,879
PRICE OF MORTGAGE	76.80%	77.12%	77.48%	77.88%	78.32%	78.82%	79.36%	79.96%	80.62%	81.35%

*Rate Scenario: Rising + + + (300 basis points beginning of second year).

Table A-22
Expected Income Statement and Margins
Amortizing Swap

	Years									
	1	2	3	4	5	6	7	8	9	10
INCOME										
FHLMC INCOME	2,144,049	2,239,174	2,126,849	2,017,437	1,910,596	1,805,991	1,703,292	1,602,171	1,502,306	1,403,373
FLOAT SWAP INC	1,619,116	2,668,352	2,391,240	2,139,201	1,909,954	1,701,423	1,511,724	1,339,141	1,182,117	1,039,234
EXPENSE										
FIX SWAP PMT REPO PMTS	(1,896,995) (1,763,089)	(1,865,504) (2,789,827)	(1,671,769) (2,650,162)	(1,495,563) (2,514,149)	(1,335,291) (2,381,362)	(1,189,503) (2,251,384)	(1,056,879) (2,123,805)	(936,223) (1,998,220)	(826,444) (1,874,227)	(726,552) (1,751,424)
NET PROFIT W/ SWAP	103,081	252,195	196,157	146,926	103,897	66,528	34,331	6,870	(16,247)	(35,369)
NET PROFIT W/O SWAP	380,961	(550,653)	(523,314)	(496,712)	(470,766)	(445,393)	(420,513)	(396,048)	(371,920)	(348,051)
NET INTEREST MARGIN IN bp W/ SWAP	41	106	86	68	51	34	19	4	(10)	(23)
NET INTEREST MARGIN IN bp W/O SWAP	152	(231)	(231)	(231)	(231)	(231)	(231)	(231)	(231)	(231)
DURATION OF MORTGAGE IN YEARS	5.045	4.983	4.913	4.833	4.743	4.641	4.527	4.399	4.257	4.098
DURATION OF SWAP IN YEARS	3.825	3.690	3.518	3.299	3.021	2.665	2.213	1.638	0.912	0.000
DURATION GAP IN YEARS	1.220	1.293	1.395	1.534	1.722	1.976	2.314	2.761	3.345	4.098
MARKET VALUE OF MORTGAGE	18,342,356	17,504,590	16,692,106	15,901,816	15,130,613	14,375,341	13,632,765	12,899,533	12,172,138	11,446,879
PRICE OF MORTGAGE	76.80%	77.12%	77.48%	77.88%	78.32%	78.82%	79.36%	79.96%	80.62%	81.35%

Chapter 18

MICHAEL F. MOLESKY

Michael Molesky is Assistant Vice President, Moody's Investors Service, responsible for mortgage credit research, including the rating of mortgage insurance companies and establishing standards for rating mortgage-backed securities. Previously he was a financial economist for the Office of Policy Development and Research at HUD. Mr. Molesky received his undergraduate and graduate degrees from Georgetown University.

An Overview of Mortgage Credit Risks from a Rating Agency Perspective

MICHAEL F. MOLESKY

INTRODUCTION

While originations of mortgages for portfolio still represent the major use of new loan product by savings and loans, the securitization of new product remains an ever growing component of the United States mortgage finance system. Indeed, S&Ls are both major issuers and investors of mortgage-backed securities—seeking greater diversification by product and geographic location.

The cornerstone of the growth of the mortgage-backed securities market continues to be the GNMA program, which combines homogeneous collateral and federal guarantees. However, conventional whole-loan, mortgage-backed securities constitute one of the fastest growing segments of the mortgage-backed securities market and may eventually replace GNMA securities as the dominant form. These instruments generally carry no federal guarantees, but are rather supported by limited guarantees of private insurance, letters of credit, or subordinated collateral.

The growth of this segment of the mortgage-backed securities market can be sustained only if investors are satisfied that credit risks have been adequately addressed. These investor concerns heightened in the mid-1980's. First, the private mortgage insurance industry has been under tremendous pressure and is only gradually returning to a stronger financial position. Second, the EPIC securities debacle has exemplified the pitfalls of inappropriate structure, as well as insufficient pool coverage relative to the underlying risk potential of the loan collateral. Finally, the effects of deflation, as well as regional economic woes connected with commodity markets, have caused a huge disparity in local housing markets. As a result, national foreclosure rates in the first quarter of 1986 were 20 percent higher than in the first quarter of 1983.

Given the extreme variance in observed default rates in today's environment, simple rules of thumb in assessing mortgage credit risks increase the chance that levels of assigned limited credit enhancement may not be sufficient to cover all default losses, resulting in lost principal and interest to investors. By developing a highly refined rating approach that addresses mortgage credit risks in a more rigorous fashion, Moody's is endeavoring to increase investor confidence in this market, and thereby expand it.

This chapter presents Moody's perspective of mortgage credit risk. First, it discusses some of the elements of mortgage credit risk. Second is a review of how Moody's uses its analysis of these elements in determining adequate pool policy coverage for whole loan pools, and finally, the chapter discusses the mortgage insurance industry and how it fits in with the future of this market.

MORTGAGE CREDIT RISK

Mortgage credit risk can be viewed in two parts: the potential claim frequency to be expected under economic stress and the loss severity under such situations.

Moody's extensive research has proven that claim frequencies are the product of the several forces. The major determinant is the net equity position over the life of the loan. (*Net equity* is defined as the market value of the home less the outstanding balance of the mortgage less selling costs. Simply stated, it's the borrower's stake in the home.)

Major factors affecting net equity over time are the initial loan-to-value, term to maturity, coupon, and home price appreciation or deflation. Differences in loan instruments are important because they affect both the borrower's equity position over time and ability to make payments. Location of the property has a decided impact on claim frequencies. The degree of local economic stability affects both the volatility in employment and the potential growth or stability in home values. Finally, occupancy status of the property has also proven to be extremely important. Investor property loans are highly sensitive to changes in local economic conditions and have had a substantially higher delinquency and foreclosure record compared to owner-occupied home loans.

To illustrate some of these observed differences, a number of figures have been included from our extensive data base on the private mortgage insurance industry.

Figures 18–1 through 18–4 display ever-to-date claim rates that are in essence weighted average claim rates by policy year for the years noted. The claim rates are calculated as the number of claims paid divided by the number of loans outstanding at the beginning of each period. These graphics are for descriptive purposes only. Our analysis looks at these data broken down by several risk characteristics by year of origination, forming in essence hundreds of static pools.

Our approach is to model the foreclosures and loss severity on such pools through the interaction of the risk characteristics with economic conditions over time. These relationships allow us to predict likely future losses under any assumed conditions.

Figure 18–1 shows claim rates for all insured loans originated between 1957 and 1977 by four original loan-to-value groups; less than 81 percent, 81–85 percent, 86–90 percent, and greater than 90 percent. Most of the loans depicted here are fixed-rate mortgages with maturities averaging between 25 and 30 years. As house values grew and balances were repaid, net equity positions grew larger, and claims frequencies declined after peaking, on average, in the third year. Notice the huge difference in claim rates between the greater than 90 percent loan-to-value loans and the 86–90 percent loan-to-value loans for only 5 percent extra down payment. The less than 81 percent loan-to-value group loans are higher than expected; claim frequencies depicted here are due to the inordinate presence of investor loans in that category. Given the higher risks associated with such loans, most lenders and insurers require higher down payments. The experience depicted in Figure 18–1 is dominated by the experience of the 1970s—a high-growth period for the private mortgage insurance industry that was also characterized as a period of low unemployment and very high home price appreication, which tended to hold claims down.

Now look at more recent experience of 1978–1985 (see Figure 18–2). This period includes the 1981–1982 recession in which there was high levels of unemployment, but also decidedly lower home price appreciation through 1985. The effect of slower net equity buildup has been to push claim rates twice as high and to shift the peak claim rates out to the fourth and fifth years. Also note how much worse the less than 81 percent loan-to-value claim rate is compared to the 1957–1977 period. It's right up there with the 91 percent–95 percent loans, and it reflects the high sensitivity of investor loans to worsening economic conditions.

The claim rates in Figure 18–2 were also greatly affected by the introduction of new loan types. These new loan types, while enabling more home buyers to enter the market, were no bargain for investors, given the higher default performance of such loans. Figures 18–3 and 18–4 compare the experience of 5 percent down, fixed-rate, fixed payment loans against the experience of other loan types between 1980 and 1985. First, compared to fixed-rate, fixed-payment mortgages, fully amortizing adjustable-rate mortgages (ARMs) were more than twice as likely to default (see Figure 18–3), while 5 percent down ARMs that permitted or scheduled negative amortization were 4.8 times as likely to default. Even more significant is the observation that these differences arose over a period—especially in policy years three through six—where United States mortgage interest rates were falling. Should such loans be faced with a period of rising interest rates, the additional payment shock and the squeeze on the net equity of negatively amortizing ARMs could push claim rates on such instruments to substantially higher levels.

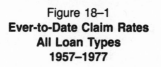

Figure 18–1
Ever-to-Date Claim Rates
All Loan Types
1957–1977

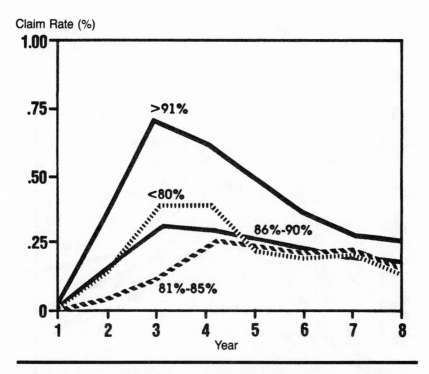

Figure 18–4 compares 5 percent down, fixed-rate, fixed-payment loans with graduated payment mortgages (GPMs), temporary buy-downs (BDNs), and growing equity mortgages (GEMs). The industry experience with GEMs and BDNs is limited. However, both instruments display claim frequencies that are higher than FRMs, a phenomenon that can be only attributed to payment shock. Buydowns reduced the early monthly payments up to three years, with yearly increases of 7½ percent, which conforms to the average scheduled increase on

Figure 18–2
Ever-to-Date Claim Rates
All Loan Types
1978–1985

Claim Rate (%)

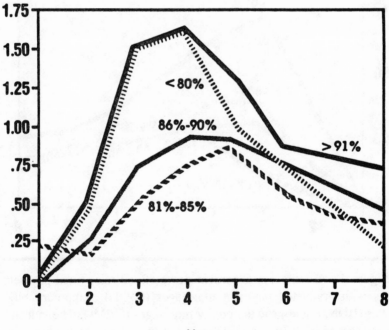

Year

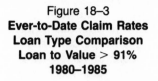

Figure 18–3
Ever-to-Date Claim Rates
Loan Type Comparison
Loan to Value > 91%
1980–1985

Claim Rate (%)

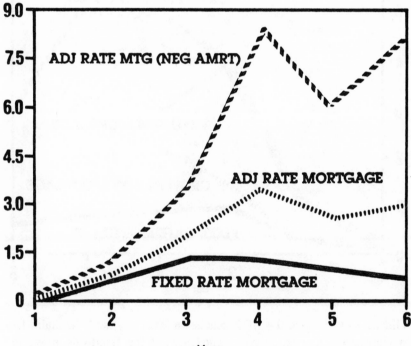

Year

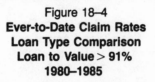

Figure 18–4
Ever-to-Date Claim Rates
Loan Type Comparison
Loan to Value > 91%
1980–1985

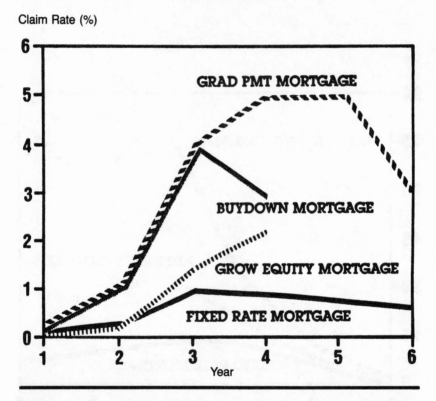

GPMs. Hence, once the BDN reaches a level payment, its claim frequency stops increasing and trends toward the fixed-rate mortgage (FRM) levels. The GPM usually levels off after five years of increases and has built in a small degree of negative amortization, which when combined with the scheduled payment increases cause the higher default rates. GEMs also have scheduled increases in principal repayments. The faster buildup in net equity helps to offset the payment shock of the increased payments.

So far we've looked at the effects of net equity, loan type, and occupancy status. That leaves location. Location is most important because the local unemployment rates and home price appreciation rates are critical in determining default frequency and severity.

Local economies in the United States are very diverse and have, therefore, supported large differences in the performance of insured mortgages. In the years 1981 to 1983, unemployment rates in all regions of the country were elevated, with the midwest being hit the hardest (see Figure 18–5). During the same years, home price appreciation rates fell as unemployment rates rose (see Table 18–1). Using Moody's mortgage insurer (MI) data base, we tracked the performance of all the states. The 10 worse-performing states (in terms of losses paid as a percentage of risk) were all in the midwest and west plus Texas and Florida, while 9 of the 10 best performing states were east of the Mississippi (see Tables 18–1 and 18–2). Interestingly, some of these same 10 worst states were among the 10 best in 1980. Very few states have consistently good or bad performances. However, there are some states that are more prone to economic cycles than others.

Therefore, one approach to avoid random adverse economic situations is to geographically diversify the mortgage pool as much as possible. But an even better approach is to pull together loans from areas that are themselves more economically diverse. Moody's has related the variance in state employment rates to individual state employment distributions by industry. This approach does two things: (1) It recognizes that concentrations in any single industry opens the possibility of unusually high unemployment rates should that industry develop problems, and (2) it recognizes that certain types of employment are less volatile than others. We believe that employment diversity is more important than population size or pure geographic distribution. This approach also permits economically feasible pool coverage for geographically concentrated pools if the local economies are sufficiently diverse.

Loss severity is the second major component of mortgage credit risk.

Figure 18–5
**Regional Weighted
Unemployment Rates
1980–1985**

Unemployment Rate

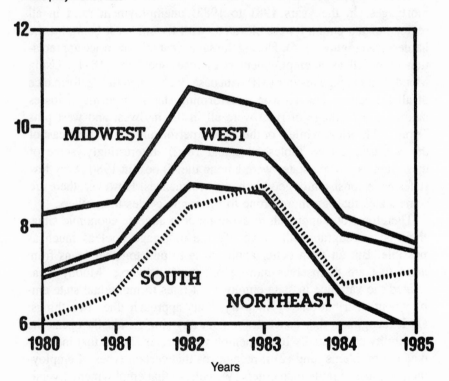

Table 18–1
Ten Worst-Performing States 1980–1985
Direct Losses Paid as a Percent of Previous Year-End Risk

Rank	State	1980	1981	1982	1983	1984	1985	1980–1985 Weighted[a] Averages
1	Wyoming	0.0%	0.2%	0.3%	2.0%	4.2%	6.1%	2.7%
2	North Dakota	1.0	1.0	1.9	2.5	2.8	2.4	2.0
3	Oregon	0.1	2.3	0.9	2.6	2.2	2.6	1.6
4	Utah	0.2	0.7	1.4	1.1	1.7	1.8	1.4
5	Nevada	0.0	0.2	0.7	1.0	1.8	2.2	1.3
6	Iowa	0.3	0.7	1.3	1.8	1.7	1.4	1.3
7	South Dakota	0.4	0.8	1.5	1.1	1.5	1.5	1.2
8	Ohio	0.4	0.7	1.4	1.8	1.4	1.0	1.1
9	Florida	0.1	0.1	0.4	1.0	1.7	1.4	1.1
10	Texas	0.1%	0.1%	0.3%	0.7%	1.2%	2.3%	1.1%

Table 18–2
Ten Best-Performing States 1980–1985
Direct Losses Paid as a Percent of Previous Year-End Risk

Rank	State	1980	1981	1982	1983	1984	1985	1980–1985 Weighted Averages
1	Massachusetts	0.2%	0.1%	0.2%	0.2%	0.1%	0.1%	0.1%
2	Delaware	0.2	0.2	0.3	0.2	0.2	0.3	0.2
3	New Hampshire	0.1	0.2	0.5	0.5	0.3	0.1	0.2
4	Wash., D.C.	0.2	0.1	0.2	0.4	0.3	0.3	0.3
5	Connecticut	0.1	0.3	0.4	0.6	0.3	0.1	0.3
6	New York	0.7	0.4	0.4	0.3	0.2	0.2	0.3
7	North Carolina	0.2	0.2	0.4	0.4	0.4	0.3	0.3
8	Georgia	0.1	0.2	0.4	0.4	0.3	0.3	0.3
9	Alaska	0.4	0.2	0.0	0.0	0.2	0.8	0.3
10	Maryland	0.2%	0.2%	0.3%	0.3%	0.3%	0.4%	0.3%

Once again, the old rules of thumb do not apply. Moody's has found that loss severity is affected by the net equity position, the interest coupon, the relative value of the property, and the average state time to foreclosure. Obviously, the greater the net equity, the smaller the losses as a result of the foreclosure process. Closely associated with net equity is the value of the property relative to the local market. Loss severity will be higher on properties originally priced high relative to local markets. The salvage value of such properties will likely be lower due to a more limited market.

Some housing analysts have suggested that the Tax Reform Act of 1986 will result in sharply higher after-tax costs of home ownership for owners of higher-priced homes. This would have the effect of pushing down or limiting the price growth of higher-priced homes. Offsetting these negative effects, of course, would be the potential deductibility of future borrowing needs and the fact that housing remains as the only significant tax shelter. Nevertheless, the 1986 tax bill is certain to have negative effects on high-priced homes located in local markets already soft because of local economic conditions. The bottom line here is that a rule of thumb approach to jumbo loan home values is once again inappropriate. The mortgage must be viewed in the context of its local market.

Interest past due, a major component of loss severity, is affected by both the size of the interest coupon and the time it takes to gain title to the property in the foreclosure process. Because the foreclosure process varies by state law, there are substantial differences in how long it takes to complete foreclosure (see Table 18–3). Thus, the higher the coupon and the longer the time to foreclosure, the greater the severity of loss.

Given this diversity of influence, it is Moody's judgment that assuming set foreclosure rates and degrees of loss severity may not be accurate. In some cases such assumptions may result in too high a pool coverage—which is good for the investor, but costly to the issuer. In those cases where the assumptions may lead to insufficient coverage, the result would be bad for both the investor and the market in general.

Moody's aproach uses as few assumptions as possible. Our assumptions center only on market conditions, such as unemployment rates,

Table 18–3
Moody's Whole-Loan Rating Approach
Time to Foreclosure

Group I (3 wks. to 3 mos.)	Group II (3 mos. to 6 mos.)	Group III (more than 6 mos.)
Alabama	Alaska	Connecticut
Dist. of Columbia	California	Illinois
Georgia	Colorado	New Jersey
Iowa	Florida	New Mexico
Maine	Hawaii	Ohio
Maryland	Idaho	Oklahoma
Michigan	Indiana	Puerto Rico
Minnesota	Kansas	Vermont
Mississippi	Kentucky	Wisconsin
Missouri	Louisiana	Wyoming
New Hampshire	Massachusetts	
North Carolina	Montana	
North Dakota	Nebraska	
Rhode Island	Nevada	
Tennessee	New York	
Texas	Oregon	
Virginia	Pennsylvania	
West Virginia	South Carolina	
	South Dakota	
	Utah	
	Washington	

direction of market values, and levels of interest rates commensurate with the economic severity one wishes the security to be able to withstand and keep investors whole. The ultimate test required for an Aaa security would be to survive conditions as severe as the Great Depression of the 1930s.

Moody's has developed a model that allows the characteristics of a pool of mortgages to react to these conditions in determining the appropriate pool coverage commensurate with the rating desired by the issuer.

To illustrate the sensitivity of the model to key elements of credit risk, let's first assume that we have a pool that is:

1. Very large in number
2. Diversified by locations commensurate with total United States employment diversification by industry
3. All mortgages on owner-occupied fixed-rate detached single-family homes of relatively equal distance from the median home price in each location
4. Economic stress commensurate with an Aa2 desired rating

With the understanding that we do not normally get such pristine pools to evaluate, let's look at the models' sensitivity to the two major factors influencing net equity over time: initial loan to value, and term to maturity. Again, net equity is the key variable to both foreclosure frequency and loss severity.

In Figure 18–6, each point represents total loss charged to a separate pool of loans of just one loan to value. Notice how fast the total loss charges goes up the higher is the initial loan to value. It reveals the exponential nature of foreclosure frequency and loss severity. Having a model that is sensitive to net equity is also very useful when we assess a pool of seasoned mortgages (*seasoned* means loans that have enjoyed a degree of home market value appreciation). Loans with greater appreciation will require smaller levels of pool coverage than fresh product with the same original loan to value, term, and coupon.

Given this nonlinear sensitivity, two pools with the same *average* loan to value could require vastly different pool coverage for the same desired rating level. Investors should know more about distributions of risk categories, not averages.

Figure 18–7 assumes a pool that is equally distributed between the various loan-to-value categories cited in Figure 18–6, plus all of the other plain vanilla and geographic considerations. This graph explores the sensitivity of term to maturity on total losses charged to the pool. As you can see, the shape of the curve moves upward as term to maturity is

Figure 18–6
**Moody's Whole-Loan Approach
Pool Coverage Requirements
Loan-to-Value Analysis**

Charge
to Pool (%)

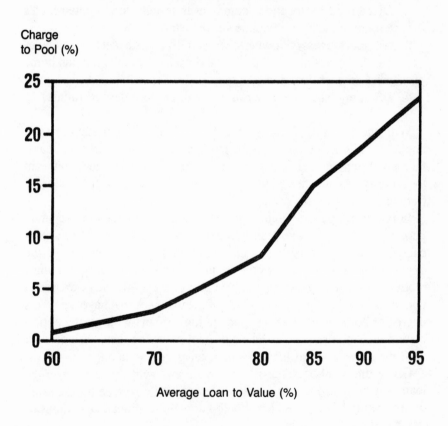

Average Loan to Value (%)

Source: Moody's 1986.

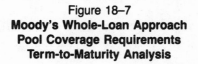

Figure 18–7
**Moody's Whole-Loan Approach
Pool Coverage Requirements
Term-to-Maturity Analysis**

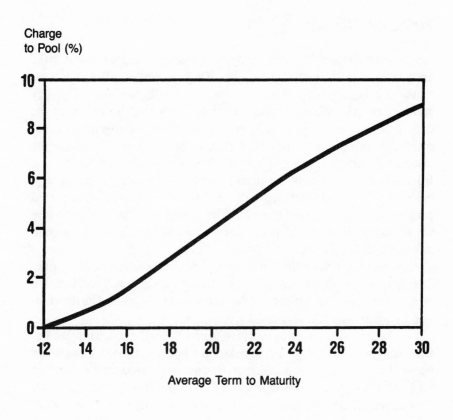

Source: Moody's 1986.

stretched out. Again, the results point to the nonlinear sensitivity of the model.

While there is a slight difference in 25-year mortgages versus 30-year mortgages, look how less risky 15-year mortgages are in comparison.

POOL CREDIT RISKS

So far this chapter has dealt only with basic mortgage credit risks associated with individual mortgages. There are other credit concerns, which can be called *pool risks*. Moody's models of claim frequency and loss severity are based on a very large data base comprised of the experience of over seven million insured loans. A specific pool of mortgages represents at most .006 percent of that base. Therefore, the chances of getting a pool that has all of the diverse attributes of the base from which our models are derived would be small. Consequently, individual pool performance will vary from what may be expected performance. If the collective claim frequencies or loss severity were worse than forecasted, the pool policy may not be sufficiently large to cover the excess losses.

Now quickly review the four major pool risk categories one by one. The first is geographic diversity. As stated earlier, local markets are quite diverse and are subject to different economic cycles. The distribution of loans by location must be considered.

The larger the number of mortgages in a pool, the more representative the pool will be of the population upon which our models are based. Moody's approach to size deficiencies is based on the standard error of the estimates of our models and the desired rating level. Consequently, Moody's does not suggest a minimum size but rather advises issuers how much coverage could be reduced if the number of loans of similar characteristics could be increased. Pool coverage is also affected by the deviation in the size of the loans. If the loan sizes are all fairly uniform, no adjustment is necessary. But should a large loan default in a pool of relatively small loans, that single default could affect the remaining balance of the pool coverage. Consequently,

Moody's examines the distribution of the pool by loan size and adjusts the pool coverage as necessary.

So far, we have looked at how much extra cushion is required. Now we must evaluate the strength of such supports. There are four major types of enhancement: (1) primary insurance on the individual loans, (2) pool insurance provided by the MI, (3) letters of credit, and (4) self insurance in the form of senior/subordinated structures. The claims-paying capacity rating is examined on both the pool and primary mortgage insurers. When a letter of credit (LOC) is used as a pool cover, the creditworthiness of the LOC bank is appraised. The provider of the LOC or pool policy must be rated at or above the desired rating on the security.

Moody's ratings of the private mortgage insurance companies are based on same analytical approach discussed earlier. Ratings reflect the high degree of industry exposure to unseasoned mortgages with high risk characteristics and a tighter overall nominal risk to capital position than was common during the 1970s. Consequently, as of mid-1986 very few MI companies (only three) had received a Moody's rating of Aa or better. It means in Moody's view, very few MIs are strong enough to provide the kind of protection required on Aaa or Aa mortgage-backed securities.

OUTLOOK FOR THE MI INDUSTRY

To gain a perspective on the MI industry and its prospects for the future, a quick look at the components of the industry's 1985 risk exposure would be helpful.

First, the industry has experienced a rapid increase in exposure to alternative mortgage instruments. As recently as 1982, conventional fixed-rate mortgages accounted for nearly 90 percent of industry risk. By the end of 1985, conventional fixed rate mortgages accounted for less than 60 percent of the industry risk (see Figure 18–8). ARMs with full amortization accounted for nearly 21 percent of the risk, with negatively amortizing ARMs for nearly 14 percent.

Figure 18–8
Mortgage Insurance Industry
Risk Distribution
Loan Type Analysis

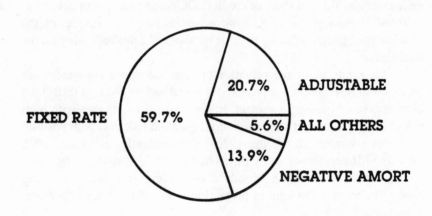

FIXED RATE — 59.7%

ADJUSTABLE — 20.7%

ALL OTHERS — 5.6%

NEGATIVE AMORT — 13.9%

Source: Moody's 1986.

Notwithstanding the industry's drive to tighten underwriting standards, 95 percent loan-to-value mortgages continued to increase as a percentage of risk to 48.15 percent, up from 45.8 percent a year before; less than 80 percent loan to value mortgages continued to decline, to 8.14 percent down from 9.8 percent in 1984. This trend reflected a move away from investor properties and vacation homes, which typically required higher down payments by most MI firms (see Figure 18–9).

The mortgage insurance industry has increased its business activity tremendously since 1982, the last year of the country's most recent and most severe postwar recession. As you can see in Figure 18–10, privately insured orgination volumes over the last three years were the highest ever recorded. As a result, the industry's risk exposure was heavily unseasoned during a period of the lowest home price appreciation since the late 1950s. Moreover, with expectations of a protracted deflationary period combined with the Tax Reform Act of 1986, which probably will soften home values even further, the industry may expect net equity buildup to remain well below previous experiece. This would tend to keep such loans more vulnerable to adverse economic events for a longer period.

Since these loans are still new they have also yet to pass through their peak loss period, which in the past had been three years, but has been extending further due to the slowdown in home prices. Consequently, the bulk of the mortgage insurance industry's risk exposure has yet to reach its peak loss period, but will do so by 1988.

While both the east and west coast economies are booming, a large part of the United States population is living in recession conditions, with some sections experiencing conditions of unemployment and home price devaluation that are commensurate with Moody's depression assumptions. With such a disparity of fortunes, the impact on the individual MI firms will depend on their exposures in such areas. As reported in Moody's 1986 annual review of the industry, there are distinct differences in company exposures by state. With more than 56 percent of the industry's exposure in the south and north central areas of the United States, the MI industry will find a return to underwriting profits a rather slow and tedious path (see Figure 18–11).

Figure 18–9
Mortgage Insurance Industry
Risk Distribution
Loan-to-Value Analysis

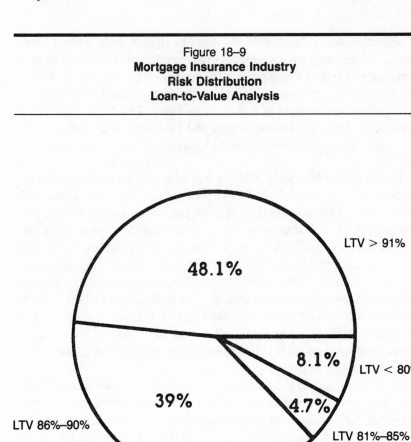

Source: Moody's 1986.

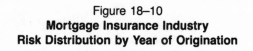

Figure 18–10
**Mortgage Insurance Industry
Risk Distribution by Year of Origination**

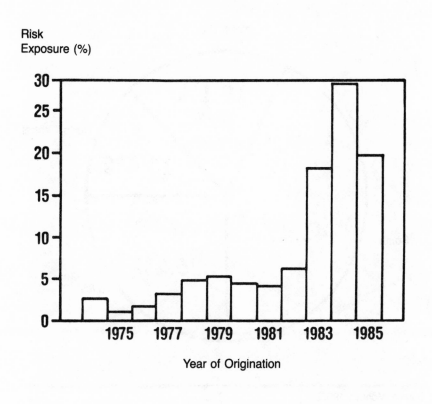

Risk
Exposure (%)

Year of Origination

Source: Moody's 1986.

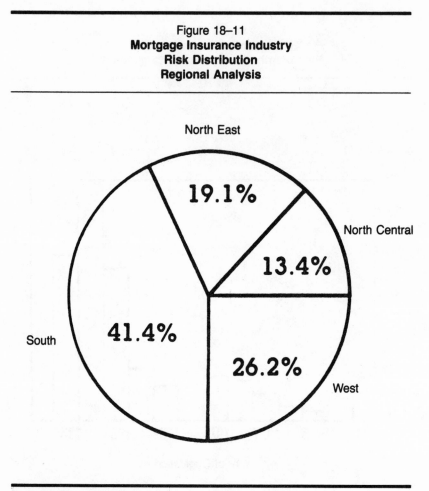

Figure 18–11
Mortgage Insurance Industry
Risk Distribution
Regional Analysis

Source: Moody's 1986.

In view of the limited number of companies strong enough to merit an Aa rating by Moody's, there has been a shift toward the use of letters of credit, which can also be designed to make up deficiencies of primary insurers and thereby afford investors extra protection. LOC-supported issues are straightforward and very easy to implement. Home Savings of California has also introduced a senior/subordinated structure—in essence, self insurance—which may be the wave of the future. While such issues are admittedly complex, such senior/subordianted structures can qualify for high ratings.

CONCLUSION

In viewing mortgage credit risk in today's increasingly fragmented market, Moody's strongly recommends that investors abandon approaches that are based on rules of thumb in favor of more careful and detailed review. It may enable investors to pick up bargains and also avoid some EPIC-type problems. For issuers, the assembly of a pool with the right characteristics could also save issuing costs or gain a higher rating and, therefore, a better price in the market.

Chapter 19

DONALD B. SUSSWEIN

*Donald B. Susswein is a partner in the New York based law firm of
Thacher Proffitt and Wood. He specializes in Federal taxation and is
resident in the firm's Washington office, which was the leading law
firm engaged in developing and shepherding the REMIC provisions
through the Congressional tax writing process. Prior to joining
Thacher Proffitt and Wood, Mr. Susswein served as Tax Counsel to the
U.S. Senate Finance Committee. He is a graduate of Columbia University and the Yale Law School.*

*Thacher Proffitt and Wood is a general practice New York firm with
a prominent role in the secondary mortgage market, representing
issuers, underwriters, purchasers and traders of mortgage securities,
as well as mortgage lenders. Through its Washington office, the firm
has represented the interests of secondary market participants in the
legislative and regulatory process. In addition to its role in the REMIC
legislation, the firm was at the forefront of the successful effort to enact
the Secondary Mortgage Market Enhancement Act.*

*The author appreciates the helpful comments and insights of Andrew
E. Furer, Vice President of Salomon Brothers Inc. Messrs. Furer and
Susswein were the principal draftsmen of the original mortgage securities industry proposal to legalize multiclass mortgage securities, which
formed the basis of the REMIC legislation.*

Using REMICs:
A Transactional Primer

DONALD B. SUSSWEIN

INTRODUCTION: WHAT IS REMIC?

REMIC (Real Estate Mortgage Investment Conduits) is the name for a new mortgage-backed security authorized by the landmark Tax Reform Act of 1986. The new tax act not only permits this new vehicle, but changes some of the rules governing existing mortgage-backed securities.

In general, the REMIC provisions liberalize prior tax law. They permit, on an elective basis, substantially greater flexibility in the use of traditional mortgage pass throughs and participations, as well as collateralized mortgage obligations (CMOs) and similar mortgage-backed debt obligations.

One significant limitation imposed by the new law is increased information reporting on CMOs issued after 1986.

Both the benefits and the detriments of the new REMIC provisions are applicable to securities issued after December 31, 1986. In some cases, however, transactions that closed before year end 1986 were structured with an eye toward the possibilities REMIC offers for restructuring in 1987 and thereafter. Although expanded information reporting will be required for CMOs issued after 1986, as well as other transactions electing the benefits of REMIC treatment, no actual reports are required by the IRS until 1988.

TRANSACTIONAL OVERVIEW: HOW REMIC CHANGES DEALS

Although REMIC is composed of a series of tax amendments to the Internal Revenue Code, its primary effect is to substantially reduce the significance of federal tax considerations in structuring mortgage securities transactions. The intent of the law, and its predominant effect, is to tax mortgage securities on the basis of their real economic substance, while allowing great flexibility to vary the form in which similar economic transactions are executed. The result is that accounting considerations, securities law considerations, regulatory concerns, and of course, the economic and financial considerations motivating the transaction, can be put in the driver's seat, while tax considerations are largely relegated to a subsidiary role in planning and structuring. A few examples will illustrate:

- Since 1984, when the Treasury Department issued the so-called "Sears" regulations, the IRS has prohibited fast-pay/slow-pay mortgage pools from using pass-through structures. Instead, issuers seeking to break mortgage pools into securities of varying maturities issued CMOs, which were transactions treated as financings for federal tax purposes. REMIC allows the creation of multiple class pass throughs and participation certificates. The advantages are that economically sound fast-pay/slow-pay transactions can be structured so that all of the mortgage cash flow goes to investors, with no equity retained by the issuer. In addition, it is expected that the issuer will be able to treat the transaction as an asset sale for financial accounting purposes, rather than a financing with added debt on its balance sheet.
- Although most issuers would prefer to issue pass throughs, others would prefer a financing structure. The most common reason would be a desire to avoid booking accounting losses on an income statement arising from the sale of below-market mortgages. REMIC allows the same "zero equity" pass-through transaction to be denominated as a bond issue. It is expected that this will facilitate the use of financing treatment for accounting purposes.

But by making a REMIC election the issuer has eliminated any risk that the IRS will question whether the bonds are true debt. Thus, whether pass-through form or debt form is chosen, the issuer is relieved of tax uncertainty, without any requirement that the efficiencies of the transaction be compromised by retaining equity in the security issued.

- Still other issuers want what they perceive to be the best of both worlds: pass-through structure and sale of assets accounting treatment, with clear-cut authorization for reserve funds, cash flow reinvestment, and the ability to sell to foreign investors free from the U.S. 30 percent withholding tax on interest paid to foreigners. REMIC allows multiple-class pass throughs to enjoy these benefits previously limited to mortgage-backed debt obligations like CMOs.

- The reason the Congress allows this flexibility ("the price") is that the investors and issuers of all of these transactions are taxed identically under the new rules: taxable gains and tax losses are recognized on the sale of interests in a REMIC mortgage pool (whether the interests are called "pass-through certificates," "participations," or "bonds"), and the new investors are taxed on their share of income from the pool regardless of the name given their investment.

REMIC BUILDING BLOCKS

The building blocks of REMIC transactions come in two basic categories: the underlying mortgage collateral that goes into the REMIC entity and the investment certificates that REMIC issues to investors.

REMIC Collateral

The basic and predominant type of collateral is called a *qualified mortgage*. This is an extremely broad category. It encompasses whole loans; 100 percent participation certificates and pass throughs; partial participations and interests in pass throughs; "stripped coupons," such as a stream of interest only on a mortgage, mortgage participation, or pass through; "stripped mortgages," such as the principal and part of the interest that remains after stripping off a stripped coupon; and senior and subordinated participations in mortgage pools. It also encompasses certain interests in other REMIC pools. (This is described in more detail in REMIC ground rules later in the chaper.)

Qualified mortgages (whichever of the forms are selected) must be secured by an interest in real property. Thus, both commercial and residential mortgage loans will qualify. However, automobile loans or installment receivables will not.

The second type of collateral is called a *cash flow investment*. In essence, this is a short-term investment in a passive, interest bearing asset made solely for the purpose of reinvesting cash flows received from qualified mortgages between regular scheduled payments to investors. Cash flow investments need not be mortgage-related in any way. They may be actual short-term securities, or third-party investment arrangements such as a guaranteed investment contract.

The third type of collateral is called a *qualified reserve fund*. This encompasses longer-term investments set aside in a reserve of reasonable size solely to fund the expenses (if any) of running the REMIC pool, or to insure investors against the risk of default on qualified mortgages. These investments can include mortgage securities or non-mortgage securities, and can also include third-party contractual guarantees to fund expenses or insure against default, such as letters of credit or pool insurance.

In addition, in the event of default on qualified mortgages, real property acquired in connection with foreclosure can be held for up to one year.

REMIC Interests Sold to Investors

Once the REMIC collateral is selected, interests in the pool can be created for investors. As with other aspects of REMICs, the hallmark of the law is substance, not form. Permissible REMIC interests can be

called bonds, participations, pass-through certificates, or even corporate stock or partnership interests for that matter. The important rules
relate to the economic differences between different types of REMIC
interests that can be sold to investors or retained by issuers.

The predominant form of investor participation in a REMIC is called
a *regular interest*. Regular interests can best be thought of as being the
economic equivalent of bonds, although they can be issued in the form
of pass throughs as well as debt obligations. In essence, a regular
interest must have an amount corresponding to the principal of a debt
obligation. It may also (but need not) provide for coupon interest on the
outstanding principal amount.

Regular interests can be issued in multiple classes. Thus, in a mortgage pool subject to prepayment, the earliest mortgages to prepay can
be assigned to the fast-pay regular interests while the last mortgages to
pay off can be assigned to the slow-pay regular interest, just like a
CMO. Regular interests can also be issued with differing priorities in
the event of defaults on qualified mortgages. Thus, senior and junior
participations in mortgage pools can be created and issued as multiple
classes of regular interests. The advantage of a REMIC senior/ junior
arrangement (as compared with similar arrangements under the grantor
trust rules) is that Congress has explicitly clarified that both the senior
and the junior classes can be freely traded. There has been some
uncertainty whether junior interests in a traditional grantor trust participation or pass through can be traded without losing pass-through treatment.

The second type of investment in a REMIC pool is called a *residual
interest*. Residual interests are statutorily defined, somewhat cryptical-
ly, as investments that are designated as residual interests and that are
not regular interests. Although some points remain to be clarified in
Treasury regulations, residual interests are generally intended to encompass rights to payments that are contingent on a certain speed of
prepayments (for example, excess servicing that will be extinguished if
prepayments accelerate; or "excess"" mortgage principal in an overcol-
lateralized structure that will be used up to make interest payments to
regular interest holders if prepayments are slower than anticipated).

In additon, residual interests can encompass the right to earnings on qualified reserve funds or cash flow investments that are not needed to pay the amounts guaranteed to holders of regular interests. In general, there are no restrictions on the size of residual interests, since the purpose of the new law was to permit the elimination of "equity" from CMO-like transactions. However there must always be one, and only one, class of residual interests. Thus, any payments that are contingent in amount on the extent of prepayments of qualified mortgages, or the amount of income earned on cash flow investments, or the risk that qualified reserve funds will be called upon to pay unexpected expenses, must all be allocated to the single class of investors who own the residual interests. Although different investors may own different size portions of the residual interest, all of their interests must be undivided, pro rata interests.

REMIC GROUND RULES

Setting Up a REMIC

A number of basic ground rules apply to setting up a REMIC pool and issuing REMIC interests to investors. A REMIC must have one, and only one, class of residual interests; regular interests can be set up without limitation.

Because of the broad definition of qualified mortgages (encompassing any mortgage participation or pass through that qualifies as a grantor trust, as well as other mortgage-related obligations) the REMIC rules permit an almost infinite series of structural options. For example, a single pool of 10 percent mortgages can be divided into a strip of 4 percent coupon interest, separate from the underlying principal and the remaining 6 percent of coupon interest. The portion representing principal and 6 percent interest can be put into a REMIC and divided up into multiple classes, including a residual interest that is contingent on prepayment experience and the extent of reinvestment earnings. The strip of 4 percent coupon interest can be sold or used as collateral for another REMIC. Moreover, regular interests in either

REMIC can serve as collateral for additional tiers of REMICs, or for pass throughs or CMOs.

Most importantly, unlike the coupon-stripping rules applicable under the grantor trust rules, the interests in a REMIC need not be interests in specifically identified principal or interest payments: as prepayments occur and the yield on cash flow investments varies, the REMIC can make payments to regular and residual holders based on the terms of the REMIC governing agreement that defines which interests are to be paid first in cases of mortgage default or mortgage prepayment.

REMICs must be structured, however, to be essentially self-liquidating pools. A REMIC is generally prohibited from buying new mortgages to add to the pool.

Starting Up a REMIC

A REMIC need not be a separate legal entity under state law. A REMIC pool can be a simple accounting entry or ledger identifying the mortgages that are set aside for the REMIC and documents specifying the interests investors will have in the pool. If a separate legal entity is established, however, it can be a participation agreement, pass through, corporation, trust, partnership, association, or indenture trust. This flexibility can allow issuers with shelf registrations to issue multiple series of REMICs under a single shelf registration.

The rights of regular interest holders must be established when the REMIC is created, a day referred to as the *startup day*. By definition, since there is only one class of residual interest and its rights are to receive whatever is not used to pay regular interests, the rights of the residual interest holders are also determined as of the startup day. This "preprogramming" ensures that the rights of different classes are not varied through active management by the REMIC, although variations on the basis of actual prepayments, reinvestment income, and default experience are permitted under the terms established on the startup day.

In general, qualified mortgages can be transferred on or before the startup day, or within the first three months after the startup day. In addition, in certain cases defective mortgages can be substituted within the first two years of the REMIC's existence.

Operating a REMIC

As a preprogrammed, self-liquidating mortgage pool, the REMIC should operate without substantial discretion on the part of its managers or trustees. Limited discretion is permitted with respect to short-term reinvestment of cash flows. But a series of "prohibited transaction" rules prevent the REMIC from acquiring new mortgage investments or selling mortgages to pay off investors early. The rules also require reserve funds to be reduced as the need for them diminishes. The REMIC is permitted, however, to substitute defective mortgages in certain circumstances, and to dispose of mortgages in connection with their default or imminent default.

The REMIC will have information reporting responsibilities to the IRS and to investors that are not currently applicable to mortgage pools structured as grantor trusts. In the case of regular interests issued at a discount, the rules may require relatively sophisticated systems for keeping track of mortgage cash flows and prepayments.

In general, the tax compliance rules similar to those applicable to debt instruments apply to REMIC interests, including restrictions and special rules regarding the sale of bearer bonds to domestic and foreign investors.

Shutting Down a REMIC

A REMIC is designed to run automatically like a complex cash flow machine, until it runs out of qualified mortgages. There is one exception, a special rule allowing for a complete liquidation of a REMIC within a 90-day period. Under these rules, the sponsors of the REMIC may adopt a plan of liquidation, sell off all of the assets and distribute the proceeds to the holders of regular and residual interests. This may be particularly advantageous if the decision to liquidate is in the hands of the residual interest holders, who may stand to benefit if market fluctuations permit regular interests to be retired at a profit.

HOW REMICS ARE TAXED

The transfer of qualified mortgages to a REMIC is generally a tax-free transaction. The transferor's unrecognized gain or loss, however, is reflected in a carryover basis in the regular or residual interests received in exchange. If and when those interests are sold, the gain or loss is taken into account over the life of the interest under special allocation rules. Issuance expenses are allowable as an immediate offset to the recognition of gain under these rules.

The REMIC itself is a tax-free entity, all of whose taxable income is passed through to the residual interest holders. That taxable income, however, is computed with a full deduction for the amount of REMIC income allocated to regular interest holders. Since the regular interests are taxed as if they were debt obligations (with interest income includable for the regular interest holders, and interest deductions made possible for the REMIC in computing how much taxable income is left to tax to the residual interest holders) the result is that the residual interests are taxed much as if they were interests in a pass-through entity issuing debt (that is, an owner's trust).

Regular interest holders are taxed much the same as a similar debt instrument would be taxed. However, new rules spell out how original issue discount is to be computed in the event the regular interests are issued at a discount with maturities that are subject to acceleration in the event of prepayments.

Residual interests are taxed on whatever is left over after REMIC income is allocated to regular interest holders by operation of the rules treating regular interests as the equivalent of debt obligations of the REMIC. Because of concerns that residual interests (which may tend to be highly taxed instruments) might be purchased by tax-exempt institutions and loss companies, special rules rules apply to limit the extent to which net operating losses can offset the income of a residual interest holder, and to require certain portions of residual interest income to be taxable for foreigners and otherwise tax-exempt entities.

In some cases, it may be preferable to issue CMOs structured as debt for tax purposes or to issue traditional pass throughs or participations, instead of using the REMIC provisions. For example, traditional financings avoid gain recognition and may facilitate the sale of residual interests to certain taxpayers. Because REMIC treatment is elective, consideration of the relative tax and structural advantages of each structure is advisable.

SPECIAL TAX CONSIDERATIONS FOR REMIC INVESTORS

REMIC interests enjoy several favorable tax attributes for certain investors.

For foreign investors, regular interests qualify as portfolio interest, exempt from the 30 percent U.S. federal withholding tax. Unlike mortgage participations and pass throughs, this exemption applies without regard to the date of origination of the underlying mortgage. Thus, by using a REMIC, mortgages originated before July 19, 1984 can be sold to foreigners free of withholding taxes. This cannot be done under current law with a pass-through or participation structure.

REMIC interests are treated as qualifying real estate loans for thrift institutions and REITS required to invest in real estate assets, as long as the underlying mortgage collateral would have qualified as such an investment.

RESTRICTIONS ON OWNERS' TRUSTS AFTER 1991

REMIC imposes restrictions—applicable in 1992 after a five-year transition period—on the use of owners' trusts and similar pass through entities that issue multiple class mortgage-backed debt obligations, and similar investments. These rules are not intended or expected to adversely affect transactions executed prior to 1992.

CONCLUSION: WHAT REMIC DOESN'T SAY

Although REMIC makes major changes in the federal tax rules applicable to mortgage-backed securities, it does not amend the federal or state securities laws, state and local tax rules that may be applicable to investment entities, ERISA rules dealing with pension fund management and fiduciary responsibilities, or accounting conventions applicable to mortgage securities transactions. Thus, REMIC is not a panacea to all legal problems and issues involving the secondary mortgage market.

In addition, there are aspects of REMIC that may still be uncertain until Treasury regulations or IRS rulings are issued.

Nevertheless, REMIC appears to have resolved the most serious federal tax impediments to the efficient and creative functioning of the secondary mortgage market.

Section III:
The Mortgage
Banking Industry

INTRODUCTION

The four chapters of Section III deal with issues of particular relevance to mortgage bankers (or institutions who act like mortgage bankers by originating loans for resale into the secondary market; these include increasing numbers of thrifts and commercial banks). Chapter 20 provides a transition from the world of mortage securities to the closely related world of wholesale mortgage bankers, which purchase loans and resell them as whole loans, participations, and securities. In this chapter, Jess Lederman advances a new theory of pricing loans in the wholesale market.

While wholesalers acquire product through the purchase of mortgage loans, the majority of mortgage bankers compete in the spot market, where the realtor is their prime customer. A smaller number of mortgage bankers, however, have found a profitable niche by servicing the builder market. This is the subject of Chapter 21, in which Joseph Garrett discusses the art of subdivision lending.

The final two chapters of Section III explore the purchase and sale of loan servicing. This is one of the most fascinating—and least well understood—subjects in mortgage finance. It is also one of the most rapidly growing markets, and an area that will amply repay careful analysis. Chapter 22 examines servicing trades from the sellers' perspective. In Part A, Hunter Wolcott makes the case that originators seeking to maximize value from the sale of servicing must master the nuances of the market by carefully analyzing and segmenting their servicing portfolios and by understanding the needs of the investor. Tim Cohane and Larry Rafferty present case studies in Part B that provide detailed examples of the quantitative analysis and legal agreements that are employed in servicing sales. In Chapter 23 Peter Ross looks at servicing sales from the buyer's perspective, and demonstrates the critical relationship between the cost of an acquisition of servicing and its ultimate profitability.

Chapter 20

JESS LEDERMAN
AND
JAMES WALTERS

Jess Lederman is Executive Vice President with Bear Stearns Mortgage Capital Corporation, a wholly-owned subsidiary of Bear Stearns & Co., Inc. Previously he was Vice President of Marketing for Sears Mortgage Securities Corporation. Before joining Sears, Lederman was Director of Pricing and Research for PMI Mortgage Insurance Co.

James Walters is Director of Pricing and Financial Analysis for Bear Stearns Mortgage Capital Corporation. Previously he was Financial Analyst for the Federal Home Loan Bank System.
  Bear Stearns Mortgage Capital Corporation is one of the nation's leading private mortgage conduit companies.

Dual Asset Pricing Theory: A New Approach to Pricing Loans in the Wholesale Market

JESS LEDERMAN AND JAMES WALTERS

INTRODUCTION

On the surface, wholesalers of any given commodity seem to face a fairly straightforward challenge: buying goods and reselling them at a markup sufficient to generate a reasonable profit. The fundamentals are the same whether we are dealing in mortgages or mushrooms: buy low and sell high. Most of the sophisticated pricing analysis that has emerged in recent years has focused on hedging price risk between the time of purchase and sale of mortgage assets. However, the great interest rate rally of 1985–86 not only challenged preconceptions of proper hedging theory, it also served to demonstrate to wholesalers that mortgage loans cannot be thought of as one indivisible asset. Rather, mortgages are a *dual asset*, with components of remarkably different character. The purpose of this chapter is to demonstrate the dual nature of mortgages, and the shortcomings of traditional techniques for pricing loans in the wholesale market.

MORTGAGES AS DUAL ASSETS: A CASE STUDY

ABC Mortgage Company is a wholesale mortgage banker that purchases 30 year nonconforming fixed-rate loans from a network of correspondents and pools loans into private securities for resale in the secondary market. Table 20–1 displays ABC's price and anticipated profit margins as of January 1:

Table 20–1			
	From Correspondents	To Investors	Spread
Net Rate	10.250%	10.000%	.250%
Price	99.000	100.000	1.000

ABC intends to earn a master servicing fee of .25 percent (ABC purchases loans servicing retained and aggregates the payments from each of its correspondents into one payment to the investor), which covers its annual costs and provides a basic master servicing profit, and a 1 percent up-front fee based on the buy-sell spread. It does not simultaneously buy and sell loans; rather, its pricing to its correspondents is based on ABC's perception of where investors would be buying its securities at any given point in time. In actuality, ABC hedges correspondent commitments by shorting Ginnie Maes in the forward market until a sufficient volume of loans has been purchased to warrant pooling for delivery. ABC is confident that this is a prudent hedge because investors have consistently purchased its packages at a stable spread over comparable coupon Ginnie Maes.

Over the next 45 days, rates rally and ABC purchases loans from correspondents at consecutively lower rates, which are shown in Table 20–2.

On February 15, ABC cuts off its accumulation to create a $6.25 milion pool for sale. Its pricing assumptions seem to have worked

Table 20–2
Purchases Between January 1 and February 15*

Net Rate	Volume of Purchases
10.250%	$2,450,000
10.125	1,750,000
9.875	750,000
9.625	1,300,000
Total	$6,250,000

*All purchases are made at a price of 99.

perfectly, for investors are not quoting a price of par for packages with a net rate of 9.375 percent. This locks in the targeted profit for the last loans purchased (at 9.625 percent at 99 percent). It appears that this same profit would be locked in for all the other, higher-rate loans.

In this case, appearances may be deceiving. ABC's investors will not purchase securities above par; therefore, the entire package must be sold with a 9.375 percent coupon at a price of par. ABC is not the only seller to confront this *par-cap phenomenon*. Most investors are reluctant to purchase mortgages or mortgage-backed securities above par, due to prepayment uncertainty, and this is especially true for less-liquid, private label issues. Table 20–3 summarizes ABC's situation at the point of sale:

ABC has consistently purchased loans at a price of 99 and is able to sell the security at par, thereby generating an up-front gain of 1 percent. This gain is more than offset, however, by a hedging loss of 2.594 percent on ABC's short position in Ginnies. If ABC had not faced the par cap, it could have sold its security with a coupon of 9.790 percent (10.04 percent less the minimum master servicing spread of .25 percent) and, if investors would purchase this coupon at the same yield as the 9.375 percent coupon, at price of 102.594, thus achieving the targeted net profit of 1 percent.

Table 20–3

Weighted Average Net Rate on Mortgages	10.040%
Less Security Coupon	9.375
Equals Master Servicing Spread	.665
Security Price	100.000%
Less Mortgage Purchase Price	99.000
Equals Buy-Sell Spread	1.000%
Loss on Hedge	(2.594%)

Two observations should be made at this point:

1. Investors in mortgages and mortgage-backed securities generally require higher yields on premiums relative to discounts or par packages.
2. Because ABC's investors will not purchase its packages above par, it has retained an excess master servicing spread of .415 percent (the difference between .665 percent and .250 percent).

The conclusion is clear: the net profitability of ABC's $6.25 million package is dependent on the value of the .415 percent excess spread, and the value of the excess spread is less than 2.594 percent. ABC will fail to realize its targeted profit margin, even though all of the variables normally analyzed in a classic hedging example behaved in "textbook" fashion.

The problem is that conventional pricing analysis has typically failed to take into account the fact that the par-cap phenomenon frequently requires wholesalers to retain significant excess servicing spreads. In effect, the packages that wholesalers sell are often "stripped securities"—instruments in which one party receives 100 percent of principal and most of the interest, while another party receives a smaller interest "strip." ABC has not simply decided to service for a higher fee on its $6.25 million package. It has retained a strip of interest with an economic value that is critical to the determination of the net profitability of the transaction.

The purchase and resale of mortgages has therefore given rise to the creation of two assets: a security and an excess interest strip. Until 1986, however, most wholesalers did not think in these terms. Excess interest strips were thought of simply as excess servicing spread. While "excess servicing" was often capitalized and taken into income, wholesalers would frequently use stock assumptions in their capitalization calculations. For example, a great deal of "excess servicing" was valued using the same prepay assumption and required yield used in selling the underlying security. This seemingly appealing approach proved particularly dangerous, because it led issuers who focused only on the reported bottom line to be indifferent between selling packages with no "excess servicing" or with significant "excess servicing" spreads.

What is the true value of excess servicing (which is perhaps better named a "100 percent interest strip")? An interest strip is an asset with characteristics very different from the underlying security. Consider a premium security—for example, a 10 percent Ginnie Mae at a price of 102.5. If the Ginnie Mae were to prepay, the investor would receive principal back at par, thereby incurring a loss equal to the 2.5 point premium, or, in percentage terms, a loss of 2.44 percent. Consider an interest strip of 0.5 percent that is purchased for a price of 2.5 percent. If the underlying security prepays, the investor in the interest strip receives nothing—the loss is 100 percent! This extreme downside risk tends to lead to higher required rates of return for interest strips than for the underlying mortgage securities. Note that in our example, if 9.5 percent Ginnie Maes were priced at par (and if 9.5 percent and 10.0 percent Ginnies had substantially similar prepayment rates), one could infer an implicit market valuation of interest strips embodied in Ginnie Mae prices. Investors would presumably be indifferent between purchasing a Ginnie Mae 10 percent coupon at 102.5 percent or purchasing both a 9.5 percent coupon at par and a .5 percent interest strip at a price of 2.5 percent.

VALUING INTEREST STRIPS

The valuation of an interest strip is, in theory, very simple: a prepayment assumption must be chosen, and the resulting cash flows must be discounted at a given rate of return. In practice, two approaches are used:

1. Assuming one "base case" prepay rate and reflecting prepayment uncertainty by using a required yield set at a higher level than the yield on the underlying security
2. Incorporating a required yield that is comparable to the yield on the underlying security, but reflecting prepayment uncertainty by using a range of prepayment scenarios, weighted by their respective probabilites

These approaches are expressed algebraically in the appendix to this chapter.

PRICE SENSITIVITY OF INTEREST STRIPS

The value of an interest strip responds to changes in market rates very differently from the underlying security. Generally, the price of a fixed-income security increases when rates decline. Mortgages, however, are complicated·instruments with durations that extend or contract as changes in market rates influence prepayment levels. Typically, the price of a mortgage sold at a discount or at or near par increases when rates decline. However, traders of premiums know that rallys can often lead to a *decline* in the price of relatively high-coupon mortgage securities. This is because a relatively high proportion of the value of premiums derives from the security *coupon*, and their price is thus correlated with the duration of cash flow. This is entirely the case with interest strips. If duration lengthens, value increases, and vice versa. A hypothetical price/yield matrix for an excess interest strip is shown in Table 20–4.

				Table 20–4					
				PSA speed					
Required Yield	100	125	150	175	200	225	250	275	300
			(Value of a 1% Interest Strip)						
10.75	5.89	5.52	5.19	4.91	4.65	4.42	4.22	4.03	3.87
11.25	5.74	5.39	5.08	4.80	4.56	4.34	4.14	3.96	3.80
11.75	5.59	5.26	4.96	4.70	4.47	4.26	4.07	3.90	3.74
12.25	5.46	5.14	4.86	4.60	4.38	4.18	4.00	3.83	3.68
12.75	5.33	5.02	4.75	4.51	4.30	4.10	3.93	3.77	3.62
13.25	5.20	4.91	4.65	4.42	4.22	4.03	3.86	3.71	3.57
13.75	5.08	4.80	4.56	4.34	4.14	3.96	3.80	3.64	3.51
14.25	4.97	4.70	4.47	4.25	4.06	3.89	3.73	3.59	3.46

THE DUAL ASSET DILEMMA

As we have seen, mortgages purchased for resale can represent a dual asset. The prices of each of the component assets are derived independently (the investors for each of the assets are likely to be different types of institutions) and will respond to changes in market conditions in very different—indeed, often opposite—ways. The crowning complication that wholesalers must face is that at the time any given loan is purchased, there is typically no way of *precisely* determining the percentage that will be sold as stripped interest and the percentage that will be sold as principal plus interest.

To see why this is so, consider our case study. The amount of excess servicing that ABC retained was entirely dependent on the extent of the interest rate rally. Furthermore, many wholesalers allow their correspondents to deliver a range of net rates that often extends over 100–200 basis points. Issuers that package loans into rated securities typically must establish a security coupon that is below the lowest net rate in the pool. All of these factors can increase the size of the interest strip relative to the underlying security.

This, then, is the "dual asset dilemma": wholesalers must price and hedge an asset that has a value and price behavior that can only be determined probabilistically. If a wholesaler issues securities that must be structured with a coupon below the lowest net rate, then the profitability of loan n will be a function not only of its own loan characteristics but also of the net rate on loan $n+1$. If loan $n+1$ has a lower net rate (whether due to interest rate fluctuations or simply to the allowance of a range of deliverable net rates), and if an interest strip has a higher required rate of return (and/or a faster prepay assumption) than the underlying security, then the profitability of loan n will decrease.

The decrease in the profitability of loan n is likely to be exacerbated in an interest rate rally due to the unique price/yield characteristics of interest strips. In a rally, wholesalers will purchase loans at consecutively lower rates, thereby increasing the dollar amount of the higher rate loans that must be sold as a higher-yielding, lower-valued interest strip. In addition, the expected duration of the interest strip will decrease, thereby reducing its value. This can lead to potentially radical changes in hedging strategy. For example, a wholesaler who anticipates a rally typically reduces or eliminates its short position to avoid hedging losses. Using dual asset pricing theory, however, the wholesaler might conceivably hedge the rally by purchasing calls!*

ANALYZING CONVENTIONAL PRICING USING DUAL ASSET PRICING THEORY

There are two pricing methods that are commonly employed by wholesalers when they purchase loans from correspondents:

---

*So much for those whimsical analysts who have dubbed this strategy a "Texas hedge"!

Yield equivalency: Often referred to as "goldbook" pricing, this involves pricing loans to produce a given mortgage yield, typically assuming a 12-year simple prepayment assumption for 30-year, fixed-rate loans.

Straight line: Under this method, correspondents are given a maximum net rate and price, as well as price adjustment factors, which indicate by how much the price will change for every ⅛ percent that the delivered net rate is below the maximum net rate.

Figures 20–1 and 20–2 illustrate the relationship between the net rate on loans purchased from correspondents and the level of profit, given the assumptions stated earlier. Note that the assumption is made that each net rate is paired with the optimal security coupon (that is, the coupon that will minimize the size of the interest strip); thus, a 10.375 percent net rate is placed in a 9.500 percent coupon security, and an 8.375 percent net rate is placed in a 8 percent security.

Analyzing Figure 20–1, it can be observed that profit stays constant between net rates of 9.875 percent and 10.375 percent. This is because the multiple received for the interest strip is exactly equal to the price adjustment factor used in pricing the mortgage loans (.125 in rate equals .625 in price). If the wholesaler receives a multiple of less than 5 for the interest strip, profitability will decline with increases in the size of the strip; if the multiple received for the strip is greater than 5, then profitability will increase. At net rates below 9.875 percent, profitability decreases. This has nothing to do with the interest strip, because below 9.875 percent there is no need to issue a security with an interest strip. The decline in profitability occurs because the price of the security falls more rapidly in response to a given change in coupon than the price of the mortgage. This is shown in Table 20–5.

How is profitability affected when correspondents deliver loans over a range of net rates under each of these pricing methods? Consider the following assumptions:

Pricing Assumptions

Mortgage Pricing

Maximum Net Rate:	10.375%
Purchase Price at Maximum Net Rate:	99.900
Net Yield for Yield Equivalency Pricing:	10.390
Price Adjustment Factor for Straight-Line Pricing:	.625

Security Pricing

Security Coupon:	We will assume that the security coupon will be set as high as possible (to minimize the size of the interest strip) so long as the security price does not exceed par; the maximum coupon is thus 9.50% (see security yield).
Security Yield:	In our first example we assume that all security coupons will be priced to achieve the same cash flow bond equivalent yield: 9.60%.
Prepayment Speed:	Prepayment speed will be held constant at a CPP of 6% for all security coupons.

Interest Strip*

Required Cash Flow Bond Equivalent Yield:	12%
CPP:	6%

---

*Note: Given these assumptions, a 0.50% interest strip will have a value of approximately 2.50—a "multiple" of 5. While the gross underlying mortgage rate will affect the valuation (and thus the precise multiple) of an interest strip to a very small degree, multiples are a convenient and accurate way to express the value of interest strips, and we will use a multiple of 5 throughout this example as our "base case."

Figure 20–1
Straight Line Pricing

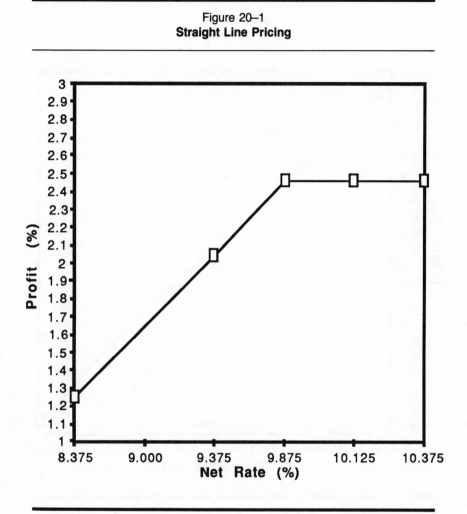

Figure 20–2
Goldbook Pricing

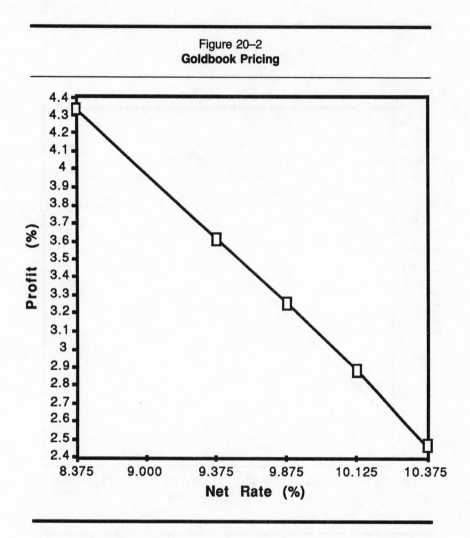

Figure 20–2 demonstrates that under goldbook pricing, profitability increases steadily as the delivered net rate decreases. This is because the mortgage price/rate multiple (the approximate change in price for a given change in rate) is about 6.5, versus a multiple of 5 for the interest strip (relevant for delivered net rates above 9.875 percent) and a multi-

Table 20–5

Net Rate on Mortgage	Mortgage Price	Change in Mortgage Price	Security Coupon	Security Price	Change in Security Price
9.875%	97.400%	—	9.500%	99.863%	—
9.375	94.900	2.500	9.000	96.943	2.920
8.375	89.900	5.000	8.000	91.194	5.749

Table 20–6
Multiple Net Rates in One Security*

Net Rate	Mortgage Price (Goldbook)	Security Price Less Mortgage Price	Value of Interest Strip	Total Profit
9.875%	96.609%	.334%	2.500%	2.834%
9.375	93.341	3.602	—	3.602
				6.436%

*Security coupon: 9.000%, security price: 96.943%.

ple of approximately 5.8 for the security (relevant for delivered net rates below 9.875 percent).

It is important to recognize that this does not mean that the delivery of a loan with a relatively low net rate will improve aggregate profitability—in fact, the reverse may be true, unless the issuer can *subdivide purchased loans into pools that are based on optimum net rate/security coupon pairings*. To understand why this is true, consider the two examples shown in Tables 20–6 and 20–7.

Table 20–7
Separate Securities for Net Separate Rates

Net Rate	Mortgage Price (Goldbook)	Security Coupon	Security Price	Profit
9.875%	96.609%	9.500%	99.863%	3.254%
9.375	93.341	9.000	96.943	3.602
				6.856%

Including the 9.875 percent net rate in the 9 percent security subopti-mizes, because the extra .500 percent in rate is worth more to the purchasers of securities than to the purchasers of interest strips.

ANALYZING THE IMPACT OF COUPON/YIELD RELATIONSHIPS

The examples discussed previously make the simplifying assumption that all security coupons are priced to achieve the same yield. In reality, the required cash flow yield for securities of different coupons can vary widely. While specific supply and demand fluctuations can distort the yield relationships between different coupons the rule of thumb is that lower coupons require lower yields than higher coupons of the same security. Lower coupons generally offer greater potential for price appreciation and often have less volatile prepayment characteristics. Figure 20–3 graphs FHLMC Participation Certificate (PC) 1 month Constant Percent Prepayment (CPP) speeds as of October, 1986 against the corresponding security coupon. One can infer from Figure 20–3 that a 50 basis point change in market rates would produce only a 200–300 basis point change in CPP for a 9.5 percent PC, whereas the same change in market rates would produce as much as a 1000 basis point change in CPP for a 10.5 percent PC.

Figure 20—3
FHLMC PC Coupon to CPP Relationship

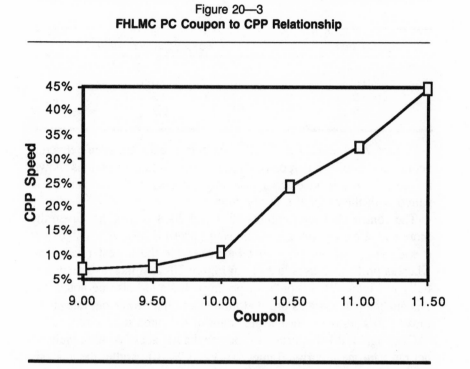

This lower coupon/lower yield phenomenon is often accentuated with private issue securities. The reason for this is that private issuers frequently package a wider spread of net rates in one security than agency issuers. As a result, the coupon on a private security is often low relative to the (WAC) on the underlying loans.

Such securities are "ideal" discounts, particularly for bullish investors. To understand why, refer to Figure 20–3, which illustrates how higher coupon loans are apt to experience a greater increase in prepayment speed than lower coupon loans for a given decline in market rates. Additionally, increases in prepayment speed provide a "yield kicker" to the purchaser of discount securities.

We can therefore add a new element to our analysis by revising our security yield assumptions, as shown in Table 20–8.

Table 20–8

Coupon	Bond Equivalent Yield
9.5%	9.6%
9.0	9.5
8.0	9.2

Figures 20–4 and 20–5 illustrate the relationship between delivered net rate and profit, incorporating the security yield assumptions shown in Table 20–8 and once again assuming that each delivered net rate is paired with the optimal security coupon.

The contrast between Figures 20–1 and 20–4 is striking. Given the more realistic coupon/yield relationship, profit is relatively stable over a wide range of net rates, but *increases* for the lowest rates. And whereas profit increases linearly in Figure 20–2, it increases expotentially in Figure 20–5 (goldbook pricing). It should also be noted that this analysis understates profits to the extent that lower net rates have lower CPPs, thus increasing the value of the interest strip.

Once again, it is important to analyze the impact of pooling multiple net rates in one security. Tables 20–9 and 20–10 parallel the analysis performed in Tables 20–6 and 20–7.

Table 20–9
Multiple Net Rates in One Security

Net Rate	Mortgage Price (Goldbook)	Security Price Less Mortgage Price	Value of Interest Strip	Total Price
9.875%	96.609%	.892%	2.500%	3.392%
9.375	93.341	4.160	—	4.160
				7.552%

Figure 20–4
Straight Line Pricing

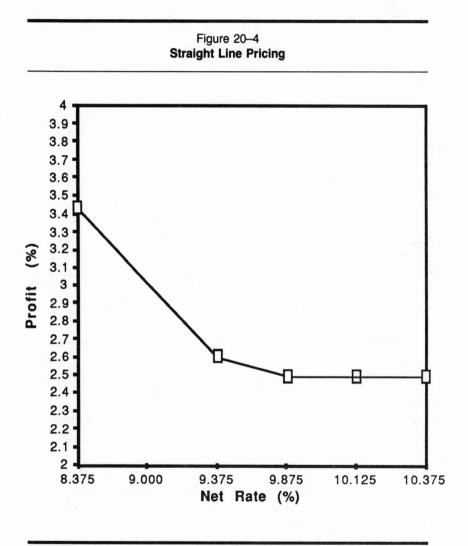

Figure 20–5
Goldbook pricing

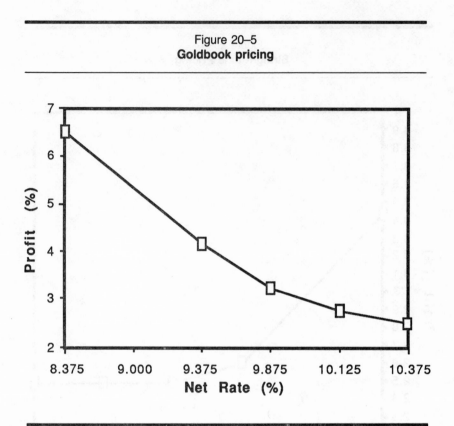

Table 20–10
Separate Securities for Separate Net Rates

Net Rate	Mortgage Price (Goldbook)	Security Coupon	Security Price	Profit
9.875%	96.609%	9.500%	99.863%	3.254%
9.375	93.341	9.000	97.501	4.160
				7.414%

Given our new coupon/yield assumptions, an issuer would be better off issuing the lowest possible coupon, thereby *increasing* the size of the interest strip. In order for an issuer to benefit from structuring a security with a coupon lower than the maximum allowable coupon (i.e., the coupon equal to the minimum net rate less servicing), the following relationship must hold:

$$P_1 - P_2 < [C_1 - C_2]E$$

Where:
P_1 = Price of security with maximum allowable coupon

P_2 = Price of security with lower coupon

C_1 = Maximum allowable coupon

C_2 = Lower coupon

E = Interest strip multiple

Note: A more sophisticated version of this equation would be derived by substituting the equation for value of an interest strip for the right hand side of the equation given above, incorporating $Iq = (C_1 - C_2)/12$

By manipulating this equation we can solve for the value of the interest strip multiple at which an issuer would be indifferent between coupons:

$$E = (P_1 - P_2) / (C_1 - C_2)$$

CONCLUSION

Whether the lessons of dual asset pricing theory are exhilarating or depressing depends on your point of view. Pricing in the wholesale market is certainly more complicated than many of us had previously thought. Most analysis to date has dealt simply with the relationship between the security price and the mortgage price, after netting out servicing and packaging (issuance) costs. But pricing analysis must go beyond that. Under dual asset pricing theory, wholesalers seek to maximize profit given their expectations for the range of delivered net rates and the relationships among the mortgage multiple, security multiple, and interest strip multiple over a range of coupons and interest rate scenarios.

APPENDIX

A-1 Definition of Interest Strips

$$I_q = [C_q - S - C_s]/12$$

Where: I_q = Interest strip on loan "q"

C_q = Net rate on loan "q"

S = Servicing Costs (insurance, trustee fees, and so on)

C_s = Security coupon

A-2 Valuation of Interest Strips

A)

$$V = \sum_{q=1}^{x} \sum_{n=c}^{m} (Bq,n \times Iq)/(1+i)^n$$

Where: V   =   Value of Interest Strip

Bq,n   =   Outstanding principal balance of loan "q" in month "n"

Iq   =   Interest strip on loan 8, divided by 12

i   =   Required yield, divided by 12

n   =   Month of loan life, from current month (c) to maturity (m)

q   =   Loans 1 through "x"

B)

$$V = \sum_{S=1}^{Z} \sum_{q=1}^{x} \sum_{n=c}^{m} [(Bq,n \times Iq)/(1+i)^n]Ps$$

Where: S   =   Scenarios 1 through "Z"

P   =   Probability of scenario "s"

A-3 Calculating Break-Even Yield Spread between Coupons

$$\Delta Y = \Delta C\,(1 - rZ)$$

Where: ΔY =   Yield on higher coupon less yield on lower coupon security

ΔC =   Higher coupon less lower coupon

r   =   Interest strip multiple

Z   =   Inverse of security multiple (1/a, where a = change in price for a change in yield equal to ΔC)

Chapter 21

JOSEPH GARRETT

Joseph Garrett, Managing Director of Hamilton Savings Bank, is a nationally recognized expert in establishing and running high volume lending operations. This has taken the form of both wholesale and subdivision mortgage banking, where he has over 11 years experience. He has been widely published in trade journals as well as the academic press. An article written in 1981 helped pave the way for builder bonds and collateralized mortgage obligations.

Subdivision Lending

JOSEPH GARRETT

The vast majority of the nation's mortgage bankers and thrifts obtain their production through what is know as *retail lending*. This means that they develop a network of loan production offices with loan officers who call on realtors, place advertisements aimed at the home-buyer, and solicit the portfolio of existing loans for refinances. Although there are countless variations, the essence of retail is originating loans one at a time.

Another source of production is commonly known as *wholesale lending*. Although more typical of the thrifts, more and more mortgage bankers have gotten involved. In this activity, a lender solicits loans from mortgage brokers or direct lenders. The loans are submitted fully processed, with the wholesaler merely doing the quality control before funding the loan. Although wholesale requires an extremely strict quality control system, its strong point is that a relatively small number of employees can obtain a high volume of loans.

While wholesale and retail lending have typically dominated the industry, so-called *builder business* or *tract lending* has long been treated as a sideline. Some lenders do not actively seek it, doing this lending only when it comes their way. Other lenders seek the business but lump it in with retail, never understanding why they are not more successful at it. With very few exceptions, each market area has a limited number of firms who dominate the business.

But builder business is profitable, and it is less prone to the cycles that cause lenders to shrink back during high interest rate environments.

EVALUATION

The potential for greater volume is the most obvious reason for entering the builder business product line. If 1 loan officer calls on 10 realtors, he or she might get loans from 5 of them. That could mean anywhere from 5 to 15 loans a month.

If 1 subdivision account officer calls on 10 substantial builders, and if a commitment is obtained from only 1 of them, that 1 source can provide 30, 40 or more loans a month, month after month. And he or she is certainly capable of handling more than one builder. Thus, 1 tract lending officer can originate as many loans in a given time period as 3 or 4 retail loan officers typically would originate.

But is it profitable? Like any business, subdivision lending can be profitable if done right. The key element is the marginal cost of originating the next increment of loans. Greater volume typically implies greater profit, and in builder business, the lender has the luxury of getting more volume from fewer sources with a smaller cadre of lending officers. For a retail office to close 100 loans a month might necessitate having 10 to 15 lending officers and 8 to 10 processors. For a builder-oriented office with 4 steady builders who sell 25 homes a month, this office might only require 2 or 3 processors.

While loan processors are the lifeblood of the real estate finance industry, there are obvious economies when they are involved in tract loans. When 1 processor is working on 25 retail loans, he or she is potentially dealing with 20 different brokers for the sellers, 20 for the buyers, probably 10 different escrow or title companies, and perhaps 10 appraisers.

In the builder business, however, examine a situation where 4 builders are closing a total of 100 loans a month. First, the processors will have contact with significantly fewer brokers. In some instances, the builder directs all contact with the processor through a central marketing director. Here, the contacts are shrunk from as many as 40 to a few as 4. And that cuts down on telephone time and paperwork.

Second, each builder typically obtains price concessions from title and escrow companies, so if there are 4 builder accounts, there might only be 4 escrow or title companies to deal with. That, too, is more efficient.

Third, the appraisal process is quicker, cheaper, and more efficient. Individual appraisers can be chosen to handle entire tracts, and once they have set up a master for each model, the ensuing individual appraisals are generated much more quickly. Lenders can obtain price concessions from appraisers for this type of business.

So while a retail processor can handle perhaps 20 loans at a time, experience has shown that processors doing strictly tract loans can handle up to 50 loans easily. When spread over a number of branches, the savings on personnel start to add up quickly.

Although homebuilders suffer greatly when rates rise, they tend not to suffer as badly as sellers of existing houses. For example, in 1982 when FNMA's 30-day net yield actually hit 19 percent, new home sales were off only 25 percent as much as sales of existing homes.

During such times, builders have many tools at their disposal, not normally available to individual homeowners, which they can use to sell homes. They can do full-term buydowns, work with temporary subsidies, and float builder bonds or warehouse loans at a low coupon. A national builder in 1982 was spending 24 points a loan to buydown rates. Although that is an extreme example, we have found that California builders typically build in between 5 and 7 points per loan to cover the cost of financing. An individual homeowner selling his or her house is already paying sales commission of 6 percent, and he or she is unable (and probably unwilling) to pay much more to provide financing concessions.

ORGANIZING FOR BUILDER BUSINESS: STAFFING AND SELECTING PRODUCTS

Assuming that a lender has decided to enter this area of mortgage banking, it must now decide how to properly structure its organization. Many companies make subdivision lending a part of their normal retail loan production office network. While this can and has worked well for many companies it can be more effective to have offices solely devoted to tract lending. The mentality of calling on realtors for loans is vastly different than that needed to call on builders. And while there are many gifted mortgage bankers who can do both, we have found it preferable if lending officers do not try to serve two masters.

Tract lending offices can be scattered more widely. It is not necessary, for example, to have an office in San Jose to handle San Jose subdivisions. The larger, more sophisticated builders have trained their sales staff to prequalify buyers and to assist them in filling out their loan applications. It may be completely unnecessary to take face-to-face applications; virtually all loans can be handled through the mail.

By its very nature, this precludes the need to have a large number of localized offices. One central office can handle all the loans of a particular builder who has eight tracts in two states—through the mail. While it is impossible to generalize for other states, experience has proven that the entire state of California can be covered with seven loan production offices.

Account Officers

I strongly recommend a network of loan offices that do no spot lending—only tract lending. In such a system, each office should have a builder account officer. He or she is responsible for obtaining business from local builders. Typically, business is generated by issuing takeout commitments. In fact, it is important that the account officers be willing to turn down spot business. The more successful companies stress a very small commission on each commitment and loan. This is meant to motivate the account officer to obtain commitments from the larger production builders.

Processors

The unheralded loan processor is perhaps as key as any element in the equation when a firm does builder business. The processor can make or break a relationship with a tract developer. Because the volume of loans is too great for the builder rep to get involved in every loan, the processor has a great deal of contact with the builder and its staff. So it is essential that the processor have the maturity to deal with a high-pressure situation.

In retail lending, there are so many one-time transactions that the temptation exists to give less than 100 percent attention to processing each loan quickly and efficiently. A processor packaging a loan to refinance a borrower's home knows that he or she will most likely never deal with that borrower again. Therefore, if the loan processing drags on an extra week, the consequences are not likely to be catastrophic.

But if that processor has been assigned to process loans under a $10 million commitment for a builder, he or she can expect to deal with upwards of 150 of loans for that builder. The very nature of built-in repeat business forces the entire processing staff to do its very best on each and every loan.

Finally, the processors might function sometimes as loan officers in a traditional retail operation. They take the applications, prequalify the borrowers, order Regulation Z disclosures, order and analyze the credit reports, verify employment, check income and sources of downpayment, and (if the borrower is self-employed), know how to analyze a tax return. Because the processor has so many responsibilities, training is critical. The processing staff should be encouraged to attend as many seminars as possible on underwriting and processing loans. Processors must be kept up-to-date on changes in FNMA's regulations in truth in lending, and in mortgage insurance requirements. In essence, they must be viewed and treated as more than clerical support. They are professionals!

Underwriters

In doing builder business, there are perhaps as many companies doing local as opposed to centralized underwriting. With the advent of VA automatics and FHA direct endorsement, it is probably impossible to avoid local underwriting in the branch. For conventionals, there are arguments to be made on both sides of the issue. But once again, the special requirements of doing builder business must be considered.

Unfortunately, there are many lenders who send their loans into the home office, only to wait for a week or more to get approval. Once again, borrowers seeking to refinance their houses may be able to tolerate such delays. A tract builder planning to sell 500 homes a year might typically be paying 2 percent interest over prime, and every day's delay adds up to a significant amount of money. Thus, while quality control must be the prime consideration in setting up an underwriting function, quick turnaround is an absolute must.

Closing Staff

Many of the same considerations go into setting up a closing department. Closing practices vary from state to state and even within states, so it is hard to make categorical statements. A major consideration might be the convenience aspect of local funding. When documents need to be redrawn, it is often easier and quicker to have them done at the local production office.

Products

Different market segments will require different products, but there will typically be certain *sine qua non* factors of doing builder business. Every lender must be able to offer some choice of fixed-rate and adjustable-rate mortgages. Depending on the price range of homes in subject tracts, FNMA and FHA/VA might be two product lines.

In areas such as Sacramento and Solano County in California, as well as areas in Texas, Arizona, and Florida, mortgage lenders have built successful builder origination offices using practically nothing but FHA products. In other areas, the same holds true for conforming FNMA products.

In recent years, mortgage revenue bond issues have also been a key ingredient. Because of the very low rates offered, most builders have participated in these programs when the local jurisdiction sponsored one. And while they may not be highly profitable for a lender, the mortgage banker should at least be capable of acting as an originator and servicer for them. This is just one aspect of trying to be a full-service takeout lender for builders. One very large California builder used a particular lender for almost all of his lending needs. But when he was told by that lender that it chose not to participate in an upcoming mortgage revenue bond issue he was forced to choose another mortgage banker. That mortgage banker, having been given the chance to do business with the builder, was able to make inroads into other product lines as well. Within a year, the old mortgage lender had lost a significant share of the builder's FHA and FNMA business.

The same is somewhat true of the various conduits that have sprung up within recent years. Such entities as HOMAC and American Southwest Financial have proven to be extremely successful in helping builders to provide below market financing. Quite often, the only requirements necessary to participate in these programs are for the secondary marketing and shipping departments to read a shipping and servicing manual and make the necessary arrangements. But as easy as it is to participte, too many lenders pass up this opportunity to get origination and servicing income.

One related activity is handling project approvals for FNMA or FHA. Although the FNMA 1026 is required typically only on condominiums or planned unit development (PUD) projects, the FHA and VA require the master conditional commitment and master certificate of reasonable value for single-family detached projects, as well. In too many instances, the process is handled sloppily, with the builder doing some of the work, the lender doing some, and the whole process ending up taking too much time.

Lenders who can provide project approvals in a timely and professional manner are providing an invaluable service to their customers. It helps to cement the relationship between builders and lenders. And if lenders get the master project approval, they can get it asigned in their name. Once this kind of process is accomplished, the builder will typically and logically originate loans through that lender.

MAKING IT WORK

Once a lender decides to get involved in doing builder business, what are the key ingredients to success? First, it is not having the lowest rates. Second, it is not being "aggressive" in the underwriting.

On the first point, it is nearly impossible to gear a long-term program to having the best prices. There will always be *some* lender willing to undercut you. Builders expect good prices, they expect competitive rates, but most of all, they crave consistency. They need a lender who is in the market year in and year out. There is nothing more disconcerting than a lender who has low rates and good programs in January, only to have them pulled back in July. Large scale builders need a consistent mortgage banking source so that it can engage in long-range sales and marketing planning. In short, builders want a long-range relationship with a lender just as much as the lender wants to develop a long-range relationship with builders.

Being "aggressive" in underwriting hardly needs elaboration. It is a short-term and self-defeating exercise. Those lenders who have made a primary market in junk loans ultimately have paid the price—either through an inability to sell their loans in the secondary market or through severe foreclosure losses. Aggressive underwriting should not be even considered, even as a shortcut to gaining entry into the market.

The key to success is having some sort of overall perspective, some overriding goal. This goal can and should be simple, so that everyone—from the account executive down to the assistant funding clerk—can understand it. As an example, one lender who has been quite successful in this area has the goal and slogan of "Meeting the Builder's Needs." It is simple. It is direct.

In what ways must a lender help to meet the needs of builder customers? First, it is important to recognize that pricing is not the dominant factor. Having the lowest rates at all times is not necessary or even possible.

Second, consistency is vital. The lender must make a commitment to being in the builder business. The firm cannot cut and run at the first uptick in rates. There were certain successful builder-oriented lenders in California who closed up offices during the 1982 credit crunch.

Many lost so much credibility that they were unable to re-enter the builder market once rates subsided.

A third component is having good organizational systems. There are countless ways to organize the process, and all of them work to a degree. But it is remarkable how many lenders lack any system at all. The flow of loans must be routinized in such a way that loans are processed quickly. This system should be devised in such a way that not only are good loans approved quickly, but bad loans are turned down early in the process. Builders know that some percentage of their buyers will not qualify for a loan, builders all accept that as part of the business. But one of the most common complaints is that lenders will spend four to eight weeks processing a loan only *then* to have it rejected by an underwriter or private mortgage insurance (PMI) company. Whatever its makeup, the system must define the flow of loans relative to log in, ordering of truth-in-lending documents, processing, approval, ordering of PMI or government insurance, documentation drawing, closing, and funding. There must be a logical and consistent flow of loans through the system.

A fourth and critical element is to develop a system for communication with the builder. It can be through a status report sent weekly for each loan, or it can mean regular meetings with the builder's staff to go over loans. Once again, there is no one right way to handle this. Perhaps the best approach is to sit down with the builder's marketing staff and ask what *they* want. However it is done, there is no such thing as too much communication. Builders do not like surprises, and if the builder has 50 loans in process with your company, he or she needs to know if they will close in time. A large dose of communication is the best way of preventing troublesome surprises.

A fifth postulate is flexibility. Every builder has different needs. Every tract has special requirements. And a loan program that works in Texas may be completely unusable in California. Within clearly defined limits, the builders must perceive lenders as being willing to negotiate almost anything.

Most of a builder's demands will be quite reasonable. Typically, they will revolve around second issues, that is, issues other than rate and price. The lender must be willing to sit down and discuss everything. If the builder requires a special kind of loan program, he or she cannot be told that such a program is not available in the program guidebook. Lenders must, at a minimum, indicate to the builder that they will discuss it with their production manager and the company's head of secondary marketing. Lenders may not always be able to ultimately offer the program, but they must be at least willing to try.

Success comes not from being a great and brilliant mortgage banker, but rather from being a great listener. If the lender will listen, truly *listen* to the builder, he or she will find out what the *builder's* needs are.

A sixth and final element is doing the small things well. When all is said and done, a builder wants to have the loans processed and funded quickly—nothing more, nothing less. And the entire process, however complex, is ultimately a series of small, almost trivial actions. It is ordering a credit report the day the loan is logged in. It is filling out the proper form when ordering private mortgage insurance. It is returning a builder's or borrower's phone call the same day. It is treating each and every loan as if it were the most important loan in the world. It is not a matter of doing anything extraordinary, it is merely doing the ordinary things extraordinarily well.

Chapter 22 (Part A)

Hunter W. Wolcott

Hunter Wolcott is President of Reserve Financial Management Corporation, the largest independent film specializing in advising institutional buyers and sellers of mortgage banking companies and loan servicing. Reserve Financial is headquartered in Miami, maintains an office in San Francisco, and serves clients nationwide. Hunter Wolcott has authoried numerous articles for leading industry journals, frequently addresses trade association meetings and is a member of the faculty of the MBA School of Mortgage Banking.

Maximizing Value from the Sale of Servicing

HUNTER W. WOLCOTT

One of the chief attractions of mortgage servicing as an investment—both for mortgage bankers and their corporate treasurers—is the use of servicing as a profit and capital planning tool. Most major originators are now at least occasionally active as buyers or sellers of servicing, and a significant percentage participate as both buyers and sellers as opportunities and needs arise.

Gaining maximum value from the sale of servicing requires that the following four areas be addressed: analysis and appraisal, marketing strategy, procedure, and presentation. The remainder of this chapter addresses each area in turn.

ANALYSIS & APPRAISAL

Many mortgage bankers and servicers leave a good deal of value on the table because they fail to inventory their servicing portfolio adequately before a sale becomes necessary. Servicing often represents 80 percent of a mortgage banking company's total value. Despite this, most mortgage bankers do not have the slightest idea of the investment characteristics of their portfolio, how its components really look and how they behave, and, most importantly, what they are worth! Imagine, if you will, how negligent the bond trader would be who did not know what bonds he owned, and who did not track their value on a continuous basis.

Step 1, then, is to continuously maintain an updated inventory of your servicing assets, with valuations conducted at least quarterly to test for changes in market value and investment suitability.

With a current inventory of servicing assets, sellers can respond to selling opportunities (or selling pressures generated by income or capital needs) quickly and accurately, because they will know their options in advance—and their likely economic consequences.

Many sellers automatically select one kind of servicing—say, GNMA—when a sale is proposed, because they mistakenly believe that it is the only kind of servicing with sufficient liquidity to meet their needs. In many cases, such narrow-mindedness may do a disservice both to the marketplace and to the seller. With the increased securitization of mortgages, most forms of mortgage-backed security (MBS) servicing are highly liquid, with FHLMC, FMNA, MBS, and GNMA MBS trading on a equal footing.

In cases where sellers have more than one type or style of servicing that can be sold, their best bet is to prioritize their sale options to try to sell servicing that has the least value to them relative to its market value. As an example, many mortgage bankers' portfolios contain relatively small fractions of some components that could be disposed of with an increase in overall efficiency. A commercial loan specialist, for instance, could profit from disposing of a relatively small residential portfolio, while a thrift with a predominantly conventional portfolio could improve operations through a sale of FHA/VA servicing.

The key to proper selection of servicing for sale is *balance*. Sellers should know, or be able to calculate, the value of any given portfolio in their hands. With updated market value analyses, sellers will know the price a given segment can be expected to bring in the open market. Good management, then, can find that point where the value of holding the servicing being sold is exceeded by the price that can be attained in the market. Selling the crown jewels every time the bottom line needs a little boost is probably not the way to a profitable future.

MARKETING STRATEGY

No single marketing strategy is effective at all times and in all markets. In the past few years the ownership of servicing and of mortgage bankers has been in almost continuous flux. One effect of this is the interesting phenomenon today that more than 80 percent of all servicing buyers are making their first or second trade ever! No longer does it suffice for a seller of servicing to scratch out a 10-line summary of a portfolio on a piece of paper and send it to the 20 largest mortgage bankers for bids. Nowadays, it seems that the top 20 themselves are the ones most likely to be for sale!

A better marketing strategy includes the following considerations.

Research

Now that the buying market is so heavily populated with newcomers, research takes on an entirely new significance. If a servicing offering is very small, for instance, its appeal could range to hundreds of smaller lenders and servicers who haven't the appetite or inclination to make large acquisitions. Medium-sized offerings ($100 to $500 million) draw from a very broad cross-section of existing mortgage servicers. With these offerings, servicers can make important additions to their portfolios in one bite, rather than dealing with numerous, smaller deals.

Very large offerings can be the most interesting of all, because their attractiveness extends beyond the universe of existing mortgage bankers to include all companies who think that they might want to *become* mortgage bankers. At $1 billion or larger, a servicing portfolio enables an entirely new entrant to delve into mortgage banking with considerable assurance of immediate servicing profitability. But buyers, no matter how eager, cannot buy what they do not see. Sound research will identify all the suitable buyer-candidates for any given offering.

At Reserve Financial Management Corp., targeting buyer-candidates is done for each deal, but the process of identifying and qualifying potential buyers is continuous.

Timing

Research identifies the knowable universe of eligible buyer-candidates, and the prospectus contains the detail a prudent buyer will require, but neither achieves full effectiveness if they are presented to the market at the wrong time. Servicing sales professinals stay abreast of *every* offering in the market, not just their own, and they can provide invaluable guidance in finding the right "window" in which to present your portfolio.

In general, selling pressure is at its highest in early December and at the end of June and September, as income-motivated sellers (who have not done their planning beforehand) rush to achieve income recognition. January is also a difficult selling period, because many financial officers are preoccupied with financial statements and audit matters they are unable to devote time to acquisitions. At other times in the year, sellers will want to be aware of—and avoid releasing their offerings on the heals of—bigger, better or cheaper comparable deals. The market is finite: it can accommodate only so many deals of one kind at a time.

Positioning

Skilled market strategists position their product in whatever fashion the market requires to get the largest possible audience of buyer-candidates, and therefore the clearest shot at the best price and terms. Frequently, this means partitioning the servicing portfolio to meet the requirements of the prospective buyers.

To use an oversimplified example, let's say that we have a seller of a $200 million portfolio that contains $100 million of loans in California, and another $100 million in Florida. There may be 200 possible buyers for the Florida portion, and 300 more for California, but of those, only a couple of dozen may really be interested in *both*! If it were operationally possible, this seller would be best advised to make a dual, simultaneous offering—permitting the possibility of one buyer winning both halves, but not foreclosing the option of selling to two, regional parties.

Positioning challenges such as this occur in many offerings. They create an opportunity for the skilled strategist to increase total gross proceeds by applying that old marketing maxim: "Don't *tell* them what they want; *sell* them what they want."

Prospectus

An *offering prospectus* contains the details of the investment opportunity presented by the servicing portfolio. An investment in servicing is an extremely complex financial proposition—and one of the most poorly understood. A prospectus has one primary purpose—to *illuminate* the facts.

When it's properly prepared, a servicing offering prospectus contains all of the material facts about the portfolio's present status: an accurate breakdown by loan type; by investor; by service fee, maturity, and coupon; by relevant geographic unit; and by an intelligent analysis of delinquencies, foreclosures, and escrows, just to name a few. A summary of current portfolio characteristics can, at best, present just a "snapshot" of the portfolio—two dimensional, and not sufficient to give a sophisticated financial analyst a feel for the investment characteristics. To do that, a historical analysis must also be prepared, showing the seasonal ebb and flow of escrows, prepayment statistics, delinquency trends, and the like.

The argument against providing proper detail runs that since some buyers are not smart enough to ask these kinds of questions, the information should therefore not be volunteered. Against that argument, several observations can be offered. First, sellers often omit good things about their servicing at least as often as bad things. Ancillary income, for instance, is often omitted, as are favorable prepayment histories and good historical escrow figures. Second, it's rare to encounter a buyer who is stupid. If they are not asking questions, it usually means that they are resolving uncertainties independently by making their own assumptions. Experience teaches that buyers tend to resolve all ambiguities *against* the seller, and that means a lower price.

A good prospectus also is sufficiently well-prepared and comprehensive so that it can stand the double test of due diligence, which is that there be no misstatement of a material fact nor any omission of a material fact, the effect of which would be misleading. All responsible buyers perform due diligence procedures prior to funding the purchase of a servicing portfolio or a mortgage banking company. Many buyers also employ experienced investment banking firms as their financial advisors, in part to guide them in that effort. Proper preparation leads to a smoother closing, with both parties satisfied.

PROCEDURE

An orderly, clearly understandable offering procedure will greatly increase the chances for a successful sale. The solicitation of offers from potential buyers should have *uniform content and timing.* A procedure for handling questions and requests for additional information should be prepared in advance, and staff should be allocated for an intensive period of scrutiny by possible buyers. No matter how well prepared your prospectus, you will never anticipate all the questions or concerns of every possible buyer-candidate, but neither can their concerns be ignored nor brushed aside.

The importance of providing a *level playing field* for contenders cannot be overemphasized. Active buyers may see 100 to 200 offerings per year, of which they may seriously pursue only a dozen and perhaps make one or two firm bids. A cursory investigation costs up to a few thousand dollars—a serious run at a big portfolio can easily cost $50,000 to $100,000 or more, including fees for lawyers, accountants, financial advisors, EDP consultants, and the like. If these serious buyer-candidates are given the feeling that the seller is shopping their proposal, that there is a potential broker conflict, or that they are not being given a fair and even-handed chance to be the successful bidder, they will drop the deal immediately.

A *deadline* should be established for closure of the investigation period, and for receipt of offers. Selecting the appropriate offering period is more art than technology. We frequently see packages brought by others to the market with 24- or 48-hour "fuses" for receipt of bids.

This is a sure sign that the seller is panicky, an amateur, or both, and usually attracts interest only from predators. Depending on the complexity of the proposition and the thoroughness of the presentation, an offering period of two to three working weeks is standard, and permits the serious institutional contenders to go through an approval process at a comfortable pace. Too long of a deadline invites procrastination or conflict with other deals coming to market. Too short of a period will make it impossible for the committee-bound buyers (who are not bad people!) to participate.

Uniform documentation is particularly valuable in this market. Buyers who are newcomers to servicing transactions welcome the guidance provided by a well-drawn and reasonably balanced bid letter. They are more likely to make a bid than if they are left strictly in the hands of their own house counsel—who, no matter how capable, may have never before seen or been a part of a servicing transaction. Uniformity has another beneficial side effect in that bids, when received, are more easily compared. If all terms in competing bids are identical, all that needs to be compared is the price offered and the credibility of the buyer.

Confidentiality should be maintained at all preliminary stages of the offering process, for two reasons. First, the financial markets are nervous, and a sale—even for the very best of business reasons—may be construed as a sign of distress by some. Second, if the seller is a large servicer believed by the market to be very sophisticated, buyers will suspect that the portfolio has been adversely selected, perhaps in some subtle, undetectable way. Either outcome is harmful to the deal. The strict maintenance of confidentiality is one of the reasons so many large buyers and sellers employ intermediaries who specialize in this complex product.

Contracting, closing, and delivery deserve mention, if for no other reason than that so many buyers and sellers tend to ignore these areas completely in the heat of the pricing batttle. Even though it possesses some annuity characteristics, servicing is not a bond that can be peddled at will. It is a business activity, and merits the same care and attention any business acquisition would receive.

Investors must be treated with the *respect* appropriate to their status, and so must mortgagors. A great servicing deal is not just a barroom story. It affects the lives of hundreds or thousands of families who have tax escrows, who want their hazard insurance maintained, who get confused and who want to be treated as adult customers, and who *vote*!

To maximize value from a servicing sale, both buyers and sellers need to adopt a set of *servicing transfer procedures* that accommodates the legitimate needs of investors and mortgagors with the greatest efficiency commensurate with their cost. Mortgagor's interests are neglected only at great peril, because they not only have the power to make a servicing transfer unprofitable, their state legislators can restrict its sale and transfer to the extent that servicing values (and, by extension, origination economics) are permanently and adversely affected.

PRESENTATION

Herschell G. Lewis, a leading consultant, has often said that the single most important word in marketing is *verisimilitude*. Verisimilitude literally means having the appearance of truth—going beyond the fact that something *is* true, but that it also *appears* to be true. The relevance of verisimilitude in marketing servicing is that your materials, actions, words, and conduct must, at all times during the deal, give buyers confidence that you are telling the truth—that you are a firm or a person with whom they can deal with confidence.

The importance of verisimilitude is most easily illustrated by its conspicuous absence in some dealings. If a seller or agent, for instance, boldly and prominently disclaims the accuracy or completeness of an offering, what message does this give a buyer? If important facts are missing or obviously misstated, can buyer confidence be sustained? If, from the other side, a bid letter is full of "weasel words," how secure can a seller be in going forward?

Finally, *personal style* is significant. Companies buy or sell servicing, but people make deals. The servicing markets are highly inefficient, and there is often a wide range between the low and high bid on a well-marketed deal. But it is not uncommon that several bids are received that could be considered basically equivalent from a purely economic standpoint. This is the point where style will separate the pros from the amateurs. A deal isn't a deal unless it can close—and it takes people to close a servicing sale. People who are experienced in the business; who understand some of the surprises that can arise and how to deal with them; and who possess that good faith, reputation, and integrity to stay the course are the ones who complete deals. People with style make more deals and better deals, because they have more to peddle than cash or servicing. And, they're lot more enjoyable to deal with!

Chapter 22 (Part B)

TIM COHANE
AND
LARRY RAFFERTY

Tim Cohane and Larry Rafferty are Senior Vice Presidents at Thomson McKinnon, where they head up the Mortgage Marketing area.

They both started their Wall Street careers at Salomon Brothers where Rafferty was in the Asset and Liability Group and Cohane was in the Mortgage Origination Group. They have been involved in over 100 mortgage servicing transactions and have spoken on numerous panels on the topic.

Before coming to Wall Street, Rafferty was President of a Division of West Point Pepperill and Cohane was head Basketball Coach at Dartmouth College.

Maximizing Value from the Sale of Servicing

Tim Cohane and Larry Rafferty

From the seller's vantage point, what could be more important than maximizing the price received from the sale of a servicing portfolio?

The first question is whether to sell, and the answer to this is usually answered by determining what a portfolio is worth. Anyone who owns a portfolio should value it quarterly. This means devising a means of gathering data by product type, investor, and maturity.

Models that compute the present value of the portfolio look for standard information. Figure 22–1 is a typical data gathering form:

Figure 22–1
PORTFOLIO EVALUATION ORGANIZER

Date of Information: _____

Product Type: _____

Principal Balance: _____

Number of Loans: _____

Average Loan Size: _____

Coupon Range: _____

Weighted Average Interest Rate: _____

Weighted Average Servicing Fee: _____

Figure 22–1 (continued)
PORTFOLIO EVALUATION ORGANIZER

Weighted Average Maturity: _____
Average Monthly Escrow Balance
  (past 12 months): _____
Principal and Interest Constant: _____

	Delinquency	
	# Loans	**% of Balance**
31–60	_____	_____
61–90	_____	_____
91–above	_____	_____
Foreclosure	_____	_____

	Loan Breakdown	
	# Loans	**% of Balance**
30–Year Fixed	_____	_____
15–Year Fixed	_____	_____
GPM	_____	_____
GEM	_____	_____
ARM (by type)	_____	_____
Other (Please Specify)	_____	_____
FHA	_____	_____
VA	_____	_____
Conventional	_____	_____
Totals	_____	_____

Let's go over some of these details:

1. *Principal Balance*—We are often asked our opinion about the optimum size for a servicing package. About $100 million keeps most buyers interested. Over $100 million cuts out the smaller bidders and under $100 million eliminates the biggest players. Your goal is to get as many institutions interested as possible.
2. *Average Loan Size*—Naturally, the larger the loan size, the higher

the price, since servicing costs increase as the number of loans increase. An interesting phenomenon has developed with the drop in interest rates. Some buyers are not as worried about loan size because lower loan size means older loans and lower prepayments.

3. *Weighted Average Interest Rates*—Most evaluators want a coupon breakdown because all the good parts of the portfolio might be in the higher coupons that may not be there next year.

4. *Weighted Average Maturity*—There is a big dropoff after 18 years.

5. *Weighted Average Servicing Fee*—There is an obvious correlation between the servicing fee and value.

6. *Escrow Balance*—One percent can serve as a plain vanilla rule of thumb. This is normally the hardest detail to get. It's important to keep accurate balances, because most evaluation models want the average balance over the last 12 months.

7. *Principal and Interest Constant*—This increases value by providing float income. In the event you don't have this figure and need a quick evaluation, you can use ⅓ of 1 percent of the principal balance.

8. *Delinquencies*—Most models are not very sensitive to delinquency changes. For one thing, your income increases with higher delinquencies, because late charges increase. But from a subjective standpoint this of course means future problems in foreclosure costs.

This average escrow balance is only important when it is related to average principal balance over the same period of time.

In the event that records are not kept, you can approximate the average balance by multiplying the constant tax and insurance input by a factor determined by how many times a year the institution is required to pay taxes according to state law.

The factors are as follow:

Once a year	5.5
Twice a year	2.5
Four times a year	1.25

The escrow figure obviously becomes less accurate the more geographically dispersed the portfolio.

It is very important to know the value of your servicing; very few institutions do. If you know the value, you can better discuss the strategic decision of whether to sell. In making that strategic decision, the most important reasons for selling are:

a. Book income
b. Increasing net worth ratios
c. Sale of cost-inefficient servicing

If you have made the decision to sell, the next question is what specific part of your portfolio should be sold. To answer this question, you must know what types of product you service most efficiently. In selecting the segment of your portfolio that will be sold, keep in mind that most buyers prefer homogeneous packages.

The next step in the process of maximizing the sale is packaging.

Perfection would be the seller hand carrying a brochure to every institution in the country and talking each through the package. If you had the time and budget to do that, it would take you 21 years and cost more money than received on the sale itself.

The next best thing you can do is professionally package the portfolio and get it in front of as many bidders as possible. Design your packages to take away most of the work for the buyer.

The package is divided (for example) into GNMA and FHLMC, and the buyers have the option of bidding on either one or both parts. This is to your advantage, because the sum of the best bids on the GNMA and FHLMC segments may or may not be greater than the bid on the undivided package.

Let us take a sample package and break it into its constituent parts. Figure 22–2 represents Part I of such a package.

Part II (Figure 22–3) begins with the GNMA Profile. There is a note rate distribution which becomes more and more a requirement in a falling interest rate environment since prepayments are more of a concern. There are some buyers who will not bid unless they can get all essential data by coupon.

Figure 22–2
Supplementary Information

Computer System	Burrough's Mainframe
	Modified Software Package (controlled by Seller)
Tax Service	Ticor Realty Tax Service
Tax Payment Cycle	Semi-annual Payment (November and March)
Escrow Analysis Schedule & Method	January—complete account analysis
	March—payment changes effective
Interest on Escrow	2% in California
Property Location	California
Percentage of Portfolio Originated by Seller	100%
GNMA and FHLMC Final Certification	Yes
Recourse and Guarantee (FNMA)	NA
Loans with Buydowns	None
235 Loans	None

Figure 22–3
GNMA Portfolio Profile

Principal Balance:	$467,150,406.93
Number of Loans:	9,956
Average Loan Size:	$46,921.50
Number of Pools:	164
Coupon Range:	(see Figure 22–1)
Weighted Average Interest Rate:	9.85%
Weighted Average Servicing Fee:	.44%
Monthly Property Tax and Insurance Average: (last 12 months)	$3,654,444
Monthly Principal and Interest Constant:	$4,319,184.70
Weighted Average Remaining Term:	278 months
Total Delinquencies	9.75%

After note rate distribution, you should include delinquencies, geographic distribution, loan characteristics and FHA–VA breakdown (Table 22–1).

The more complete the data the better chance a buyer will be interested in the package. See Figure 22–3 for Part II of the package.

Part III, shown in Figure 22–4, entails a sensitivity study on the four most sensitive details—servicing cost per loan, earnings on impounds, prepayments, and discount rate.

Servicing cost per loan was derived from the data on the operations of large mortgage bankers. The economies of scale associated with servicing portfolios of large magnitude render a $50 servicing cost per loan, which is a realistic and achievable figure.

Table 22–1
GNMA Note Rate Distribution

Note Rate Range	Number of Loans	Dollar Amount	Percentage of Total Loans
7.99 or less	316	5,547,900	3.17
8.00– 8.99	3,967	142,862,220	39.85
9.00– 9.99	2,616	124,771,567	26.28
10.00–10.99	1,703	102,952,057	17.11
11.00–11.99	639	41,394,878	6.42
12.00–12.99	116	8,188,762	1.17
13.00–13.99	378	26,055,823	3.80
14.00–14.99	154	10,642,376	1.55
15.00–15.99	45	3,190,867	.45
16.00–16.99	19	1,349,888	.19
17.00–17.99	3	194,328	.03

GNMA Delinquencies

Days Delinquent	Number of Loans	Percent
31–60	636	6.39%
61–90	118	1.19%
91 and above	882	8.86%
Net Delinquency	89	.89%
Total Delinquency	971	9.75%

GNMA Geographic Distribution

State	Number of Loans	Percent of Total
California	9,956	100%

GNMA Loan Characteristics

Loan Type	Number of Loans	Percent of Balance
30–Year Fixed	9,045	90.85%
15–Year Fixed		
GPM (21 pools)	911	9.15%
FHA	4,677*	46.98%*
VA	5,279*	53.02%*

*Estimated

Figure 22–4
Analysis of the GNMA Portfolio

The following "base" assumptions were employed for the initial analysis of the GNMA segment:

1. Servicing Cost per Loan	$50
2. Earning on Impounds	10%
3. Prepayment (CPR)	2.35%
4. Discount Rate	11%

Earnings on impounds assumes a "base" rate of 10 percent. Individual bankers use rates from 9 percent to 12 percent. Many savings and loans associations assume a more aggressive position and employ higher rates. Thus, a "base" rate of 10 percent is a more conservative and generally applicable case.

Prepayments have been analyzed on the basis of historical data for the weighted average coupons of the individual segments. On a constant prepayment basis (CPR), the GNMA portion exhibits an historical prepayment level of 2.35%. This rate was derived from the five-year historical prepayment levels for the weighted average portfolio coupon product type.

Sensitivity analysis was performed on the key variables of servicing cost per loan, earnings on impounds, rate of prepayment and the after tax discount rate.

Servicing Cost Per Loan:
a. *30 percent tax rate:* An increase or decrease of $3 per loan per year changes value by $197,841, or 4.2 basis points. The internal rate of return changes 34 basis points.
b. *48 percent tax rate:* A change of $3 per loan per year in either direction changes value by $146,957, or 3.1 basis points. Return changes 30 basis points.

Earnings on Impounds:

a. *30 percent tax rate:* A 1 percent change in either direction produces a $282,606 (6.1 basis point) difference in value. Return changes 47 basis points.

b. *48 percent tax rate:* An increase or decrease of 1 percent changes value by 209,944, or 4.5 basis points. The portfolio return changes 44 basis points.

Prepayment Rate:

a. *30 percent tax rate:* Altering the level by 50 basis points produces a change in value of $252,371, or 5.4 basis points. Return changes 44 basis points.

b. *48 percent tax rate:* A 50 basis point change results in a value difference of $187,482, or 4.0 basis points. Return is altered by 40 basis points.

Discount Rate:

a. *30 percent tax rate:* A 1 percent changes value by $563,713, or 12 basis points. The after tax internal rate of return remains the same.

b. *48 percent tax rate:* A 1 percent difference changes value by $468,289, or 10 basis points. Return is not affected.

Tax Rate:

A decline from a 48 percent tax rate to a 30 percent tax rate increases value by $1,204,647, or 26 basis points. The associated return increases 230 basis points.

We then follow the same procedure for FHLMC, beginning with Figure 22–5.

Table 22–2 details note rate distribution, delinquencies, geographic distribution, loan characteristics, and FHA–VA breakdown for FHLMC delinquencies.

The next part of the package includes an analysis of the FHLMC portfolio. See Figure 22–6.

Servicing cost per loan was derived from the data on the operations of large mortgage bankers. The economies of scale associated with servicing portfolios of large magnitude render a $50 servicing cost per

---

Figure 22–5
FHLMC Portfolio Profile

Principal Balance:	$225,700,035.27
Number of Loans:	6,121
Average Loan Size:	$38,873.06
Number of Pools:	148
Coupon Range:	(see Table 22–2)
Weighted Average Interest Rate:	9.97%
Weighted Average Servicing Fee:	.3898%
Monthly Property Tax and Insurance Average: (last 12 months)	$1,327,931.66
Monthly Principal and Interest Constant:	$2,177,300.65
Weighted Average Remaining Term:	264 months
Total Delinquencies	3.15%

---

loan, which is a realistic and achievable figure.

Earnings on impounds assumes a "base" rate of 10 percent. Individual bankers use rates from 9 percent to 12 percent. Many savings and loans associations assume a more aggressive position and employ higher rates. Thus, a "base" rate of 10 percent is a more conservative and generally applicable case.

Prepayments have been analyzed on the basis of historical data for the weighted average coupons of the individual segments. On a constant prepayment basis (CPR), the GNMA portion exhibits an historical prepayment level of 2.35%. This rate was derived from the five-year historical prepayment levels for the weighted average portfolio coupon product type.

Table 22–2
FHLMC Note Rate Distribution

Note Rate Range	Number of Loans	Dollar Amount	Percentage of Total Loans
7.99 or less	2,069	36,444,702	33.80
8.00– 8.99	1,579	59,191,352	25.80
9.00– 9.99	1,176	56,171,771	19.21
10.00–10.99	519	27,306,664	8.48
11.00–11.99	249	13,525,079	4.07
12.00–12.99	328	22,400,698	5.36
13.00–13.99	66	3,923,001	1.08
14.00–14.99	57	3,411,515	.93
15.00–15.99	53	3,335,275	.87

FHLMC Delinquencies

Days Delinquent	Number of Loans	Percent
31–60	138	2.25%
61–90	24	.39%
91 and above	8	.13%
Net Delinquency	170	2.77%
Foreclosures	23	.38%
Total Delinquencies	193	3.15%

FHLMC Geographic Distribution

State	Number of Loans	Percent of Total
California	6,121	100%

FHLMC Loan Characteristics

Loan Type	Number of Loans	Percent of Balance
30-Year Fixed	6,121	100%
15-Year Fixed		
FHA	1,090*	17.81%[8]
VA	1,082*	17.68%*
Conventional	3,949	64.52%

*Estimated

Figure 22–6
Analysis of the FHLMC Portfolio

The following "base" assumptions were employed for the initial analysis of the FHLMC segment:

1. Servicing Cost per Loan	$50
2. Earning on Impounds	10%
3. Prepayment (CPR)	6.5%
4. Discount Rate	11%

Sensitivity analysis was performed on the key variables of servicing cost per loan, earnings on impounds, rate of prepayment, and the after tax discount rate.

Servicing Cost Per Loans:
a. *30 percent tax rate:* An increase or decrease of $3 per loan per year changes value by $89,996, or 4.0 basis points. The internal rate of return changes 68 basis points.
b. *48 percent tax rate:* A change of $3 per loan per year in either direction changes value by $66,835, or 3 basis points. Return changes 30 basis points.

Earnings on Impounds:
a. *30 percent tax rate:* A 1 percent change in either direction produces a $93,100 (4.2 basis point) difference in value. Return changes 69 basis points.
b. *48 percent tax rate:* An increase or decrease of 1% changes value by $69,160, or 3.1 basis points. The portfolio return changes 60 basis points.

Prepayment Rate:
a. *30 percent tax rate:* Altering the level by 50 basis poitns produces a change in value of $55,590, or 4.2 basis points. Return changes 42 basis points.
b. *48 percent tax rate:* A 50 basis point change results in a value difference of $41,299, or 18 basis points. Return is altered by 37 basis points.

Discount Rate:
a. *30 percent tax rate:* A 1 percent change affects value by $129,211, or 5.7 basis points. The after tax internal rate of return remains the same.
b. *48 percent tax rate:* A 1 percent difference changes value by $110,088, or 4.9 basis points. Return is not affected.

Tax Rate:
A decline from a 48 percent tax rate to a 30 percent tax rate increases value by $216,107, or 9.6 basis pints. The associated return increases 288 basis points.

Finally, Figure 22–7 illustrates a typical bid letter.

It is most important to standardize the bid. *You* tell the buyer how you want the caveats to be structured. This helps eliminate negotiable caveats and unwanted bids. The objective is to have apples to apples comparisons.

In conclusion, it's advisable to use one consultant to package and market your product. The main reason for this is that you can only motivate consultants 100 percent if they know they will be paid if there is a sale. Otherwise the salespeople will simply not make the calls, or, if they do, it will be a rushed, sloppy approach.

Furthermore we suggest you use a specialist who deals only in servicing transactions. He or she will be aware of correct market conditions and market psychology.

With your advisor, establish a minimum so the buyer will know there will be a sale—buyers do not want to go to all the trouble of preparing a bid only to know it really isn't a sale.

Figure 22–7
Sample Letter of Intent

Date: _____

RE: Mortgage Servicing Offering

Gentlemen:

The information you provided us concerning the above servicing offer has been reviewed by our executive staff.

This letter confirms our offer and intent to purchase from the seller the servicing rights totaling approximately _____ covered by the attached offering of Thomson McKinnon Securities Inc. on the terms and conditions expressed in this letter.

1. *Purchase Price:* The purchase price shall be calculated by multiplying the bid percentage of X% by the unpaid principal balance of all loans, except for those past due for ninety days or more, in litigation or in foreclosure as of the transfer date. Payment of the purchase price will be scheduled as follows:

    a. 5% of the purchase price upon acceptance of my bid to be held in escrow by Thomson McKinnon Securities Inc. until the sale date.

    b. The remainder of the purchase price is due to the seller on the sale date.

2. *The sale date* wil be designated as the date of execution of the Loan Servicing Purchase and Sale Agreement. All rights to the servicing will transfer to the purchaser upon execution of this agreement.

3. *The transfer date* shall be the date the purchaser begins servicing the loan portfolio.

4. The seller is responsible for servicing the loan portfolio prior to the transfer date and must adhere to all applicable FHA, VA, GNMA, or FHLMC regulations and procedures. Additionally, the seller retains such rights, benefits, and duties inherent in this servicing. These include the right to earn and receive servicing fees and other associated income. Seller and purchaser agree to execute an acceptable interim servicing agreement covering the period between the sale date and the transfer date.

5. As of the transfer date, the seller retains responsibility for servicing all loans in the process of foreclosure. Further, the seller retains responsibility for any and all losses incurred by foreclosure action on loans delinquent for 90 days or more on the transfer date.

6. Purchase of the servicing rights is contingent upon:

    a. Purchaser's determination that the books, records, and accounts of the seller concerning the pools are in order and acceptable to the purchaser. Further, the purchaser's verification that the information conveyed within the offering package is substantially valid;

    b. Seller's delivery to the purchase of GNMA's, FNMA's and FHLMC's written approval of transfer of issuer/servicer and seller/servicer rights and responsibilities, and private investors' approvals as necessary;

    c. Execution by purchaser and seller of a Loan Servicing Purchase Agreement that is mutually acceptable to both parties. This agreement shall include the seller's agreement to hold purchaser harmless, through loan repurchase or other means, for any and all expenses incurred from seller's improper or inadequate origination and servicing prior to the transfer date in accordance with HUD, FHA, VA, FNMA and GNMA rules, regulations, and guidelines;

    d. Mutual approval and acceptance by purchaser and seller of any and all documentation to conclude the sale and assignment of the servicing rights by seller to purchaser;

    e. Seller's transfer to purchaser on the sale date all loan escrow monies and unearned fees which are deemed earned as collected in immediately available funds.

7. Seller claims to have the sole right and authority to sell the servicing rights. Further, seller has no prior contractual obligation to sell the rights to another party.

8. The costs of obtaining GNMA's, FNMA's, FHLMC's and private investors' approval including any transfer fees due them are the responsibility of the seller. Costs associated with preparing and recording assignments of mortgages as required shall be paid by the seller. Where permitted, the seller may employ blanket assignments. Fees due Thomson McKinnon Securities Inc. shall be paid by seller. Other than as provided within this letter of intent, neither party is obligated to pay any broker's or other fees on this transaction.

Figure 22–7 (continued)
Sample Letter of Intent

Upon acceptance, this letter of intent constitutes a binding agreement between the parties for the purchase and sale of servicing.

With regard to this servicing offering, I would like to submit the following bid(s) as a percentage of the outstanding loan balance:

GNMA Portfolio
  Purchase Price   _____ %

FHLMC Portfolio
  Purchase Price   _____ %

Total Portfolio
  Purchase Price   _____ %

Purchaser   Date: _____

By: _____
Title: _____
Accepted: _____

Seller   Date: _____

By: _____
Title: _____
Accepted: _____

The specialist will now send out the package to all possible buyers and establish a bid date, and salespeople will follow up to make sure the package is received and answer any questions.

On the bid date, receive the bids in confidence and submit the winning bid. Now it is important to get the bid in writing along with a 5 percent good faith deposit.

It is now time to arrange for a due diligence inspection and to work out details of the contract.

There are as many contracts as there are deals, and it is important to use your specialist to assist you. You can eliminate any potential losses through the use of a standard bid letter.

Chapter 23

PETER M. ROSS

Peter M. Ross is a Senior Vice President of Goldome Realty Credit Corp. Peter's duties include the overseeing of the Residential and Commercial Servicing operations of GRCC.

In that capacity, he oversees mortgages totalling $8.5 billion or 157,000 individual mortgagors. He also serves as Vice Chairman for the Mortgage Bankers Association of America's Servicing Committee; Chairman of the Computer Power Inc. User Group and President of the Empire State Mortgage Bankers Association.

Goldome Realty Credit Corp. is the 11th largest mortgage banking firm in the country and is lcoated in Buffalo, New York.

Measuring the Cost Impact of a Mortgage Servicing Acquisition

PETER M. ROSS

This chapter discusses methods for calculating the actual cost impact of a contemplated servicing acquisition. Such analysis is especially useful when you are considering a mortgage servicing acquisition, because the extent of an increase or decrease to your average costs can dramatically affect profitability.

First you'll see how to arrive at fixed versus variable cost for your company. Then, this analysis will be applied to a specific acquisition example, thus translating theory into a practical application.

Next, using adjustable-rate mortgages (ARMs), the chapter examines the cost impact of product type on servicing cost. Last, the chapter discusses the proper determination of conversion costs and their impact on cost analysis.

Note at the onset that few, if any, mortgage servicing firms have an entirely accurate handle on all costs. My firm, however, employs certain methods of analysis that allow us to better estimate the costs of certain activities and their resultant impact. These methods are the basis for my discussion.

DETERMINING VARIABLE COSTS

The first step in determining applicable costs is to decide which costs in your company are fixed and which are variable. The proper scope for this determination is the planned activity itself set against your own corporate structure. Following is an example.

Several years ago, Goldome Realty Credit Corp. purchased and then renovated a former high school for its corporate headquarters. The capacity of that location is somewhere in the neighborhood of 180,000 loans. The facility's variable cost from an acquisition before volume reaches 180,000 loans is very, very small. It may include additional utilities, some furniture expense, but it would not entail any additional rental space or the construction of an additional building. As volume approaches 180,000 loans, the company must recognize that additional growth will entail the acquisition of additional space. At that time, the facility cost—and thus variable cost—will increase accordingly.

That increase can be handled several ways. If Goldome chooses to purchase or rent an additional 20,000 square feet, and the planned activity will only use 10,000 of that additional space, we could charge the total 20,000 square feet additional cost to the first additive activity or a managerial decision could be made to analyze the additional cost by averaging it over a period of time. More specifically, if that 20,000 square feet cost $5 per square foot, the $100,000 additional annual expense could be charged, in total, to the new planned activity. Alternatively, Goldome could divide that $100,000 charge between the planned activity and an investment in future expansion space. In other words, we would charge $50,000 to the planned activity and divide the other $50,000 corporate-wide.

I have purposely selected this example to get you to consider that fixed and marginal cost figures are really very relative and situational. A method of analysis should allow you to arrive at a cost structure that you as a manager feel comfortable with.

Certain variable costs are controlled managerially. One example in mortgage banking is customer service. Although customer demand for customer service should be directly proportional to the number of loans serviced, management can decide to restrict the level of availability of that customer service. Specifically, management can reduce the customer service costs by reducing the number of incoming telephone lines or by reducing the number of customer service representatives available to handle those calls. This is not in any way endorsing such restrictions; such a decision is not effective in the long run. However, it illustrates that if managers only seek to reduce cost, there are available methods.

There is another important cost factor to consider, called the "rubber band effect." Basically, as you expand you will find certain points where you can sandwich in additional volume without proportional additions to staff. There's no science here; it really comes from managerial experience.

If you employ such a concept, it is equally important that you watch several critical gauges. For example, if you are stretching the hazard area, it is important to know the backlong of unpaid hazard bills. Similarly, if you are stretching the collection area, you must be extremely sensitive to months where not all 30-day accounts have been contacted. Such indicators gauge whether the staff has reached its limits at this level of productivity.

Experience often proves that if you choose to stretch further, that rubber band may indeed break, and the operational disruption of an exhausted and destroyed staff could cost you far more than any additional, potential savings.

REDUCING DOWN TO MARGINAL COST

In 1985 Goldome Realty Credit Corp. (GRCC) purchased an operation in Orange County, California. In analyzing the purchase of that corporation, it was important for us to analyze the difference between the average cost for GRCC and the additive cost that will result from this purchase.

At that time, our fully loaded average cost was in the neighborhood of $75 per loan. Since average cost calculations can vary greatly, the exact dollar figure cited is not nearly as important as the reduction in that dollar figure by employing a marginal cost analysis.

To understand fully, read the following explanation and follow Table 23–1. We found that when expanding, we could add loans (using the rubber band effect) at slightly better than our average of 800 loans per person. In fact, at that time, we felt that we could add loans at approximately 1,100 per person. So too, we felt management costs were fixed in a 10,000 loan change. Certainly if the scope of change would have been 100,000 loans versus 10,000, we would have needed additional supervisory and managerial talent. However, at this growth level the additive or variable cost for management would be zero. Benefits, a variable cost, should follow personnel and be tied to the number of staff added.

Based on our experience over the last several years, overtime and outside help appeared to run at two thirds of personnel growth expense and was reflected accordingly in the analysis.

Nonpersonnel expenses varied widely. As already mentioned, this facility was below the 180,000 loans capacity and, therefore, additional occupancy cost was zero. We even analyzed the need for additional furniture and found that that cost would also be zero. Telephone, office supplies, postage, data processing, and other fixed expenses were viewed as variable, tied to loan volume. Therefore, these costs increased in direct proportion to the contemplated growth.

The bottom line here is that, as indicated in Table 23–1, through a marginal cost analysis the average cost figure of approximately $75 had been legitimately lowered to an additive cost of approximately $40. Now, in reality, when placing the bid, we tempered this slightly, premising the bid more in the middle $40s because we felt that we needed a cushion for the unknown. But most important, as a management team, after conducting such an analysis, we felt comfortable in reducing our cost assumptions for this acquisition to a much lower figure than the previous average.

ARMs—COST OF SERVICING

Just as mortage servicing firms analyze the marginal impact on average cost produced by a particular activity or economic situation, so too

Table 23–1
**Reconciliation of Marginal versus Average Cost
10,000 Loan Portfolio**

Average Cost—$78.00

Personnel

Staff—9 people @ $12,000 average = (1,100 vs. 750)	$108,000	
Management	–0–	
Benefits (25% × 108,000) =	27,000	
Overtime & Outside Help = (2/3 × .05% (108,000)	3,602	
Total Personnel		$138,602

Nonpersonnel

Occupancy =	–0–	
Telephone ($3.20 per loan) =	32,000	
Office Supplies & Postage ($5 per loan) =	50,000	
Data Processing ($11 per loan) =	110,000	
Other (nonforeclosure expense) ($6.50 per loan) =	65,000	
Total nonpersonnel		257,000
Total Additive Costs		395,602
Divided by 10,000		39.56

must they assess the (often dramatic) impact of product type on cost.

Table 23–2 reproduces an internal study conducted several years ago on GRCC's cost of ARM servicing. By the end of 1984, GRCC added over 21,000 ARM loans to its total portfolio. We needed to determine whether this new product's additive costs were offset by the additional 1/8th percent servicing fee that we were collecting.

Table 23–2
ARM Cost Study Approach

Department	Cost Description	Assumption Explanation	Amount	Method of Calculation
New Loans	Additional time to set up an ARM	Setting up an ARM requires 10% additional time to research and select basis codes	$ 2.46	Multiply the cost of setting up a loan by 10% to arrive at the additional ARM costs
Mortgage Servicing Systems	Computer enhancements and in-house programming	Enhancements and in-house programming help to automate ARM servicing for better efficiency	.20 (2.00)	Add programming costs and/or enhancement costs. Amortize these costs by the straight-line method for 5 years and divide by the number of ARMs
Loan Administration Training	Training to educate staff	Training is necessary to keep the staff educated on ARM products	1.02	Assuming training for ARM education is 10% of this department's budget, multiply the budget by 10% and divide by the number of ARMs
Payment Administration	Additional time on ARM payments rejected from normal processing (suspense)	ARMs are 25% more likely to go into suspense and this requires additional staff time for research	.24	Multiply the average amount of time spent on suspense items by 25% for additional time spent on ARMs. Multiply this time factor by the wage plus 22% for benefits and divide by the number of ARMs

Escrow Analysis	Additional time on ARM processing and additional coupon book ordering	In 25% of ARMs serviced, manual escrow analysis adjustments are needed. In 75% of ARMs serviced, there is no change in escrow analysis procedures but an additional coupon book is ordered	.41	Determine the amount of time spent in each activity; do a weighted average between these activities and then multiply the wage plus 22% for benefits and divide by the number of ARMs.
Investor Reporting	Investor-required reports on ARMs	Additional reports are required by investors, and adjustments are needed	$ .13 (9.30)**	Multiply the average amount of time spent on research and reports by wage, adding 22% for benefits and divide by the number of ARMs
Customer Service	Additional contacts with customers	With payment changes, the number of calls and letters from customers increases. Training is also needed to educate customer service representatives	Calls .50 Letters .54 Train. .14	Multiply the time spent on calls, letters of training by wage, adding 22% for benefits and divided by the number of ARMs. Training requires 15 additional hours for CSRs
Delinquency	Additional staff time for delinquent ARMs	Delinquent ARMs require additional attention due to customer confusion and subsequent follow-up calls required from the collection area	.05	Multiply the amount of time by wage, adding 22% for benefits, and divide by the number of ARMs

*Note: These figures are not based on actual costs and are being presented to demonstrate a methodology that could be utilized in an individual company.

**This amount represents more complex investor reporting requirements, such as guaranteed-yield sales.

Table 23–2 (continued)
ARM Cost Study Approach

Department	Cost Description	Assumption Explanation	Amount	Method of Calculation
Foreclosure	ARMs are more likely to hit foreclosure	If ARMs are more likely to hit foreclosure, they become more costly to service	6.61 (21.52)	Using the ratio of (a) number of ARMs in foreclosure/total number of ARMs, compare this ratio to (b) number of fixed rate loans in foreclosure/total number of fixed rate loans. This shows that ARMs are currently 50% more likely to go into foreclosure. Therefore, if there are approximately 460 loans in foreclosure and ARMs represent 14% of the portfolio, then there are 60 more ARM foreclosures than the average. Multiply this number by $2150 (the MBA statistic assuming a pass through) and divide by the number of ARMs
ARM	Servicing activities for ARMs only	Because of notice requirements, P & I changes and system maintenance and research, all such ARM activites are centralized	12.90	Total expenses including salary, benefits, and operating costs charged to the ARM cost center plus an approximation of management expense

Payoff

Acquisition cost $ 50.00

Assume ARMs are paying off
twice as fast as the entire
portfolio. Therefore, we need
to recognize an increased
amortization of our cost to
originate/acquire the loans

Using the difference between the
average life of a fixed-rate loan (12
years) and the average life of an
ARM (6 years), the amortization
rate is increased by 1/12. Therefore, if the cost of origination is 1%
and the average loan is $60,000,
$1/12 \times (1\% \times 60,000) = \$50.000$

To analyze this additive cost, we studied those aspects of the product that would be different from a normal "vanilla" mortgage. We analyzed the impact of ARMs on each of the major functions within servicing. For example, in the new loan area, we looked at the additional time necessary to set up an ARM loan. More specifically, we analyzed the additional work necessary to research and set up an ARM rate change index in our computerized system. Then we timed the setup on several ARM loans and arrived at a general average increase of 10 percent. At that time, the cost to set up a new loan in our servicing system was averaging $24.60. As it was taking 10 percent longer to set up an ARM loan, it was assumed for the purpose of the study that the added cost would be $2.46.

When we examined the mortgage servicing systems and programming costs, we were surprised. We had thought that the cost of computer enhancements to handle the new ARM product would be extremely large. However, as a CPI client, we benefited (along with many computer service bureaus servicing shops) from the fact that the service bureaus can divide the enhancement cost between many clients. Therefore, when we took our CPI-shared client enhancement cost of $20,000 and divided it against the number of loans serviced (20,000), and then depreciated that over a five-year usable life, the managers saw that the cost of programming, although huge to CPI, effectively measured a meager $.20 a loan per annum for GRCC.

In the table note the $2 for mortgage servicing. What this means is that even if we had not shared the cost with other CPI clients, and we had sustained the full developmental cost of $200,000, the per loan cost would not have increased that significantly because of the loan volume and because costs are being amortized over a five-year useful life. The $2 additive cost for programming would still have been less than the additional cost for the ARM new loan set up.

As we turned our attention to Mortgage Loan Administration training, we saw that ARM servicing did indeed require additional training. In fact, our training department dedicated 10 percent of its training time to ARM servicing. This $1.02 additive cost reflects that portion of the budget so dedicated.

The increased costs in payment administration were almost nothing. So too, escrow analysis costs were very minimal. The $.41 cited here is merely the additional cost for a coupon book to be sent out at the time of payment change.

The investors reporting cost illustrates how you can structure a deal to reduce cost. We found that on most of our deals, the secondary marketing people had structured investor reporting to be a fairly simplistic, single-debit type reporting; therefore, the additive costs were minimal. However, in certain deals, where secondary marketing had cut a guaranteed yield, customized reporting structure, the resulting manual effort literally cost hundreds times more to service. The $9.30 figure in the table reflects that additive cost for those loans that require such specialized servicing.

Initially, customer service impact appeared to be very large, because telephone calls involving ARMs were complex, and customer service representatives remembered them when they were casually interviewed. However, a sampling of customer service volume by type of call proved very quickly that the number of ARM calls, although memorable, were not as frequent as perceived; hence, the additive cost was only $1.18.

Analysis of delinquencies showed no significant effect on cost. In foreclosure, however, there appeared to be a dramatic increase. When we analyzed the approximately 460 loans in foreclosure, the ARM foreclosure portfolio totaled 60 more loans than the proportional share of ARMs to the total portfolio. Multiplying this number by $2,150 (the company's cost to foreclose a mortgage) then dividing it back over the portfolio, we arrived at a $6.61 additive cost.

We then examined the impact of real estate owned (REO) responsibilities. In such a situation—where we have the responsibility of not only foreclosing but also absorbing any possible REO expense—the cost per loan increased to over $7,000. In such a situation, the additive cost to service an ARM increased by an astronomical $21.52. The point here is that the arrangement concerning foreclosure expenses with your investor is critical to your ARM servicing cost.

Due to the volume of ARM servicing, we were able to centralize all payment change and detailed ARM research functions. When analyzing that department's budget and divided it by the volume, we learned that that area's additional cost was $12.90.

The last concept that we explored during this study was the recovery of origination expense. Generally, the net cost of origination for GRCC, like many other firms, was somewhere in the neighborhood of 1 percent. If indeed it is 1 percent, and the ARM loans are originated with an average principal balance of $60,000, then we have invested $600 in the origination of that product. That investment is worthwhile because GRCC will make a much larger profit on the mortgage during its servicing life.

However, this study of the discharge rate for ARM loans indicated that they tended to discharge (or refinance to a fixed-rate loan) twice as fast as did the firm's fixed-rate product. In other words, if a portfolio overall was prepaying at a rate such that a loan averaged a 12-year life, normally that $600 origination investment had to be amortized at a rate of 1/12 per year ($50 per annum) over 12 years. However, with the ARM portfolio's average life in the neighborhood of 6 years, that investment had to be amoritzed in half the time of a fixed-rate loan, or at the rate of $100 per year. That additional cost of $50 was perhaps the most significant cost of ARM servicing.

The analysis of the additional cost of ARM servicing taken by itself is not a useful management tool. What is helpful is to take that additional cost and plug it into a projected income stream. Table 23–3 attempts to accomplish just that. This example involves $100 million in ARM servicing. The service fee of .5 percent results in $500,000 in income. Late charges and other ancillary income adds $40,000 to that income stream. In addition, the $900,000 in escrow balances allows the GRCC to buy down a similar amount of warehouse line with a resultant effective savings of $54,000.

Direct expenses cited include such items as cost of service. In this particular example, $100 is the cost of service. That would be made up of the $40 additive or marginal cost discussed in the first example plus $60 in additional costs selected from the additive ARM cost study. We could have easily used a figure of $125 or $150, depending on which combination of additive costs applies to the exact type of ARM being

Table 23–3
Projected Income Flow

	First Year →	Second Year →
Income:		
Service Fee:		
.5% × 100,000 =	$500,000	
Ancillary Income:		
8% of S.F. =	40,000	
Warehouse Effect (Escrow $ × 6%)	54,000	
Total Income:	$594,000	
Expense:		
Cost to Service:		
(100,000,000 ÷ 80,000) × 100 =	125,000	
Amortization of Acquisition:	300,000	
Total Expense:	425,000	
Net Income:		$169,000

analyzed. Note, too, the need to show the amortization of any proposed acquisition expense. Alternately, if GRCC originated the product, it must amortize the effective investment resulting from the origination process.

Then the total expenses would be substracted from total income to arrive at a net income for the first year. That same process could be used through each subsequent year, discounting that cash flow back to decide whether the product under this cost structure is profitable.

CONVERSION COSTS

When analyzing an acquisition of servicing rights, it is very important to also analyze the immediate cost impact of the servicing transfer itself.

Table 23–4 attempts to detail some conversion costs that may be applicable to any proposed acquisition. First and foremost is due diligence. No matter how concise or how thorough an analysis you have made of the proposed purchase, it is essential that top managers from your company examine the proposed acquisition on site. *Top managers* of the company does not necessarily mean the *most senior*. The people selected for a due diligence trip should be those individuals who can test the operational capacity of the company and who can assess the managerial strengths and weaknesses quickly, arriving at a bottom line on whether your analysis and cost assumptions are indeed correct for this portfolio.

For the acquisition described in this chapter, the servicing operation selected eight individuals for a four-day, on-site due diligence inspection. The $10,000 expended for that activity is minimal compared to the purchase price of over $10 million. Despite this relatively small cost, many companies do not go on site to test the quality of their analytical assumptions.

The conversion team expense cited reflects a typical on-site management. As the team was winding down the operation of moving the servicing portion to Buffalo, they placed on site six trained individuals to operate in the area and prepare the site for computerized conversion.

Table 23–4
Conversion Costs
(Additive)

Due Diligence		
8 people for 4 days on site at @ $200 =	$ 6,400	
Travel @ $400 per person =	3,200	
Conversion Team		
6 people on site @ $1,000 per week (4 weeks) =	24,000	
Conversion Programming Expense	16,500	
Tax Service Setup ($25 per loan)	250,000	
File Buildup and Correction ($2 per loan)	20,000	
Assignment Processing ($.50 per loan)	5,000	
Contingency Reserve (10m × 65m × 1.7 × 3%)	331,500	
Total		$656,000
Divided by 10,000		65.66
Optional Costs		
Conversion Team Salary $20,000 × 6 × 6/52 =	13,846	
Due Diligence Team @ $40,000 × 8 – 52 weeks =	6,153	

In such a conversion, they employ computer programming through CPI that allows them to merge and scrub the computer records of the targeted firm.

Tax service setup is many times forgotten by a company in its cost analysis. However, it can be extremely costly. In this particular example, the 10,000 loans in this portfolio cost $250,000 ($25 per loan) to be setup.

A data base frequently must be built up or cleared of inaccurate information upon (or prior to) the completion of a conversion. If so, significant amounts will need to be subjected for temporary and/or overtime expense. In this particular case, a cost of $2 per loan was sufficient to clean the existing company's data base to the team's standards. Furthermore, investors frequently require that assignments be prepared to reflect the new servicer. Hence, the $5,000 cost was budgeted.

An essential inclusion in the conversion cost is a contingency expense; in this case, the team set aside approximately 3 percent of the purchase price. That contingency expense reserve allowed them to have a cushion for the unexpected—which always occurs in the acquisition of a company or a portfolio.

It is interesting to note that dividing the total conversion cost of $656,000 by the 10,000 loans yields a per-loan conversion cost of $65 or approximately one year's servicing expense. Despite that significant dollar figure, frequently companies analyze the flow of net income but not the conversion expense when they analyze the profitability of a particular activity.

CONCLUSION

This chapter discussed the impact of a servicing acquisition on cost structures. It also suggested several tools for your own company's analysis whenever you consider the additive costs from acquisition of servicing.

In summary, this approach calls for examining your own company's cost structure to determine the actual additive cost. Then you examine the characteristics of the product whose servicing you are acquiring to test whether there are special additive costs associated with the product.

Finally, you should remember that there are very large costs associated with the actual transfer. The failure to properly account for any of these can turn a projected profit into a significant loss.

This explanation attempted to demonstrate that there is no set rule for analysis, only effective approaches. There is no one set answer; rather, you can select among an array of answers applicable to your company in a particular situation.

Section IV:
The Thrift and Commercial Banking of Industries

INTRODUCTION

The 1980s have been a tumultuous decade for thrifts and commercial banks, a period of time when a record number of institutions failed or were merged out of existence. Yet, paradoxically, it has also been a decade of spectacular advances, of new products, technologies, and strategies that some have used to dramatically *increase* profitability and market share. One such strategy has been to develop an increased presence in mortgage banking—the origination of loans for resale, rather than for portfolio, which is the subject of the first two chapters in Section IV. In Chapter 24, Kevin O'Neil makes the case that mortgage banking subsidiaries can be very profitable for thrifts and commercial banks, but warns that parent companies must understand the criticial differences between mortgage banking and their own businesses. Joel Rosenberg follows in Chapter 25 with a detailed analysis of the many alternatives that thrifts and commerical banks should consider for funding their mortgage banking operations.

Many thrifts and banks have continued to prosper while continuing to hold mortgages in portfolio. Gone are the days, however, when institutions could safely originate 30-year fixed-rate mortgages and finance them with short-term liabilities.

The final three chapters of Section IV discuss many of the new strategies and tactics that successful thrifts and banks have developed to deal with a volatile, deregulated economic environment. In Chapter 26, James Montgomery makes the case for adjustable-rate mortgages, and argues that the payment-capped, cost of funds indexed ARM best meets the needs of borrowers, originators, and investors.

In Chapter 27, William Longbrake and Peter Struck present an analytical framework for restructing mortgage portfolios to achieve an optimum balance between minimizing interest rate risk and maximizing profit. Section IV concludes with Chapter 28, authored by Gregory Coleman and Robert Hunter, which examines state-of-the-art techniques that have been developed to finance mortgage portfolios by tapping the money and capital markets.

Chapter 24

KEVIN J. O'NEIL

Kevin O'Neil has served as President of Goldome Realty Credit Corp. since its formation in January 1983. Prior to his appointment as President of Goldome Realty Credit Corp., he served as Group Vice President for Mortgages at Goldome, FSB and earlier, as Goldome's Senior Mortgage Officer.

Before joining Goldome in 1981, Mr. O'Neil served as Senior Vice President and Treasurer of Women's Federal Savings and Loan Association of Cleveland, Ohio. Prior to joining Women's Federal he was a Vice President of Citizens Mortgage Corp., where he managed the company's publicly owned real estate investment trusts.

Mr. O'Neil, a graduate of Canisius College of Buffalo, New York, received his M.B.A. in finance from Harvard University. Mr. O'Neil has also completed the Advanced Management Program at Harvard University.

He is a member of the Mortgage Bankers Association of America and currently sits on its Legislative Committee. Mr. O'Neil also serves on the Board of Governors for the Mortgage Bankers Association and is also a Board Member on the PMI Advisory Board. He recently served on the MBA's Ad Hoc Committee on Computerized Loan Origination Systems.

Profit Opportunities for Thrifts and Commercial Banks in the Sale or Acquisition of Mortgage Banking Operations

KEVIN O'NEIL

The mortgage banking industry has always been attractive to both thrifts and commercial banks. As savings and loan associations began to expand their national mortgage lending activities in the late 1960s and 1970s, many of them started mortgage banking operations. This enabled them to originate in areas other than their home office. It also gave them the vehicle to originate more loans than they could fund themselves, because they could sell the loans in the secondary market.

Commercial banks, on the other hand, primarily entered the mortgage banking field through acquisitions of existing mortgage banking companies. With the formation of many bank holding companies in the 1960s and 1970s, the banks' diversification efforts often turned to the acquisition of existing mortgage banking companies. Notable among the early acquisitions were Citibank's purchase of Advance Mortgage Corporation and Manufacturers Hanover's acquisition of Citizen's Mortgage Corporation. Numerous other commercial banks followed suit. The commercial banks believed that mortgage banking would provide a better return on equity than their basic banking business, enable them to build off balance sheet value in the servicing portfolio, and provide synergy with their other banking and nonbanking activities.

Mortgage banking companies in themselves can be very profitable. Returns on equity in good years when interest rates are favorable, as in 1985 and 1986, often exceed 20 percent. In addition, the mortgage banking company's value will increase over time as the servicing portfolio grows. Today, with regulators putting pressure on both thrifts and commercial banks to increase their capital, a number of banks and thrifts have sold their mortgage banking operations at a handsome profit. In the mid-1980s, Manufacturers Hanover, Crossland Savings, Pittsburgh National Bank, and Florida National Bank disposed of their mortgage banking subsidiaries, reportedly at a considerable profit.

As this is being written in 1986, Commonwealth Savings is attempting to spin off a portion of its mortgage banking operation into a limited partnership in which Commonwealth will be the general partner. This will enable Commonwealth to realize a profit on the portion that is sold, retain control through its role as general partner, and, finally, maintain some ownership by buying some percentage of the limited partnership shares being offered to the public. If this vehicle can be successfully marketed, it may become a method for many other thrifts and commercial banks to capitalize on the profitability inherent in the servicing portfolios of the mortgage banking operations, while, at the same time, participating in future profits.

The acquisition of a mortgage banking company by a commercial bank or thrift gives that institution access to a large consumer base, that is, to all the individuals whose mortgages are being serviced. In addition, the information on each individual is extremely voluminous, including income and credit history. On the other hand, the information is not kept up-to-date and becomes stale rather quickly. There are, however, a number of cross-selling opportunities for the commercial bank or thrift. The most obvious is the extension of additional credit such as second mortgages, home improvement loans, home equity lines of credit, auto loans, and credit card lines. If the mortgage banker operates nationally, however, the thrift or commercial bank may have difficulties, both legal and practical, in extending credit to this customer base. Another obvious opportunity for cross-selling is insurance. Every individual who takes out a mortgage loan needs one thing—a new homeowner's policy. On the other hand, most thrifts and commercial banks are severely restricted in entering the insurance field.

Many commercial banks and thrifts have looked at their mortgage banking companies as a way of getting a jump on interstate banking. They can open mortgage banking offices in states where they cannot open retail banking branches. The thought is that when interstate banking finally does become the law of the land, mortgage banking companies will already have a presence in areas other than their home state. Although the existence of a mortgage banking office gives the institution retail presence and name recognition in the area in which it operates, most offices of mortgage bankers could not easily be adapted into deposit-gathering facilities. However, they could easily become outlets for other types of lending, particularly consumer lending. If the mortgage banker has commercial offices, these could probably be adapted for non-real estate commercial lending, leasing, factoring, and so forth.

Commercial banks and thrifts have also been attracted to mortgage banking companies because of the huge escrow accounts that mortgage bankers maintain. Normally, escrow deposits—together with the float obtained by the mortgage banker between the receipt of the payment from the borrower and the remittance to the investor—total 2 percent of the amount of the dollar volume of the loans being serviced. In other words, a $5 billion servicer would probably generate escrow accounts in excess of $100 million. These escrow deposits can be a very inexpensive source of significant deposit dollars for the parent thrift or commercial bank. On the other hand, most mortgage banking companies use their escrow balances to buy down the rate on their warehouse lines of credit; thus the balances are not really available to the parent.

The net interest margin earned by the mortgage banker normally is a substantial part of its profitability. If regulations allow, the parent could achieve additional profitability by being the warehouse lender for the mortgage banking subsidiary. A note of caution here—laws requiring interest to be paid on escrow accounts already exist in a number of states, and there is consumer sentiment to enact such statutes in other states. Another threat to escrow balances is a proposal that has surfaced in several states, but that has not yet been enacted, which would require escrow accounts to be used for various types of low-income housing.

Commercial banks and thrifts have also been attracted to the mortgage banking industry as a means of increasing fee income. All origination fees on mortgages can be credited to income at the time when the loan is sold to the ultimate investor. This is in contrast to portfolio lending, in which a substantial amount of the fees would have to be taken into income over the life of the loan. This will become particularly significant in light of the 1986 FASB Proposal, which would require that virtually all origination fees be deferred and recognized by the interest method over the life of the related loan as an adjustment to yield. This requirement will be particularly onerous for many thrifts, a substantial amount of whose income consists of origination fees taken on loans that they are putting into their portfolio. The likelihood is that more thrifts will be involved in mortgage banking, or at the very least in secondary marketing, selling at least a portion of the loans they originate. It is even conceivable that certain thrifts, in order to circumvent the regulation, will originate and, in effect, swap loans with each other so that they can recognize the income once the loan has been sold to another investor.

Asset-liability management has also played a significant role in why commercial banks and thrifts want to be involved in mortgage banking. Although a mortgage banker may be originating 30-year, fixed-rate mortgages, the banker can eliminate interest rate risk by entering into commitments to sell fixed-rate loan production. In effect, the mortgage banker is actually making 60- to 90-day loans, because it has a chance to refix the rate on its warehouse portfolio at least every 60 or 90 days. Mortgage bankers, however, still can run into asset-liability mismatches in periods of extremely high short-term rates. On a number of occasions, short-term rates exceeded (at least for a short period of time) long-term rates, resulting in a negative spread on loans in warehouse. Mortgage bankers attempted to react to this situation by speeding up the turnover of loans and by charging a fee to the borrower to cover the cost in the warehouse. These strategies were only partially successful. Fortunately, the inverse yield curve, in which short-term rates were higher than long-term, normally did not last for a significant period of time.

As previously indicated, in recent years mortgage banking companies have generated excellent returns on equity. The profitability of the mortgage banking subsidiary of a parent commercial bank or thrift can also be enhanced through a number of strategies. One would involve selling a portion of the servicing portfolio each year. Traditionally, mortgage bankers retain their servicing and realize a significant capital gain only when the entire company is sold. In recent years, however, sales of portions of servicing portfolios have become extremely common. GNMA servicing, in particular, is readily saleable, and in excess of $100 billion of that servicing has changed hands in recent years.

Another strategy used to increase earnings by certain mortgage banking companies involves capitalization (and, thus the immediate recognition as income) of so-called excess servicing fees. In other words, if a loan is originated at 10.5 percent and sold to an investor at 10 percent, the 50 basis point spread could be recognized annually as servicing income. Another acceptable accounting treatment suggests that the servicing fee would only be half of the 50 basis points, or 25 basis points, and that the other 25 basis points would represent excess yield. The present value of this excess yield can be capitalized and taken into income in year 1. The capitalized value would then be amortized over a period of years. Certain mortgage companies have been very aggressive in using this technique, allowing for only 10 or 12 basis points as the normal servicing fee, and capitalizing (and thus taking into income) any amount in excess of the "normal" servicing fee. There is a serious question, however, whether 10 or 12 basis points would represent a sufficient amount of servicing revenue to offset costs over the entire life of the loan, particularly in the case of ARMs, which are more expensive to service than fixed-rate loans.

A number of mortgage banking companies also used capitalization for part of the 44 basis point servicing fee on GNMA servicing. It was anticipated that FASB would rule on this issue, but as of mid-1986 no ruling was forthcoming.

For those commercial banks or thrifts that are contemplating an entry into the mortgage banking business, there should be a recognition that mortgage banking truly differs from commercial banking or thrift banking. The management of the parent institution must recognize these differences and deal with them. I have come up with what I shall call the 10 commandments of mortgage banking for a commercial bank or thrift. They are:

1. *Thou shalt originate quality product.* Remember, it's not for the portfolio. The costs of handling delinquencies and the ultimate costs of foreclosure far exceed the servicing fees obtained on those loans. Because inflation has been brought under control, there is a sharply increased emphasis on quality among ultimate investors in mortgage loans such as FNMA and FHLMC. The mortgage banker who is not originating quality product, or who is even not documenting properly, runs the risk of investor rejects and a veritable mountain of unsaleable loans in the warehouse.

2. *Thou shalt have the capacity to handle wide swings in volume.* Mortgage lending, particularly mortgage banking, has always been extremely cyclical. Swings in interest rates drastically impact the volume of loans originated. The decrease in interest rates in 1986 not only sparked housing sales, but also a tremendous surge in refinances. Most mortgage bankers found their volume had more than doubled since 1985. FNMA and FHLMC found a similar increase in their purchase volume. The lesson here for the bank or thrift is that the mortgage company must be able to move extremely rapidly to marshal resources, including the addition of staff and the renting of temporary space. Ponderous, committee-type decision-making processes will severely hinder the ability of the mortgage banker to react to changes in volume. Some of the problems inherent in rapid expansion and contraction can be alleviated somewhat if the mortgage banker has a combination of both direct originations and purchases from other mortgage bankers. Purchased loans do not involve an origination or processing function, and they do not affect the volatility of operations as much as does retail origination.

3. *Thou shalt minimize secondary marketing risks.* The mortgage banker's business is to originate loans and service them. The mortgage banker should avoid taking any unnecessary market risks. If the parent institution wants to take a position on interest rates, it should normally be done through the parent's investment department. The use of a mortgage pipeline to take interest rate risks is inherently inefficient, since many mortgage loans will not close in a period of rapidly declining interest rates. Borrowers walk from their commitments. The corollary here is that the mortgage banker must have a very sophisticated tracking system so that it is aware of what is being originated and therefore can obtain appropriate coverage.

4. *Thou shalt manage the servicing portfolio just like a bond portfolio.* The rapid decline in interest rates in 1986 prompted a tremendous amount of refinancing, and the servicing of high-rate loans acquired just a few short years ago went by the boards as these loans were refinanced. The objective of the mortgage banker should be to maximize the amount of servicing it has at lower rates and minimize the servicing of higher-rate portfolios. Thus, when rates are high, the mortgage banker should sell servicing and should sell a high percentage of new production servicing released. This might involve a no-growth policy for the servicing portfolio, or it might even result in a decrease in the servicing portfolio. In the long run, however, this produces a more profitable servicing portfolio and tends to insulate the mortgage banker from rapid runoff of the portfolio. In addition if a mortgage banker is *buying* servicing, and paying a premium, the banker will want to sell off servicing in high-rate periods so that the capitalized cost of the servicing will not have to be written off when interest rates decline and there is substantial refinance activity.

5. *Thou shalt maintain a high-quality, expert staff in the mortgage banking operation.* Stated another way, keep the parent's personnel department out of the mortgage banking subsidiary. The mortgage banking industry has traditionally been driven by incentive compensation related to production and profitability,

much more so than the commercial banking industry or thrift industry. Similarly, mortgage bankers have been paid somewhat lower benefits than thrift or commercial banking personnel. In addition, employment has traditionally been less stable in the mortgage banking industry, due to the volatility of production in good and bad years. Although the differences between the personnel practices of mortgage bankers and commercial banks and thrifts may be decreasing somewhat, differences still remain. During periods of high activity, there is tremendous raiding of personnel among mortgage banking companies. The mortgage banker must be able to adjust salary ranges for key personnel such as underwriters, processors, and secondary marketing personnel very quickly. These ranges will have to vary in different geographic areas in the country. In short, the mortgage banker needs more flexibility in personnel administration than traditionally exists in the commercial banking or thrift industry.

6. *Thou shalt maintain an adequate capital base.* There is some misconception among commercial bankers and thrift executives that mortgage banking companies can be run with little or no capital. This in fact is not the case and is becoming increasingly less so. The mortgage banker must have sufficient capital to support warehouse lines. Debt-to-equity ratios in excess of 10 to 1 or 12 to 1 begin to strain the mortgage banker and make lenders reluctant to extend additional credit. The nature of the equity base is also important. If the company is initially capitalized with a large amount of purchased servicing and a substantial portion of the net worth consists of an intangible (mainly purchased servicing rights) the ability of the mortgage banker to leverage that equity base will be somewhat diminished.

In today's mortgage banking arena, most or virtually all government loans and a substantial portion of conventional loans are sold in mortgage-backed securities. When any of these securitized loans go delinquent, the mortgage banker must advance the payment to the ultimate investor. The banker must keep advancing payments until such time as it can recoup advances, either because the account is brought current or because the property is foreclosed and ultimately sold. Again, such advances require the mortgage banker to maintain additional capital or see a reduction in the warehouse capability, because it will have to devote lines of credit to these advances.

7. *Thou shalt maintain adequate external lines of credit.* Although there is a tendency on the part of commercial banks and thrifts to finance the needs of the mortgage banker internally, the use of external lines of credit from other commercial banks should not be discarded. The rates and terms negotiated with outside lenders will demonstrate to both the mortgage banker and its parent commercial banker or thrift the true market rates for such credit. This then can form the basis for any intercompany transactions between the parent and the mortgage banker. In addition, the needs of the subsidiary mortgage banking company for additional funds may come at exactly the wrong time for the parent bank or thrift. At the very least, the mortgage banker should probably maintain standby lines of credit that could be drawn on in the event of unexpected cash needs. In 1986, when GNMA extended the time it took to issue commitments and securities, mortgage bankers found that they needed substantially increased lines of credit. The parent commercial bank or thrift should carefully evaluate whether it can really fill the needs of the mortgage banking subsidiary without resort to any external credit.

8. *Thou shalt keep the computer systems of the mortgage banker current and separate from the parent.* Although most commercial banks and thrifts have sophisticated data centers, their computer operations are likely to be somewhat different from those of the subsidiary mortgage banker. In the origination area, the mortgage banker needs state-of-the-art software to track the mortgage pipeline so that it can obtain adequate coverage. The industry is also moving toward distributive processing so that it can put access devices in the offices of its brokerage and mortgage correspondent customers. Bank and thrift data centers, on the other hand, tend to be highly centralized. Systems and programming

personnel need to be dedicated to the mortgage banking operation, so they can become knowledgeable in the unique requirements of mortgage banking.

9. *Thou shalt keep a keen eye trained on Washington and Wall Street.* Increasingly, the residential mortgage is becoming a commodity sold through Wall Street in securitized pools both whose timely and ultimate payment are guaranteed by various governmental or quasigovernmental agencies such as FHA, VA, GNMA, FNMA, or FHLMC. The mortgage banker needs to be cognizant of the ever-changing scene in Washington with respect to these agencies, both with regard to their funding and their regulations. The commercial banking and thrift executives should also recognize that their legislative and regulatory goals may be at variance with those of the mortgage banker. The easier it is for the mortgage banker to sell its production, the more difficult it will be for the thrift to originate for portfolio. The senior thrift executives must determine where their priorities lie and act accordingly. Additionally, the mortgage banker and its commercial bank or thrift parent must cultivate and maintain a close working relationship with a number of Wall Street firms. Wall Street will continue to increase its activity in and impact on mortgage banking, and the mortgage banker must be alert to new developments from Wall Street.

10. *Thou shalt recognize mortgage banking for what it is—a unique business with substantial profit opportunities as well as substantial inherent risks—a business that needs to be managed as a separate business and not as a division of the parent commercial bank or thrift.*

Chapter 25

JOEL L. ROSENBERG, CFA

Joel Rosenberg is Senior Vice President and Treasurer for ComFed Savings Bank in Lowell, Massachusetts. He is responsible for overall asset/liability management, portfolio strategies and executions, liability pricing, cash management, investor relations and non-retail deposit liability acquisitions. Prior to his association with ComFed Savings Bank, Mr. Rosenberg was Vice President and Treasurer for the Federal Home Loan Bank of Boston. There he was in charge of asset/liability management, interest rate swap programs, financial futures and options, lending programs, financial forecasting and cash management.

Mr. Rosenberg has a Masters of Science in industrial administration from the Graduate School of Industrial Administration of Carnegie-Mellon University. He has a Bachelors of Science in economics from Rensselaer Polytechnic Institute. He is also a chartered financial analyst. He holds an Adjunct Faculty Appointment in Finance at Bentley College and is an Associate Editor of Bank Asset/Liability Management Newsletter.

Funding Mortgage Banking Operations by Thrifts and Commercial Banks

JOEL L. ROSENBERG, CFA

During the 1980s, many thrifts and commercial banks have organized mortgage banking subsidiaries. These subsidiaries are either established as separate legal entities as a division of a holding company structure or as an integrated part of the bank or thrift. The purpose of these subsidiaries or divisions is to perform the traditional mortgage banking operations of originating loans and selling them into the secondary market. This does not mean origination for the intent of sale sometime in the undefined future, but actual near-term sale into the secondary market. The result of these mortgage banking subsidaries and divisions is the creation of a new type of asset called a "warehouse pipeline." It includes loans originated but not yet sold, in which funding has been disbursed to the mortgagors and the loans are now in the process of being packaged and sold into the secondary market. This asset can become a significant and profitable part of an institution's asset structure. The purpose of this chapter is to discuss means by which thrifts and commercial banks can fund this asset.

Mortgage banking involves receiving an application for a mortgage loan, processing that application, and funding the application to create a mortage loan. Although this early stage is similar to mortgage lending performed by most thrifts and banks, the second stage becomes critical in mortgage banking. That is, this stage comprises selling off the mortgage loan, either through direct sale to another institution (whether it be thrift, federal agency, bank trust department, pension fund, or other source) or creation of a mortgage-backed security, which is then sold in the secondary market. The time period between disbursing funds to the mortgagor and the receipt of funds on the sale of the mortgages or mortgage-backed product in the secondary market creates this warehouse pipeline, which is similar to the inventory of an industrial company. As in a manufacturing firm, this inventory can take several forms. In the first form, it may be basic mortgages, which are similar to raw material. In a second stage, the mortgages may be identified and allocated for being placed in a mortgage-backed security, similar to goods in process. In the third stage, as with the finished products of a manufacturing company, mortgages are sold in their final form (usually mortgage-backed securities). Just as with a manufacturing company, the inventory of a mortgage banking operation must be financed. Fortunately, the mortgage banking subsidiary or division of a financial institution has several advantages over an independent mortgage banking company: it has a greater number of viable alternatives for funding this pipeline and is able to benefit from greater flexibility and, often, a significantly cheaper source of funds.

Depending on the structure of the mortgage banking operation, the ability to tap these funds may vary. However, the traditional means is through a loan or disbursement of funds from the parent thrift or commercial bank to the mortgage banking division or subsidiary. For the traditional thrift, the source of these funds is the deposit liabilities of that institution, which are readily available and relatively inexpensive funds.

However, a thrift or commercial bank must look beyond its traditional deposit base to other alternatives. For a successful mortgage banking operation, the pipeline can be a very significant part of an institution's balance sheet, and alternative sources can become a very cost-effective means of funding this pipeline. There are several reasons why an institution needs to examine the alternative sources of funding its mortgage banking pipeline and operation. These are:

1. Deposits may not meet pipeline requirements.
2. Alternative sources can often be raised more rapidly.
3. Alternative sources may offer a rate advantage.
4. There may be lower overhead expense with some sources.
5. The alternative sources may be more secure and flexible.
6. The institution may gain valuable exposure.

Alternative sources of funds can vary, including such possibilities as: borrowing from larger commercial banks, reverse repos, and borrowing from the Federal Reserve. One of the first advantages of using an alternative source of funds rather than deposits is that an institution may not want to use its deposit flows in funding mortgage banking operations. Perhaps sources of funds raised through deposit are fully allocated to other areas of an institution's operation. It may not be feasible, as such, to raise sufficient funds through the deposit mechanism for the mortgage pipeline.

The graph in Figure 25–1 shows the flows associated with mortgage banking operations. As can be seen, in a typical mortgage operation, disbursements for mortgages occur somewhat regularly throughout the month. Receipts of funds through the sale of mortgages, however, are often received on one or only a few days towards the end of the month. As a result, the outstanding pipeline or warehouse of mortgages available for sale fluctuates during the month from a relatively low level near the end to a relatively high level in the middle. Since it takes on average anywhere from 30 to 60 days from the times funds are disbursed for the mortgage until the time that funds are received from sale, this pipeline can be a significant drain on an institution's resources.

The second advantage of alternative sources is that they can be raised quickly. Raising deposits require some effort, and, although through the manipulation of rates one can retain, increase, or chase away some deposit flows, this is not necessarily an instantaneous process. Alternative sources of funds can be quickly raised and/or paid off when they are no longer needed.

Given these speed considerations, there can often be significant rate advantages to raising funds through alternative sources rather than deposit mechanisms. Rates on deposits are often as greatly influenced

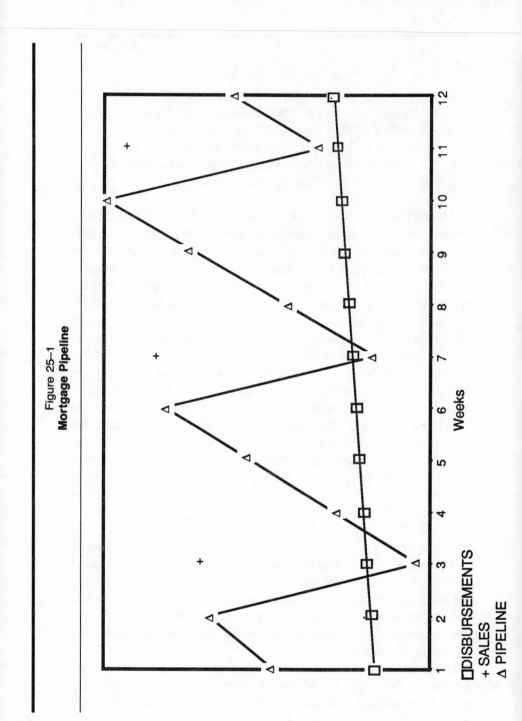

Figure 25–1
Mortgage Pipeline

Weeks

□ DISBURSEMENTS
+ SALES
△ PIPELINE

by "irrational" pricing of competitors as by general market rates and requirements. Often, alternative sources provide a less expensive means of funds acquisition than the traditional deposit mechanism.

Raising funds through alternative sources does not involve the expensive branch network usually associated with deposit gathering. One does not need a staff of tellers, managers, and ATMs; there is no need for leased or owned office space. In fact, what is often needed is only a telephone, typewriter, calculator and, perhaps a personal computer. Therefore, one does not face the dilemma of increasing staff. All that is needed is part-time involvement of one or possible two individuals, usually the treasurer, chief financial officer, or the portfolio manager. Depending on the alternative source used, the overhead or direct and indirect costs can be as little as zero to perhaps as great as 100 basis points, which compares favorably with the cost of raising deposits (which usually runs around 100 basis points).

Alternative sources also have the advantage that the institution generally controls their maturity and/or when these sources are to be paid. The problem with deposits is that it is the *customer's* decision to withdraw the money; an institution has little control (except perhaps by paying extraordinarily high rates). Alternative sources can be much more secure, and the institution is in control of when the alternatives will be liquidated. In addition, on longer-term sources, one does not have the fear of the customer prepaying the funds.

Finally, particularly for public companies, there is the exposure afforded by using alternative sources. Instead of being known to just the depositors, you will now be known to financial institutions and major suppliers of funds. For public companies, these financial institutions may also be those that buy equity, so this provides greater familiarity to the marketplace. It also may add some valuable indirect familiarity to the marketplace for your mortgage banking operation and subsidiary. Your name can become better known and, assuming you have reasonably good financials, more trusted. This can help increase the universe of institutions who can supply you with funds and/or business.

There are numerous alternative sources of funds, and this chapter deals with only the major ones. However, with changes in the financial markets over time, and with new and expanded powers for thrifts and commercial banks, there may soon be other alternatives available that are not discussed here. The following are the major shorter-term alternatives, listed in approximate order of overall cost:

1. Borrowing from a Federal Reserve bank
2. Reverse repurchase agreements
3. Fed funds from thrifts and commercial banks
4. Borrowing from a federal home loan bank
5. Commercial paper issuance
6. Prime base loans from commercial banks and/or insurance companies
7. Broker and institutional sales of jumbo short-term certificates of deposit

The following are sources of long-term funds on a floating-rate basis that can satisfy the permanent, outstanding level of the pipeline:

- Floating-rate medium-term notes
- Variable-rate mortgage-backed bonds
- Adjustable-rate preferred stocks

Each of these alternatives can be structured slightly differently, depending on the form of the bank or thrift and its relationship to its mortgage banking division or subsidiary. In addition, certain legal or technical requirements may prohibit the use of some of these alternatives. For instance, to borrow from the federal home loan bank, an institution must be a member of this organization, and commercial banks cannot legally become members. In addition, minimum size considerations may prohibit some of these alternatives from effective use by your organization. An example is commercial paper issuances, in which it is relatively uneconomical for total outstandings to be in amounts less than $25 million.

The first and perhaps the least costly means of raising funds is borrowing from the Federal Reserve bank. Unfortunately, this is comparable to a Russian purchasing consumer goods—the list price on the goods may be inexpensive, but they are usually not available. The Federal Reserve bank is there to meet an "emergency" need for funds, and it is not meant to be a permanent source for mortgage pipelines. In addition, the Fed is used by the bank or thrift and not by the mortgage company subsidiary. To the extent that the subsidiary's books are mixed with the bank's books, funds become intermixed. However, the Fed takes a very dim view if its discount loans are outstanding for more than a day, and they will "counsel" borrowers who frequently need to tap this source of funds. Finally, to borrow from the Fed, one cannot be in a liquid position by being a net seller of Fed funds and/or have large unused borrowing capacity that has not been tapped.

The Federal Reserve can, however, be a viable source in an emergency situation when more permanent sources of funds are expected to be available within a day or two. In addition, borrowing from the Fed is generally available later in the day than are some of the alternative sources. Besides certain legal documents that all institutions should have on file with the Federal Reserve, one must also have collateral available to be placed against these loans. The Fed's preferred source of collateral is generally wirable securities, such as U.S. Treasury or agency securities. However, if safekept by the Fed, collateral can include money market securities, mortgages, GNMA and certain other marketable secured notes. Finally, the rate is extremely attractive, being anywhere from 25 to 50 basis points below Fed funds. Except perhaps for passbook savings, this is the cheapest source of funds around.

The most readily available source of funds, as well as one of the least expensive, is the reverse repurchase (repo) transaction. A reverse repurchase agreement is a collateralized short-term borrowing between the financial institution and a security dealer, another financial institution, or even an individual. One provides collateral generally in the form of marketable securities or mortgages that are in turn assigned to the lender. In return, a sum of money is received that is equal to the market value of the underlying collateral and any accrued interest. When reverse repurchase agreements extend beyond a week or two, the collateral may be periodically "marked to market" with marginal changes made in the amount lent. At the time of termination, the security is returned to the borrower upon repayment of the borrowing.

Although reverse repurchase agreements have received bad press—given incidents relating to Drysdale, ESM, and others—in almost all situations, there is little risk to the borrower or the lender. As long as the amount lent is approximately equal to the market value of the security plus any accrued interest, potential loss to either party should be minimal.

The following five major subtypes of reverse repurchase agreements are similar in structure but differ in the type of collateral and interest rates charged:

1. Treasury and agency
2. Mortgage-backed securities
3. Money market securities
4. Whole-loan reverses
5. GNMA dollar rolls

The first subtype of Treasury and agency reverses is relatively easy to execute and the least expensive of any reverses. It involves an institution's most readily marketable securities, these being Treasury and agency (FHLB, Farm Credit, FNMA, and others), bills, notes, and bonds. These are wirable securities and are transferred over the Federal Reserve book entry system. Generally, the savings institution or commercial bank wires or has its safekeeping agent wire these securities to the lender's safekeeping agent. The cash borrowed is exchanged at the same time the security is transferred and, as such, is payment on receipt. At the termination of this transaction, securities are returned when the lender receives the amount borrowed plus interest. Reverse repos can have a fixed rate for anywhere from one day to one year or longer. In addition, the reverse can be "open," in which case the rate is adjusted daily based on the then-prevailing repo rate. U.S. Treasuries as collateral generally involve rates slightly below Fed funds. The use of U.S. agencies involves an interest rate that is at or slightly above Fed funds. Since this involves wirable securities, these reverse repos should be executed early in the morning for same day funds. The standardized trade is $5 million, although reverses can be done in smaller amounts.

This market is very liquid, with funds available to meet that day's immediate needs of a warehouse line. In addition, the reverse repo can be structured so it terminates upon receipt of funds from mortgages or mortgage-backed securities sold from the pipeline.

The second subtype of reverse repos uses mortgage-backed securiteis as collateral. These are generally FHLMC or FNMA, which are wirable securities, and GNMA, which is in definitive (paper) form. This type of reverse repo is very similar to the Treasury and agency reverse repos. For the wirable securities, funds are exchanged with the receipt of the securities that are wired through the Fed system. GNMA securities, which are physically transferred, are treated similarly. In addition, on GNMA securities, the PD Form 1832 must be signed and attached to the certificate. Occasionally, GNMA securities that are reversed frequently are placed in a segregated third-party safekeeping account. The major difference between this and the first subtype is that the cost of the second subtype generally runs 10–25 basis points above Fed funds rates.

The third subtype involves "bearer" short-term money market securities, primarily bankers' acceptances, negotiable Euro and domestic CDs, and commercial paper. These securities are transferred to the lender's safekeeping agent or may be held in a segregated account with a third-party agent. As with mortgage-backed securities, the rates on money market repos generally run slightly above Fed funds rates. Otherwise, this type of reverse repo is similar to those involving GNMA securities.

The fourth subtype is of relatively recent vintage and uses whole-loan mortgages. In this case, the borrower provides as collateral, through the use of a third-party safekeeping agent, mortgages generally held in the portfolio of the pipeline. This often involves nonconforming, fixed or adjustable-rate mortgages that will be sold on a whole-loan transaction. Again, these mortgages are marked-to-market and held by a third-party safekeeping agent, along with assignment forms. Although this is physically somewhat more cumbersome than the use of wirable securities, the structure is similar to any type of reverse repo. However, because of the use of many mortgages to support the reverse, it is advisable to have pretransferred the underlying collateral to a third-party safekeeping agent prior to a transaction. It may be difficult, if not impossible, to transfer the mortgages and receive the funds on the same day, given the physical form. In addition, it is generally advisable to execute this kind of reverse repo at a fixed rate or open for some stated term. This type of reverse repo, because of the physical safekeeping and number of documents, generally results in a rate that runs anywhere from 25 to 50 basis points above a comparable Fed funds rate. Since the underlying collateral is generally not as readily marketable as Treasury securities, this will not affect an institution's liquidity ratios.

The last subtype of reverse repo includes GNMA dollar rolls. In this form of reverse repo, GNMA certificates are used for a stated term. This term is generally set to mature on GNMA settlement day. The difference between this and other types of reverses is that the collateral sent out may not be exactly identical to the collateral received, although if 9 percent GNMAs are used, 9 percent GNMAs will normally be received. However, they may not be the exact pool that was originally pledged as collateral. This may mean that the collateral received could be inferior to the collateral originally pledged, in terms of prepayment speed. In addition, since GNMAs have monthly principal payment of both normal amortization and prepayment, speed of prepayment can affect the expected cost. The advantage of this type of reverse is that the rates offered can be considerably below Fed funds and may, in fact, be as low as 2 or 3 percent below, depending on the underlying collateral coupon. If, however, an institution fails to abide by certain accounting and regulatory pronouncements, this transaction can be considered a sale. Also, when dealing in reverse repos, you should receive financial statements from the lending party.

The appendix to this chapter has a sample reverse repo agreement developed by the Public Security Association (PSA). In summary, reverse repos can be a good source of inexpensive, immediately available funds to meet the short-term funding nature of the mortgage pipeline.

A third alternative short-term source of funds is buying Fed funds (borrowing) from another commercial bank or thrift. Although this is standard practice by larger commercial banks to fund their loan portfolios, most small commercial banks and thrifts generally only sell (lend) Fed funds. Buying Fed funds can be done daily or using a term of up to three months. This is an unsecured source of borrowing in which lenders use a much stricter credit approach. The first requirement is to establish Fed funds lines with several commercial banks and thrifts. This can be difficult, particularly for smaller institutions and for thrifts. While larger commercial banks are generally very happy to buy Fed funds, they often take a dim view of selling them to others, including their correspondents. Smaller institutions spend a great deal of time and effort convincing financial institutions that they are worthy of consideration and not likely to fail in the near future. It is usually easiest to start with an institution's correspondent commercial banks. Depending on the correspondent's policies, they have a better knowledge about your institution's operations and its financial well-being. However, developing lines with a group of fellow thrifts or commercial banks of similar size is also a viable alternative.

Even though a line has been established, there is no guarantee that an institution will sell you Fed funds on the day you need them. Obviously, the institution needs to be in a selling mode at the time you are seeking to buy Fed funds. They may have other uses for their funds; they may believe that the time and the day that you want to purchase or the rate you want to offer is not optimal in terms of where they see the market or expect it to go. However, where there are good working relationships, Fed funds can become an immediate source of funds to temporarily fund one's pipeline. In addition, Fed funds transactions may be done as late as 6:30 p.m. to meet unexpected funding requirements. Generally, the rate an institution will pay should be only 5 to 10 basis points greater than rates paid by major money center banks at a particular time of the day.

The federal home loan bank system is a traditional alternative source of borrowing. Funds from the federal home loan bank represent thrifts' second most important source of liabilities. The federal home loan bank offers several different types of short-term lending programs at rate levels of approximately 75 to 100 basis points above the Treasury yield curve. Although the federal home loan bank will not necessarily loan directly to the mortgage banking subsidiary, it will lend to the savings bank or savings and loan, which can recycle the money to the division. Besides a slightly higher rate, the biggest disadvantage of using a federal home loan bank is that you must be an eligible member. As such, any commercial bank or credit union is eliminated from this source, as are certain state-chartered savings banks. However, for eligible institutions who are having severe earnings problems or low net worth, the federal home loan bank may be the only alternative source of funds. A major advantage is that there is no transaction limit either on the up or down side, loans as small as $50,000 can be applied for, while $100 million loans are not uncommon. There is relatively little legal work involved and collateral requirements are minimal for institutions with moderate to strong net worth. For smaller institutions, this may be the least expensive and most efficient means of funding mortgage pipeline activity. There are several different types of programs with differing maturities, from a daily Fed funds type borrowing to short and intermediate term, fixed-rate programs. In addition, funds can often be acquired on the day they are applied for, if not the following day.

Larger institutions have the alternative of issuing commercial paper. For many larger commercial banks, commercial paper is sold on an unsecured basis. Unfortunately, for most thrifts and smaller commercial banks, this is generally done on a collateralized basis. This may take the form of a security bond, a letter of credit or a pledge of mortgage-backed securities. A well-collateralized commercial paper program or uncollateralized paper issued by a strong institution can provide attractive stated rates. These rates are often comparable to high-quality banker acceptances of term Fed funds. However, there is a certain amount of legal, trustee, and other costs associated with commercial paper that can raise the stated rates by 50 to 70 basis points. In addition, the need to maintain a relatively active program results in a minimum total outstanding of at least $25 million, with an average outstanding close to $50 million. Commercial paper can be sold with a maximum maturity of 270 days, but generally has a maturity range of 5 to 90 days. If sold early in the morning, the paper can provide same-day funds.

Although the commercial paper market experienced some problems in the early 1970s with the case of Penn Central, it has grown significantly. Many larger commercial banks and some thrifts have successfully tapped this market. Except for the largest of programs, it is generally advisable to use a dealer to handle all transactions. It is also advisable to establish the commercial paper program as an obligation of the subsidiary or holding company. Commercial paper can be a good program, with rates not much different than those charged by the federal home loan bank system.

Another alternative is the issuance of jumbo CDs. In order not to conflict with local efforts, they are generally issued through brokers or institutional dealers. Although there has been abuse of these programs, if used in moderate size to fund pipeline needs, this can provide a very viable cost of funds that can be properly spread against one's mortgage pipeline. Generally, the CDs are for periods of one month and longer, although the maturity can be adjusted to match times of expected inflows. The cost of using a dealer can be anywhere from 25 to 50 basis points above the stated coupon rate. This is usually paid up front and needs to be considered when one judges the overall rate attractiveness of these programs.

The final short-term alternative is direct borrowings from commercial banks, insurance companies, or other lenders. The major example of this is prime-based warehouse lines. In this case, a commercial bank provides funds at a point or two over the prime rate. This line is often collateralized by assignments on the mortgages in the warehouse line. These lines are often written so that they're paid off from the proceeds of loan sales into the secondary market. This alternative should generally be avoided by most institutions, given the high costs involved. In addition to the stated rate, there may be other requirements, such as compensating balances at the commercial bank in the form of the institution's general operating funds or escrow deposits on the mortgages serviced. The advantages of these loans are that they're generally available when needed, and borrowing often takes the form of instructing the bank to transfer funds or credit an institution's demand deposit account. An institution can also enter into arrangements with insurance companies and pension funds. In addition, loans may be available on a selective basis via security dealers through which one intends to sell mortgages. In this case, upon consummation of the sale, the dealer often offsets the funds received against the loan. However, because of the high costs and the other alternatives available to most commercial banks and savings institutions, this type of borrowing to support warehouse loans should generally be used as a last resort. Only if it appears that one has used up all the other resources and still has funding needs, should one turn to this type of borrowing.

The level of an institution's warehouse line rises and falls over the month, season, and year. As discussed earlier, this rise will generally be largest prior to actual receipt of funds from the sale of mortgage products into the secondary market. For those institutions who package their products into mortgage-backed securities, settlement is often the last third of a month. Some base level of the pipeline will always exist and to fund this, one should examine floating-rate, longer-term funds. There are, as mentioned earlier, three sources that can meet the longer-term nature of the mortgage warehouse line.

One source is floating rate, medium-term notes—self-registered notes with a maturity of 18 months to 5 years. They are sold by a security dealer based on the term decided by the institution, and they are often collateralized by existing mortgages or mortgage-backed product. However, it is possible to move new production into a collateralized account while one takes older production out upon sale. These notes can be sold on either fixed-rate or floating-rate basis that is indexed off of Treasury bill rates or LIBOR. Although the medium-term notes can be sold at different times, one can set specified periods for the reset period (such as the 15th of the second month of every quarter). The cost of this debt varies upon collateralization, the size of the program, and the credit quality of the institution. Medium-term notes can be structured as direct obligations of the bank or thrift or the mortgage company subsidiary. Because of size limitations, these programs are more advisable for larger mortgage banking operations. Finally, in calculating the overall cost, one must add another 50 to 75 basis points for legal, safekeeping, and dealer costs.

While the level of medium-term notes can be increased or decreased over time, a second alternative is to sell a mortgage-backed bond that is collateralized by existing mortgages. Generally, there is an over-collateralization requirement. Again it is possible to add new mortgages as they are made and have them replace mortgages that are being sold. This mortgage-backed bond can be sold on either a fixed- or a floating-rate basis. This type of deal is generally underwritten by a syndicate of security dealers, and the minimum size of an issuance is at least $10 million. The bond can also contain certain call features that allow early prepayment if the size of one's institution's warehouse line drastically declines.

For institutions with net loss carry forwards or low taxable income, adjustable preferred stock may make sense. Besides providing funds on a floating-rate basis, preferred stock may increase an institution's capital position, thereby permitting further growth or allowing it to satisfy certain regulatory net worth requirements. For stock instittutions, adjustable-rate preferreds can be established with a convertibility feature to the institution's common stock. It may also have call features or a sinking fund that allow earlier redemption of the outstanding issue when the institution no longer needs the funds or finds itself in a higher tax situation. As with mortgage-backed bonds, preferred stock is sold by a syndicate of security dealers. Because of the present 85 percent divided exclusion for corporations, adjustable-rate preferred stock can be sold at signficiant yield advantages to any other type of borrowing with rates equivalent to or below those of high-grade municipal general obligations.

This chapter dealt with alternative sources of funds that an institution can use in funding its mortgage banking subsidiaries or divisions' mortgage warehouse pipeline. As thrifts and commercial banks become more involved in mortgage banking, the funding for their inventory (the pipeline) becomes more and more important. Traditional deposit sources may no longer be adequate or may be earmarked for other uses, so the alternatives discussed here can provide funds to meet an institution's cash flow needs. As can be seen, there are a variety of alternatives that can be used, either in conjunction with one another or separately. In selecting a source of funding, management must, in addition to cost, analyze the economic environment and the institution's current operating requirements.

APPENDIX

MASTER REPURCHASE AGREEMENT

Dated as of _____ ____, _____

Between:

_____

and

_____

1. Applicability

From time to time the parties hereto may enter into transactions in which one party ("Seller") agrees to transfer to the other ("Buyer") securities or financial instruments ("Securities") against the transfer of funds by Buyer, with a simultaneous agreement by Buyer to transfer to Seller such Securities at a date certain or on demand, against the transfer of funds by Seller. Each such transaction shall be referred to herein as a "Transaction" and shall be governed by this Agreement, including any supplemental terms or conditions contained in Annex I hereto, unless otherwise agreed in writing.

2. Definitions

(a) "Act of Insolvency", with respect to any party, (i) the commencement by such party as debtor of any case or proceeding under any bankruptcy, insolvency, reorganization, liquidation, dissolution or similar law, or such party seeking the appointment of a receiver, trustee, custodian or similar official for such party or any substantial part of its property, or (ii) the commencement of any such case or proceeding against such party, or another seeking such an appointment or the filing against a party of an application for a protective decree under the provisions of the Securities Investor Protection Act of 1970, which (A) is consented to or not timely contested by such party, (B) results in the entry of an order for relief, such an appointment, the issuance of such a protective decree or the entry of an order having a similar effect, or (C) is not dismissed within 15 days, (iii) the making by a party of a general assignment for the benefit of creditors, or (iv) the admission in writing by a party of such party's inability to pay such party's debts as they become due;

(b) "Additional Purchased Securities", securities provided by Seller to Buyer pursuant to Paragraph 4(a) hereof;

(c) "Buyer's Margin Amount", with respect to any Transaction as of any date, the amount obtained by application of a percentage (which may be equal to the percentage that is agreed to as the Seller's Margin Amount under subparagraph (q) of this Paragraph), agreed to by Buyer and Seller prior to entering into the Transaction, to the Repurchase Price for such Transaction as of such date;

(d) "Confirmation", the meaning specified in Paragraph 3(b) hereof;

(e) "Income", with respect to any Security at any time, any principal thereof then payable and all interest, dividends or other distributions thereon;

(f) "Margin Deficit", the meaning specified in Paragraph 4(a) hereof;

(g) "Margin Excess", the meaning specified in Paragraph 4(b) hereof;

(h) "Market Value", with respect to any Securities as of any date, the price for such Securities on such date obtained from a generally recognized source agreed to by the parties or the most recent closing bid quotation from such a source, plus accrued Income to the extent not included therein (other than any Income credited or transferred to, or applied to the obligations of, Seller pursuant to Paragraph 5 hereof) as of such date (unless contrary to market practice for such Securities);

(i) "Price Differential", with respect to any Transaction hereunder as of any date, the aggregate amount obtained by daily application of the Pricing Rate for such Transaction to the Purchase Price for such Transaction on a 360 day per year basis for the actual number of days during the period commencing on (and including) the Purchase Date for such Transaction and ending on (but excluding) the date of determination (reduced by any amount of such Price Differential previously paid by Seller to Buyer with respect to such Transaction);

(j) "Pricing Rate", the per annum percentage rate for determination of the Price Differential;

(k) "Prime Rate", the prime rate of U.S. money center commercial banks as published in *The Wall Street Journal*;

(l) "Purchase Date", the date on which Purchased Securities are transferred by Seller to Buyer;

(m) "Purchase Price", (i) on the Purchase Date, the price at which Purchased Securities are transferred by Seller to Buyer, and (ii) thereafter, such price increased by the amount of any cash transferred by Buyer to Seller pursuant to Paragraph 4(b) hereof and decreased by the amount of any cash transferred by Seller to Buyer pursuant to Paragraph 4(a) hereof or applied to reduce Seller's obligations under clause (ii) of Paragraph 5 hereof;

(n) "Purchased Securities", The Securities transferred by Seller to Buyer in a Transaction hereunder, and any Securities substituted therefor in accordance with Paragraph 9 hereof. The term "Purchased Securities" with respect to any transaction at any time also shall include Additional Purchased Securities delivered pursuant to Paragraph 4(a) and shall exclude Securities returned pursuant to Paragraph 4(b);

(o) "Repurchase Date", the date on which Seller is to repurchase the Purchased Securities from Buyer, including any date determined by application of the provisions of Paragraphs 3(c) or 11 hereof;

(p) "Repurchase Price", the price at which Purchased Securities are to be transferred from Buyer to Seller upon termination of a Transaction, which will be determined in each case (including transactions terminable upon demand) as the sum of the Purchase Price and the Price Differential as of the date of such determination, increased by any amount determined by the application of the provisions of Paragraph 11 hereof;

(q) "Seller's Margin Amount", with respect to any Transaction as of any date, the amount obtained by application of a percentage (which may be equal to the percentage that is agreed to as the Buyer's Margin Amount under subparagraph (c) of this Paragraph), agreed to by Buyer and Seller prior to entering into the Transaction, to the Repurchase Price for such Transaction as of such date.

3. Initiation; Confirmation; Termination

(a) An agreement to enter into a Transaction may be made orally or in writing at the initiation of either Buyer or Seller. On the Purchase Date for the Transaction, the Purchased Securities shall be transferred to Buyer or its agent against the transfer of the Purchase Price to an account of Seller.

(b) Upon agreeing to enter into a Transaction hereunder, Buyer or Seller (or both), as shall be agreed, shall promptly deliver to the other party a written confirmation of each Transaction (a "Confirmation"). The Confirmation shall describe the Purchased Securities (including CUSIP number, if any), identify Buyer and Seller and set forth (i) the Purchase Date, (ii) the Purchase Price, (iii) the Repurchase Date, unless the Transaction is to be terminable on demand, (iv) the Pricing Rate or Repurchase Price applicable to the Transaction, and (v) any additional terms or conditions of the Transaction not inconsistent with this Agreement. The Confirmation, together with this Agreement, shall constitute conclusive evidence of the terms agreed between Buyer and Seller with respect to the Transaction to which the Confirmation relates, unless with respect to the Confirmation specific objection is made promptly after receipt thereof. In the event of any conflict between the terms of such Confirmation and this Agreement, this Agreement shall prevail.

(c) In the case of Transactions terminable upon demand, such demand shall be made by Buyer or Seller, no later than such time as is customary in accordance with market practice, by telephone or otherwise on or prior to the business day on which such termination will be effective. On the date specified in such demand, or on the date fixed for termination in the case of Transactions having a fixed term, termination of the Transaction will be effected by transfer to Seller or its agent of the Purchased Securities and any Income in respect thereof received by Buyer (and not previously credited or transferred to, or applied to the obligations of, Seller pursuant to paragraph 5 hereof) against the transfer of the Repurchase Price to an account of Buyer.

4. **Margin Maintenance**

(a) If at any time the aggregate Market Value of all Purchased Securities subject to all Transactions in which a particular party hereto is acting as Buyer is less than the aggregate Buyer's Margin Amount for all such Transactions (a "Margin Deficit"), then Buyer may by notice to Seller require Seller in such Transactions, at Seller's option, to transfer to Buyer cash or additional Securities reasonably acceptable to Buyer ("Additional Purchased Securities"), so that the cash and aggregate Market Value of the Purchased Securities, including any such Additional Purchased Securities, will thereupon equal or exceed such aggregate Buyer's Margin Amount (decreased by the amount of any Margin Deficit as of such date arising from any Transactions in which such Buyer is acting as Seller).

(b) If at any time the aggregate Market Value of all Purchased Securities subject to all Transactions in which a particular party hereto is acting as Seller exceeds the aggregate Seller's Margin Amount for all such Transactions at such time (a "Margin Excess"), then Seller may by notice to Buyer require Buyer in such Transactions, at Buyer's option, to transfer cash or Purchased Securities to Seller, so that the aggregate Market Value of the Purchased Securities, after deduction of any such cash or any Purchased Securities so transferred, will thereupon not exceed such aggregate Seller's Margin Amount (increased by the amount of any Margin Excess as of such date arising from any Transactions in which such Seller is acting as Buyer).

(c) Any cash transferred pursuant to this Paragraph shall be attributed to such Transactions as shall be agreed upon by Buyer and Seller.

(d) Seller and Buyer may agree, with respect to any or all Transactions hereunder, that the respective rights of Buyer or Seller (or both) under subparagraphs (a) and (b) of this Paragraph may be exercised only where a Margin Deficit or Margin Excess exceeds a specified dollar amount or a specified percentage of the Repurchase Prices for such Transactions (which amount or percentage shall be agreed to by Buyer and Seller prior to entering into any such Transactions).

(e) Seller and Buyer may agree, with respect to any or all Transactions hereunder, that the respective rights of Buyer and Seller under subparagraphs (a) and (b) of this Paragraph to require the elimination of a Margin Deficit or a Margin Excess, as the case may be, may be exercised whenever such a Margin Deficit or Margin Excess exists with respect to any single Transaction hereunder (calculated without regard to any other Transaction outstanding under this Agreement).

5. Income Payments

Where a particular Transaction's term extends over an Income payment date on the Securities subject to that Transaction, Buyer shall, as the parties may agree with respect to such Transaction (or, in the absence of any agreement, as Buyer shall reasonably determine in its discretion), on the date such Income is payable either (i) transfer to or credit to the account of Seller an amount equal to such Income payment or payments with respect to any Purchased Securities subject to such Transaction or (ii) apply the Income payment or payments to reduce the amount to be transferred to Buyer by Seller upon termination of the Transaction. Buyer shall not be obligated to take any action pursuant to the preceding sentence to the extent that such action would result in the creation of a Margin Deficit, unless prior thereto or simultaneously therewith Seller transfers to Buyer cash or Additional Purchased Securities sufficient to eliminate such Margin Deficit.

6. Security Interest

Although the parties intend that all Transactions hereunder be sales and purchases and not loans, in the event of any such Transactions are deemed to be loans, Seller shall be deemed to have pledged to Buyer as security for the performance by Seller of its obligations under each such Transaction, and shall be deemed to have granted to Buyer a security interest in, all of the Purchased Securities with respect to all Transactions hereunder and all proceeds thereof.

7. Payment and Transfer

Unless otherwise mutually agreed, all transfers of funds hereunder shall be in immediately available funds. All Securities transferred by one party hereto to the other party (i) shall be in suitable form for transfer or shall be accompanied by duly executed instruments of transfer or assignment in blank and such other documentation as the party receiving possession may reasonably request, (ii) shall be transferred on the book-entry system of a Federal Reserve Bank, or (iii) shall be transferred by any other method mutually acceptable to Seller and Buyer. As used herein with respect to Securities, "transfer" is intended to have the same meaning as when used in Section 8-313 of the New York Uniform Commercial Code.

8. Segregation of Purchased Securities

All Purchased Securities in the possession of Seller shall be segregated from other securities in its possession and shall be identified as subject to this Agreement. Segregation may be accomplished by appropriate identification on the books and records of the holder, including a financial intermediary or a clearing corporation. Title to all Purchased Securities shall pass to Buyer and, unless otherwise agreed by Buyer and Seller, nothing in this Agreement shall preclude Buyer from engaging in repurchase transactions with the Purchased Securities or otherwise pledging or hypothecating the Purchased Securities, but no such transaction shall relieve Buyer of its obligations to transfer Purchased Securities to Seller pursuant to Paragraphs 3, 4 or 11 hereof, or of Buyer's obligation to credit or pay Income to, or apply Income to the obligations of, Seller pursuant to Paragraph 5 hereof.

9. Substitution

Seller may, subject to agreement with and acceptance by Buyer, substitute other Securities for any Purchased Securities. Such substitution shall be made by transfer to the Buyer of such other Securities against simultaneous transfer to the Seller of such Purchased Securities. After substitution, the substituted Securities shall be deemed to be Purchased Securities.

10. Representations

Each of Buyer and Seller represents and warrants to the other (i) it is duly authorized to execute and deliver this Agreement, to enter into the Transactions contemplated hereunder and to perform its obligations hereunder and has taken all necessary action to authorize such execution, delivery and performance, (ii) it will engage in such Transactions as principal (or, if agreed in writing in advance of any Transaction by the other party hereto, as agent for a disclosed principal), (iii) the person signing this Agreement on its behalf is duly authorized to do so on its behalf (or on behalf of any such disclosed principal), (iv) it has obtained all authorizations of any governmental body required in connection with this Agreement and the Transactions hereunder and such authorizations are in full force and effect and (v) the execution, delivery and performance of this Agreement and the Transactions hereunder will not violate any law, ordinance, charter, by-law or rule applicable to it or any agreement by which it is bound or by which any of its assets are affected. On the Purchase Date for any Transaction Buyer and Seller shall each be deemed to repeat all the foregoing representations made by it.

11. Events at Default

In the event that (i) Seller fails to repurchase or Buyer fails to transfer Purchased Securities upon the applicable Repurchase Date, (ii) Seller or Buyer fails, after one business day's notice, to comply with Paragraph 4 hereof, (iii) Buyer fails to comply with Paragraph 5 hereof, (iv) an Act of Insolvency occurs with respect to Seller or Buyer, (v) any representation made by Seller or Buyer shall have been incorrect or untrue in any material respect when made or repeated or deemed to have been made or repeated, or (vi) Seller or Buyer shall admit to the other its inability to, or its intention not to, perform any of its obligations hereunder (each an "Event of Default"):

(a) At the option of the nondefaulting party, exercised by written notice to the defaulting party (which option shall be deemed to have been exercised, even if no notice is given, immediately upon the occurrence of an Act of Insolvency), the Repurchase Date for each Transaction hereunder shall be deemed immediately to occur.

(b) In all Transactions in which the defaulting party is acting as Seller, if the nondefaulting party exercises or is deemed to have exercised the option referred to in subparagraph (a) of this paragraph, (i) the defaulting party's obligations hereunder to repurchase all Purchased Securities in such Transactions shall thereupon become immediately due and payable, (ii) to the extent permitted by applicable law, the Repurchase Price with respect to each such Transaction shall be increased by the aggregate amount obtained by daily application of (x) the greater of the Pricing Rate for such Transaction or the Prime Rate to (y) the Repurchase Price for such Transaction as of the Repurchase Date as determined pursuant to subparagraph (a) of this Paragraph (decreased as of any day by (A) any amounts retained by the nondefaulting party with respect to such Repurchase Price pursuant to subparagraph (d)(i) of this paragraph, and (C) any amounts credited to the account of the defaulting party pursuant to subparagraph (e) of this paragraph) on a 360 day per year basis for the actual number of days during the period from the date of the Event of Default giving rise to such option to the date of payment of the Repurchase Price as so increased, (iii) all Income paid after such exercise or deemed exercise shall be retained by the nondefaulting party and applied to the aggregate unpaid Repurchase Prices owed by the defaulting party, and (iv) the defaulting party shall immediately deliver to the nondefaulting party any Purchased Securities subject to such Transactions then in the defaulting party's possession.

(c) In all Transactions in which the defaulting party is acting as Buyer, upon tender by the nondefaulting Party of payment of the aggregate Repurchase Prices for all such Transactions, the defaulting party's right, title and interest in all Purchased Securities subject to such Transaction shall be deemed transferred to the nondefaulting party, and the defaulting party shall deliver all such Purchased Securities to the nondefaulting party.

(d) After one business day's notice to the defaulting party (which notice need not be given if an Act of Insolvency shall have occurred, and which may be the notice given under subparagraph (a) of this Paragraph or the notice referred to in clause (ii) of the first sentence of this Paragraph), the nondefaulting party may:

(i) as to Transactions in which the defaulting party is acting as Seller, (A) immediately sell, in a recognized market at such price or prices as the nondefaulting party may reasonably deem satisfactory, any or all Purchased Securities subject to such Transactions and apply the proceeds thereof to the aggregate unpaid Repurchase Prices and any other amounts owing by the defaulting party hereunder or (B) in its sole discretion elect, in lieu of selling all or a portion of such Purchased Securities, to give the defaulting party credit for such Purchased Securities in an amount equal to the price therefor on such date, obtained from a generally recognized source or the most recent closing bid quotation from such a source, against the aggregate unpaid Repurchase Prices and any other amounts owing by the defaulting party hereunder; and

(ii) as to Transactions in which the defaulting party is acting as Buyer, (A) purchase securities ("Replacement Securities") of the same class and amount as any Purchased Securities that are not delivered by the defaulting party to the nondefaulting party as required under or (B) in its sole discretion elect, in lieu of purchasing Replacement Securities, to be deemed to have purchased Replacement Securities at the price therefor on such date, obtained from a generally recognized source or the most recent closing bid quotation from such a source, against the aggregate unpaid Repurchase Prices and any other amounts owing by the defaulting party; and

(iii) as to Transactions in which the defaulting party is acting as Buyer, (A) purchase securities ("Replacement Securities") of the same class and amount as any Purchased Securities that are not delivered by the defaulting party to the nondefaulting party as required hereunder or (b) in its sole discretion elect, in lieu of purchasing Replacement Securities, to be deemed to have purchased Replacement Securities at the price therefor on such date, obtained from a generally recognized source or the most recent closing bid quotation from such a source.

(e) As to Transactions in which the defaulting party is acting as

Buyer, the defaulting party shall be liable to the nondefaulting party (i) with respect to Purchased Securities (other than Additional Purchased Securities), for any excess of the price paid (or deemed paid) by the nondefaulting party for Replacement Securities therefor over the Repurchase Price for such Purchased Securities and (ii) with respect to Additional Purchased Securities, for the price paid (or deemed paid) by the nondefaulting party for the Replacement Securities therefor. In addition, the defaulting party shall be liable to the nondefaulting party for interest on such remaining liability with respect to each such purchase (or deemed purchase) of Replacement Securities from the date of such purchase (or deemed purchase) until paid in full by Buyer. Such interest shall be at a rate equal to the greater of the Pricing Rate for such Transaction or the Prime Rate.

(f) For purposes of this Paragraph 11, the Repurchase Price for each Transaction hereunder in respect of which the defaulting party is acting as Buyer shall not increase above the amount of such Repurchase Price for such Transaction determined as of the date of the exercise or deemed exercise by the nondefaulting party of its option under subparagraph (a) of this paragraph.

(g) The defaulting party shall be liable to the nondefaulting party for the amount of all reasonable legal or other expenses incurred by the nondefaulting party in connection with or as a consequence of an Event of Default, together with interest thereon at a rate equal to the greater of the Pricing Rate for the relevant Transaction or the Prime Rate.

(h) The nondefaulting party shall have, in addition to its rights hereunder, any rights otherwise available to it under any other agreement or applicable law.

12. Single Agreement

Buyer and Seller acknolwedge that, and have entered hereinto and will enter into each Transaction hereunder in consideration of and in reliance upon the fact that, all Transactions hereunder constitute a single business and contractual relationship and have been made in consideration of each other. Accordingly, each of Buyer and Seller agrees (i) to perform all of its obligations in respect of each Transaction hereunder, and that a default in the performance of any such obligations shall constitute a default by it in respect of all Transactions hereunder, (ii) that each of them shall be entitled to set off claims and apply property held by them in respect of any Transaction against obligations owing to them in respect of any other Transactions hereunder and (iii) that payments, deliveries and other transfers made by either of them in respect of any Transaction shall be deemed to have been made in consideration of payments, deliveries and other Transactions hereunder, and the obligations to make any such payments, deliveries and other transfers may be applied against each other and netted.

13. Notices and Other Communications

Unless another address is specified in writing by the respective party to whom any notice or other communication is to be given hereunder, all such notices or communications shall be in writing or confirmed in writing and delivered at the respective addresses set forth in Annex II attached hereto.

14. Entire Agreement; Severability

This Agreement shall supersede any existing agreements between the parties containing general terms and conditions for repurchase transactions. Each provision and agreement herein shall be treated as separate and independent from any other provision or agreement herein and shall be enforceable notwithstanding the unenforceability of any such other provision or agreement.

15. Non-assignability; Termination

The rights and obligations of the parties under this Agreement and under any Transaction shall not be assigned by either party without the prior written consent of the other party. Subject to the foregoing, this Agreement and any Transactions shall be binding upon and shall inure to the benefit of the parties and their respective successors and assigns. This Agreement may be cancelled by either party upon giving written notice to the other, except that this Agreement shall, notwithstanding such notice, remain applicable to any Transactions then outstanding.

16. **Governing Law**

This Agreement shall be governed by the laws of the State of New York without giving effect to the conflict of law principles thereof.

17. **No Waivers, Etc.**

No express or implied waiver of any Event of Default by either party shall constitute a waiver of any other Event of Default and no exercise of any remedy hereunder by any party shall constitute a waiver of its right to exercise any other remedy hereunder. No modification or waiver of any provision of this Agreement and no consent by any party to a departure herefrom shall be effective unless and until such shall be in writing and duly executed by both of the parties hereto. Without limitation on any of the foregoing, the failure to give a notice pursuant to subparagraphs 4(a) and 4(b) hereof will not constitute a waiver of any right to do so at a later date.

18. **Use of Employee Plan Assets**

(a) If assets of an employee benefit plan subject to any provision of the Employee Retirement Income Security Act of 1974 ("ERISA") are intended to be used by either party hereto (the "Plan Party") in a Transaction, the Plan Party shall so notify the other party prior to the Transaction. The Plan Party shall represent in writing to the other party that the Transaction does not constitute a prohibited transaction under ERISA or is otherwise exempt therefrom, and the other party may proceed in reliance thereon but shall not be required so to proceed.

(b) Subject to the last sentence of subparagraph (a) of this paragraph, any such Transaction shll proceed only if Seller furnishes or has furnished to Buyer its most recent available audited statement of its financial condition and its most recent subsequent unaudited statement of its financial condition.

(c) By entering into a Transaction pursuant to this paragraph, Seller shall be deemed (i) to represent to Buyer that since the date of Seller's latest such financial statements, there has been no material adverse change in Seller's financial condition which Seller has not disclosed to Buyer, and (ii) to agree to provide Buyer with future audited and unaudited statements of its financial condition as they are issued, so long as it is a Seller in any outstanding Transaction involving a Plan Party.

19. **Intent**

(a) The parties recognize that each Transaction is a "repurchase agreement" as that term is defined in Section 101(39) of Title 11 of the United States Code, as amended (except insofar as the type of Securities subject to such Transaction or the term of such Transaction would render such definition inapplicable), and a "securities contract" as that term is defined in Section 741(7) of Title 11 of the United States Code, as amended.

(b) It is understood that either party's right to liquidate securities delivered to it in connection with Transactions hereunder or to exercise any other remedies pursuant to Paragraph 11 hereof, is a contractual right to liquidate such Transaction as described in Sections 555 and 559 of Title 11 of the United States Code, as amended.

[Name of Party]   [Name of Party]

By _____   By _____

Title _____   Title _____

Date _____   Date _____

[Annex I, "Supplemental Terms and Conditions," and Annex II, "Names and Addresses for Communications Between Parties," would follow as needed.]

Chapter 26

JAMES F. MONTGOMERY

Mr. James F. Montgomery is Chairman and Chief Executive of Great Western Financial Corporation and its subsidiary Great Western Savings. He was elected a director and President of the company in 1975, the Chief Executive Officer in 1979 and the Chairman of the Board of Directors in 1981.

His leadership has been recognized by the Wall Street Transcript, *which named Mr. Montgomery "Outstanding Chief Executive Officer" in the savings and loan industry for four years. It has cited him for keeping Great Western's "balance sheet one of the strongest in the S&L industry."*

Mr. Montgomery's financial experience spans more than 25 years. After graduating from the University of California, Los Angeles, he began his career with the accounting firm of Price Waterhouse and Company, and in 1960, he joined Great Western Financial Corporation as Assistant to the President. Before rejoining Great Western in 1975, Mr. Montgomery was a Director and President of United Financial Corporation and its subsidiary, Citizens Savings and Loan Association, serving those companies from 1964–1975.

Currently, Mr. Montgomery is a director of the Federal Home Loan Bank of San Francisco, advisor to the Federal Reserve System in Washington, D.C., and a past member of the executive committees of both the California and the United States Leagues of Savings Institutions. He also serves as director of the California Economic Development Corporation and the California Chamber of Commerce.

Adjustable-Rate Mortgages: Buying the Best on the Market

JAMES F. MONTGOMERY

The adjustable-rate mortgage (ARM) has been extremely important to me for most of my years in the savings and loan business. I remember being a relatively young person in the business when the industry first went under savings rate control in 1966. Frankly, borrowing short and lending long under a federal regulatory umbrella made me nervous. That is why I have been a believer in variable-rate mortage (VRM) lending since 1968 when we began the first program of variable-rate mortgage lending at old United Savings and Loan Association. My feeling for the need for variable-rate mortgages never diminished, even though for years my firm was essentially all by itself in this feeling. When I rejoined Great Western Savings in 1975, it, along with several others in California, entered into VRM lending in a major and successful way.

HELPING TO MAKE THE ARM A STANDARD PRODUCT

Today we are offering a relatively new, much more flexible product in the marketplace—the adjustable-rate mortgage. However, in 1975, the VRM, which was by law quite limited in its variability, was much more of a substantial breakthrough for its time than the ARM was to be.

One important similarity, which needs to be emphasized, is the tremendous number of misconceptions and prejudgments about both the old variable-rate mortgages and today's ARM. In 1975, I heard that the variable-rate mortgage wouldn't be accepted in the marketplace, yet we proceeded, in the most competitive real estate market in the country, to convert more than 70 percent of Great Western's loan portfolio from a fixed rate to variable. We did so in less than five years.

In the midst of that successful conversion, the skeptics warned that, while the public was accepting the VRM, consumers didn't really understand it. "Wait until you try to increase rates—that's when they will tear your buildings down." Unfortunately, we had to raise rates over a period of years a total of 10 times—the maximum number of increases allowed. While borrowers didn't like to have their rates increased, they understood. Because the fact is, the people who took out a VRM during the times of higher interest rates have historically fared better than if they had taken out a fixed-rate loan during the same period.

I was also told, and there is an important similarity here, that the VRM wouldn't sell in the secondary market.

This is another prejudgment that has proven false. We have sold virtually all of our VRMs in the secondary market. As a matter of fact, prospective purchasers were offered the option of acquiring a variable interest in VRMs or fixed-rate participations. There were buyers of both types, but needless to say, the happiest buyers were those who bought the variable rate participation.

That old VRM, with its severe limits, was not variable enough, but nonetheless Great Western was considerably better off during the high interest rate environment of the late 1970s and early 1980s as result of that program.

IN OUR HANDS

Now, in this era of nearly complete deregulation, we can offer for the first time a truly flexible mortgage—the adjustable-rate mortgage. For the first time, the professionals who originate home mortgages have been able to design a loan, rather than have it created by the political process. The result is a mortgage loan that is the most sensible quid pro quo between borrower and lender yet developed.

Allowing lenders to design their own loan products is a mixed blessing, of course, because it produces both a variety of instruments in the market and considerable confusion. But I believe there is clearly a "best" ARM for borrowers and investors—one tied to the 11th District Cost of Funds (COF) Index. This is the ARM Great Western and a few other major California savings and loans offer.

How do I know this is the best one? We at Great Western have learned a lot in recent years about adjustable-rate mortgage lending, becoming one of the country's largest originators of ARM loans. In 1985, virtually all of our $6.7 billion in mortgage lending was in adjustable-rate products. In 1986, despite what some have called a fixed-rate environment, this particular ARM remains popular with the public and is considered by most investors to be the best kind of ARM available.

Prudent, sucessful lenders know that the intelligently constructed ARM is the only logical way for a mortgage portfolio lender to operate in an era of true deregulation. But is the type of ARM that is best for consumers and portfolio lenders necessarily the best ARM for the secondary market? Compelling evidence suggests that this one particular ARM is best for consumers, lenders, *and* the secondary market.

NOT ALL ARMS ARE CREATED EQUAL

Because not all ARMs are alike—and there are more than 100 different ARMs on the market today—it is important to examine the adjustable-rate mortgage so buyers can determine what kind of ARM they are taking off the shelf.

Perhaps the single most important feature of an ARM is the index to which it is tied. Yet few people thoroughly understand the impact the different indexes have on mortgage instruments, and in turn, how these indexes can affect the borrower, the lender, and its attractiveness to the secondary market.

Fortunately, a few analysts are looking closer at the indexes. What they have found is that the majority of ARMs—which are most often tied to a Treasury index—may not lock in a profit margin during all phases of the monetary cycle, and are prone to high levels of delinquency and foreclosure when interest rates rise rapidly. Conversely, ARMs that are tied to the 11th District COF index are being called by these same analysts the best ARM in the secondary market.

This particular ARM best accomplishes the objectives that lenders are trying to achieve. Ideally, lenders should offer ARMs that lock in a spread over the cost of their money and tie the ARM to an index that best tracks the lender's cost of funds. Surprisingly, relatively few lenders have done this.

COST OF FUNDS ARMs

Ironically, despite this experience, lenders are still fighting the idea that there is a better index than the COF index. If there is, lenders haven't found it.

Why do some lenders think the COF index is the best index available today? What lenders are trying to do with adjustable mortgages is develop and maintain a reasonable spread between the price of their finished product and the cost of their raw materials. The difference with a mortgage loan is that when lenders invest a group of dollars at a certain raw material cost in 1986, we must be prepared to leave those dollars invested in a mortgage until well past the year 2000—knowing that the cost of those dollars will be variable on almost a daily basis. Lenders need to vary the yield on the mortgage loan in which they invest those funds. What more sensible index to choose than the cost of funds over the entire life of this contractual arrangement?

History does, and I believe will continue to, underscore the desirability of the COF index. It has been the most stable of indexes to which ARMs are tied. While the commercial bank prime rate reached almost 21 percent, and the 1-year T-bill exeeded 16 percent in 1982, the highest the 11th District COF index ever reached was 12.673 percent—and then only for one month.

The best argument for why the CQF index is a better index for the consumer than the 1-year T-bill is to look at the record since 1979. If two borrowers had identical $100,000 ARMs—one tied to the 11th District COF index, the other to the 1-year T-bill—the borrower with the ARM tied to the COF index would have saved $120.44 more *per month* from 1979 to midyear 1985. That represents a total savings of nearly $8,000 during this 66-month period.

DRAWBACKS OF OTHER INDEXES

I would worry about tying my adjustable mortgages to an index that may have a historical correlation to my cost of funds but that may operate differently in the future. I would hate to tie my adjustable mortgages to an index that is declining when my cost of funds is rising.

Of course, that should never happen. We could never have a time when Treasury bill rates, for instance, are going down significantly faster than my cost of funds. But that is exactly what has happened to many lenders in the mid-1980s!

There is another practical reason why the COF index works at Great Western, based on several years of experience with borrowers. In the past, when rates rose on VRMs and ARMs and people called the loan service department to inquire about the increase, the dialog went something like this: "Why did you raise my mortgage rate?" The answer was simple: "Because our cost of money went up."

People may not like this, but they understand it, because it is logical. If loan service people had to say something like, "because the Moody's composite bond index went up," the conversations would be considerably longer and more difficult, and the firm would need a much larger loan serving staff.

A MODEL ARM

Specifically, how does the typical COF ARM work? A Great Western ARM adjusts monthly and generally has a 500 basis point lifetime cap. Monthly payments adjust only *once* a year, and are limited to adjustments of 7.5 percent per year. In times of rapidly escalating interest rates, the borrower is given the option of deferring interest.

We believe that this ARM design strikes the proper balance between the needs of the borrower and the lender. Borrowers are protected from payment shock, and lenders are protected from underwriting losses.

Due to the cyclical nature of interest rates, history has shown that ARMs tied to the COF index are a better choice for everyone, over an extended period of time.

To determine this for yourself, you only need to run five-year scenarios of rising and falling interest rates, compaing ARMs with different indexes. What you will find is that the type of ARM just described not only looks more attractive to the borrower, but to the lender and buyer as well.

How successful is our type of ARM in the secondary market? A premium is being paid for it. Although Great Western does not yet offer ARMs in any substantial quantity in the secondary market, other California institutions that offer similar products have found that demand exceeds supply.

UNDERSTANDING THE DIFFERENCES

To better acquaint yourself with the nuances of adjustable-rate mortgages, and what makes some work better than others, look closely at some other important features. This should also help to dispel a litany of prejudgments and misconceptions that exist.

One of the most talked about features of the ARM is *deferred interest* or *negative amortization*. It is also the most misunderstood. Negative amortization is actually the most important consumer benefit in the ARM. What it really means is that, if the interest rate on a mortgage increases faster than the borrower's ability to absorb changes in his or her monthly payment, he or she may voluntarily limit the change in monthly payment and have interest added on a regular basis to the mortgage until either interest rates or another anniversary of monthly payment changes comes around.

Why do some insist that this is anticonsumer? Many borrowers, when given the choice, elect to have their monthly payments increased to the point that negative amortization does not occur. They don't like the idea of their mortgage getting moderately larger, even temporarily. This is the point that is so important—the decision is totally within the borrower's control.

In fact, although some have questioned negative amortization, the ARM experience in recent years has been very favorable. Thousands of consumers with ARMs collectively have saved millions of dollars because of declining interest rates, and in effect, have experienced "positive amortization."

PAYMENT VERSUS ANNUAL INTEREST RATE CAPS

Even some learned members of the academic community are confused about the terms "percent" and "percentage points" in discussing ARMs and use them interchangeably.

They talk about a 2 percent annual interest cap, which is common in a lot of mortgages, when they really mean a two *percentage* point annual interest cap. A 2 percentage point interest increase in a year, which would bring a 10 percent mortgage to 12 percent, is really a 20 percent increase in interest, and, if negative amortization is not allowed, it's a 20 percent increase in the monthly payment. A 7.5 percent increase in monthly payments, which exists in Great Western's mortgage instrument, means that at a borrower's option at the end of the year, a monthly payment of $100 can only be increased to $107.50 a month—which is less than the payment increase that could result from a 1 percentage point increase in the interest rate.

I have attended a number of meetings around the country where the terms are freely interchanged in a haphazard way, and the misunderstanding that exists is quite significant.

NO DELINQUENCY PROBLEMS

Some people suggest that all ARM loans, with their specter of future payment shock, represent serious actual and potential delinquency problems.

This dialog was conducted with a number of consumer advocates in the 1970s about the variable rate mortgage, conjuring up hypothetical situations in which mass foreclosures would result from the rate increase in the VRM. The worse-case scenarios, by the way, generally did not contemplate a 20 percent-plus bank prime rate. So what happened? The bank prime rate topped 20 percent, and lenders still didn't experience any unusual increase in foreclosures with the variable rate mortgage.

Notwithstanding that experience, doomsayers predict mass delinquency and foreclosures with the ARM. What are the facts? Great Western's experience is limited to only five years and $14 billion in adjustable-rate lending, it has had an excellent collection and delinquency experience. Indeed, as of mid-1986, our ARM portfolio has a delinquency rate of .25 percent—the lowest of any segment in the portfolio.

What part of that portfolio has the highest delinquency ratio? It is the loan that was most commonly used after deregulation and just before the ARM was introduced: that is, the fixed-rate loan with a 30-year amortization schedule, all due and payable in 7, 5, or even 3 years.

Earlier I said lenders must protect ARM borrowers from payment shock. There is no payment shock possible with the COF index.

Payment shock truly is the fixed-rate loan with a 30-year amortization schedule, all due and payable at the end of 5 years, with no assurance of refinancing in an uncertain interest rate environment. That represents real payment shock! And, if you think about it, if ARMs are limited or eliminated, that will be the only type of mortgage written by portfolio lenders.

It is hoped that lenders have all learned the lesson that making fixed-rate loans with a 30-year amortization schedule that really lasts 30 years is called "bet the company." By the way, some have made that "bet the company" gamble in recent years and lost.

THE FUTURE IS THE ARM

The industry's future is the adjustable-rate mortgage. Despite reports to the contrary, the ARM did not disappear when interest rates fell. In fact, as recent as August 1986, nearly 90 percent of approximately $1 billion in home loans funded by Great Western were ARMs.

As an ARM seller-to-be, Great Western is reluctant to part with this mortgage. Once an ARM with an acceptable spread over the COF index is added to the portfolio, we like to keep it. There is strong demand in the marketplace for these ARMs—more demand than supply. It is clear that people want to buy this ARM for the same reasons lenders want to make them.

The future has never been brighter for these mortgage instruments.

Chapter 27

WILLIAM A. LONGBRAKE
AND
PETER L. STRUCK

William A. Longbrake is presently Senior Executive Vice President for Distribution and Operations, and is part of a three-member Office of the President management team of Washington Mutual Savings Bank, Seattle, Washington. Previously he served as Executive Vice President for Finance. Prior to joining Washington Mutual in August 1982, Mr. Longbrake served in several positions in the Office of the Comptroller of the Currency including Senior Deputy Comptroller for Resource Management, Acting Senior Deputy Comptroller for Policy and Deputy Comptroller for Research and Economic Programs. Mr. Longbrake also served as Special Assistant to the Chairman of the FDIC from 1977 to 1978 and as Acting Controller. He has written articles on banking, cost accounting and related topics and has taught courses in financial institutions and financial management. He currently is a member of the Editorial Advisory Board of issues in Bank Regulation.

Mr. Longbrake received a B.A. in economics from the College of Wooster; an M.A. in economics and an M.B.A. in finance from the University of Wisconsin and a D.B.A. in finance from the University of Maryland. He is married and has four children.

Peter L. Struck is the Vice President and Manager of Secondary Marketing at Washington Mutual Savings Bank, Seattle, Washington. Prior to joining Washington Mutual, Dr. Struck was a manager in the Economic and Policy Analysis group at the Office of the Comptroller of the Currency, Washington, D.C. He has written extensively on banking and finance-related topics. Dr. Struck holds a Ph.D. from the University of Wisconsin–Madison.

Analyzing and Restructuring Mortgage Portfolios for Thrifts and Commercial Banks

WILLIAM A. LONGBRAKE AND PETER L. STRUCK

For many thrift institutions, the mortgage portfolio represents the single largest asset on the balance sheet. Traditionally, a mortgage portfolio of fixed-rate loans had produced attractive returns in a stable interest rate environment where an upward-sloping yield curve was the norm.

With the advent of deposit-rate deregulation in the late 1970s brought on by double-digit interest rates and a negative-sloped yield curve, however, the fixed-rate mortgage portfolio became an ever-tightening noose around the necks of many thrifts and commercial banks. Indeed, out of that environment arose the initial need to restructure the mortgage portfolio.

The objectives of restructuring a mortgage portfolio irrespective of whether the firm is a thrift or commercial bank can be multifaceted. In examining those objectives and, more importantly, in making decisions on restructuring, it is crucial to have a sound, analytical framework to make those judgments. Such a framework is set forth in this chapter.

OBJECTIVES OF RESTRUCTURING

The decision to restructure a mortgage portfolio can be designed to achieve one or more of the following objectives:

- Reduce sensitivity of income to fluctuations in interest rates
- Achieve a (greater) positive spread between yields earned on mortgages and the rates paid for funds
- Maintain adequate capitalization
- Raise additional funds

The selection of a particular objective or a set of objectives depends mainly on the institution's current capital position, profitability level, exposure to interest rate risk, and liquidity. More importantly, management should have a clear focus on the institution's direction. Decisions need to be made regarding whether the institution will have a retail or wholesale orientation; whether the institution will be a portfolio lender or act more like a mortgage banker; or, whether the institution expects to pursue a rapid growth strategy. Answers to strategic questions like those will provide a valuable backdrop to determining the objectives of restructuring the mortgage portfolio.

MEASURING INTEREST RATE SENSITIVITY

Background

The key concept to understanding the mortgage portfolio restructuring process is measuring interest rate sensitivity and its incumbent factors. Before thoughtful and *profitable* restructuring can be accomplished, however, two requirements must be met.

First, a wealth of information must be extracted from an institution's data base. Without the appropriate information about the complexion of the mortgage loan portfolio, restructuring decisions can inadvertently be erroneous. Of primary importance is the expected pattern of cash

flows from the mortgage loans. That pattern consists of two elements—the stated contractual cash flow of interest and principal, and
unscheduled prepayments of principal whereby the borrower exercises
a call option (the right to make principal payments at par at any time).
Furthermore, the coupon interest rate associated with those cash flows
needs to be known, as does the current market interest rate. The current
market rate will serve as a discount rate for calculations of present
value.

The second requirement is an understanding of fundamental financial management concepts pertinent to mortgage restructuring. The
first concept, the *lending spread*, represents the difference between
asset and liability rates of the *same* maturity. Figure 27–1 shows how to
measure the lending spread. A four-year asset yielding 12 percent is
being funded with a one-year liability costing 8.5 percent. Abstracting
from the difference in maturity between the asset and liability, the
lending spread, as measured in the first year, is 2 percent or an asset
yield of 10.5 percent less the liability cost of 8.5 percent. Ideally, the
lending spread compensates a lender for taking on credit and liquidity
risks, but not the difference in maturities or yield curve spread.

The second concept, the *yield curve spread*, measures the difference
in stated interest rates due to mismatching asset and liability maturities.
Referring to Figure 27–1 again, the yield curve spread defines the
difference between the actual asset yield of 12 percent and a maturity-
matched, one-year asset of 10.5 percent. The value of the yield curve
spread can change dramatically in response to shifts in the yield curve.
Figure 27–2 overlays a downward-sloping yield curve on the original
situation portrayed in Figure 27–1. Now, the one-year liability costs
10.5 percent, and a one-year asset yields 12.5 percent. The yield curve
spread has been totally eliminated, and the institution must rely solely
upon its lending spread to achieve its profitability levels.

Consequently, when one examines restructuring decisions, it's important to distinguish between the lending spread and the yield curve
spread. Historically, most thrifts achieved acceptable levels of profitability by receiving a yield curve spread in addition to a lending spread.
As was demonstrated so harshly in the early 1980s, however, that
combination should no longer be relied upon.

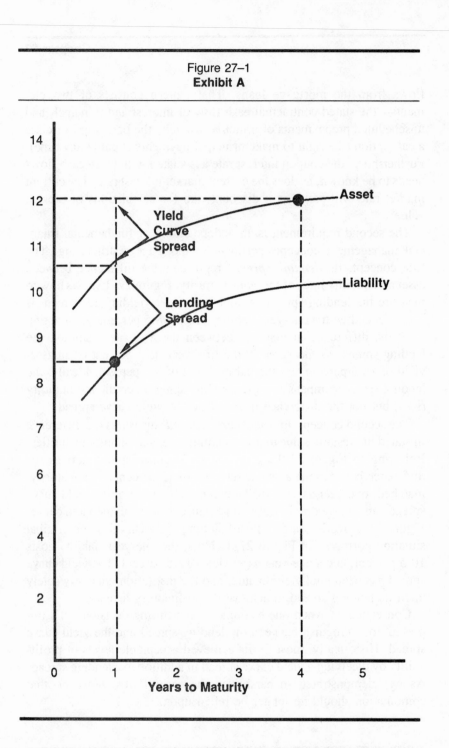

Figure 27–1
Exhibit A

14

12 ━━━━━━━━━━━━━━━━━━━━━━━━━━━● **Asset**

**Yield
Curve
Spread**

11

10   **Liability**

**Lending
Spread**

9

8

7

6

4

2

0   1   2   3   4   5
Years to Maturity

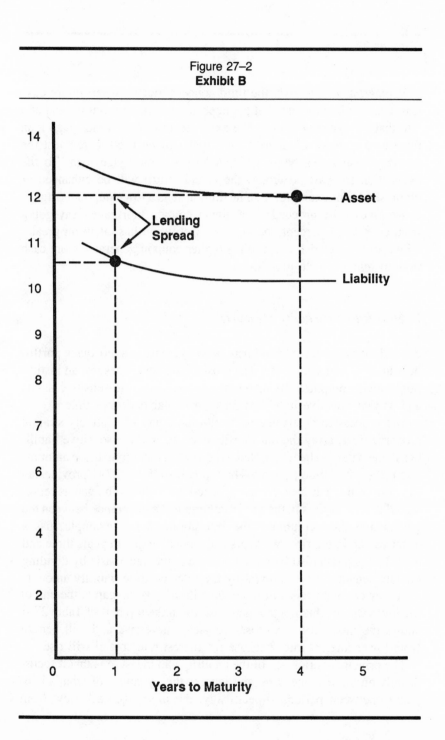

Figure 27–2
Exhibit B

Reinvestment rate risk, the third concept, occurs when future cash flows cannot be reinvested at the expected future rate, but instead at a rate that is higher or lower. The expected return on a mortgage loan requires a forecast of interest rates that will be used to reinvest the monthly cash flows being generated by the mortgage loan. To the extent that forecast is wrong, the actual return will be enhanced or diminished. For example, if an institution sells a low-coupon mortgage and reinvests the proceeds in a higher coupon mortgage—say going from an 8 to 12 percent coupon—the institution has taken on greater reinvestment rate risk because the higher coupon generates more cash flow to reinvest each month.

Interest Rate Sensitivity Measures

Several measures have been formulated to measure a mortgage portfolio's interest rate sensitivity. The most elementary measure, an institution's *gap*, computes the difference between its rate-sensitive assets and its rate-sensitive liabilities for a particular period of time.

The process to determine an institution's gap is relatively straight forward. First, array the rate-sensitive assets and rate-sensitive liabilities in the balance sheet by stated maturities. Then group those amounts into preselected time periods. The top half of Table 27–1 provides an example of the gap measure using stated maturities. The gap as represented in total dollars in the fourth column is the difference between the second and third columns. The institution, in this example, has a negative gap in the first two years and a positive gap in years three and four. The gap can also be measured on a percentage basis by dividing the rate-sensitive asset amount by the rate-sensitive liability amount.

A very common focus of many practitioners is the gap at the end of the first year. Evaluating that gap position in the top half of Table 27–1 shows the institution is exposed to yield curve risk and will benefit from lower interest rates because its interest rate spread will rise.

The principal deficiency of the maturity gap measure is that it focuses only on the balance sheet and ignores the dynamics of what's happening between periods—specifically, the mortgage cash flow from

Table 27–1
Gap—Maturity Basis

Year	Assets	Liabilities	$ Gap	% Gap
1	$ 200	$ 400	(200)	.50
2	300	400	(100)	.75
3	400	100	300	4.00
4	100	100	0	1.00
	1000	1000	0	

Gap—Cash Flow Basis				
1	$ 286	$ 455	(169)	.63
2	316	380	(64)	.83
3	327	90	237	3.63
4	71	75	(4)	.95

scheduled interest and principal repayments, and unscheduled principal prepayments. To take account of that fact a cash flow gap measure can be calculated. As presented in Table 27–2, the procedure involves three steps. First, determine the amounts of assets and liabilities maturing in each period just as in the maturity gap procedure; second, determine the interest flows for each period; and third, determine the present values of cashflows.

A comparison of the two gap measures, referring back to Table 27–1, reveals that the cash flow gaps are different, as one would expect. By incorporating the interest cash flows and taking into account the timing of all cash flows through the use of present value, the cash flow gap measure shows an institution that is slightly less sensitive to fluctuations in interest rates than the maturity gap measure.

A further extension of the cash flow gap measure is time weighting the present value of the cash flows. Such a measure is called *duration*. Although the duration concept is beyond the scope of the present undertaking, suffice it to say that duration has the unique property of

Table 27–2
Gap—Cash Flow Basis

Assets

Year	Principal	Interest	Cash Flow	Discount Factor 12%	Present Value
1	$ 200	$ 120	$ 320	.893	$ 286
2	300	96	396	.797	316
3	400	60	460	.712	327
4	100	12	112	.636	71
	1000	288	1288		1000

Liabilities

Year	Principal	Interest	Cash Flow	Discount Factor 12%	Present Value
1	$ 400	$ 100	$ 500	.909	$ 455
2	400	60	460	.828	380
3	100	20	120	.751	90
4	100	10	110	.683	75
	1000	190	1190		1000

measuring changes in asset or liability values to changes in interest rates.

Following the format of Table 27–2, Table 27–3 extends the example to include duration. When an institution's asset duration exceeds its liability duration, it will benefit from declining rates as the interest spread is expected to increase.

BENEFITS AND COSTS OF RESTRUCTURING

Before proceeding with mortgage portfolio restructuring, it is vital to understand both the *present* and *future* benefits and costs of restructuring. For each restructuring strategy identified below, there entails different risks and costs.

Table 27–3
The Impact of Duration

Year	Cash Flow	Discount Factor 12%	Present Value	Time Weighted Present Value
Assets				
1	320	.893	286	286
2	396	.797	316	632
3	460	.712	327	981
4	112	.636	71	284
	1288		1000	2183*
Liabilities				
1	500	.909	455	455
2	460	.826	380	760
3	120	.751	90	270
4	110	.683	75	300
	1190		1000	1785†

*Duration = 2.183 years
†Duration = 1.785 years

One strategy focuses on the asset side of the balance sheet. By selling (generally) longer maturity fixed-rate assets—principally mortgages—and reinvesting the proceeds in assets that match the maturity of liabilities—adjustable-rate mortgages (ARMs) for example—an institution can reduce its interest rate sensitivity. The cost of implementing such a strategy is a likely reduction in the interest spread. In many instances, short-term assets have lower spreads than their longer-maturity counterparts.

A key asset product to achieve a better match of assets and liabilities is the adjustable-rate mortgage. The two principal types are those that limit the rate adjustment and those that limit the payment adjustment.

Rate-capped ARMs are not totally rate sensitive; thus, the institution has not shifted all of the interest rate risk to the borrower. In a rising rate environment, the duration of an ARM may be longer than one year because it will take longer than one year for the ARM rate to reach a market rate.

In contrast, payment-capped ARMs may have negative amortization, or a growing loan amount, if the payment limit is less than the payment implied by the current rate on the mortgage. The risk inherent in payment-capped ARMs arises from negative amortization. Negative amortization erodes the equity cushion the lender has in the property.

An offshoot of selling assets is offering incentives to borrowers to refinance existing mortgages. Such a program may be less costly than the outright sale of assets, although it requires a longer period of time to accomplish. The upgrading of an existing mortgage portfolio should be undertaken irrespective of what other restructuring options are pursued. The objectives of such an undertaking are to:

- Raise the overall yield on those portfolios
- Reduce maturities
- Qualify those loans for secondary market sale
- Include due on sale clauses
- Provide fee income

A second general strategy alters the institution's liability structure to more closely match the asset side. The restructuring of the liability side can often be more easily accomplished than asset restructuring. The range of options is much greater and transactions are completed more quickly. Those advantages arise from the much greater participation of investment bankers in offering liability products.

A variety of sources in the cash market may be tapped to extend liabilities. Those sources include:

- Federal home loan bank advances
- Retail term CDs
- Mortgage-backed securities—repo and swap
- CMOs

- Collateralized preferred stock
- Subordinated debt
- Real estate-based equity participation certificates

The particular use of those sources requires an analysis of their cost, availability, liquidity, and marketability. Marketplace dynamics are such that the relative attractiveness of a particular source changes over time. Moreover, diversification of liability sources is a worthwhile approach to pursue.

More often than not liability extension through the cash market is coupled with portfolio growth rather than just serving as a replacement for short-term liabilities.

The use of the noncash liability market alters the maturity characteristics of existing liabilities without requiring the actual sale of those liabilities. Three major noncash sources are interest rate swaps, futures, and options.

Interest rate swaps, or more technically, interest rate exchange agreements, enjoy a well-developed and liquid market. Swaps can generally reduce borrowing costs by matching parties with specific advantages in different maturity markets. For example, thrifts and banks can raise inexpensive retail customer short-term deposits that then can be extended in the swap market.

Interest rate futures are aimed at protecting values of assets or liabilities. The futures market is extremely well-developed and very liquid. Moreover, there is virtually no credit risk with futures. The major risks in using futures are market volatility and basis risk. Basis risk, especially, has become a difficult element to manage as the different markets move in unpredictable patterns.

Options can be substituted for futures to protect values. Unlike futures, the total cost of an option is known up front through the payment of a premium by the purchaser. Options can be used to purchase and sell mortgages. By locking in a particular price or yield level, an option purchaser has effectively bought insurance.

In addition to the three major noncash sources, there are a myriad of derivative products being developed. As one example, rate-capped options pay the difference to a purchaser between a current short-term rate and a preset level for that rate. For a fee premium, one party may be willing to pay the difference between the current six-month LIBOR rate and nine percent. This agreement may be for a period of two years with the payment frequency set for a quarterly rate. Such an agreement may provide ARMs with better interest rate sensitivity in a rising rate environment.

A third strategy entails a growth orientation whereby the addition of new assets is purposefully matched with similar liabilities. In the process of growing, an "old" mismatched portfolio shrinks and becomes less of a problem relative to the whole portfolio.

By default, the final strategy is to do nothing. Euphemistically, the institution is "rolling the dice" or betting that interest rates behave in a favorable manner.

In choosing a particular strategy to follow, an institution must consider the effect of that strategy on its financial performance. Does the institution have sufficient capital to absorb losses if assets are sold? Moreover, can the institution realize the tax benefits that accrue from taking losses? What is the impact on the net interest spread? Does the institution have sufficient revenue to cover noninterest expenses? How are profits and the expected valuation of the firm affected? Indeed, taking large losses today may have a larger effect on valuation than spreading out the losses over time.

An Example of Portfolio Restructuring

Table 27–4 presents the assumptions for the example:

- The institution currently owns an old four-year asset with a coupon rate of 9 percent that pays interest once a year.
- The current market rate on four-year assets is 11 percent so that the market value of the four-year asset is $937.95 per $1000 of face value.
- The asset is being financed with a one-year liability that has a coupon rate of 8 percent.

Table 27–4
Costs/Benefits of Restructuring Assumptions*

	Coupon Rate	Market Rate
Old 4-year Asset	9%	11%
New 1-year Asset	10	10
New 1-year Liability	8	8
New 4-year Liability	9	9

*Market value old asset = $937.95; reinvestment rate = 10%; and tax rate = 30%.

- The institution is able to reinvest cashflow at a 10 percent rate on a one-year matched liability maturity basis.
- The tax rate is 30 percent for both capital gains and ordinary income.

Table 27–5 presents Case I, the naive restructuring strategy of "doing nothing." At the end of four years when the asset matures, the institution will have recorded $31.08 in income. In doing nothing, the institution maintains a mismatched portfolio and benefits from a positive yield curve spread.

Table 27–6 shows the asset-side restructuring case in which the old asset is sold at a loss, and the remaining proceeds are reinvested in a one-year asset yielding 10 percent. Assuming a stable interest rate environment, income of $5.23 is recorded after four years.

In comparison with the "do nothing" strategy of Case I, Case II shows an improved interest spread of 2 percent (10.0% − 8.0%) versus a 1 percent spread in Case I (9.0% − 8.0%). The improvement in spread is partially deceiving, because if the loss on the sale of asset is taken into account, the net interest margin only rises from 1 percent to 1.57 percent. More important, however, is the fact that the institution

Table 27–5
Case I: Status Quo—Keep Old Asset

Year	Assets 9%	Funds 8%	Reinvestment 10%	Taxes	Total
1	$ 90	$ 80	$ .00	$ 3.00	$ 7.00
2	90	80	.70	3.21	7.49
3	90	80	1.45	3.44	8.01
4	90	80	2.25	3.67	8.50
					$31.08

Table 27–6
Case II: Sell Old Asset—Buy 1-Year Asset

Year	Assets 9%	Funds 8%	Reinvestment 10%	Taxes	Total
0					($43.44)*
1	$ 95.66	$ 80.00	$ .00	$ 4.70	$ 10.96
2	95.66	80.00	1.10	5.03	11.73
3	95.66	80.00	2.27	5.38	12.55
4	95.66	80.00	3.52	5.75	13.43
					$ 5.23

*Loss on sale $= (1{,}000 - 937.95) \times (1 - .30)$

Table 27–7
Case III: Convert Liability to 4-Year

Year	Assets 9%	Funds 9%	Reinvestment 10%	Taxes Taxes	Total Total
1	$ 90.00	$ 90.00	$ .00	$ .00	$ .00
2	90.00	90.00	.00	.00	.00
3	90.00	90.00	.00	.00	.00
4	90.00	90.00	.00	.00	.00
					$ .00

has matched its maturities and is not particularly vulnerable to changing levels of interest rates. The cost of that matching was a significant drop in income as the asset maturity was shortened up and the yield curve spread was forsaken.

With Case III, shown in Table 27–7, a liability-based restructuring strategy can be employed to match the asset. To convert the existing one-year liability to a four-year maturity, an interest rate swap agreement is entered into. Under that agreement the institution agrees to pay the four-year liability rate of 9 percent and the other party consents to pay the one-year rate of 8 percent. By executing such a swap, the institution keeps its one-year liability on the balance sheet but it now carries a four-year rate and it behaves like a four-year instrument.

Income in Case III declines to zero as the interest spread is also zero—the asset and liability carry the same rates. Income decreased because the effective liability maturity moved up the yield curve to achieve a better match with the asset. In the process, the institution gave up its yield curve spread.

By using an interest rate swap or some other noncash transaction, no gain or loss is recorded and there is no tax effect with which to be concerned. Moreover, the book value of capital is unaffected. Such a

Table 27–8
Costs/Benefits Recap

	Rates Constant	Rates Rise
Case I	$ 31.08	($ 13.89)
Case II	5.23	4.27
Case III	0.00	0.00

strategy may be preferred if tax benefits cannot be realized or the institution's capital ratio is low.

Table 27–8 summarizes the three cases; with the assumed interest rate levels, the most profitable strategy was Case I—do nothing. If interest rates were to rise after the first year by 2 percent, however, the results of the three strategies change. For Case I, the yield curve spread becomes negative and a loss is recorded. In Case II, income drops slightly as the present value of the tax benefit declines at higher rates. Case III shows no change, because four-year rates were locked in and the increase in rates after the first year has no effect on the cash flow stream.

The benefit of restructuring the mortgage portfolio was easily illustrated in the example, as it minimized the sensitivity of income to fluctuations in the level of interest rates. Also observed was the primary cost of restructuring—the loss of the yield curve spread.

SUMMARY

Analyzing a mortgage portfolio for possible restructuring requires two elements: an ability to skillfully extract the relevant asset and liability cash flow data and the knowledge to understand how those cash flows can be manipulated to achieve one's objective. Once those elements have been mastered, it's then necessary to simulate the potential costs and benefits of executing a particular strategy—such as selling assets or extending liabilities. Guiding the choice of a particular strategy, however, are the institution's objectives for attempting a portfolio restructuring.

Chapter 28

GREGORY L. COLEMAN
AND
ROBERT W. HUNTER

Gregory L. Coleman, CFA, serves as Executive Vice President, Director of Investments and Asset Liability Management. In this capacity, Mr. Coleman has overall responsibility for all investment functions, including asset/liability management, measurement of the company's interest rate sensitivity, and many corporate finance duties.

Prior to joining Northeast Savings in 1983, Mr. Coleman was with Southeast Bank, N.A. of Miami, of Florida for four years, where he served most recently as Senior Vice President and Manager of the Funds Management Department.

A cum laude graduate of Michigan State University, with a Bachelor's Degree in Business Administration, Mr. Coleman also holds an M.B.A. from the University of Michigan. He is a member of the institute of Chartered Financial Analysts.

Robert Hunter is First Vice President with Northeast Savings since a merger in October 1982. Prior to that, he was Vice President of Secondary Marketing at Freedom Federal Savings & Loan of Worcester, Massachusetts.

Mr. Hunter is responsible for managing Northeast's approximately $3 billion mortgage-backed securities and purchased loan portfolios.

He is a 1985 M.B.A. graduate of Clark University in Worcester, Massachusetts, as well as a 1976 graduate of the Mortgage Bankers Association School of Mortgage Banking.

Innovations in Mortgage Financings for Thrifts

GREGORY L. COLEMAN AND ROBERT W. HUNTER

In the late 1970s, both thrifts and commercial banks were frequent issuers of mortgage-related debt. Bank of America, based largely on the success of the Government National Mortgage Association (GNMA) and Federal Home Loan Mortgage Corporation (FHLMC), issued the first nongovernment pass-through security in September 1977. Although Bank of America and several other private issuers were active over the balance of the decade, the success and cost effectiveness of the agency pass-through programs largely confined private issuance to the jumbo loan market.

Thrift institutions, on the other hand, began issuing mortgage backed bonds in October 1975 and have increased their presence since that time via a cadre of mortgage-backed borrowings. Collateralized mortgage obligations, collateralized commercial paper, and collateralized backed letters of credit are recent variations on the original mortgage-backed bond, to name only a few. In addition, while the collateral on earlier issues was comprised largely of federal agency-backed pass-through securities, recent offerings have included fixed- and adjustable-rate whole loans, as well as mortgage participation certificates from nongovernment agencies.

Ironically, it was the deregulation of interest rates and the subsequent havoc it brought to the viability of the thrift industry that led to the numerous structured financial innovations that thrifts now use. This allowed access to the capital markets during very difficult times and has burgeoned with today's more sanguine markets.

Commercial banks, by contrast, have remained content to use their large holdings of Treasury and agency securities to secure repurchase agreements, almost exclusively. In the long-term debt markets, banks have generally found that using mortgage-backed securities (MBSs) or Treasuries as collateral is an inefficient means of acquiring funds.

It is easy to understand why this is the case. Figure 28-1 compares single "A" rated commercial bank debt to that of nonrated, or below investment grade thrift debt, from January 1983 to August of 1986. During this period, "A" rated commercial banks were able to borrow, on average, at slightly less than 100 basis points above the comparable maturity U.S. Treasury. Thrifts, by comparison, could only raise long-term funds on an unsecured basis at yields that exceeded Treasury yields by over 500 basis points (before steep underwriting commissions).

Consequently, the liquification of thrifts' mortgage assets was a very attractive alternative to that of borrowing on an unsecured basis. Banks, appropriately, elected to use MBSs almost exclusively for repurchase agreements, where overcollateralization is at minimum levels.

Another important factor in the growth of thrift issued mortgage backed bonds is the position of the Federal Home Loan Bank Board (FHLBB) as it relates to actions that could be taken in cases of a thrift insolvency by the FSLIC as receivor. Sections 109(b) (2) and (d) of the U.S. Bankruptcy Code exclude thrifts from the Code's authority. This is critical, because Section 362 (a) of the Code imposes an automatic stay on foreclosure of collateral by a secured creditor. Further, Section 542 of the Code could require that a secured creditor return collateral to the debtor.

It is equally important that there is nothing evident in the applicable FHLBB regulations that would allow a thrift receiver to use similar powers provided in the Bankruptcy Code. To that point, in a letter dated December 12, 1983, Norman H. Raiden, general counsel to the Federal Home Loan Bank board, stated to Neil D. Barron of Booth and Baron that "Collateral that secures a valid claim of a secured creditor (of a

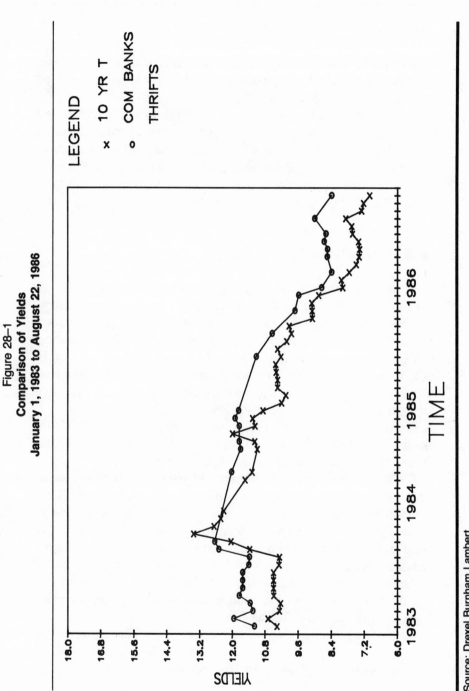

Figure 28–1
Comparison of Yields
January 1, 1983 to August 22, 1986

LEGEND

x 10 YR T

o COM BANKS

   THRIFTS

TIME

YIELDS

Source: Drexel Burnham Lambert

thrift) must be utilized solely for the satisfaction of such secured claim up to the full principal amount owed plus interest at the contractual rate through the date of payment."*

Given the extraordinary cost savings available to a thrift and the lack of investors on an unsecured basis, it is apparent why the proliferation of collateralized borrowings has flourished. What follows is a detailed description of some of the programs that thrifts have undertaken to unlock the attractive borrowing potential of the high-quality mortgage assets on their balance sheet.

MORTGAGE BACKED BONDS

Since its initial development in 1975, when California Federal Savings & Loan issued the first public offering backed by mortgage collateral, the market for mortgage-backed financings has skyrocketed, particularly after the development of the Collateralized Mortgage Obligations (CMOs) in 1983. These mortgage-backed transactions have been issued with the highest credit ratings from S&P and Moody's and have allowed even small thrifts and builders the opportunity to raise new funds in the capital markets at the lowest possible cost.

The top rating on these transactions has been based upon: (1) the amount of excess collateral required over the amount funded, and (2) the marketability and liquidity of the collateral.

The initial mortgage-backed bonds (MBBs) had a single maturity structure, usually 7–10 years. The bonds typically had an overcollateralization requirement of 150 percent—175 percent of the amount financed, generally backed by GNMA MBSs. This basic structure used in the initial MBB offerings has spawned many derivations in collateralized financings. This evolution reduced issuers' financing costs and collateralization requirements. However, the key ingredient to the success of these transactions has continued to be the high-quality mortgages used as collateral for the financings.

The *builder pay-through bond* was one of the first derivations used in

---

Banking Law Report, 1, Number 4 (July 1984), Neil D. Baron, NY, NY.

1981 by the builder community to help finance their housing sales. The builder bond program combined the single-maturity structure of a MBB with the prepayment characteristics of the mortgage collateral. As the underlying collateral reduced in principal value, the builder issuer paid down the debt. This pay-through structure allowed collateral levels to be reduced to the 110 percent–125 percent level, thus lowering the overall costs of the bond as compared to the straight MBB. However, the overcollateralization requirement made this financing attractive to only the well-capitalized builders.

The most successful derivation of the MBB structure is the CMO. First issued in 1983 by FHLMC, the CMO combines mortgage collateral with a multimaturity cash flow bond structure. This structure has attracted additional investors into the mortgage market. As of August 31, 1986, almost $45 billion in CMOs had been issued, and the market was absorbing an additional $4 to $5 billion per month. Under this structure, collateral requirements have been reduced to the lowest levels to date, allowing the issuers to lower effective financing costs.

The issuers of MBB financings have had several similarities. They all owned high-quality mortgage assets, and they sought new and better ways to finance these assets than the market had previously allowed. The MBB market has allowed them to do this. At the same time MBB investors have found an opprotunity to receive a superior market rate given the credit quality of these investments.

THE EUROBOND MARKET

During 1984, as many thrifts sought to broaden their funding sources, they began issuing debt securities in the Eurobond market. This new source of funding was aided by the 1984 Tax Reform Act (TRA) and the desire of international investors to acquire high quality agency backed securities.

Prior to the TRA passage, a thrift institution had to enter the Euromarket via an offshore subsidiary, usually a Netherlands Antilles (NV) corporation. This circuitous route was established so that investors were not subject to a 30 percent tax on U.S. source interest income. By issuing through an NV subsidiary, the tax was eliminated. However, much of the savings that an issuer could obtain from lower cost Euro-dollar funds were eroded by the cost of setting up and maintaining the NV subsidiary.

The TRA eliminated the tax for certain "portfolio interests" paid on obligations issued after July 18, 1984. This repeal generally applies to bonds issued by corporations after that date.* Issuers could then issue eligible obligations in the Euromarket without the additional cost previously associated with such transactions.

Finally, the Euromarket requires less documentation, produces lower issuance costs, and provides for a faster turnaround time from formulation to launch. This faster, simpler procedure allows issuers to take advantage of rate differentials in the Euromarket versus the domestic market.

The first Eurobond MBB transactions were similar in structure to their American counterparts: the issues were AAA rated; had final maturities of 7–10 years with call protection of 4–7 years; and the collateral was predominantly mortgage-backed securities (FNMA, GNMA, or FHLMC). However, there were few transactions done in the fixed-rate market, because it again became more attractive to issue domestically. In late 1985, thrifts capitalized on the opportunity to issue floating-rate notes (FRNs) at a time when other FRN issuers were decreasing their issuance. Thrifts were willing to issue on a floating-rate basis because they were originating large amounts of adjustable-rate mortgages (ARMs) and needed a long-term funding source with similar repricing terms. As Figure 28–2 shows, this trend has continued as FRNs compose in excess of 60 percent of the S&L new issue volume.

As a commentary on the viability of the thrift sector of the Euro FRN market, in December 1985, Northeast Savings (NES) issued the first FRN based on a one-year London Interbank Offered Rate (LIBOR), as well as the first issue backed predominantly by nonagency pass throughs. The transaction had a 10-year final maturity and could not be called for 5 years. This financing provided the issuer with a long-term

---

*49 C.F.R. 33228 (August 1984).

Figure 28–2
U.S. Savings and Loan Institutions
Euromarket New Issue Volume
1980 to 1986 (July)

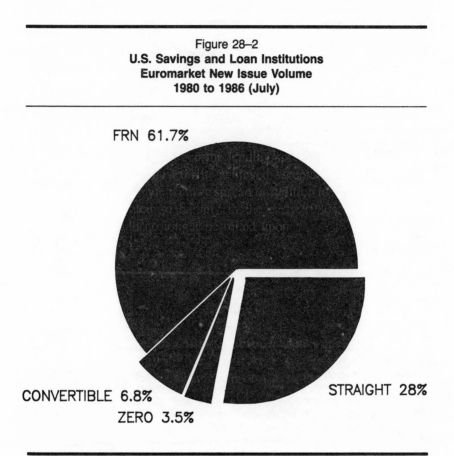

FRN 61.7%

CONVERTIBLE 6.8%

ZERO 3.5%

STRAIGHT 28%

Source: Credit Suisse First Boston

source of funds, lower cost annual interest payments, and an efficient use of previously used collateral.

NES is a large originator and purchaser of one year ARMs. By securing funds with an interest rate that adjusted annually, NES was able to offset a major portion of the interest rate risk associated with using money market borrowings to fund such loans. Additionally, the all in cost of the transaction, based on the first year's coupon rate, was approximately 50 basis points less than a similar financing from the FHLB. While annual and lifetime interest rate caps could limit full

Table 28–1
Annual Average

Year	1-Year Treasury	1-Year LIBOR	Fully Indexed ARM[a]	Capped 1-Year ARM[b]
1979	10.69	11.55	13.44	13.44
1980	12.10	13.17	14.85	14.85
1981	14.84	15.80	17.59	16.85
1982	11.36	12.38	13.90	14.85
1983	9.57	10.03	12.32	12.85
1984	10.89	11.56	13.64	13.64
1985	8.56	9.20	11.31	11.64

Source: Merill Lynch Capital Markets (1985).
[a] A 1-year ARM indexed to the 12-month Treasury with an adjustment over the Treasury index of 275 basis points. There are no limits on rate changes.
[b] A 1-year ARM indexed to the 12-month Treasury with an adjustment over the Treasury index of 275 basis points. There are rate adjustment limits of 2% per year and 5% over the initial mortgage rate.

yield adjustments during periods of rapidly rising interest rates, a historical analysis of standard ARMs versus one-year LIBOR shows otherwise (see Table 28–1). This is particularly significant, because the interest rate environment from 1979 to 1985 was one of the most volatile in our history.

The specific collateral that was used to back the financing, however, was the driving force that motivated the transaction. Up to that time all AAA rated mortgage-backed Euro issues were composed almost entirely of agency securities. Whole loans, while qualifying as eligible collateral (with requisite increases in overcollateralization levels), required a level of documentation and data collection that was complicated and time consuming. Northeast found a hybrid solution by using 100 percent loan participation certificates that met S&P's AAA rating requirements. The majority of the mortgage assets were unrated participation certificates.

This collateral is different in structure from previous issues, but it continued to meet the general criteria that S&P requires:

1. The collateral must be either highly liquid or marketable. The underlying participations were in a tradable format, were principally purchased through Wall Street dealers and were standard fixed-rate and adjustable-rate loan programs.
2. The servicers must have the proven servicing capabilities needed for the transaction. The participations were all transacted with substantial, quality servicers who made strong representations and warranties to the participant regarding the quality of the loans (similar to those required by FNMA/FHLMC). The loan agreements provide for a modified MBS pass through. In addition, the servicing of the collateral was spread among seven or eight servicers, giving the underlying collateral further diversification.
3. There must be a perfected first security in the collateral. This is the most important aspect of the collateral, as far as the rating agencies are concerned. The participation format requires a third-party custodian, recordable assignments of the underlying loan documents, and last, allows for the participation interest to be readily transferred from the thrift into the benefical ownership of the bond trustee. The participation format facilitates transfers of ownership much more readily than the standard whole-loan format. Therefore, if the trustee has to liquidate the collateral because of an issuer default, the transfer to a new owner is much smoother than the transfer of more cumbersome whole-loan collateral. This is of particular importance at the time of any default, since the trustee wants to ensure transfer of ownership and sale in a prompt manner.

Until this transaction, Wall Street had perceived that, other than agency MBS collateral, mortgage whole loans represented the most suitable, secure quality collateral available for thrift's collateralization requirements. When examined further, however, all the standard safeguards that made mortgage-backed transactions secure were available under the participation format that our firm had used on most of its purchases. These safeguards were developed with the idea of protecting nontraditional mortgage investors' interests when they purchased loans. That is the same principle under which the rating agencies developed their guidelines.

COLLATERALIZED COMMERCIAL PAPER

Commercial paper (CP) is an unsecured promissory note generally issued by large firms with established credit ratings as a lower cost alternative to commercial bank loans. The maturity on CP runs from one to 270 days, though in practice the average maturity is in the 45-day range. The short-term maturity of the CP market makes it similar to the GNMA/FNMA/FHLMC (MBS) repo market, with the exceptions that CP is an unsecured line of credit, and secondly, because the CP issuers carry a published credit rating, it has typically carried a lower cost of funds than the repo market.

Although thrifts have had legal authority to issue commercial paper since 1979, they did not use this funding source because few thrifts carried ratings of investment grade or higher. In order to enter the CP market and gain a yield advantage over the repo market, an issuer must qualify for a top rating from S&P, Moody's, or Fitch. To obtain this coveted rating, thrifts had to contrive a means by which their mortgage assets could be used as credit enhancements.

Such a mechanism was devised in 1984 by Merrill Lynch Money Markets (MLMM). A special-purpose corporation was established to act as the issuer of commercial paper backed by collateral loaned (sold under agreement to repurchase) to the corporation by the ultimate borrowers, the S&Ls. In the first six months of the program, MLMM issued approximately $3.3 billion of commercial paper using this technique. Since that time, the program has had approximately $1.8 billion in average daily outstandings.

The success of the program can be attributed to the credit rating that the issue receives; the lower rate of the CP versus alternative short-term funding sources for the participating thrifts; and the special purpose corporation that MLMM implemented to protect the investors who purchased the commercial paper.

All of the issues to date have been rated A-1 + by S&P, and P-1 by Moody's, the highest rating available for commercial paper by either rating agency. This rating is obtained because of the structure that has been established to protect the noteholders. This structure involves four parties and offers maximum protection to the noteholders. Under the program, a financial institution (thrift) pledges to the issuer government or agencies securities (principally mortgage-backed). This collateral is used to both issue the CP, as well as to secure a line of credit from a commercial bank for up to 25 percent of the borrowing facility. The issuer (the funding corporation) is a special-purpose subsidiary of MLMM, set up at arm's length from the financial institution. Therefore, the issuer is "insolvency proof" from FDIC and FSLIC liquidation. The level of overcollateralization required to obtain the A-1 + /P-1 rating varies with the type and valuation frequency of the collateral, but would typically fall within a range of 130 percent–160 percent. A depository bank holds the securities for the funding corporation; serves as trustee for the noteholders; marks the collateral to market on a timely basis; and acts as issuing and paying agent for the noteholders. Figure 28–3 outlines the procedure under which the program will typically function.

This type of security has allowed thrifts to garner funds from many nontraditional sources. In 1985, a year in which the financial news headlined large losses in the repo market associated with ESM and Bevel Bresler, 27 percent of the transactions under the program were done with municipalities and tax exempt, nonprofit corporations. Another 25 pecent of the transactions were done with bank trust departments and insurance companies, neither of which would likely engage in wholesale repos with a nonrated thrift.

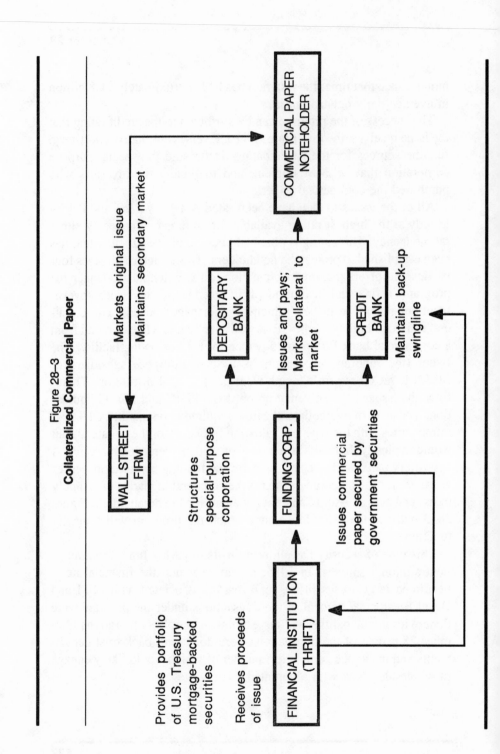

Figure 28–3
Collateralized Commercial Paper

Thus, the noteholders are protected by substantial overcollateralization, a backup commercial bank line of credit, and a special-purpose corporation that facilitates liquidation should the financial institution fail.

Once the facility is in place, the issuer can borrow up to the limits of the facility, without the attendant paperwork and delivery problems that occur in a typical repo transaction. In a sense, the program is an insolvency-proof, streamlined repo facility.

Cost is the second advantage of the program. As shown in Figure 28–4, thrift collateralized commercial paper has yielded, on an unadjusted basis, an average of 26 basis points below LIBOR from January 1985 to July 31, 1986. When the issuance costs and the ongoing expenses for the trustee and the standby credit facility are included, the total cost, based on an average outstanding of $200 million, is still 16 basis points below comparable LIBOR. This savings is even greater when compared to other alternatives such as federal home loan bank advances.

The proceeds from the CP issuance have been used as an effective funding vehicle for adjustable-rate mortgage product that the issuers have added to their portfolios. Further, thrifts can use short-term cash raising liability programs, such as commercial paper, along with interest rate swaps and caps, to fund long-term mortgage backed assets on a hedged basis.

COLLATERALIZED CREDIT FACILITIES

Backup lines of credit are a useful cash management tool for financial and nonfinancial institutions alike, particularly those with limited access to the money markets. While a number of thrifts have successfully negotiated unsecured lines of credit from commercial banks, the cost of such lines is quite high, typically in excess of prime. Recently, a few savings institutions have established revolving credit facilities in the Euromarket. In so doing, thrifts are leveraging their success achieved in the FRN market. These revolving facilities can support either regular

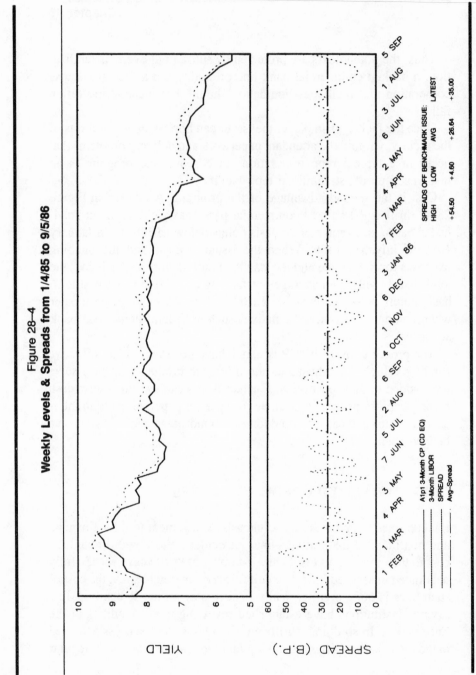

Figure 28-4

Weekly Levels & Spreads from 1/4/85 to 9/5/86

YIELD

SPREAD (B.P.)

A1p1 3-Month CP (CD EQ)
3-Month LIBOR
SPREAD
Avg-Spread

SPREADS OFF BENCHMARK ISSUE:			
HIGH	LOW	AVG	LATEST
+54.50	+4.60	+26.64	+35.00

Source: Salomon Bros. Inc.

note issuance or a standby facility for bank borrowings for Euro commercial paper.

The latest variation on the revolving credit facilities, however, is the securing of the facility with nonagency mortgage assets of the thrift. Because such facilities are not rated, the documentation is less onerous and overcollateralization levels are lower than those typically required by the rating agencies for collateralized FRNs. This type of financing facility will grow over time as foreign investors become more receptive to mortgage-backed assets in general, especially considering the superior rates of return and credit quality available to investors on these financings.

SYNTHETIC MORTGAGE-BACKED BONDS: RATE SWAPS AND REPURCHASE AGREEMENTS

The purchase of mortgage-backed securities funded via repurchase agreements (using the purchased securities as collateral) has long been an efficient means by which thrifts could acquire and finance mortgage assets (efficient in the sense that all repo participants borrow at ostensibly the same rate). This is the case because it is the government collateral securing the repo that investors looked to in the transaction. What was needed was a means by which savings institutions could alter the already large interest rate risk exposure that such purchases funded by repo engendered.

The burgeoning interest rate swap market offered just such a vehicle. With few exceptions, thrifts' only sources of long-term, fixed-rate funds had been the district federal home loan bank or local depositors. By entering into a swap agreement as the fixed-rate payor, the interest rate risk associated with the short funding of the MBSs was greatly reduced. This is known as controlled risk arbitrage (CRA).

The interest rate swap market has evolved such that most large thrifts do not pay any "credit premium" in addition to the going market rate. A counterparty may require collateral but it can take the form of corporate bonds with limited lost opportunity cost. Smaller institutions may be required to obtain a letter of credit on 10 percent–15 percent of the notional amounts from their district FHLB, but the basis point cost is minimal relative to the entire transaction. Thrifts have been such large participants in the swap market that, at year-end 1985, the FHLBB estimated that thrifts had booked $22 billion in interest rate swaps.

In effect, thrifts can receive the benefits of their comparative cost advantage (1 percent–5 percent overcollateralization) in the repo markets over a 3–10 year period by using rate swaps to synthetically lengthen these money market borrowings. There is, of course, some basis risk that is assumed since the repo rate will not move in lock step with their floating rate receipt, typically LIBOR.

The greater risk inherent in the transaction, however, is the prepayment risk associated with the purchase of the mortgage assets. The meteoric rise in mortgage prepayments associated with the huge mortgage refinancings of 1985 and 1986 has caused investor nightmares. What started out as an asset with the duration characteristics of a 10-year treasury was transformed into a money market instrument. Specifically, thrifts that had duration-matched MBS purchases with 5–7 year bullet liabilities in 1984 found that they had high-cost funds supporting assets representing only a fraction of the original mortgage balance 2 years later.

Ironically, thrifts are perhaps the only financial institution that can view such massive prepayments with ambivalence. At the microlevel, such match-funded arbitrages may not have proved profitable. However, given the liability-sensitive nature of a thrift's balance sheet, the decline of interest rates and subsequent widening of thrift margins more than offset the loss due to prepayments.

Recent refinements in the CRA arena have further reduced the effect of an adverse move in interest rates. By laddering rate swap maturities to coincide with the estimated cash flow of the mortgage asset, an institution can be both duration and cash flow matched over the investment horizon. Figure 28–5 depicts a typical $500 million CRA using laddered funding sources. Such a strategy, coupled with the purchase of discount mortgage assets, can reduce the variability in returns over a wide range of interest rate scenarios. This method also reduces the expected value of the match-funded spread versus current coupon MBS, which is the cost of increased certainty.

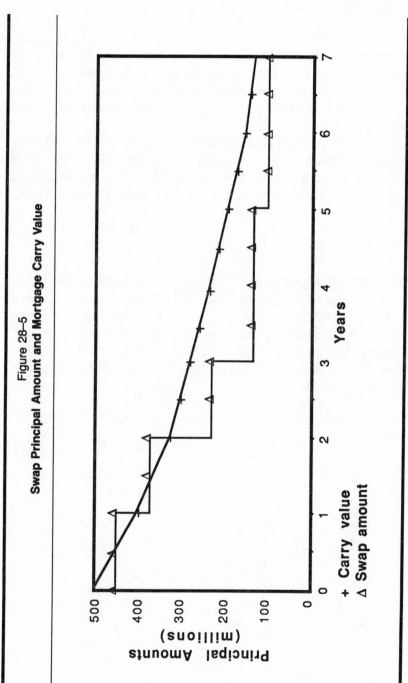

Figure 28–5
Swap Principal Amount and Mortgage Carry Value

+ Carry value
△ Swap amount

Principal Amounts (millions)

FHLBB regulatory changes have provided further incentives for repo/interest rate swap transactions. As part of the revised net worth regulation, thrifts with lower levels of interest rate risk receive a substantial direct reduction in their required net worth levels, to as low as 4 percent.

The repo/interest rate swap transaction does not solve all thrift funding and rate risk management issues. It increases rollover risk and is only well suited to agency MBS assets. Still, it is an increasingly important tool in the liability management process of today's thrift.

CONCLUSION

The tremendous growth of the secondary mortgage market in the 1980s, coupled with increased competiton for funds, has created a need for thrift institutions to develop new funding sources and mechanisms to meet their financing needs. These mortgage-backed financings have provided thrift institutions with viable sources at attractive interest rates, allowing them to take maximum advantage of their high-quality mortgage portfolios.

Section V:
The Mortgage
Insurance Industry

INTRODUCTION

Section V presents an overview of an industry that is at a crossroad, wracked by record losses in the early and mid-1980s and challenged by a proliferation of alternative credit enhancement vehicles. Roger Blood explores the art and science of managing insured mortgage risk in Chapter 29, and makes the case that MI companies will have to find a new balance between marketing and risk management as they strive to increase market share while continuing to reduce losses. Chapters 30 through 33 offer the viewpoints of four of the leading companies in the MI industry. In Chapter 30, Earl Corkett discusses the new products that PMI Mortgage Insurance Co. developed to meet the challenges of a changing environment. William Lacy presents MGIC's view of critical underwriting issues in Chapter 31. In Chapter 32, Diane Cortes asks: Has the MI industry entered a fundamentally new and different world of risk management, or is it simply returning to the basic precepts on which it was founded? Finally, Chapter 33 offers a concluding essay by Robert Hastings that examines the questions that everyone involved in the industry must consider to avoid repeating the mistakes of the past.

Chapter 29

ROGER BLOOD

Roger Blood, Senior Consultant to Temple, Barker & Sloane, Inc., specializes in the mortgage insurance industry.

Previously, Mr. Blood was Senior Vice President, Risk Management for Investors Mortgage Insurance Company. His responsibilities included product development, pricing, underwriting, quality control, claims, and reserve development.

Earlier, Mr. Blood was Senior Analyst and Project Director for Morton Hoffman and Company, Urban and Economic Consultants. Among other duties, he performed housing market analyses and feasibility studies for clients in the public and private sectors.

Mr. Blood has published several articles on mortgage risk and insurance and co-authored The Private Insurance of Home Mortgages *(The Institute for Environmental Studies and MGIC). He has also served on the Advisory Board of the Federal National Mortgage Association, Southeast Region.*

For the past 12 years, Mr. Blood has been active in MICA, the mortgage insurance industry trade association. He has worked on, or led, MICA committees on risk management, appraisal standards, adjustable mortgages, Fannie Mae/Freddy Mac and mortgage banker liaison, and mortgage-backed securities.

Mr. Blood received a B.A. in economics from Clark University, where he was elected to Phi Beta Kappa. He earned an M.B.A. in real estate finance from the Wharton Graduate Division at the University of Pennsylvania. He also received a Strathcona Scholarship, under which he attended a program in transportation management at the Yale University Graduate School of Economics.

Temple, Barker & Sloan, Inc. is one of the largest independent general management consulting firms in the United States. The TBS Financial Services Industry Group serves the banking, insurance, securities, thrift, and mortgage insurance industries.

Managing Insured Mortgage Risk

ROGER BLOOD

INTRODUCTION

A radical shift in mortgage insurers' priorities, from an industry driven essentially by sales volume goals to one emphasizing control and quality, began slowly in 1984 and gained momentum throughout 1985. Responding to unprecedented claims levels and the first operating losses ever, owners of mortgage insurance (MI) firms and their chief executives began to demand that their organizations improve control over the risks being assumed.

Tighter underwriting policies were only the most visible change; the mandate to manage risk more effectively has brought pervasive alterations throughout most MIs. The precipitous drop in private MI market shares during 1986, however, will probably force MIs to deal with their risk-related challenges in a more strongly marketing-oriented context in the late 1980s.

This chapter focuses on several anticipated risk managment developments that will significantly affect how mortgage insurers relate to their customers. Among the issues and opportunities addressed are: MI underwriting of lenders; the pivotal role of risk sharing, or coinsurance; increased attention to regional underwriting, and even regional pricing; and the likely renewal of interest in automated processing and delegated underwriting.

A business is inevitably driven by its numbers. The dramatic change in mortgage insurance follows an equally dramatic jolt in the industry's most basic measures of performance.

MIs booked total losses of just $39 million in 1979; by 1982 losses had jumped over fivefold to $210 million, according to *Moody's*. The industry's loss ratio (losses booked as a percent of premiums earned) grew from 13 percent to a record high 60 percent during the same period. In 1982 alone, the loss ratio more than doubled from the previous year, triggering the industry's first underwriting loss—$40 million—versus a $70 million gain in 1981 and a $122 million gain in 1979. Both these totals and their causes strongly suggested that the industry needed a solution better than a strong dose of new business volume. The housing recovery and record new business volumes could not match the rampant increase in claims. By 1985, the industry loss ratio had redoubled to 120 percent, with total losses topping $1 billion. Operating losses (including EPIC) reached $480 million.

The industry's most sobering losses before 1983 were caused by a cyclical downturn in the mid-1970s that never drove loss ratios as high as 40 percent of earned premiums. Half a dozen years of accelerating inflation in home prices immediately following, plus the entry of several new competitors into the marketplace, made cautious underwriting increasingly hard to justify as the 1980s began. However, by 1983 the rapid rise in foreclosures signaled fundamental market changes, not just another cyclical housing recession.

Almost without exception, mortgage insurers were structured and conditioned to reward those who contributed most to a growing market share. Without actual experience factors to support intuition and judgment, all too often MI underwriting became a process of rationalization. Underwriters sometimes modified, but rarely refused to accept, the risk on loans whose viability depended on continued inflation. Most MIs recognized the dilemma in 1983. But individual companies could not take appropriate risk management actions without a basic change in lender and investor attitudes regarding loan quality, unless they were prepared to virtually stop writing new business. With underwriting rejects running 1 percent or less, the MI user had simply become too conditioned to doing business with totally accommodative carriers.

By mid 1986, MIs had completed the major revamping of their underwriting policies, and originators of insured loans had experienced, at least briefly, the first effects of these changes. MIs will continue to refine their policies while addressing a broad range of related risk management issues. In evaluating the MIs' actions and reactions in managing their risks, several questions must be asked. Have these actions been responsive to the new market forces that presented such massive risks to the MIs in recent years? Or has there been an overreaction to temporary or cyclical risks that have since changed or abated? Conversely, are some risks still inadequately addressed?

Further, has a proper balance been established between MI underwriting and risk management on the one hand, and marketing and service responsiveness on the other? Are we experiencing—or about to experience—a further swing of the pendulum, either to a more conservative extreme or back toward a more accommodating posture? What forces are operating to suggest or warrant further changes?

We can begin to address these questions by looking first at the current scope of risk management in mortgage insurance. Then, following a closer view of the underwriting actions and issues, we will examine several broader risk management concerns that are likely to affect the way MIs do business in the late 1980s.

THE GROWING SCOPE OF RISK MANAGEMENT

Risk falls into four broad categories:

1. Normal risks—a small percentage of mortgage loans that become delinquent and develop into claims as a result of individual borrower circumstances, such as divorce, illness, or unemployment.
2. Cyclical risks—Foreclosures concentrated in a region, or nationally, as a result of cyclical adverse economic conditions.
3. Catastrophic risks—A severe and extended drop in property values caused by economic depression regionally or nationwide.
4. Fraud—The emergence of significant default patterns caused by

deliberate misrepresentation of credit or property information necessary to conduct prudent underwriting. This risk is not intentionally covered by mortgage insurers, but it is often difficult to identify and avoid.

Risk management, as applied to mortgage insurance, has changed. Risk management is not to be confused with underwriting, although underwriting is its central component. When the term first emerged in the MI industry in the mid-1970s, *risk management* meant the application of claims experience and quality control post-underwriting audit findings to the formulation and implementation of current underwriting policies.

During the late 1970s, many MIs created risk management units encompassing the traditional claims and underwriting departments, including the quality control audit function. Interestingly, by the mid-1980s several leading MIs had separated the organizational marriage between underwriting and claims, no longer assigning overall responsibility for risk management to a single executive. This move reflects more the growing demands of claims as a major corporate function than any diminution of corporate attention to risk management.

Today's concept of mortgage insurance risk management is broader and more complex. Arguably, it includes the following functions:

1. Individual loan underwriting
2. Project approval
3. Lender evaluation, approval, and tracking
4. Regional market analysis
5. Underwriting policy development
6. Appraisal review (quality control)
7. Credit review (quality control)
8. Pricing
9. Insurance product design (the establishment of policy terms that define the assumption of liability)
10. Claims (loss) management, including fraud investigation and litigation and real estate owned (REO) management

11. Management of risk concentrations (geographic, lenders, servicers, projects, borrowers, insurance product lines)
12. Reinsurance
13. Incentive compensation as it affects business risk

On the basis of this broader-based concept of risk management, the "risk management officer" is—almost inevitably—the CEO!

Establishing an appropriate balance among these functions is critical. For example, to meet a threshold rate of return on investment, MIs face many choices—for example, raising prices, underwriting more stringently, offering the product in selected areas, or not offering it at all.

Viewing risk management as balancing or selecting different vehicles to achieve a desired profit margin, MIs could also develop a variety of ways to attack a problem such as fraud and misrepresentation. To date, the major response has been to tighten and enforce policy terms more strictly; to document underwriting better; to audit more; and to investigage and deny claims aggressively.

These actions are valid. However, the risk of fraud is perpetual; the need for protection against fraud will always exist. Standard & Poor's and Moody's are especially sensitive to this uninsured risk in rating mortgage-backed securities. MIs could decide to evelute this risk and cover (and charge a premium for) it separately.

Such an initiative could be accompanied by an activity typically associated with risk management in casualty insurance: client education. MIs could work with clients to establish fraud detection and prevention activities, perhaps turning one serious MI headache into a future market opportunity.

TIGHTER UNDERWRITING

Announced policy changes in how individual loans will be underwritten may be only the most visible aspect of the current MI underwriting transition. No less critical will be the continued strengthening of lender underwriting, as discussed later. MIs are increasingly relying on lenders to underwrite loans thoroughly and service them conscientiously. Therefore, insurers are likely to become more selective in establishing underwriting relationships with individual lenders. The system of lender warranties that underpins lenders' selling contracts with the FHLMC and FNMA appears to be setting a pattern for lender-insurer relationships as well.

The underwriting changes instituted during 1984–1986 have touched nearly the entire array of specific requirements covering individual borrower, property, and loan terms. The following areas, having been the subject of major rules changes, will continue to receive closer underwriting scrutiny:

1. 95 percent loan-to-value (LTV) ratio loans
2. Adjustable payment instruments
3. Cash equity and borrower liquidity
4. Seller contributions
5. Appraisals and appraisers
6. Cash out refinances
7. Nonowner-occupied properties
8. Self-employed borrowers

A recent shift in underwriting emphasis may continue into the late 1980s. While continuing the more traditional evaluation of borrowers' ability to repay their loans, more attention is being given to indicators of borrowers' *willingness* to repay. Many risk managers believe that borrower equity probably offers the best proxy for personal commitment. This helps explain the greater emphasis on such factors as appraisal quality, cash down payments, seller contributions, cash out refinances, and, of course, 95 LTV ratio loans.

REGIONALIZED UNDERWRITING

Insurance transfers risk from a single policyholder to an insurer who spreads risk through the law of large numbers. Theoretically, no single risk jeopardizes the insurer's viability, because its total financial exposure is spread among many diverse risks. Like casualty insurance, private mortgage insurance must be spread geographically. Housing market dynamics being far more regional than national, one of the mortgage insurer's primary functions is to protect policyholders from regional recessions, or even depressions.

From the Rust Belt to the Oil Patch, MIs have fulfilled this critical functional admirably. However, they have only recently begun to address how to anticipate and avoid excessive or unnecessary losses arising from regional downturns. What range of underwriting and other risk management actions are likely to be most effective in preserving profitability or minimizing losses at the regional level? What early indicators and other analytical techniques should be used to trigger appropriate management action? The most extreme option is to withdraw from and re-enter regional markets as cyclical conditions warrant. Past experience, however, suggests that mortgage insurers cannot stop accepting new business temporarily and then readily recapture terminated accounts as part of a strategy for managing regional risks. A more acceptable alternative recently pursued by many MIs is to close and consolidate regional underwriting offices. In 1984, the industry maintained about 225 service facilities nationally. By the end of 1986, fewer than 100 branch offices will be processing new business.

There are risk management considerations behind this trend, in addition to the obvious cost-cutting objectives. Closing an underwriting facility in a problem market area reduces the flow of new business. More important, perhaps, consolidation of field facilities helps to improve corporate controls over underwriting in terms of system management, personnel administration, and staffing quality and consistency. Some MIs discovered, upon intense examination of the causes of rapidly rising defaults in 1984–1985, that poor controls—poor implementation of established underwriting policies and procedures—might be causing as many losses as overly liberal guidelines.

The trend toward fewer regional offices operating with larger staff and tighter controls will probably continue. It may be complemented by a greater reliance on automated processing and delegated underwriting, as discussed later. Regional underwriters may spend more time with lenders, evaluating the quality of their operations and reviewing and auditing—often on-site—loans and projects already insured. Lenders who seek the best available MI products and services should prepare for, and welcome, more regular and substantial face-to-face interaction with MI underwriters and risk managers whose objective is greater reliance on the lender to control default risks.

For the first time in 1986, some MIs adopted major variations in underwriting policies and limits on a region-specific basis. Not surprisingly, the first important targets for regional restrictions were 95 percent ratio loans and condominiums. A logical defense against falling property values and eroding borrower equities is the reduction of maximim insurable LTV ratios. For example, in 1986 a 90 percent insurable LTV ratio was instituted by some MIs in problem housing markets, such as parts of Texas and Oklahoma. In some cases, MIs have correlated high defaults with the condominium segment of the market—or certain portions thereof, such as condo conversions of small projects. As a result, they have targeted condos for stricter underwriting limits in particular regions.

This important MI initiative is likely to expand considerably in the latter 1980s. It does complicate life somewhat for originators operating in multiple markets, not to mention the added complexity of administration. However, industrial and economic volatility and the risk of falling real property values throughout a metropolitan market or region may be greater today than at any other time during the postwar period. Consequently, most MIs believe they can no longer afford the luxury of a single set of national underwriting standards.

The need for timely adoption of appropriate regional underwriting criteria has spawned a renewed MI demand for the skills of professional appraisers. Such in-house expertise had become a casualty of the inflation of the late 1970s at many MI home offices. We can expect to see MIs not only recruiting more designated appraisers, but also taking earlier and more careful heed of their advice regarding metropolitan and regional housing market trends.

The MIs have only begun their efforts to base underwriting policies on regional economic forces. We can expect the industry to develop and use relevant regional and metropolitan area data to identify earlier, and to act upon, both adverse and favorable mortgage risk trends.

REGIONALIZED PRICING

In contrast to the general consensus on the need for more regionalized underwriting policies, there are very differing views on whether mortgage insurance premium rates should vary by state or region.

In theory, a geographic area that exhibits higher claims rates over time should be subject to higher premium rates to offset the added risk. Certainly other major forms of insurance have always varied their rates geographically. At least one major MI has concluded that this practice is warranted for mortgage insurance as well. It established higher premium rates for California and indicated that other state or regional rate *increases* or *decreases* may follow.

There is an interesting precedent to this voluntary pricing decision. About a decade ago, the state of Wyoming directed all MIs licensed in that state to reduce their rates substantially. The regulator's justification was that claims losses in Wyoming had been exceedingly low for many years, and that to charge Wyoming policyholders national rates was to make them pay for overbuilding in Sunbelt cities or for unemployment in Rust Belt states.

This argument may have sounded plausible at the time, especially to people accustomed to casualty insurance practices. But recent developments have also illustrated the main reason why most MIs have not implemented regionalized pricing. Following the energy crisis of the mid-1970s, the successive energy industry growth and depression has created classic "boom and bust" economic conditions in many energy-producing states, including Wyoming. Mortgage default rates in Wyoming have risen substantially above the national average.

The main argument against regional pricing variations stems from the unusually long "tail of risk" inherent in mortgage insurance. A policy, once written, cannot be canceled, not can the premium be changed, even though that risk may remain in force for 10 to 15 years or longer. Similarly, the complete cycle of risk in a regional market may take a generation or more to unfold. In the shorter run (up to a decade or more!), mortgage insurers do effectively cross-subsidize cyclical regional risks. A uniform national premium rate structure, combined with stiff regulatory requirements for building long-term contingency reserves from currently earned premiums, provides the needed cushion against a regional depression *anywhere*.

Another critical element of geographical risk variations *at the state-specific level* has received little attention. Both the severity and frequency of mortgage insurers' losses on claims probably have been adversely affected by certain features of state foreclosure laws.

An obvious example is the state laws mandating unusually long foreclosure and redemption periods. Insurers' standard policies make them liable for substantial interest and other time-related accruals, such as property taxes, insurance, and maintenance in the event of a foreclosure and claim. A 1975 Federal Home Loan Bank Board study of foreclosure costs in three states revealed that average foreclosure costs varied from a low of about 15 percent of the loan balance in the state with the most expeditious process, to a high of about 50 percent of the loan amount in the state with the longest foreclosure and redemption period. A long foreclosure process not only costs more, but also precludes the mortgage insurer from mitigating its losses by securing a third-party buyer for the property.

An even more pernicious feature in some foreclosure statutes is restrictions on personal recourse against the defaulting borrower. In California, for example, the lender who acquires title to a property through foreclosure waives its rights to pursue the borrower for a deficiency judgment—even if the borrowers misrepresented their credit standing to secure the loan. This type of contractual relationship between borrower and lender seems to engender borrower attitudes throughout an entire market that the personal cost of a mortgage default is minimal. Under moderately adverse personal circumstances—including a perception that stagnant property value may have eroded home equity—borrowers may be more inclined to walk away from their obligations with less fear of longer-term consequences.

These are examples of *noncyclical* causes of long-term incremental risks at the regional or state level. If a state, in the interest of consumerism, opts to retain very tough foreclosure laws, the insurers should be justified in covering these incremental claims costs from incremental premium rates in that state.

We may see some further regional pricing differentials. However, regionalized underwriting will probably be far more pervasive than regionalized pricing over the next few years.

AUTOMATED PROCESSING AND DELEGATED UNDERWRITING

Whether and how much a mortgage insurer should rely on computer processing and delegation of insurance underwriting authority to its lender-customers continues to be debated. It hinges on the more basic question of how risk management and underwriting should be balanced and blended with sales and marketing.

The mortgage insurance industry has been experimenting in this area for nearly a decade. Delegated underwriting and automated processing relegated to the actual underwriting function fell out of favor by the mid-1980s for obvious reasons. However, data-communications technology has been successful in the delivery of the insurance certificates *after* the underwriting decision has been made. For example, in 1986 one MI promoted three different versions of this type of service, including use of an on-line terminal or PC.

Before the recent flood of claims, industry management almost fully agreed that automated processing and delegated underwriting was essential for any company to remain competive. In the late 1970s, American Mortgage Insurance (now GEMIC) launched the industry's first delegated underwriting program. With the consent, if not the enthusiasm of FNMA and FHLMC, most other MIs followed suit. One insurer experimented with an automated underwriting and processing service known as "The Blue Box" that struck fear in competitors' hearts. It consisted of a microcomputer affixed on-site to the lender's mainframe processing unit that issued commitments based on an abbreviated underwriting matrix and then telecommunicated batch-processed data to the insurer's mainframe computer. Another MI marketed with some success a computer timesharing system, employing freestanding terminals on the lenders' premises that accessed an on-line underwriting matrix and produced immediate printed commitments.

Other efforts to capitalize on the constantly improving technology of facsimile transfer of documents were less successful. In fact, none of the computer-automated services offered by MIs fulfilled the hope—or fear—that they would replace the reviewing of individual loan packages by regional underwriting personnel. As instruments become more complex, risks increased, and regional office networks—complete with courier pickups and delivery—saturated the country, automated processing and delegated underwriting receded into the background.

Conditions may be ripe for renewed attention to automated processing and delegated underwriting, for several reasons:

1. Competition from FHA's Direct Endorsement program is strong and enduring. It could be years (if ever) before originator abuse would cause FHA to retrench in this area.
2. Cost pressures within the industry will cause MIs to seek ways of reducing unit production costs. High loss ratios have driven combined loss and expense ratios over 100 percent at most firms. As a result, expense ratios are receiving more attention. Following the lead of FNMA and FHLMC, the industry, in the face of continued high volumes, will probably seek the means of automating production, while controlling excessive risk.
3. The industry has begun to invest heavily in evaluating and tracking lender quality. As these skills become honed, MIs can create closer business relationships with selected clients that include forms of delegated underwriting and automated processing not yet fully developed. These relationships may also rest on innovative coinsurance arrangements, as discussed later in this chapter.
4. The advancement of FNMA and FHLMC into essentially electronic data communications relationships with volume customers may serve as a bellwether for the mortgage insurers. For example, the acquisition by FNMA of Financial Software, Inc., and the apparent strategic positioning of automated document prep-

aration, loan tracking and delivery, and loan servicing as part of FNMA's mainstream programs set the stage for greater MI involvement in these areas.

5. The market still wants the fastest service at the lowest possible cost. One of the few possible areas for improving is advances in delegated underwriting and automated processing. MI advertising in 1986 confirms this.

6. The increasing volume and share of the market involving mortgage-backed securities has been accompanied by closer relationships between MIs and their parent companies and major Wall Street firms. Inevitably, the immense state-of-the-art information-processing capabilities of these firms will further integrate the mortgage insuring function with the larger process of converting individual home mortgages into investment-grade securities (or, as someone once said, "turning frogs into princes").

Insuring, like purchasing loans, is essentially the generation of documents based on a structured flow of information—subject, of course, to a controlled environment; a strict, clear set of rules; and effective audits. Mortgage insurance managers, customers, and investors must become involved in, or at least stay well informed about, new developments in automated processing and delegated underwriting.

MANAGING RISK CONCENTRATIONS

MIs have traditionally viewed, and reported on, risk concentrations mostly in terms of geography. Freddie Mac's *Eligibility Requirements for Private Mortgage Insurers* restricts the degree of risk concentration an MI may have in a given state, metropolitan statistical area (MSA), or individual project complex. State regulations also restrict the amount of risk an MI may have in one project or in contiguous projects.

The EPIC debacle dramatized the fact that MI exposure to risk concentration embodied more dimensions than geographic. One longer-term effect will be the greater attention that MIs and regulators, rating agencies, and investors will devote to the control of adverse risk concentrations.

EPIC was essentially a *borrower* concentration, albeit a remarkably complex and hybrid form, that failed. While lender failure was a factor, it was the inability of limited partnership borrowers and their underlying real estate holdings to service the insured mortgage debt that caused the losses. Before EPIC, most MIs did not have information systems that were sophisticated enough to monitor and control borrower concentrations. This risk management technique is now becoming standard operating procedure for every MI.

MIs will also examine more closely their concentration of risk in *projects*. While project approval has traditionally been a part of the underwriting process for most MIs, the industry is now investing more resources in practical systems that track accumulations of business and risk experience at any given project location.

Adequate tracking of risk concentrations with individual *lenders* has become surprisingly complicated, yet necessary. The fluid state of the market in terms of lender mergers and acquistions, nationwide lending organizations, loan sales with and without release of servicing, and the role of third parties such as mortgage brokers, makes the task of defining insured lenders, let alone adequately understanding them, exceedingly difficult. Lenders can be defined in a variety of ways, including:

- An entire mortgage lending organization, including all branches, affiliates, subsidiaries, and regions
- An originating branch or a region with multiple branches
- An originating affiliate or subsidiary
- A servicing organization
- A mortgage investor
- A housing finance agency or MBS conduit
- An originating broker

MIs will continue to develop management information systems and operating policies that effectively define lender accounts, measure their profitability, and alert MI managers to potential problem lenders.

However, large concentrations of insured risk with a single lender—while necessary to track—are not as critical as risk concentrations with a single borrower or in a single local market or project complex. The reason is simple: If a large borrower, a project complex, or a local market with a heavy concentration of insurance risk fails, payments stop; the properties cannot be moved somewhere else, and the bad loans are not likely to be assumed without loss by another borrower.

By contrast, when a lending institution fails, which has been occurring with growing frequency, the *deposit insurer* is far more likely to suffer losses than the mortgage insurer. If the loans were well underwritten—that is, if properties and credits are sound—lender failure can be almost transparent to the insurer as the lender is merged or acquired, or the loan portfolio is assigned intact to another servicer.

For this reason, concentration of risk with a single *loan servicing* entity should warrant greater attention than concentration with a loan originator or investor. Servicer failure, whether the result of outside forces, poor management, or negligence, can present considerable risk to the unwary MI. Any breakdown in collections, foreclosures, or remittance procedures could create substantial risks for an insurer with thousands of policies under a single servicer. Furthermore, servicing concentrations are more likely to occur under mortgage-backed securities or tax-exempt housing finance programs where coverages are generally deepest and coinsurance is minimal. For this reason, I believe MIs will be monitoring servicer risk concentrations much more aggresively, including on-site audits of high-volume servicers.

A related challenge is underwriting the quality of the lender. MIs have made major strides in screening lender quality and reviewing lender performance. Armed with more reliable data on individual lender quality, MIs will be competing more keenly to establish relationships with the better quality lenders. Originators of higher-risk loan products, on the other hand, may encounter growing difficulties in securing mortgage insurance. Because imposing higher premium rates on high-risk producers tends to be difficult, MIs may be even more restrictive in terms of whom they will seek, or accept, business from.

Many insurers will focus on originating branches of approved lenders that are either new or the source of rapid volume increases, are remotely located from the lender's home office or regional headquarters, do not service loans, or rely on brokers for originations. Rapidly developing concentrations of inferior risk can emerge unexpectedly, even though the prevailing quality of loans from the lender itself is good. Quality rating of branches is more a facet of lender underwriting than a control of risk concentrations. Once a lender has proved itself by producing consistently high-quality product and demonstrating prudent policies and strong management controls, the question of accepting excessive concentrations of business may become almost moot.

We can also expect to see a much greater MI focus on the metropolitan statistical area (MSA, formerly SMSA). The state has always been a poor measure of geographical risk concentration, due to diversity of size and poor matching of state boundaries with individual housing markets. Until recently, however, suitable data were available and reported only at the state level (in part because insurance is state-regulated). Most insurers have now enhanced their information systems to report extensively at the MSA level. Improved management of geographic risk concentrations will be but one of many future benefits from new MSA-based information systems.

LOAN SERVICING AND CLAIMS MANAGEMENT

Several trends in the area of loan servicing and claims bear attention.

Continued stronger enforcement of policy terms relating to loan servicing and claims processing is likely. With the growing recognition that inadequate loan servicing can cause very great risk for MIs will come increased attention to who performs the servicing. In this regard, MIs will generally exercise more control over the transfer of servicing of insured loans. In fact, servicers are likely to be approved by MIs in much the same way as loan originators.

MIs will expect servicers to devote sufficient personal attention to collections and counseling of delinquent borrowers—that is, to invest more in curing delinquencies, even though the loan is insured against loss. Some MIs are instituting programs to assist servicers directly in dealing with delinquent borrowers. In this regard, most MIs will seek closer communications between servicing and claims units, including timely notice of defaults, foreclosures, and claims. Servicers who do not adhere to reasonable standards of timeliness on both notifications, and on the collections foreclosure process, may encounter more reduced claims settlements, if not outright denials.

We are likely to witness more and earlier collaboration between servicers and insurers regarding the early sale and disposition of foreclosed properties to halt unnecessary cost accruals and to mitigate losses to all parties. FNMA and FHLMC in the past may have seemed ambivalent about structuring working agreements with the MIs regarding servicers' handling of the property disposition aspect of claims. The trend will be to more standardized procedures and a greater cooperative effort to move distressed properties quickly to third parties.

Continuing to gain further acceptance will be the premise that originators of insured loans are responsible for all material information submitted to an MI for underwriting—even information from such third parties as borrowers, brokers, and appraisers. Probably more claims will be denied and even litigated because of misunderstanding or disagreement over this critical point.

MIs will continue to investigage extensively default situations that suggest the presence of fraud or misrepresentation. Discussion continues within the industry regarding the potential benefits and risks of developing an information bank on so-called bad actors, such as exists in the medical malpractice field. However, no dramatic developments are likely to occur soon in this area.

For MIs, loss management—managing delinquent loans, claims, and real estate—can have as much impact on the bottom line as does underwriting.

COINSURANCE: POSSIBLE MARRIAGE OF MARKETING AND RISK MANAGEMENT?

Private mortgage insurance was founded on the principle of coinsurance, or risk-sharing, with the insured lender. Insuring the top 20 to 25 percent of a high-ratio loan caused most lenders to be prudent in their underwriting and *servicing* of insured loans. The beneficial results were twofold: (1) faster insurance service because the MI could rely on the lender's underwriting; and (2) lower premium rates attributable to a more efficient insuring operation.

Various market forces, mainly related to the growth of secondary marketing and mortgage-backed securities, have eroded the coinsurance feature of the MI product. Typical of this trend has been the advent and growth of pool insurance and 100 percent coverage. Meanwhile, 24-hour service and reliance on lender underwriting has not changed—nor will the market permit it to change—despite the enormous rise in claims. MIs have, to date, pursued alternative avenues—such as sharply higher premiums, tougher underwriting rules, and stricter policy terms. I believe that a major risk management and market opportunity for MIs and their customers will be coinsurance and performance-based pricing.

Market developments in the mid-1980s constricted the private MIs' market share. MI premium rate increases between 1984 and 1986 averaged 50 to 100 percent. The FHA's Direct Endorsement (delegated underwriting) program for the first time is generating serious service competition from the government sector of the business. As a result, private insurers are likely to encounter growing market pressure to offer better service at a lower cost.

Further, government insurance is not the only alternative in a market that now widely perceives private mortgage insurance to be both expensive and difficult to secure. For example, the highly rated Home Savings MBS offering in 1985 embodies a form of self-insurance by means of a subordinated participating retention.

Just as alternative competitively priced sources of energy began to appear when the price of oil skyrocketed, so too can alternative forms of financial guarantees emerge, if a window of opportunity opens. No matter that current MI premium rates can be actuarially justified by recent losses; if market alternatives can be structured with less risk and lower costs, they will be. In fact, the highest-quality originators and servicers of insured mortgages are most likely to judge today's MI product as too expensive and inflexible and, therefore, to design alternative sources of ratable coverage.

A critical challenge and opportunity for MIs will be to retain their highest quality lender clientele by offering innovative, cost-effective, and quality-sensitive insurance programs.

How? Reinstituting risk-sharing in forms suitable to today's (and tomorrow's) market environment can help dramatically to improve relations between insurer and insured. Properly done, such actions will create incentives for users to write insured buiness that produces fewer claims. It follows that those lenders who are willing *and able* to produce quality loans and to share the (reduced) risks should be able to secure mortgage insurance at a lower cost. Soundly implemented, such a plan would produce several benefits, including acceptable MI profit margins with lower probability of severe variances, and greater business volumes. From the lender' standpoint, participation in a coinsurance program in a secondary marketing or MBS context would require *both* superior loan underwriting and servicing units and substantial financial capacity to credibly support retention of risk. The lender's superior capabilities would be rewarded in its lower cost to produce an investment-quality product.

Coinsurance and performance-based pricing may be to mortgage insurance in the late 1980s what the advent of conventional mortgage-backed securities was to mortgage lending in the late 1970s. The frequency and seriousness of discussion about the feasibility—and the inevitability—of a conventional mortgage-backed security grew noticeably in the mid-1970s. Then in 1977, with little advance publicity, Bank of America and MGIC overcame the final obstacles to issuing a rated conventional mortgage pass-through security with the invention of pool insurance. Many other successful issues soon followed. Without the creative participation of a private insurer to meet the need, chances are that Bank of America—or others—would have launched the conventional MBS era without mortgage insurance.

A similar scenario may be developing now. Mortgage insurers can use their expensively acquired risk management knowledge and ability to develop a highly risk-sensitive product line for their best customers—or their best customers may very will find another way to get the job done. Creative coinsurance can provide the critical link.

INCENTIVE COMPENSATION AS A RISK MANAGEMENT TOOL

This discussion of risk management trends and prospects has focused almost entirely on external MI actions that directly affect the customer. Organizational issues—that is, internal actions—can also significantly affect an MI's management of risk. Perhaps the most potent is the application of financial incentives effectively geared to achieve corporate risk management goals.

By the late 1970s, sales-driven MIs had become highly adept at designing tantalizing carrots to spur new business production. Only recently have some carriers begun to explore seriously the potential of incentive compensation as a risk management tool. Early experiments seem to produce positive results. Quality incentives have been structured for a wide range of responsibilities, including sales management, direct sales, underwriting, claims, and of course senior management.

Quality-directed incentive schemes have included the following diverse features:

1. Profit sharing for regional managers, based on various definitions of an operating profit—including claims losses.
2. Differential sales commission rates, depending on the risk rating of various lines of business produced—for example, a lower commission rate on 95s than on 90s.
3. Incentives geared to attracting specially targeted customers.
4. An offset to new production incentives based on the level of early default activity.
5. Underwriter performance awards for successfully combining productivity with quality results.
6. Incentives for MI field personnel to help cure delinquencies by working with lenders and borrowers.

7. Incentive bonuses to claims personnel for mitigating loss by negotiating third-party sales.

In short, emerging quality- and profit-based compensation plans may exert as much influence on MI customer relationships as do new production incentives. Such plans can cross many department lines, even altering the direction of the direct sales function.

Incentive bonus and commission structures may seem an unusual domain for a risk manager. However, risk managers with a good base of experience factors and a sense of the relationships between loan quality and profitability can contribute much to improved profit performance by helping to establish strong, quality-based incentives.

CONCLUSION

Risk management actions during the latter half of the 1980s may be more subject than in the recent past to marketing considerations. Market share, both as a company and an industry yardstick, is no longer the paramount measure it once was. But the rapidly falling share of privately insured loans as a share of total residential originations is, in the mid-1980s, a very real issue. Industry market penetration for the entire 1973–1983 decade fell within a range of 13 to 21 percent. After peaking at 33 percent in 1984, it fell to 20 percent in 1985. The steep slide in industry penetration continued through the first half of 1986, dropping to an estimated 11 percent, the lowest share since 1971.

This dramatic decline results from many factors, including such external and temporary market forces as the recent massive wave of refinancings. However, at least some of the shrinkage is attributable to market perceptions that mortgage insurance has become difficult to secure, because of tough and sometimes inflexible underwriting, and expensive, following several rounds of price increases. Few would argue about the wisdom of today's specific underwriting policies or premiums rate levels; but there are indications that government insurance, and to a small but growing degree, self-insurance, is siphoning off a meaningful volume of loans that MIs would like to underwrite.

Therefore, at least some risk management initiatives are likely to be directed toward the recovery of good business, rather than just the elimination of higher risk business. As a result, the job may become even more complex, but in a positive sense.

In summary, the MIs will become more sophisticated in selecting—or in a growing number of cases, creating—insurable risks. Several significant developments are likely to emerge or continue:

- While continuing to refine underwriting policies at a national level, calibration of underwriting limits is more likely to be concentrated at the regional and metropolitan level, based on more effective definitions of leading housing market indicators.
- Improved information systems will be used to better measure, audit, and control MI operations, especially functions that entail risk assumption. Improved and timely recognition and control of emerging adverse risk concentrations should be one major benefit from these initiatives.
- Considerable additional research into the structural causes of regional risk differentials is likely. Some further experimentation with regional pricing, if and where warranted, may be one result of such research.
- Further research and development in the area of automated policy generation and delegated underwriting appears likely. This could include significant new operating relationships with various third-party users of MI. Competitive forces, both within the industry and between the private and government sectors, could cause such activity to gain momentum, despite reservations by some risk managers.
- Greater attention to the MI claims function is probable—not so much in the direct processing of claims as in the effort to induce more effective loan servicing by the insured. The main objective: avoidance of unnecessary claims by curing more delinquencies, and the mitigation of unnecessary losses through the expeditious resale of foreclosed properties. In addition, we should see stepped up efforts to contain losses involving fraud. Initiatives may in-

clude more in-house and professional investigations leading to claims denial and negotiation. They may lead as well to the possible development of "recovery units" that pursue various other parties to the loan for recovery after payment of the claim to the lender.

- Experimentation with different organizational approaches to the overall risk management function should continue. For example, to achieve quicker and more effective use of risk and market data, some nontraditional positioning of the data processing function within the overall organization may occur. Also, more MIs may adopt a variety of creative incentive plans designed to foster a greater commitment to loan quality and profitability, both in sales and throughout the organization.

- Coinsurance promises to be one of the most attractive MI opportunities. Conditions appear ripe for intensive MI efforts in development viable risk-sharing programs. Whether the coinsurance takes the form of deductibles, retrocession of risk, performance-based pricing, or some other innovation or combination is not known. But the risk-sharing concept has been proved in other forms of insurance, and it seems to contain the basic ingredients needed to solve many of the current risk marketing issues facing MIs today.

The MI industry seems to be at a turning point. After half a dozen years of successively higher claims and poorer financial results, some modest improvement seems to be in store in 1986 and 1987—but probably not enough improvement to produce an underwriting profit.

The industry as a whole has retained its financial credibility. Most elements of redirection in risk management have begun; the next stage is one of implementation. Less well defined, ironically, but equally in need of clear new directions, may be the marketing arm of the business. More than ever before, the marketing of mortgage insurance will be shaped by its inevitable—and one hopes permanent—partnership with risk management.

Chapter 30

C. Earl Corkett

C. Earl Corkett is Chairman and CEO of The PMI Group of Companies. Previously he was Vice President and Treasurer of Budget Industries. Mr. Corkett received his B.S. from Oregon State University and is a graduate of Harvard's Advanced Management Program.

Breaking with Tradition: New Mortgage Insurance Products for a Changing Environment

C. EARL CORKETT

INTRODUCTION

Private mortgage insurance is a changing industry in a changing environment. The last decade has seen an important transition. During much of the 1970s, the industry's primary function was risk-sharing with portfolio lenders; in today's market it is best characterized as credit enhancement aimed at facilitating secondary market transactions. Risk is still being shared, but now the investor in the mortgage is typically someone different from the originating lender. Thus, mortgage insurers, through the evaluation and sharing of risk, help solve an information problem that might otherwise create a barrier to the flow of new capital into the mortgage market.

The social role of the industry, however, remains largely the same: making home ownership available to hundreds of thousands of American households who might not otherwise qualify for a conventional mortgage. As of mid-1986, over three million families had mortgages that were covered by private mortgage insurance.

The private mortgage insurance industry and the secondary mortgage market have grown up together, the growth of each nurturing the development of the other. Over the last several years the annual volume of private mortgage insurance has been three to four times as large as the level of the early 1970s. This directly parallels the growth of secondary market activity.

This era of growth has also been one of enormous environmental and economic changes. The eighties began with an explosion of new, untested mortgage instruments that saw lenders, borrowers, investors, and insurers searching for common ground in the design of these instruments. New loan types were only a part of the impact of financial deregulation, which saw the rules of the game in real estate and mortgage markets change dramatically. These structural changes occurred simultaneously with some of the widest swings in interest rates and inflation in the history of the U.S. economy. Between 1980 and 1986, mortgage rates went from 10 percent to 15 percent and back again, while inflation rose to double digits before falling to its lowest levels since the early 1970s. Perhaps most important, home appreciation, which rolled along at double-digit rates for most of the 1970s, slowed dramatically in the 1980s. As a result, the housing market has experienced the most severe dislocations since the Great Depression, with significant declines in value in a number of major markets.

One consequence of these changes has been the enormous increase in mortgage defaults and mortgage insurance claims. In 1985, for the first time in its history, the mortgage insurance industry operated at a net loss. During the early to mid-1980s, the industry experienced loss ratios four to five times higher than those during much of the 1970s. We have seen, for the first time, a major company in the industry forced into conservatorship. And, in a related event, we witnessed the default on a set of widely held mortgage-backed securities as the EPIC syndications unravelled.

The mortgage insurance industry has responded to these challenges in several ways. The first response I would characterize as a gradual transition from an industry that perceived itself as primarily in the financial services busienss to an industry that now understands (at least in most quarters) that its business is insurance, and that our pricing, underwriting, and claims procedures must be expanded and adapted to that role. Secondly, the industry and its clients have learned clearly that each mortgage insurer's most important asset is its financial strength, and each company must run its operations with the primary aim of preserving the integrity of its long-run financial position. This is critical if we are to ensure the continued flow of capital into the industry necessary to meet the demands of the market. Finally, we are learning that innovation is essential. The old ways do not meet the new needs. New ideas—in products, services, programs and technology—will be the foundation of the industry's future.

UNDERSTANDING RISK IN TODAY'S MARKETPLACE

Like much else about the real estate and mortgage markets of the 1960s and 1970s, the concept of mortgage insurance risk was less complex than in today's market. The 30-year, fixed-rate loan had dominated the market for decades, and actuarial studies of historical data seemed to provide a reasonable guide to the probable incidence of default. Loan-to-value (LTV) ratios were typically the only way in which loans were distinguished from one another for the purposes of risk classification and pricing. In underwriting, the focus was almost exclusively on the borrower's ability to pay. Credit and employment histories, along with debt-to-income ratios, were viewed as the key indicators of risk. Unemployment and divorce—the two forces creating the greatest change in a family's financial position—were thought to be the primary causes of mortgage delinquencies. The broad, persistent increase in home prices, together with what was viewed as a strong social stigma attached to default, meant that willingness to pay had not yet surfaced at the key determinant of mortgage default.

As we entered the late 1980s, our conception of risk was remarkably different. At some large insurers today, risk classification and pricing by loan type, property state or region, and lender are all now essential parts of operations. They serve to ensure that managers are appropriately matching premiums to risk and enable them to maximize the service we provide to our client base.

In 1984 PMI expanded its rate structure to allow for pricing by type of loan instrument. We did this based on data that had already begun to show that most of the alternatives to the fixed-rate, fixed-payment mortgage carried a substantially higher risk of borrower default. In addition, we had the commonsense view that loans with negative amortization built in, designed to be effective instruments when property appreciation is high, carry an enormous risk potential if the anticipated appreciation does not materialize. And as we looked at the large buy-down features of the instruments that were being used to qualify those borrowers who could not afford the first year payments on a 14 or 15 percent mortgage, we saw that trouble was in the offing if the real economic value of a property was being muddied with the value of discount financing.

The data available in 1986 strongly supported the necessity for categorizing risk by type of loan instrument. For example, according to a study of industry statistics compiled by Moody's, ARMs that permit negative amortization are almost five times as likely to default than fixed-rate, fixed-payment loans.

PMI is also be strongly committed to the analysis and pricing of risk based upon property state or region. For decades, the mortgage insurance industry operated, with only minor exceptions, with a uniform schedule of national prices. The story typically used to justify this practice had two parts:

1. All regions experience economic cycles, so that while at any moment losses would be higher in some places than others, in the long run loss ratios would be about the same everywhere.
2. Even if losses are different among regions, the differences are impossible to predict and, therefore, to price.

These two statements are best characterized as myths that have outlived their usefulness. All regions *do* experience economic cycles, but the frequency and amplitude—that is, how often and how severe— differ greatly by region. Since the upside benefit to mortgage insurers is limited (you can't do any better than 0 percent defaults), the main concern is with the potential severity of the downside of the cycle. Here regions differ *dramatically*, and in ways readily projectible into the future, including the diversity of the regional economic base, the role of local governments in regulating growth and development, and the past performance of the construction and lending industries.

In 1985, PMI instituted a systematic policy of pricing on a state or regional basis consistent with the risk analysis associated with each individual market. Acknowledging the differences in risk among regions means simply that the firm is not asking borrowers and lenders in low-risk areas to subsidize the risks being taken on in other parts of the country. The analysis of geographic risks has a long history in a variety of insurance lines, and while firms like PMI are leading the way, its incorporation into mortgage insurance is inevitable.

The analysis of risk by loan type and property region bring the borrower's willingness to pay to the forefront of the discussion. Sound mortgage financing must allow borrowers to develop and maintain a substantial net equity position in their home. For decades a majority of American households have used their mortgage payments as their primary vehicle for savings, and this has been one of the key motivations for owning rather than renting. When after several years of payments, a borrower discovers that the savings is illusory, the results are often foreclosure and an added bit of tarnish to the American dream. How do we act to minimize these occurrences? We cannot guarantee homeowners that there will be property appreciation. But we can:

- Encourage the use of mortgage instruments that allow for a faster repayment of principal
- Insist that appraised values reflect the real economic value of the housing services being provided, not the value of discouinted financing or anticipated appreciation
- Avoid responding to a small increase in market demand with a glut of overbuilding that plants the seeds of value deflation.

In a perfect world, we might do all of these at all times. In our imperfect world, we must at least acknowledge the additional risks that are created when we do not.

In 1986 PMI instituted what is perhaps its most decisive break with the pricing and risk analysis traditions of the industry: a Performance Incentive Program designed to provide lower premiums for lenders who have a history of providing us with quality business.

This program begins to make explicit what are really some fundamental issues of risk for our industry. For one, the *lender* is the insured party in mortgage insurance. It is only natural that the characteristics of the insured, insofar as they are relevant, should be taken into account in pricing the product. And there are many relevant issues here. For one, lenders differ in their cost of doing business. For those lenders where we need to underwrite two loans in order to write one policy because such a large portion of the applications do not meet our guidelines, the cost of business begins to skyrocket. Even more important, differences in deliquency and claim rates among lenders are not accidental. Often, the quality of the servicing that a lender provides is a key determinant of whether a loan remains current. And, most significantly, the lender who underwrites its business carefully before submitting it for insurance is likely to have the best performing business. Mortgage insurance underwriting, done at a distance, was always meant to serve as a second look at the loan package. And what we do can never replace the opportunity that the lender has for personal communication with the potential borrower. In all these ways, lender behavior is a key determinant of cost and risk. Pricing based on lender performance is therefore simply another natural extension of basic insurance principles.

PRODUCT AND SERVICE INNOVATION

The Performance Incentive Program demonstrates PMI's willingness to lower prices were appropriate; it is, therefore, the best example of how risk-based pricing benefits lenders. The program offers initial premium discounts of 10 percent or 20 percent based on PMI's experience with insured loans originated by a lender and all of the lender's affiliates within a specific state. Once qualified for a discount within a particular state, a lender remains qualified for a year. Re-evaluation of a lender's business occurs annually. A lender who qualifies for continued eligibility is again eligible for the discount for an entire year. To ensure that lenders are aware of their performance and the likelihood of requalifying, the firm sends monthly status reports to all program participants. This gives lenders the ability to monitor the status of their loans insured with PMI.

With the Performance Incentive Program, lenders who qualify can offer their borrowers lower mortgage insurance premiums. Risk-based pricing benefits the lenders by providing them with a competitive edge in their marketplace.

A mortgage insurer cannot base product changes solely on risk considerations. To be successful, mortgage insurers must offer products and services that reflect the changing needs of their clients. Recent innovations from my firm that will benefit residential mortgage lenders include three programs: Accelerater Coverage, SHARP, and the Timesaver Series. All were designed to meet specific needs in the marketplace. Accelerater Coverage is targeted to a very specific customer: the portfolio lender who has considered foregoing mortgage insurance coverage. Under this program, the amount of mortgage insurance coverage starts below standard levels and rises annually until standard levels are reached in either the third or fourth year. For instance, rather than beginning with the standard coverage of 20 percent on a loan with a 90 percent loan-to-value ratio, the Accelerater 90–10–15–20 plan provides 10 percent initial coverage. Coverage then increases annually, as long as payments on the loan are current, until the standard level of 20 percent coverage is reached in the third and subsequent years.

Lenders for whom this coverage was developed are confident that the quality of their underwriting and appraisals protect them from foreclosure losses. This confidence, coupled with their wish to avoid higher mortgage insurance premiums, has tempted some portfolio lenders to bear the entire risk of low-downpayment, high-ratio loans. There are several problems with this approach, however, which Accelerater Coverage overcomes. First, quality underwriting and appraisal practices do limit the risk of default, particularly in a loan's early years. No amount of careful analysis however, can fully account for unforeseen future events such as divorce, recession, unemployment, and decreasing property values, particulary when any of them is coupled with the behavior of today's alternative mortgage instruments, such as ARMs.

Mortgage insurance exists to protect against these future risks and to provide risk diversification should an insured's market suffer from an economic downturn. It is really catastrophe insurance, and the Accelertor is the ultimate form of catastrophe insurance. It offers coverage congruent with risk. With Accelerater, lenders who feel that their risk of default is limited by their loan origination standards and who don't need standard coverage for secondary sales, can save on their initial mortgage insurance premium and still have deeper coverage when they really need it, in the unknown future.

A second potential problem for the portfolio lender who wants to forego mortgage insurance is also handled by the Accelerater. In today's market it is an unusual lender who never sells loans. Many portfolio lenders will sell seasoned loans from their portfolio when market conditions and asset management considerations make such a sale attractive. Buyers usually require mortgage insurance—even on seasoned loans—when the LTV ratio exceeds 80 percent. Given this requirement, the seller with uninsured loans must limit the loans sold to loans with lower LTVs or must obtain mortgage insurance on a number of loans within a short time frame. Obtaining this mortgage insurance coverage could be complicated by changes in underwriting guidelines that may have occurred after the loans were originated. With the Accelerater, this complication is avoided. Even if coverage has not yet reached standard levels, conversion to a standard level is available through the Instant Acceleration feature.

The Accelerater was introduced in response to the need of a segment of the market. More important, perhaps, are the new services that have been developed for the firm's existing client base. Entering the 1980s the national foreclosure rate for conventional loans published by the Mortgage Bankers' Association of American was .07 percent with a total conventional delinquency ratio of 2.66 percent. In the fourth quarter of 1985, the foreclosure rate was .16 percent and the percent of loans with payments past due had reached 4.10 percent. In some states, particularly those with heavy oil industry involvement, these rates were much higher. In Oklahoma and Texas, for instance, the foreclosure rates at the end of '85 were .52 percent and .45 percent, respectively.

Certainly, a high foreclosure level does not benefit mortgage insurers. Just as certainly, the negative impact is not confined to our industry. It affects everyone—the borrower, the servicing lender, the investor, and, ultimately the community. That is why new approaches to the default problem, such as PMI's Saving Homeownership and Repayment Program (SHARP) program, have been developed. Through SHARP, PMI works with lenders and borrowers to prevent foreclosures. The program is targeted at homeowners who, although delinquent, have the ability to maintain future payments on a loan. Where a loan modification or a refinance will enable a borrower to handle future mortgage payments, PMI works with the lender and the borrower to make it happen. PMI may assist by making the delinquent payments or paying back interest and refinance fees.

In cases where borrowers must sell their home but find the market value of the homes is less than the amount owed plus the selling costs, PMI works with the borrowers to provide the funds to enable a sale to take place. The borrower's credit history is saved from the stigma of a foreclosure, the investor is saved from a possible loss, and the servicing lender from the time and expense involved in handling a foreclosure. And, of course, PMI is able to mitigage a loss and conserve capital. Today, lenders should look to mortgage insurers to provide more than a claim check. The value of mortgage insurance can and should be measured in more than claims dollars.

The level and quality of service provided is not only important on the claim end. The record number of loan originations in 1986 emphasized the need for mortgage insurers to simplify the mortgage insurance process whenever possible. This was the genesis of the Timesaver Series of programs, introduced in 1986 with the Rapid-Refi, Instant Modification, and Alternative Documentation Programs.

In essence, these programs embody a commonsense approach to obtaining mortgage insurance coverage. They reduce the time and paperwork involved without sacrificing the quality underwriting that we have all learned is vital. In fact, PMI's Timesaver Series is based on a belief that by simplifying the mortgage insurance process, lenders can concentrate on the most important aspect of lending—the actual evaluation of risk.

In the long run, computers probably offer the greatest opportunity to increase processing efficiency. Another Timesaver introduction in 1986, the Electronic Delivery Program, or EDP, uses the Mortgage Bankers' Association's Echo I communication network to electronically transmit mortgage insurance certificates. The EDP allows lenders to receive insurance certificates in minutes, enabling them to complete their file the same day they receive mortgage insurance approval.

Automating processes to increase efficiency is not only applicable to loan origination. Servicing lenders are only too aware of the time and effort that it can take to process mortgage insurance renewal premiums and cancellation requests and comply with delinquency reporting requirements. To help in servicing, my firm offers computerized tape-to-tape renewal billings in lieu of paper renewal billings; in 1986 PMI significantly expanded the number of customers using this service. Also in 1986, PMI developed computerized delinquency reporting through two major service bureaus. In the years ahead, this service will be expanded to other lenders.

Perhaps as important as the development of automated delinquency reporting is the hoped for by-product of this effort. In response to lenders' complaints about the different reporting requirements within the mortgage insurance industry, mortgage insurers are joining in the effort to automate delinquency reporting. Customers cannot fully capitalize on the efficiencies of computerization unless insurers achieve a degree of standardization.

LOOKING TOWARD THE FUTURE

The recent changes within the mortgage insurance industry have set the stage for the late 1980s and beyond. The lending community has recognized that we are indeed insurers and will judge us as such.

Financial strength will not decline in importance, nor will the need to manage risk.

Leading insurers will continue to tailor their prices and guidelines to reflect the actual risk insured. Implict in this approach is a commitment to the ongoing analysis of loan characteristics, markets, and lenders. This analysis will serve as an early warning system, alerting insurers to potential problems before they occur. The results will no doubt lead to future adjustments in pricing and underwriting guidelines, but the magnitude of these changes should be less than what we have experienced in the mid-1980s. Lenders are now positioned to proactively adapt to change before it causes severe dislocations.

Lenders who have a record of originating high-quality loans and providing effective loan servicing will continue to benefit from their expertise. Their borrowers will not only benefit from lower mortgage insurance premiums but from more efficient processing of their loans. Increased computerization of the loan origination and mortgage insurance processes will eliminate many of the delays that are common today. Such efficiencies as the computerized exchange of underwriting data will be just one of the services provided for the quality lender.

Competition and cost control measures within the residential lending industry will translate into a continued emphasis on increased efficiency in all aspects of lending, including mortgage insurance. This in turn will lead to future product innovations and an increased dependence on technology.

As important as technology will be in the future, it will not and cannot replace the people who provide the mortgage insurance products and services. Mortgage insurers will be even more dependent on knowledgeable, experienced professionals to ensure that they can respond rapidly to the needs of their client base. Whether we are working to keep homeowners in their properties or are developing mortgage insurance coverage for a new form of mortgage security, a mortgage insurer's human resources are as important as financial strength. The lender of the future will recognize that importance and demand high levels of services, support, and innovation from their mortgage insurer.

The changes of the 1980s have indeed affected the mortgage insurance industry. Given the high level of claims over the last few years, the impact has now always seemed positive. As the industry faces the future, however, it does so with a new health and vigor. Lenders who have created the challenges of the '80's as opportunities are better able to meet the future needs of mortgage customers.

Chapter 31

WILLIAM H. LACY

William H. Lacy is the President and Chief Executive Officer of Mortgage Guaranty Insurance Corporation. He is also Executive Vice President and Chief Operating Officer of MGIC Investment Corporation.

Lacy joined MGIC in 1971 and held several sales and marketing positions with the company before being named President in 1982. He was named Chief Executive Officer in March 1985.

Lacy attended the Air Force Academy and is a graduate of the University of Wisconsin.

Attention to Primary Market Risk Management Helps Strengthen Secondary Market Performance and Potential

WILLIAM H. LACY

From the perspective of private mortgage insurers, risk management is the keynote of the 1980s, whether you're involved in the primary mortgage market, the secondary market, or both. It's the ability to manage risk successfully that's going to separate the winners from the losers in the complex, competitive mortgage industry.,

The emphasis on risk management is one that's been growing in scope and in intensity, particularly since 1984. So it's not really a new story. But it is an important one, and my MGIC believes it's worth stressing. Each player with a stake in the game—borrower, lender, investor, insurer—benefits when risk management becomes the name of the game.

THE NEW ENVIRONMENT

The lending climate of the 1980s has proven to be more risky than any other period in recent history. High interest rates and deregulation

589

during the decade spurred the development of new mortgage instruments and creative financing techniques whose effects are just now becoming clear. And while high interest rates were less of an issue in 1986, low housing appreciation continued to adversely affect borrowers and lenders across the country.

MGIC is ready to insure mortgage lenders against the risk of borrower default, especially during this period of increased risk. But, to prevent an inordinate exposure to risk as we move into the late 1980s, we are focusing on three important areas of underwriting concern:

- Local market conditions
- Individual loan features
- Lender quality control

In this chapter I want to share with you the experience and knowledge MGIC has gained through managing a well-diversified $77 billion book of business. By examining MGIC's experience as it relates to the three underwriting areas, you can gain a clearer understanding of a large insurer's underwriting direction, use the same information to evaluate and refine your own underwriting guidelines and risk management philosophy, and become a more knowledgeable buyer and seller of loans in the secondary market.

THE 1970s VS. THE 1980s

There has been a definite shift toward instruments and loan-to-value (LTV) ratios that represent a much higher risk of default. According to Moody's Investors Service, adjustable-rate mortgages (ARMs) and graduated-payment mortgages (GPMs) accounted for less that 1 percent of the mortgage insurance written in 1979, compared to 1983's 30 percent share. And by 1986 loans with LTVs greater than 90 percent had grown to represent about 40 percent of the mortgage insurance in force.

The presence of more high-risk mortgage instruments and more high-risk credit situations is further complicated by a general lack of housing appreciation. This is an important contrast to the 1970s when 10 percent annual property appreciation provided ample opportunity for homeowners to sell their properties and pay off their loans rather than permit foreclosure. Even when foreclosure did occur, the high appreciation of the 1970s protected lenders and mortgage insurers from excessive losses. That protection simply no longer exists in most areas of the country, and we cannot depend on it to continue indefinitely in those few areas that enjoy strong appreciation today.

These three factors—a shift toward more risky loan programs, a shift toward higher LTVs, and lack of housing appreciation—have pushed many insurers' claims incidence in the 1980s to three times that of the late 1970s.

PROFITABILITY: THE KEY TO FUTURE CAPACITY

Premium income can only tolerate a certain level of claims, and current premium tolerances are such that an increased claims incidence of just 1 or 2 loans per 100 would mean the difference between profit and loss. Without profits, mortgage insurers can neither generate earnings to add to capital surplus nor attract the outside capital that is necessary to provide new insurance capacity. Clearly, the future of conventional high-ratio lending depends on the profitability of the mortgage insurance industry.

As of 1986, MGIC has the capacity to write over $20 billion in new insurance, and by maintaining profitability, generate sufficient earnings to write more than $70 billion in new insurance over the next five years. To ensure our ability to generate future capacity, MGIC continues to evaluate risk in relation to premiums and to identify and control those risk factors that lead to excessive defaults and claims.

LOCAL MARKET CONDITIONS

At any one time, certain areas of the country represent a greater mortgage insurance risk than others. However, some areas that were once risky improve, and vice versa. The level of "local market risk" has a high potential for change over the life of a mortgage.

Unlike other types of insurers, mortgage insurers are unable to adjust premiums or cancel coverage on existing policies to compensate for changes in local market conditions. Therefore, the only prudent way to distribute credit risk over time and over geography is to base premiums on national loss experience and general economic conditions.

Even though local markets have a good chance of recovering over a period of years, it would be dangerous to knowingly originate and insure marginal loans during such local market downturns. So to protect borrowers, lenders, potential investors, and ourselves from an inordinate exposure to risk, my firm considers local market conditions when it makes underwriting decisions and from time to time establishes special, temporary underwriting guidelines for specific markets.

Oversupply of housing and single-industry economies are two common local market conditions that are of concern.

Declining property values and subsequent equity erosion are the major problems that occur when housing supply greatly exceeds housing demand. The southern Florida condominium market, which experienced 40 percent price reductions in many projects, provides a powerful example of how overspeculation and overbuilding can affect market values. But the situation need not be that severe to significantly increase the risk of foreclosure.

The borrower in Table 31–1 experiences only a 3 percent annual decline in market value over two years, largely due to discounted prices on builder spec homes in his subdivision. If he is forced into a selling situation at this point for whatever reason (divorce, interruption of income, or job transfer), two scenarios present themselves: he can allow foreclosure and lose his $5,000 equity, or he can sell the property at the current market price and lose $12,700 (lost equity plus selling costs).

Many borrowers are unable to obtain the several thousand dollars needed to settle a loan under these circumstances. Other borrowers may have the means to settle the loan but are unwilling to do so. In either case, the probability of foreclosure is much higher in markets where oversupply of housing threatens property value.

Table 31–1

1983 purchase price:	$ 100,000
1983 mortgage amount:	$ 95,000
1985 market price:	$ 94,090
Less brokerage fee and closing costs(8%):	$ (7,527)
	$ 86,563
Less 1985 mortgage amount (12% 30-year fixed):	$ (94,267)
Net sales proceeds:	$ (7,704)

Also a concern are cities or regions whose economies depend on a single employer or a single industry. Consider Oklahoma City and Detroit. In 1981 and 1982 the American auto industry experienced huge layoffs, sending Detroit's unemployement and default rates skyrocketing. At the same time, Oklahoma City's oil-related economy boomed, and its default rate was extremely low. Today, less than five years later, the two markets have experienced significant changes.

In areas currently experiencing economic problems, MGIC informs lenders of specific underwriting modifications. However, single-industry local economies are an underwriting concern even when current conditions are favorable, especially if there is a history of cyclical upturns and downturns. MGIC encourages lenders to underwrite with the same factors in mind, denying credit to marginal borrowers whose ability to repay depends entirely on the future of one industry.

INDIVIDUAL LOAN FEATURES

Several factors related to individual loan features increase the likelihood of default and foreclosure. Some of the factors have already been addressed through specific underwriting guidelines. Others are areas of concern that help determine the overall strength or weakness of the insurance application.

In today's lending environment, an underwriter must be satisfied that a mortgage program will not exceed the future financial capabilities of the borrower. Underwriting guidelines should seek to minimize two problems that are most often caused by the mortgage program itself: equity erosion and payment shock.

Negative amortization and its effect on borrower equity become important factors in the borrower's *willingness* to repay once a default situation occurs. The equity erosion caused by negative amortization is further amplified when housing appreciation is flat. For borrowers who start out with less than 10 percent equity, the combination of negative amortization and little or no appreciation is often too much to overcome, and the typical result is abandonment. Guidelines by the insurer on negative amortization should help everyone avoid the unprofitable process of foreclosure caused by equity erosion.

Payment caps are very effective in reducing the potential for *payment shock* and the subsequent risk of default. However, payment caps without rate caps can create substantial negative amortization, especially when the loan is originated during a low rate period that is followed by a rapid increase in rates. Underwriters should consider both the positive and the negative effects of payments caps in evaluating the overall risk of the loan package.

Temporary buydowns on fixed-rate instruments and low introductory interest rates on ARMs increase the risk of default due to payment shock. In fact, discounted start rates on ARMs can turn a sound mortgage program into a risky one, even under relatively stable interest rate conditions.

If the index rate increases just .5 percent per year on the ARM in Table 31–2, monthly payments will increase from $764 to $1,009 after

Table 31–2

Assumptions:

- One-year ARM with 2%/5% caps
- $95,000 loan amount
- 2.5% rate concession
- Index plus gross margin—11.5%
- Initial rate—9.0%
- Index increases total of 1%

	Interest Rate	Principal and Interest	Increase in Monthly Payment	Percentage Increase
1st Year	9%	$ 764.39		
2nd Year	11%	902.59	$138.20	18.08%
3rd Year	12½%	1,008.89	106.30	11.77%
Total increase after 24 months			$244.50	29.85%

only 24 months—an increase of $245 or nearly 30 percent. Such an increase would strain the resources of most borrowers and must be considered beyond the means of the marginal borrower.

Temporary buydowns on fixed-rate instruments can cause similar problems. A typical 3–2–1 buydown on a $95,000, 30-year loan at 12 percent will guarantee a payment increase of $212 after 36 months (almost a 28 percent increase). Whenever discounted initial payment rates are used to qualify borrowers, MGIC takes a close look at the borrower's projected ability to meet the higher payments.

VALUE ISSUES

The cost of a seller contribution is almost always built into the sales price of the property. The result is a sales price that exceeds the property's true market value, causing instant equity erosion for the borrower. This can become an exceptionally serious problem for borrowers with 95 percent LTV loans—a problem that can easily change a 5 percent equity position into a 0 percent equity position if the seller contribution is 5 percent or more. By comparing the claims incidence on new homes versus existing homes, one can see when and to what extent builder/seller contributions have affected claims.

In its 1985 report on the mortgage insurance industry, Moody's concluded that default rates tend to react exponentially when negative risk factors are combined. This is exactly what happens when builder/ seller contributions are used with adjustable-rate mortgages; the ARM introduces the risk of payment shock while the builder/seller contribution threatens the borrower's equity position.

Guidelines by the insurer should limit the use of builder/seller contributions because of their potentially serious negative impact, especially in those situations that already represent a higher exposure to risk.

Equity refinances have long been recognized as a substantially more risky class of business. MGIC attempted to deal with the problem by limiting LTVs to 80 percent and by pricing accordingly. But the result has been that lenders only insure the most risky equity refinances, making our exposure to risk on this class of business worse instead of better. In fact, an analysis of MGIC's insured refinances originated from 1980 through 1984 shows that equity refinances resulted in claims twice as often as purchase money loans. The failure of pricing and underwriting to adequately control this higher risk within my firm has resulted in a decision to discontinue insuring equity refinances.

LTV loans of 95 percent can be a profitable class of business. However, they definitely represent a higher exposure to risk and thus require more conservative underwriting and appropriate pricing.

The major problem with 95 percent LTV loans is that once default occurs, there is a better than 50 percent chance of foreclosure, largely because of the borrower's inability to sell the property at a price high enough to cover the remaining loan balance plus selling costs and delinquent interest. The key, then, is to control those risk factors that increase the likelihood of default, and in effect stop the foreclosure process before it starts.

A recent study of the 95 percent LTV loans insured by MGIC identified four specific loan characteristics that tend to increase the likelihood of default:

- Gifts used for downpayment
- Lack of cash after closing
- Seller contributions greater than 3 percent
- Origination by broker

Any loan feature that assures or introduces the potential for payment increases also heightens the risk of default and must be carefully evaluated when used in conjunction with 95 percent LTV loans (that is, artificially low start rates on ARMs, temporary buydowns, graduated payment features, and so on).

The objective is to encourage the use of prudent and conservative mortgage programs so that borrowers with 95 percent LTV loans can meet their credit obligations throughout the mortgage term.

PROPERTY ISSUES

Claims MGIC has paid show that investor loans originated in the 1980s were responsible for a highly disproportionate number of claims. One logical explanation of this experience is that most investors are interested primarily in capital gains and tax shelter, and they are therefore more likely to default when those benefits vanish—even if they have the means to cure the loan. The Tax Reform Act of 1986 may make investor loans all the more fragile.

Because of their demonstrated high degree of risk and their potential for even higher risk in the future, MGIC is no longer providing insurance for investment properties; instead, it uses capacity for borrowers who intend to occupy the homes they purchase.

Under the right circumstances, condominiums purchased as a primary residence represent a fairly normal mortgage insurance risk. But factors such as heavy investor concentration in a project, oversupply of housing in the local market, and price competition between like units have made condominium loans a higher-than-average risk as a class of business.

Research in the relative risk of various condominium projects identified three characteristics that indicate a need for special underwriting attention:

- *Investor concentration above 20 percent*—this may affect the physical maintenance of the project and often encourages other owners to move out and rent their units.
- *Unit price under $60,000*—the low price tends to eventually attract investors.
- *Surrounding land use greater than 80 percent commercial*—this may affect future property values.

Because condominiums also tend to be more price-sensitive to local market conditions, many insurers pay particular attention to property values and project viability when they underwrite condominium loans, and the insurers may establish special guidelines for markets that show signs of softening condominium prices.

LENDER QUALITY CONTROL

The driving force in the mortgage lending industry has definitely shifted away from high-volume originations and toward high-quality originations. Nowhere is this more apparent than in the secondary market community. Fannie Mae's overall tightening of underwriting guidelines in 1985 and its particular concern with 95 percent LTV loans is strong evidence of the desire for better quality control. Freddie Mac's mandatory buyback provision for loans that default within the first four months after purchase and new restrictions by some of the private conduits are further evidence of this trend.

As the primary underwriter, the originating lender is in the best position to make judgments about quality and potential for foreclosure. Its loan officers and underwriters know the local employment conditions, the market values, and the appraisers. They have the opportunity to meet with the borrower face to face and thoroughly investigate the borrower's credit history.

MGIC acts solely as a review underwriter in this process, relying heavily on the representations made by the originating lender. Because our exposure to risk is so dependent on lender underwriting, those lenders who fail to provide adequate quality control jeopardize their ability to obtain MGIC mortgage insurance in the future and ultimately jeopardize the long-term viability of their own best interests in today's quality-conscious environment. Lenders must always underwrite as if the loans were entering their own portfolios.

MORTGAGE DEFAULT CONTROL PROGRAM

A new and growing Mortgage Default Control Program gives MGIC an effective way to work with lenders to solve delinquency problems and reduce the potential for losses. A key element of the program, borrower counseling, provides direct counseling support to delinquent borrowers. Borrower counseling helps identify reasons for default as well as work out solutions to avoid foreclosure. Working in cooperation with collection department personnel, MGIC selects and arranges contacts as early as possible before the borrower becomes hopelessly in arrears. While counseling does not eliminate defaults, in many cases it can lead to a solution that avoids the trauma and expense of foreclosure. Direct involvement by a third-party specialist like a mortgage loan counselor can often provide the extra effort needed to save the loan.

This program is designed to complement the lender's servicing efforts by jointly servicing mortgages MGIC has insured. MGIC experts, supported by state-of-the-art equipment, offer prompt, personal attention to delinquent borrowers while providing up-to-date recordkeeping and reporting to lenders. Briefly:

- Representatives working in lender offices provide summary reporting on the activity of loans referred by the lender.
- Counselors discuss the status of individual cases with their counterparts in the lender's office.
- Representatives are ready with current and detailed information on the status of each case if a lender has specific questions.

The team concept means insurers working together with lenders. Counselors' recommendations to borrowers are tailored to the lenders' policies, and approval is obtained from the lender before taking effect. The success of the program is dependent upon a cooperative effort. Toward this end, MGIC asks lenders to:

- Continue their normal collection activities
- Discuss their collection policies and procedures with insurer representatives
- Provide case information at an early stage in the delinquency
- Advise representatives of any investor constraints

This program is designed to solve delinquency problems and reduce the potential for losses. Through the program's team concept, lenders and insurers work together. The program can produce a winning situation for everyone, saving homes for borrowers, minimizing losses for lenders, and reducing the number of future claims for insurers.

BENEFITS OF PRUDENT RISK MANAGEMENT

MGIC's prudent risk management philosophy and strong underwriting guidelines reflect our dedication to the long-term success of high-ratio mortgage lending. By adopting this quality-conscious approach, everyone involved in the mortgage industry will benefit:

- Borrowers will purchase homes with financing they can afford now and into the future
- Lenders' loan and servicing portfolios will remain profitable

- MGIC will continue to build capacity for future high-ratio mortgage lending
- Especially important for secondary market participants, the residential mortgage loan will maintain its reputation as a premium-quality investment.

Like other types of insurers, mortgage insurers are in the business of taking risk, and we continually evaluate the relationship between that risk and our underwriting guidelines and premiums. As we move into the late 1980s, MGIC will continue to work closely with lenders and investors to ensure the long-term success and profitability of the entire mortgage lending industry.

Chapter 32

DIANE L. CORTES

Diane Cortes is Senior Vice President for General Electric Mortgage Insurance Co. responsible for strategic planning and marketing mortgage insurance programs. She received a B.A. from the University of Wisconsin and an M.B.A. from Duke University.

Risk Management — A Brave New World or Just Back to the Basics?

DIANE L. CORTES

The first half of the 1980s brought about the most rigorous challenge ever to be faced by the mortgage market. The decade began with the U.S. economy being propelled into a deep recession unparalleled by any previous economic cycle. The real estate lending market reverberated from the effects of this severe economic downturn.

For many thrift institutions this economic fallout came at the worst and best of times. Traditionally, thrifts had built and maintained huge mortgage portfolios of fixed-rate mortgages. However, as interest rates stalled in the 14–16 percent rate level for a two-year period in the early 1980s, the underwater portfolio* became a seemingly permanent problem and a topic to be dealt with at management and board of directors' meetings. Underwater portfolios became the catalysts that brought about numerous thrift closings. On the brighter side, deregulation of the thrifts provided new ground for the industry to restructure portfolios, generate interest rate-sensitive assets, and diversify its income-producing activities.

---

*The term *underwater portfolio* was coined in the early 1980s to describe the situtation thrifts faced as yields on mortgage loan portfolios fell significantly below that of their cost of deposits and borrowings.

Unlike thrifts, mortgage bankers were not saddled with the burden of underwater portfolios. But neither did they escape the drastic effects of the failing economy. While their lifeblood servicing portfolios seemed to remain healthy (prepayment runoff rates even decreased significantly), new origination volume dropped off substantially. Abnormally high interest rates precluded tapping a ripe and highly desirous population of baby boomers that were coming into their prime home-buying years. Thus, mortgage bankers had to scale down loan production staffs as a response to dramatically lower originiation volume. At industry conferences attendees spoke of "skinnying down to skeleton staffs."

And mortgage insurers (MIs)—how were they affected by the recession of the early 1980s? Like mortgage bankers, MIs experienced a reduction in volume, although the volume of privately insured loans did not shrink as much as total loan origination volume (see Table 32–1). What was more pronounced was the shift in the type of mortgage volume that was being *insured* compared to the past years' insured portfolios. The MIs' insured volume of 95 percent loan to value (LTV) loans increased from about one-third to over one-half of their total volume. Adjustable-rate mortgages (ARMs), only recently introduced, began to make up nearly 50 percent of the insurers' volume (see Table 32–2). Most significant, however, was the MI industry's annual doubling of losses that began to occur in 1980, catapulting the industry from a 25-year uninterrupted period of operating profits to its first underwriting loss in 1982. The industry continued to incur operating losses for the next four years (see Table 32–3).

Since the start of the decade, thrifts, mortgage bankers, and mortgage insurers collectively have been faced with mortgage delinquency and foreclosure rates that have remained at historically high levels despite the economic recovery of recent years. Recovery indicators such as tumbling interest rates, waning unemployment rates, and increased home sales and loan originations have signaled improvement since 1984, yet delinquency and foreclosure rates remained at all-time highs (see Table 32–4).

This uncharacteristic break in the traditional cyclical correlation between the economy and mortgage debt performance has prompted

Table 32–1
Mortgage Originations of 1–4 Family Homes ($ Million)

Year	Total	Privately Insured
1978	$185	$27
1979	187	25
1980	134	19
1981	98	19
1982	95	19
1983	191	43
1984	199	63
1985	247	51
1986 (Est.)	381	46

Source: GEMICO Research Dept.

Table 32–2
**Privately Insured New Mortgage Insurance Volume
by LTV Ratio and Product Type**

Year	95% LTV of Total Volume	% ARM of Total Volume
1979	33%	Less than 1%
1980	38	2
1981	40	6
1982	40	26
1983	46	27
1984	53	58
1985	51	48
1986 (3rd Qtr.)	32	20

Source: GEMICO Research Dept.

Table 32–3
Operating Performance of MI Industry ($ Millions)

Year	Losses	Expenses	Underwriting Profit (Loss)
1980	$ 59	$141	$111
1981	94	161	75
1982	210	175	(36)
1983	357	191	(99)
1984	472	265	(97)
1985	971	296	(362)
1986 (3rd Qtr.)	946	206	(436)

Table 32–4
Annual MBA Delinquency Survey Ratios

At Year-End	% Loans Delinquent (30 days or more past due)	% Loans with Foreclosure Started
1979	4.7%	.14%
1980	4.9	.15
1981	5.2	.16
1982	5.7	.20
1983	5.7	.21
1984	5.8	.19
1985	5.7	.21
1986 (3rd Qtr.)	5.4	.27

Source: GEMICO Research Dept.

mortgage insurers to begin underwriting mortgage default risk. The emerging need for risk management has caused the philosophies, principles, and methods of mortgage insurers to change significantly. A close examination of risk management in the industry reveals that the change is not a retrenchment, nor a retrogression to the operating modes of the 1960s and 1970s, but a total rethinking and repositioning of the industry.

The major factors driving this necessary mortgage insurance industry metamorphosis are:

- The prolonged effect of minimal housing appreciation on the high-ratio lending market
- The effect of new mortgage instrument structures on the borrower's ability or willingness to pay
- The growing disparity in the quality and performance of mortgage originators
- The exposure to smaller geographic market catastrophes
- The effect of tax reform on homeownership

Many of these factors are interrelated and some create a "chicken or the egg syndrome." But, undeniably, these are the issues in the forefront of the MI industry, and they must be addressed if this industry is to continue to be viable for the remainder of the 1980s and beyond.

DOES NO APPRECIATION LEAD TO NO 95 PERCENT LTVs?

The cooling down of inflation to almost non-existent levels has put a significant damper on housing appreciation rates in most markets. There is every indication that inflation will be tightly controlled over the next few years. This situation has impacted mortgage insurance risk across the board, but never more severely than in the high-ratio loan segment.

Past housing appreciation rates afforded lenders and insurers wide margins of error in loan underwriting decisions (see Figure 32–1).

When appreciation rates were robust, even a 95 percent levered borrower who could not make his/her mortgage payment often cured the default by selling out before foreclosure was initiated. The accelerated equity buildup fueled from housing appreciation provided the incentive for the homeowner to sell the property, recapture his or her initial equity and sometimes even realize appreciation of equity. This phenomenon certainly contributed significantly to why the MI industry's claims incidence rates averaged only 2–3 percent during the 70s. However, the continued absence of high annual appreciation rates and the concern that housing appreciation rates will continue to be minimal in the next few years revises the scenario dramatically. In the 1980s the highly levered borrower who has difficulty meeting his or her mortgage obligation evaluates the traditional "pre-sale option" only to find that he or she frequently cannot recoup the initial equity stake and may very well have to incur additional out-of-pocket costs to sell the home prior to the lender initiating formal foreclosure. This 95 percent borrower is indeed most vulnerable, particulary when the vast majority of mortgage defaults occur within the first three years following the home purchase. The insured portfolio statistics have born out this new scenario, as demonstrated by the industry's claims rates. These rates have risen to 5 percent on average for all loans insured. For 95 percent LTV loans, claims rates have well exceeded 7 percent in recent years.

Historically, the 95 percent LTV loan has been known to have a propensity to default that is two to three times greater than for lower loan-to-value loans. Contributing to this higher default probability is the fact that a greater percentage of 95 percent borrowers are first-time homebuyers, who normally have both less employment tenure and lower liquidity after closing compared to higher downpayment borrowers. So, irrespective of housing appreciaton rates, these borrowers can be more susceptible to defaulting on their loans, and there is a lesser probability that they will be able to cure a default. Add to this the impact of low property appreciation on default and claim incidence, and the question arises as to whether 95 percent LTV loans are still viable, and, if so, how this increased default risk can be underwritten by mortgage insurers.

An absolute affirmation that 95 percent LTV loans can exist in an

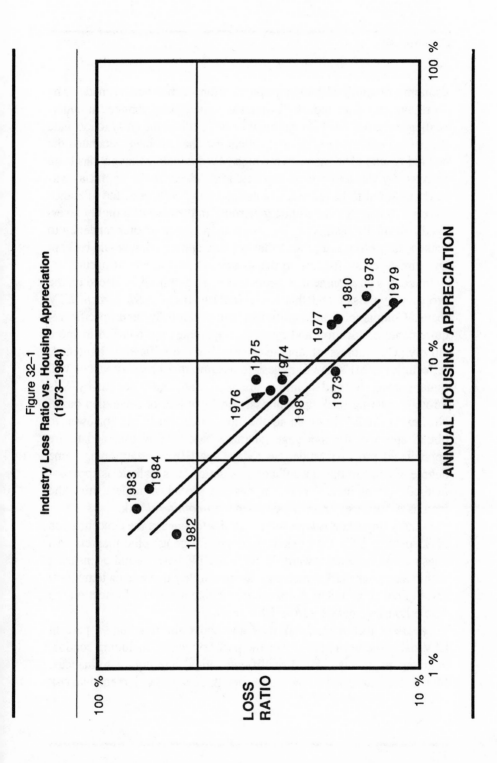

Figure 32-1
Industry Loss Ratio vs. Housing Appreciation
(1973-1984)

economy of minimal housing appreciation cannot yet be made. The mortgage insurance industry has made some drastic changes in underwriting these lowest-downpayment loans, but it is too early to evaluate the data to conclusively determine that the changes have generated the desired results. The manner in which MIs evaluate collateral has been affected by the absence of appreciation. Whereas the appraisal was never held out to be an exact valuation of the collateral, the tolerance for error was historically quite generous. In the case of a highly leveraged marginally qualifying borrower, there was a greater tendency to make a subjective assumption that housing appreciation would bail out an ultimate claim for loss to the insurer, should a default occur.

In today's environment, a good deal more emphasis is placed on the property appraisal, and this is particularly true for 95 percent LTV loans. Comparables are scrutinized more carefully, and specific requirements of location and age of comparables are adhered to more closely. Currentness of appraisals has been significantly tightened, reflecting the MI's unwillingness to assume that property values will remain level. Second opinions are more frequently sought by MIs through ordering back-up appraisals on a random or scheduled basis. No "extra credit" is given to the marginally qualified borrower to obtain approval for mortgage guaranty based on an assumed future appreciated property value. So today, apart from ascertaining some degree of comfort that the collateral valuation is as realistic as appraisal methods can estimate, more emphasis is placed on underwriting the loan as a borrower *credit* risk rather than *collateral* risk.

Equally important is an insurer's ability to manage the concentration of 95 percent LTV loan risk within specific geographic markets. An unusual convergence toward 95 percent LTV lending and/or insuring within a smaller market increases the possibility that even a temporary and limited economic disturbance can create a snowball effect on the whole housing market across LTV levels.

Layers of incremental risk over and above the baseline 95 percent LTV risk have been added over the past few years, including condos, nonfixed payments, liberal qualifying ratios, and equity refinances. Mortgage insurers have now pared back these layers of incremental risk in order to better underwrite and control 95 percent LTV loan default and claims risk.

Mortgage insurers have also recognized that these underwriting changes are not enough without reinstating the operating principle of pricing for risk. In 1984, the first price increases ever experienced in the industry since its emergence in 1957 took place. Reflecting the greater propensity towards claims incidence for 95 percent LTV loans, insurance rates for these loans were generally increased proportionately higher than for other LTV categories.

MORTGAGE PAYMENT VARIABILITY AND ITS IMPACT ON DEFAULT RISK

The high risk interest rates of the 1980s spurred the development of alternatives to the fixed-rate, fixed-payment (FRFP) loan structure due to two primary factors:

1. Portfolio originators and nonoriginating mortgage investors were hurting from the rapid escalation in interest rates. They began to demand interest rate-sensitive loan instruments/investments to keep their investment yields in line with their costs of funds.
2. Mortgage originators felt pressured to create new loan structures that would qualify homebuyers who were locked out of fixed-rate lending due to high interest rate levels and/or to encourage homebuyers who were forestalling their purchases due to high fixed interest rates.

The pronounced proliferation of ARMs in the 1980s led to the use of a wide range of instrument structures, extending from the conservative to the exotic. Graduated-payment features were combined with ARMs to create what is proving to be the riskiest loan instrument ever originated, the graduated-payment, adjustable-rate mortgage (GPARMs). Homebuilders, anxious to reduce their large inventories of new homes, expanded interest rate buydowns to such depths that advertisements for this type of buydown financing appeared to be erroneous because rates were so low. Mortgage insurers, operating under the erroneous assumption that the normal economic cycle would mitigate the ultimate defaults and claims on these loans, and also feeling the pressure to support the frail origination market, blithely acquiesced to market demands for all these new mortgage instruments. In some instances insurers were directly involved in creating the abominations of exotic loan instruments that were originated.

As experience has proven, the market can and did create uninsurable risk via the more exotic alternative mortgage instruments. The performance results of several instrument structures such as GPARMs has led to a general mortgage insurance industry prohibition against insuring these loan types.

The market has quickly backed away from originating GPMs/ GPARMs in the past year because of the adverse "double whammy" effect on the borrower. The successive annual payment increases associated with GPMs/GPARMs caused lenders and insurers to question the affordability of rising annual payments, especially since the borrower was qualified at a low initial payment rate. Then, the steeply increasing negative amortization accrual characteristic of the GPM/GPARM loan structure also gave rise to collateral value shock. The GPM/GPARM's negative amortization accrual has caused borrowers who experience payment difficulty during early loan years to lose incentive for keeping up on a loan obligation that has very obviously outstripped their home's value. Features such as negative amortization, which are dependent on some level of housing appreciation, have been found to be inappropriate in today's economy.

The GPM/GPARM with its negative amortization also can be compared to the fixed-rate loan with a temporary buydown to some degree. The fixed-rate loan with a temporary interest rate buydown has been demonstrated through portfolio studies to have the same double adversity factors working against the borrower as with a GPM/GPARM. The common annual payment graduation for a buydown is 7½ percent, just as in the case of the typical GPM/GPARM. And, the cost of the temporary interest rate buydown is usually built into the home's selling price. Therefore, on a 95 percent LTV fixed rate loan with an interest rate buydown, the property in effect has negative amortization built into the financing from the loan origination date. The contemporary issue of appraisal valuation only further compounds this situation. A few builders, for instance, operate on significantly smaller profit margins than others and therefore don't have the buydown cost built into the home's selling price, and if such a property is used as a comparable in another appraisal, the appraiser does not have access to that information.

No evidence today confirms that the default risk of all ARMs—and other mortgage structures that have variable payments—make such instruments uninsurable risks. The more rational ARM loan plans that limit the maximum periodic payment and interest rate changes, as well as the maximum rate change over the life of the loan, appear to be performing as well as, and in some cases better than, the FRFP mortgage structure. However, the ARMs that have been adjusting to market rate indexes, which were originated without initial interest rate subsidies by way of teaser rates, have for the most part had decreased payments to date. The true test of the viability of these instruments will only come in a rising interest rate environment.

Mortgage insurers have reacted to the growth of the alternative mortgage loan market in three basic ways:

1. The industry's insurance premium pricing structure now reflects the incremental default risks that are created through alternative loan structures with adjusting payments and/or interest rates. For example, a typical 95 percent LTV ARM loan commands a first-year premium of 1.8 percent of the loan amount, as opposed to a 1.0 percent premium for the fixed-rate, fixed-payment loan (see Figure 32–2).
2. Insurers are specifically defining those loan instrument features that are acceptable for insurance through loan product guidelines. Generally, the industry has set up procedures to review alternative loan structures on a case-by-case basis. The alternative loan features within an instrument are interdependent, and the limits on each feature must be weighed both independently *and* collectively.

Figure 32–2
Illustration of Mortgage Insurance Premiums

	Fixed-Rate, Fixed-Payment Loan	ARM Loan
Loan Amount	$60,000	$60,000
First Year Premium Rate	1.0%	1.8%
First Year Premium	$600	$1080
	$480	(+80%)

3. Insurers have begun to comingle loan product guidelines with credit/collateral underwriting guidelines. For instance, on loans that allow adjustments to payments, tighter housing debt-to-income and total debt-to-income qualifying ratios are enforced. This ensures that if a payment increase occurs within the first year of the loan term, the borrower's income level will have a greater cushion to absorb the payment increase. Liquidity requirements net of cash required for closing are also generally higher if the loan structure does not have level payments.

The alternative loan lending market has caused insurers to add a new dimension to their underwriting process that did not exist prior to the 1980s; they now underwrite loan product risk. Although an extraordinary level of alternative lending experimentation has occurred in the last five years, the lack of standardization has made it difficult, if not impossible, to fully evaluate the performance of each loan type. Some basic groups of alternative loan structures have proven to be uninsurable risks, and others need a rising interest rate cycle for the risks to be fully assessed.

THE 80/20 RULE IN MORTGAGE INSURANCE

The age-old axiom of 80 percent of something is created by 20 percent of a group applies to the mortgage insurance industry. Eighty percent of the mortgage insurance volume is generated from 20 percent of the states in this country. In most companies, 80 percent of the insurance premiums are generated from 20 percent of the insurer's customer base. And unfortunately, recent experience has shown that 80 percent of an insurer's losses are driven by 20 percent of its customers.

Some mortgage insurance companies are implementing policies and procedures to break this axiom as it has applied to claims payments, or at least to improve the situation by ensuring that the group producing the losses also is the highest premium-producing customer group. Ways to ensure the quality of lenders in the 1980s are developed very differently by the companies within the industry. To assess the overall quality of a lender requires analyses beyond the calcuation of loss ratios from an MI's insurance claims. A fair assessment of a lender's quality will include analysis of:

- Delinquency ratios (by total insured portfolio, by year of origination, by early term*, by loan product type, by LTV)
- Mortgage insurance application rejection ratios (although an MI can ferret out poor quality through its own underwriting, lenders that fail to prescreen applications will incur high rejection ratios and cause an MI's productivity to decline significantly)
- Claims payments ratios
- Concentrations of higher-risk characteristics within their insured portfolios (95 percent LTVs, investor loans, self-employed borrowers, and so on)
- Loan servicing quality (adherence to MI's delinquency reporting requirements, frequency and quality of delinquent borrower contact, experience of servicing personnel and depth of capacity, procedures for loss mitigation, and other factors)

---

*An early-term default is classified as a loan that is in default prior to at least 12 payments being made or having at least 1 year of seasoning.

Several major market changes have caused the range in the quality of lenders to expand. There has been an onslaught of loan brokering, and the market also has seen exponential growth in loan correspondent lending relationships. Growth in these two segments has reduced the traditional "co-insurance" relationship that had previously existed between originator and insurer. In recent years, some loan brokers and correspondents have developed a higher degree of insensitivity toward loan origination quality. Since brokers and correspondents will not be servicing their originations, they may be less motivated to seek out the level of quality that a portfolio originator would, because they do not rely on loan income from servicing.

The expansion of the secondary market has further diluted the co-insurance relationship between lender and insurer. Originators that become pressed to "make the market" or avoid "missing the market" through loan sales might adversely impact loan quality by taking short-cuts in the origination process. Lenders that sacrifice quality control procedures instead of changing their processes and retaining their standards are showing up as poor quality accounts.

The occurrence of misrepresentation and fraud is thought to be higher today than in the past. Fraudulent originations as a percentage of total originations are quite small, and they have been highly concentrated within relatively few lenders, as opposed to being evenly distributed among all originators.

The transfer of loan servicing also has increased. Most such transfers have not impacted quality. However, forced servicing transfers due to failure of an institution and/or a lack of capacity have also occurred.

Finally, most lenders' loan servicing capabilities were strained by significant increases in delinquencies between 1984 and 1986. Growth in staffing and systems support has lagged behind the growth in delinquent loans in many shops. Inadequate servicing, which results in such cases, has been shown to significantly impact the percentage of lenders' delinquencies that end up as MI claims.

The argument that the MI has as much responsibility to reject poor quality loans as the originator is valid. However, most insured loans today are being underwritten under a number of differing underwriting guidelines. Guidelines are just that; they are not absolute minimums or maximums. Because each loan insurance approval decision is independent of the next, often it is hard to identify a lender's trend toward impaired quality if it should occur. And since the bulk of an MI's defaults don't occur until the 36th month, it is difficult to realize a deterioration in quality until after the risk is already assumed. Finally, lending quality goes beyond the point of origination. Due to the continued high level of delinquencies and claims, loan servicing has become an integral part of the lender quality assessment.

The specific ways that MIs are dealing with the lender quality issue are unique to each company. Generally however, the industry has taken the following directions:

1. MIs have rewritten master policy* contracts to define fraud and misrepresentation and strengthen their defense against the occurrence of fraud. Also, master policies now require prior approval of portfolio servicing transfers in order to ensure that the MI recognizes the new servicer as qualified.

2. MIs have reduced the maximum insurance coverage on each insured loan to reinforce the "co-insurance" concept. When total (or even deep) coverage is not permitted, poor quality origination and servicing will impact the lender as well as the insurer.

3. MIs have actively sought to establish minimum quality control origination standards through revisions of underwriting guidelines. Specific credit, collateral and loan product guidelines spell out minimums for loan insurance eligibility. MIs no longer maintain static guidelines. Between 1984 and 1986, frequent guideline changes have been made by the majority of insurers, reflecting the fine-tuning of risk management efforts.

4. Some insurers are refusing to do business with lenders whose experience shows they lack the capability or incentive to originate quality loans or they lack the capacity to service insured loans.

5. Insurers are actively assisting lenders in delinquent loan servicing. Some MIs have provided lenders with consultative loan servicing support, including servicing systems/procedures cri-

---

*A master policy is a contractual agreement between a mortgage originator and private mortgage insurer. Terms of performance requirements and obligations are detailed in this contract.

tiques and analyses, and loan restructuring programs. Others are providing direct delinquent borrower contact and counseling services.

The lending market will continue to see heightened activity by MIs in quality control as it relates to both origination and servicing areas. Mortgage insurers are more than anxious to prevent another EPIC* debacle. The MIs are not alone in this area. FHA, VA, FHLMC and FNMA have all initiated separate actions to identify and act on situations in which lender quality and performance fall short of minimum expectations.

FUTURE HOUSTONS?

It is not realistic for an insurer, much less anyone else, to be able to predict geographic market downturns. When markets start to show signs of souring, it is too late for an insurer to escape the ramifications. In fact, in the years just prior to severe economic slumps, markets such as Houston, Miami, and San Diego were experiencing a *boom* in housing. Most insurance risk had already been placed in portfolio in these markets in 1978, 1979, and 1980, before the market crisis hit.

The only real lesson to be learned from what occurred in Houston during the mid-1980s is not unique to mortgage insurers. A geographic market's dependency on one industry (oil in the case of Houston) creates a separate risk classification that must be managed differently than markets with greater economic diversification.

In retrospect, the preponderance of 95 percent LTV loans, particular-

---

*Equity Programs Investment Corporation (EPIC) was a real estate syndication group that purchased large numbers of real estate investment/rental properties during the late 1970s and 1980s. The EPIC loans were securitized and sold. In August 1985, EPIC defaulted on the pass-through payments to the investors. Many of the properties, which are located in depressed real estate markets, have current values significantly below the original purchase prices. A formal bankruptcy workout plan was adopted. However, the claims for loss on the insurance coverage for EPIC properties has caused two MIs to date to go into conservatorship. Total MI losses could be as high as $394 million.

ly in the condominium housing market in Houston, should have been tightly controlled. Investment property lending, the most vulnerable in Houston's case, could have been more contained. Geographic risk dispersion is much like borrower risk dispersion in the nondiversified economic markets. An insurer must continuously look at these particular SMSAs or cities as if they were one borrower, and assess the impact on the company's staying power in a severe downturn.

Because there always will be some geographic markets that are booming while others are in a slump, the necessity for broad insurance risk diversification will remain a basic precept for a mortgage insurer.

TAX REFORM ACT AND HOMEOWNERSHIP

The final major issue that may affect MIs is the Tax Reform Act of 1986. Tax authorities remain undecided on whether the real estate market will be aided or harmed by the new tax structure. One area that is almost certain to experience a negative impact is the nonprimary housing segment (investment and/or resort/vacation homes). The overall tax shelter advantage in this segment is being curtailed, and tax losses from real estate investments for the most part have been eliminated. However, the predominant portion of the real estate market—the primary housing market—is being affected to the extent that the tax deduction for interest expenses continues to make owning a home a better investment than the renting alternative.

The impact of the new Tax Bill on housing will probably not be realized until the market has fully adjusted to its effects over a period of several years. One area of tax reform that is affecting the mortgage insurance industry is the new limit on the amount of equity that a borrower can extract from a home in order to finance consumer purchases. There may be a high motivation to lever up more highly on the initial financing of the home purchase in the future to avoid these limitations. This may skew MIs' insured portfolios more heavily into the highest-risk LTV category even further than it has gone in recent years.

CONCLUSION

Without a doubt, the mortgage insurance industry has implemented such wide-ranging operational changes between 1984 and 1986 that it is hard to even compare it to prior years' experience or standards.

While obviously many of the changes were promulgated on the basis of severe adverse financial performance, the mortgage insurance industry is still committed to supporting the high ratio lending market. Some friction initially was created when the insurance industry did an about-face with lenders on the type of risk it would assume and the price it would command for the guaranty product. However, with the demise of two insurers in the mid-1980s, the recognition that these changes were long overdue generally has become accepted, and there is a high degree of cooperative effort among the market participants to build a sounder loan product.

The industry still must prove that it can make prudent underwriting decisions to provide mortgage guaranty in an environment of minimal or nonexistent housing appreciation. The incrementally higher default risk of alternative mortgage instruments must be assessed and quantified to validate their insurability. The range of lender quality must be actively managed by insurers so that the market is not curtailed. Neither should the market have to bear the penalty through higher insurance premiums if a small segment of poor originators causes a large loss impact on insurers.

Risk dispersion must be controlled to deemphasize the insurers' vulnerability to catastrophies in limited geographic markets. Finally, the impact of tax reform should be measured by insurers to ensure that industry policies and philosophies complement the new tax structure as it pertains to homeownership.

As of early 1987, the economy is continuing to gain strength, and the outlook is promising. However, mortgage insurance risk must continue to be underwritten and managed with new standards. The risk-versus-reward ratio must be kept in relative balance in order to sustain a viable industry. The issues that have surfaced during the first half of the decade will continue for the second half. The mortgage insurance industry cannot be classified as getting back to the basics. The basics have changed, and we are entering a brave new world.

Chapter 33

ROBERT L. HASTINGS

Robert Hastings is Chairman of the Board of Foremost Guaranty Corporation, a mortgage guaranty company based in Madison, Wisconsin. His career includes 20 years in mortgage guaranty insurance, 7 years in banking, and 9 years in real estate. Mr. Hastings is a graduate of the University of Wisconsin, and has completed the Graduate School of Banking at the University of Wisconsin. He holds the SREA designation from the Society of Real Estate Appraisers and served as its International President in 1978. Mr. Hastings also holds the MAI designation from the American Institute of Real Estate Appraisers.

The Changing Face of Risk Management

ROBERT L. HASTINGS

At the start of this decade Peter Treadway, PhD, chief economist at the Federal National Mortgage Association, said, "The future isn't what it used to be." Those of us who have made it to 1987 and expect to survive beyond know that Treadway was right. Things have changed in the residential lending industry. Every lender, investor, appraiser, and risk manager knows it.

In this brief chapter I would like to shed some light on the changes and what they mean. Let me make it clear that I do not profess to have all of the answers. Frankly, I would be very content if I prove able to determine the right questions.

SOME BACKGROUND

Prior to the 1970s, the concept of home ownership was wrapped up along with the flag, apple pie, and motherhood. The concept of "A man's home is his castle," prevailed as a prime force motivating home ownership.

As we moved into the 1970s, the situation changed. With the median price of a new home moving from approximately $23,000 in 1970 to nearly $65,000 in 1980, the credo became, "A man's home is his castle and a highly attractive investment when leveraged." The fact that you could make money from your home became Common Knowledge. (Like most such "facts" that make cocktail party and barbeque conversation circuit, it was common, but it wasn't really knowledge.)

The heady environment of rising home prices during the 1970s made it hard to see the top. It seemed like things would continue to get better and better. The cycle was not unlike that of the stock market during the 1920s. But not many people made the analogy, since speculating in stocks seemed quite flimsy next to the purchase of a home. There's always something substantial about bricks and mortar.

At the risk of appearing to hoist my industry—private mortgage insurance—on its own petard, I should point out that much of the leverage was made possible by our facilitating the purchase of homes by buyers using low downpayments. (But then, we might be blameless as we would have never flourished had it not been for the fact the Freddie Mac and Fannie Mae started buying privately insured mortgages in the 1970s.)

In retrospect, it is easy to wag a finger and say "shame!" to those who fostered the conditions of the 1970s. However, that would be almost sheer hypocrisy. Times were good and most of us were making a fine living out of the prevailing conditions. Most cannot honestly say that we wish that we had done otherwise; rather, what we *really* wish is that the good times could have continued, providing uninterrupted prosperity. That's normal.

By the end of the 1970s, the lender's world had changed dramatically. The cost of funds had crept up. The spread squeeze pinched profits. Alternative mortgage instruments (AMIs) were created to meet the challenge. A plethora of AMIs was developed. They both solved and created problems.

The major problem for AMI lenders and mortgage insurers was determining how increases in payments would affect default ratios. There was no empirical data available for making reliable actuarial forecasts. This problem was compounded, in many cases, by the needs of lenders to induce customers into the instruments with various concessions. Lenders were under tremendous pressure because they not only had to think about eliminating the interest rate spread squeeze, but about the consequences of poor risk management, as the vast majority of AMIs were to be kept in portfolio.

It was clear that at the beginning of the 1980s, the once tranquil world of residential mortgage lending was, like one well-known era, gone with the wind.

THE PROBLEMS

Double-digit inflation of the 1970s was followed by an inflation-breaking recession in the early 1980s. While inflation slowed, housing prices continued to historic highs. As disposable income did not keep pace with this increase, affordability became a major issue for homebuyers and originators.

A major question became how to manage the risks presented by this unprecedented situation. Answers were not immediately forthcoming. This should not be too surprising, as it took a while for the problems to become apparent. Too, there was the natural tendency for many of us to assume that the situation was an aberration, that things would get back to "normal."

Normalcy was not going to be the case. Each year of the 1980s has presented its particular challenges.

In 1980, mortgage interest rates began their steep climb. The cost of funds put additional pressure on the thrifts. The need for AMIs began to build.

During 1981–1982, interest rates for fixed-rate mortgages (FRMs) reached 17 percent, levels hitherto reached only by MasterCard or VISA. Originations of FRMs ground to a virtual halt. Borrowers were not quick to embrace AMIs. A variety of incentives to induce them to do so were initiated. Incentives only addressed a part of the problem; affordability with payment increases was still a fundamental problem.

By 1983–84, the AMI was gaining acceptance among home buyers. Lenders knew how to sell the instrument. While the AMI might be gaining in favor, underwriting it presented a definite risk.

Necessary data was absent from the decision-making process. Among those missing elements were:

- Track record for the instruments
- Secure assumptions about home values; most predictive scenarios called for values to increase
- Reliable data due to hidden buydown concessions
- A guarantee that borrower income would keep pace with payment increases

Given these missing elements, coupled with the cumulative experience of the 1980s up to 1984, people began to understand what Dr. Treadway meant when he said the future was not what it used to be.

As 1985–86 rolled around, lenders, investors, appraisers, and risk managers sought to make sense out of seeming chaos. Pressure built up to return to the "basics" regarding underwriting. Changes were needed.

And changes have been made.

THE CURRENT SITUATION

More risk and actuarial analysis of overall portfolio performance is being done than ever before. All aspects of loans are being scrutinized carefully. Old assumptions are no longer regarded as operative until they have been tested for new conditions.

The most outstanding example that comes to mind is the revised definition of market value agreed to by Freddie Mac and Fannie Mae. Previously, *market value* had been defined as the highest price that a property will bring. The new definition states that it is the most probable price that a property should bring.

While some might regard this change as one of semantic hair splitting, it is not. Rather, it is a profound reorientation for appraisers in how they evaluate a property. It permits the appraiser to take into account the true nature of the market, rather than channeling the conclusion of value along the lines of determining what a property would bring in the classic situation where the buyer and seller are engaged in a hypothetical, basically perfect transaction.

Further, appraisers are being directed to make adjustments for financing concessions based upon market conditions. This, too, is a departure from the traditional appraisal technique.

The result of the changes in the appraisal approach will have a definite impact on the underwriting process. It will be enhanced. However, it should not be construed as a panacea that will somehow relieve the responsibilities of the risk manager. Instead, it will enable the risk manager to do the job at hand more effectively.

While it may be embarrassing to admit it, some of the errors that existed as a result of past lending, appraising, private mortgage insurance underwriting, and risk management practices were actually corrected only through inflation. With inflation under control at this economic moment, the fallacy of that thinking becomes evident—very evident.

Now, the time has come for risk managers to take advantage of the computer's ability to handle data quickly. Defaulting or delinquent loans must be analyzed in order to see what their characteristics are. Questions that must be answered include:

- What property types tend to go into default/delinquency most frequently?
- Where are delinquent/defaulting properties located?
- What loan-to-value ratio results in the most defaults/delinquencies?
- Is there a borrower profile that indicates potential for a problem loan, if the loan is not made correctly?
- Is there a pattern to default/delinquency among certain types of mortgage instruments?
- Are there particular macro- and/or microeconomic features that spell trouble or prosperity in a given area in the future?

The relative value of these questions will vary from risk manager to risk manager, depending upon the portfolio objectives, that is, the degree of risk sought.

There is a problem inherent with any screening process where lending is involved. It is that of discrimination. In no way should the changing needs of risk management be construed to condone discrimination in any form. It is not intended to be so. Rather, the application of new techniques to risk management should permit lenders to take better informed steps in the direction of helping lendable funds reach the entire universe of borrowers most effectively.

At the outset of this essay I said that I would be content if I could simply pose the right questions that we should be asking about the changing face of risk management. I hope that I have raised at least some of those issues.

Having been active in the appraisal, private mortgage insurance, and banking industries, as well as growing up in the real estate business, I've had a front-row seat to see what changes have occurred. I have also seen the extent to which we have had false starts toward changing the basics, when the need has arisen.

Today is no time for false starts or for wishing that the good old days would return because the new times that we face are somewhat distressing. Even if we were to return to a period of mild inflation for the housing industry, we will be doing ourselves a severe disservice if we forget the lessons of 1980–1986.

At this juncture we know that the fixed-rate mortgage is not the only salable mortgage type in the secondary market; we know that the days of borrowing long and lending short are in the past; we know that certain property types just don't make good loans during certain economic scenarios; we know that there are mortgage types that are literally time bombs in any portfolio. And each of you may know something else that is the key to success for you and your operation.

Given what we know, the inevitable question must be, why do we still make mistakes? The answer is easy. . . .

We just have to remember what we know and apply it consciously and consistently.

The home finance market will range from $200–250 billion annually during the late 1980s and probably beyond. This demand for capital represents the largest debt market in the nation today—one of the largest in the world. The business of mortgage securitization has expanded from virtually nothing 10 years ago to somewhat more than $140 billion in 1985. Such activity requires vigilant risk management.

We have the tools to do the job. We have people with the necessary experience. All we have to do is apply our resources and remain unafraid to innovate, and we will have the situation well in hand.

The future isn't what it used to be. It's better.

Index

Index

Dynamic hedge(s) GNMA 8 versus, T-Note futures analysis illustrating a, September 1986, 55-56

E

Early-term default, 617
Economic activity of a region as it affects the yield on mortgage-backed securities, 197-211
80/20 hedged position, 41-50
11th District Cost of Funds (COF) Index, 497
Equity Programs Investment Corporation (EPIC), 561, 575, 620
Eurobond market, 531-32, 533
Excess servicing fees, 365
  capitalization of, 455
Expected value, 26-32

F

Fannie Mae. *See* Federal National Mortgage Association (FNMA)
Federal Home Loan Bank system
  Bankruptcy Code, 528
  borrowing by thrifts and commercial banks from the, 473-74
  Freddie Mac securities to collateralize advances from the, 224
  insolvency regulations of thrifts under the, 528
  1975 study of foreclosure costs by the governing Board of the, 558
  regulation of savings institutions under the, 175
Federal Home Loan Mortgage Corporation (FHLMC)
  amortization schedule of a generic PC offered by the, 275
  analysis of a portfolio containing securities issued by the, 417-21

as collateral for Treasury tax and loan accounts, 225-26
Eligibility Requirements for Private Mortgage Insurers (EPIC) published by the, 561, 575, 620
evolution of swap programs by the, 136
investor payments scheduled by the, 234-35
mortgage-backed securities marketplace participation by the, 135
new issues volume of the, 1981-1983, 137
PCs offered by the, 136, 215-26
probability distribution for five prepayment rates under different interest rate scenarios for a PC issued by the, 277-79
repo rate of the, 277
securities used as collateral for Treasury tax and loan accounts, 225-26
security guaranty provided by the, 233
Federal National Mortgage Association (FNMA- 625. *See also* Loan(s), securitization of
ARM and VRM programs offered by the, 238
auction activities of the, in the mid-1970s, 135
Customer Service Trading Desk (CSTD) of the, 241
delivering against the commitment and effecting the security issuance of an MBS by the, 239-41
evolution of swap programs by the, 136
foreclosure servicing options provided to lenders by the, 238-39

Index

Index

Index

Index

Risk
  associated with GPMs and GPARMs, 614-15
  basis, 11, 13, 71
  control program to lessen mortgage, 599-601
  curve, 71
  dispersion in MIC trading operations, 127
  fine tuning of, 72
  hedging as a means of decreasing, 71
  intermarket spread leading to increased, 71
  investment property insurance, 597-98
  lender quality control to lessen, 598-99
  loan features that lead to an increase in foreclosure, 594-95, 597, 610
  management, 552-53, 589-601, 625-31 mortgage, 551-53
  to a mortgage pipeline with different interest rates and different hedge positions, 22-52
  95 percent LTV, 609-613, 615
  regional differences in mortgage, 201-4, 327-28, 317-41, 578-79, 592-93 *See also* Mortgage insurance
  regional unemployment affecting mortgage, 325-28
  potential claim frequency analysis of mortgage, 318-24
  understanding, 577-80

Risk/return
  analysis in secondary marketing, 36-39
  curves, 33-36, 70
  return trade-off, 33-36

Roberts, Blaine, 202

S

Salomon Brothers, Inc., 247, 251-52
Savings institutions (SIs)
  deregulation of interest rates and the effect on, 175, 527
  investment grade thrift debt charted against that of single "A" rated commercial bank debt, 528-29
  use of repurchase agreements by, 541-43
Sears Mortgage Securities, 137-38
"Sears" regulations, 346
Seasonal effects, 201-2
Securities, components of the return on nonmortgage, fixed-income, 157-58
Securitization
  applied to commercial properties, 251-53
  commercial loan, 231-35, 249-50
  equity loan, 253-54, 596-97
  Fannie Mae loan selection and, 237-40
  mortgage, 215
  mortgage-backed securities', 245-55
Sellers of mortgage-backed securities
  defining investor criteria by, 100-2
  marketing decisions of, 102-4
  sales and servicing agreements of, 104-7
Short-term mandatory delivery commitments
  maximizing profits for using, 81
  for unclosed loans, 79
Single loan delivery commitments (SLCs), 78
  mandatory, used with pair offs to manage the risk of loan fallout, 86-88
  optional delivery, used for recouping commitment fees, 87, 89

Index

assets in the, 463
funding of the, 476-77
Whole loan market
  importance and size of the, 126
  MIC's activities in the, 126
  negotiated transactions in the, 111-16
  secondary market for, 250-51
Woodward and Lothrop, Incorporated, 253

Y

Yield(s)
  analysis of cash flow and, by Wall Street of mortgage loans, 137
  curve spread, 509-11
  15-yr. private sector loans vs. 7-yr. Treasury, 129
  MIC whole loan, 127
  spread combined with total return analysis, 157-59
  spreads between mortgage and treasury, 144, 148, 156-57
  30-yr. private sector whole loan vs. 10-yr. Treasury, 128
Yield equivalency pricing method, 369

Z

Zero coupon bonds, 252

Dear Customer:

Probus is thoroughly committed to publishing the highest quality materials for professionals in the Mortgage-Backed Securities and Secondary Mortgage markets.

As such, we would like to keep you (and your firm) abreast of forthcoming publications in this fast moving area. In order to do this we ask that you supply us with your name, firm and address.

Thank you; we look forward to serving you.

Name _____

Firm _____

Address _____

City _____ State _____ Zip _____